IET COMPUTING SERIES 64

Intelligent Multimedia Processing and Computer Vision

Other volumes in this series:

Intelligent Multimedia Processing and Computer Vision

Techniques and applications

Edited by
Shyam Singh Rajput, Chen Chen and Karm Veer Arya

The Institution of Engineering and Technology

Published by The Institution of Engineering and Technology, London, United Kingdom

The Institution of Engineering and Technology is registered as a Charity in England & Wales (no. 211014) and Scotland (no. SC038698).

First published 2023

The Institution of Engineering and Technology
Futures Place
Kings Way, Stevenage
Hertfordshire SG1 2UA, United Kingdom

www.theiet.org

British Library Cataloguing in Publication Data
A catalogue record for this product is available from the British Library

ISBN 978-1-83953-725-7 (hardback)
ISBN 978-1-83953-726-4 (PDF)

Typeset in India by MPS Limited
Printed in the UK by CPI Group (UK) Ltd, Eastbourne

Cover Image: MF3d / E+ via Getty Images

Intelligent Multimedia Processing and Computer Vision

Techniques and applications

Edited by
Shyam Singh Rajput, Chen Chen and Karm Veer Arya

The Institution of Engineering and Technology

Published by The Institution of Engineering and Technology, London, United Kingdom

The Institution of Engineering and Technology is registered as a Charity in England & Wales (no. 211014) and Scotland (no. SC038698).

The Institution of Engineering and Technology
Futures Place
Kings Way, Stevenage
Hertfordshire SG1 2UA, United Kingdom

www.theiet.org

British Library Cataloguing in Publication Data
A catalogue record for this product is available from the British Library

ISBN 978-1-83953-725-7 (hardback)
ISBN 978-1-83953-726-4 (PDF)

Typeset in India by MPS Limited
Printed in the UK by CPI Group (UK) Ltd, Eastbourne

Cover Image: MF3d / E+ via Getty Images

Contents

About the editors

Shyam Singh Rajput is an assistant professor at the Department of Computer Science & Engineering (CSE), National Institute of Technology Patna, India. His research interests include image processing, computer vision, *ad-hoc* networks, and information security. He has published over 45 journal and conference papers in the areas of image processing, computer vision, wireless *ad-hoc* networks, and information security. He holds an Indian Patent and has edited a book on *Digital Image Enhancement and Reconstruction*. He is a member of the IEEE and the ACM. He earned his PhD degree in CSE from the ABV-Indian Institute of Information Technology and Management, Gwalior, India.

Chen Chen is an assistant professor at the Center for Research in Computer Vision (CRCV), University of Central Florida, USA. His main research interests include computer vision, image and video processing and machine learning. He is an associate editor for the *IEEE Journal on Miniaturization for Air and Space Systems*, *Journal of Real-Time Image Processing*, *Signal, Image and Video Processing*, and *Sensors Journal*. He is a member of the *SIAM, IEEE, ACM*, and *IET*. He holds a PhD degree in electrical engineering from the University of Texas at Dallas, USA.

Karm Veer Arya is a professor at the ABV-Indian Institute of Information Technology & Management (IIITM), Gwalior, India. He has published several books including *Security in Mobile Ad-hoc Networks*, *Emerging Wireless Communication* and *Biometric Computing*, as well as book chapters and over 200 journal and conference papers in the areas of image processing, biometrics, and information security. He is on the editorial board of international journals and is a member of organizing committees and programs committee for conferences and workshops. He is a senior member of the *IEEE*, fellow of the *IETE*, fellow of the IE and life member of the ISTE. He holds a PhD degree in Computer Science and Engineering from the Indian Institute of Technology Kanpur, India.

Foreword

Multimedia (and more generally multimodal data) stands as one of the most demanding and exciting aspects of the information era. The processing of multimedia has been an active research area with applications in secure multimedia contents on social networks, digital forensics, digital cinema, education, secured e-voting systems, smart healthcare, automotive applications, the military, finance, insurance, and so on. The advent of the Internet of Things (IoT), cyber-physical systems (CPSs), robotics, as well as personal and wearable devices, now provides many opportunities for the multimedia community to reach out and develop synergies.

Our book series comprehensively defines the current trends and technological aspects of multimedia research with a particular emphasis on interdisciplinary approaches. The authors will review a broad scope to identify the challenges, solutions, and new directions. The published books can be used as references by practicing engineers, scientists, researchers, practitioners, and technology professionals from academia, government, and industry working on state-of-the-art multimedia processing, analysis, search, mining, management, and security solutions for practical applications. This will also be useful for senior undergraduate and graduate students as well as PhD students and postdoctoral researchers.

This book entitled *Intelligent Multimedia Processing and Computer Vision: Techniques and applications* focuses on state-of-the-art research in various fields of multimedia processing and computer vision along with the applications of artificial intelligence, machine learning, and deep learning to perform various processing tasks in numerous applications. The unique contribution of this volume is to bring together researchers from distinct domains that seldom interact to identify theoretical, technological, and practical issues related to the *Intelligent Multimedia Processing and Computer Vision*. The book is intended to enhance the understanding of opportunities and challenges in intelligent multimedia processing and its applications at the global level. We hope that the readers will find this book of great value in its visionary words.

Dr. Amit Kumar Singh, Book Series Editor
Department of Computer Science and Engineering
National Institute of Technology, Patna 800005, India

Prof. Stefano Berretti, Book Series Editor
Department of Information Engineering
University of Florence, Florence 50139, Italy

Chapter 1

Introduction

Shyam Singh Rajput[1] and Karm Veer Arya[2]

Multimedia stands as one of the most demanding and exciting aspects of the information era. The processing of multimedia information has been an active research area contributing to many frontiers of today's science and technology as well as many real-world applications. Traditional multimedia and intelligent multimedia are two different areas of multimedia.

Traditional media encompasses the display of images, graphics, audio, and video with possibly touch and virtual reality (VR) linked in. Intelligent multimedia involves computer processing and the understanding of perceptual input from speech, text, and images. Reacting to these inputs is much more complex and involves research from engineering, computer science, and cognitive science. This is the newest area in multimedia research that has seen an upsurge over the last few years and the one where most organizations, universities, and R&D agencies do not have proper expertise.

With increasing use of intelligent multimedia processing techniques in various fields, the requirement for fast and reliable techniques to analyze and process multimedia content for various purposes is also increasing day to day. For this purpose, artificial intelligence (AI) and machine learning (ML) techniques have been gaining prominence in recent years. This book sheds light on different AI and ML techniques used for intelligent multimedia processing and analysis. Multimedia processing deals with the analysis of images and videos to extract useful information regarding numerous applications, including medical imaging, robotics, remote sensing, autonomous driving, augmented reality/VR, law enforcement, biometrics, multimedia enhancement and reconstruction, agriculture, and security.

This book presents state-of-the-art research in various fields of multimedia processing and computer vision along with the applications of AI, ML, and deep learning (DL) to perform various processing tasks in the abovementioned areas. This book also provides a detailed discussion of the latest trends in processing tools required for computer vision applications. This is an attempt to provide a practical and an

[1]Department of Computer Science and Engineering, National Institute of Technology Patna, India
[2]Department of Computer Science and Engineering, ABV-Indian Institute of Information Technology and Management, Gwalior, India

adequate platform for researchers and practitioners from all over the world working in the fields of image processing, biometrics, computer vision, ML, and DL.

This book covers cutting-edge research from both academia and industry with a particular emphasis on interdisciplinary approaches, novel techniques, and solutions to provide intelligent multimedia for potential applications. We first cover recent trends, new concepts, and state-of-the-art approaches in the field of multimedia information processing for various emerging applications. We end the book with a chapter on future perspectives and research directions. A brief discussion of the major topics covered in this book is given below.

Chapter 2 presents the analysis of state-of-the-art ML techniques for image segmentation. Image segmentation is the process of extracting a set of desired pixels (objects, lines, and curves) that render useful information for computer vision tasks. It often includes the segregation of foreground from the background or clustering areas on the basis of color, gray level, contrast, texture, brightness, and shape similarity. It is used as the preprocessing step in many areas of computer vision and pattern recognition. The main applications are medical image analysis, automatic license plate recognition, video surveillance, hyperspectral image analysis, and autonomous driving. The epithelial and stroma segmentation from hematoxylin and eosin (H and E) staining images plays a pivotal role in cancer diagnosis. The detection of microcalcification regions in the mammogram is another important biomedical segmentation application. In the remote sensing scenario, land use/land cover area classification is an important area of research. Face segmentation is a key area of biometric research that finds application in sentiment analysis, facial pose and expression recognition, facial landmark detection, etc. The image segmentation task can be divided into three categories: semantic segmentation, instance segmentation, and panoptic segmentation. A detailed discussion on this topic is provided in Chapter 2.

Computer vision is a part of AI that helps computers to interpret, understand, and develop intuition about real-world objects and scenes to annotate, classify, and identify them with accurate precision. Computer vision techniques have been gaining popularity since their inception and have become a fundamental part of technological development and digital transformation. Biometrics recognition employs various aspects of AI to enable a computer system to recognize a biometric pattern for identification purposes. It is an inevitable part of multiple applications, such as border control cyber security, 3D faces modeling and recognition, intelligent video surveillance, finger vein recognition, and forensic biometrics where vision techniques have been integrated with and instilled into the biometrics systems in order to perform the desired tasks. Chapter 3 introduces biometrics-based computer vision and discusses the essential components of biometrics technologies for computer vision. The discussion also includes different processes, state-of-the-art techniques, challenges of biometrics-based computer vision, application areas, the selection criteria of suitable biometrics, and the future of biometrics-based computer vision applications.

Deep models are state-of-the-art models for fingerprint preprocessing. However, these models have a very high number of parameters, usually in millions.

As a result, redundancy is observed among the features learned by DL-based fingerprint preprocessing models. Channel refinement is a state-of-the-art method to help deep models learn distinct and informative features. Therefore, Chapter 4 delves into presenting a detailed study illustrating the usefulness of channel refinement in reducing redundancy and imparting generalization ability to fingerprint enhancement models. Furthermore, this chapter extends this study to assess whether channel refinement generalizes on fingerprint ROI segmentation. Extensive experiments on 14 challenging publicly available fingerprint databases and a private database of fingerprints of the rural Indian population were conducted to assess the potential of channel refinement on fingerprint preprocessing models.

Chapter 5 presents a brief review of DL approaches for video-based crowd anomaly detection. In recent years, the video surveillance system has gained huge attention in public and private places to provide security and safety. Video-based crowd anomaly detection (VCAD) is one of the crucial applications of a surveillance system whose timely detection and localization can prevent the massive loss of public or private properties and the lives of many people. Crowd anomalies or abnormal activities can be defined as irregular activities that deviate from normal crowd behavior patterns. Some abnormal activities in crowd scenes include panic, fights, stampedes, congestion, riots, and abandoned luggage, whose real-time detection is paramount. Crowd anomaly detection (CAD) becomes a more challenging task due to the dynamic nature of the crowd, the effect of the cluttered background, daylight changes, shape variation due to perspective distortion, and lack of large-scale ground-truth crowd datasets. Both conventional ML and DL approaches have been explored to provide different solutions for crowd anomaly detection. The current research trend shows the vast development of DL approaches for CAD. However, state-of-the-art reviews still need to address the comprehensive analysis of DL models, performance evaluation methodologies, open issues, and challenges for VCAD. Therefore, the main objective of this chapter is to provide an insightful analysis of several DL models for VCAD, their comparative analysis on different datasets based on various performance metrics, and to discuss future research scope for VCAD. A detailed discussion on this topic is provided in Chapter 5.

Every natural language presents certain regularities that have been studied for years. From statistical approaches to ML, many authors have found that automatic processing is far more complex than any other brain production. Despite the current status in the field, many applications like chatter-bots, speech recognition, and sentiment analysis show that there is still an interesting gap between the analysis and production of sentences. Despite the solutions being used nowadays, the deep essence of linguistic reasoning dynamics keeps mostly not revealed, and many of the current approaches involve the conception of restricted patterns for human linguistic reactions, usage, and interpretation. Hence, Chapter 6 presents a perspective of this problem centered on the idea followed by many authors that consider the brain as a complex device working under some kind of fractal rules, and deeply related to entropy. A detailed discussion on this topic is given in Chapter 6.

Chapter 7 gives a detailed discussion of AI and ML in medical data processing. A seizure is defined as a sudden synchronous activity of a group of neurons causing sudden movement of the body. Nearly 10 million people from India are suffering from epilepsy. EEG is a noninvasive technique to measure the neural activity of the brain. EEG signal processing and speech signal processing have application in seizure detection. Sudden neural activity in the brain is reflected in the EEG signal and is processed using ML and DL techniques for efficient seizure detection. This chapter gives an overview of different speech-processing and signal-processing techniques for seizure detection. DL and ML techniques are implemented and the results are discussed in this chapter. Different techniques are compared to give a future direction to the researcher to work in this field.

As the use of DL techniques in digital pathology for the detection of chest radiographs is increasing day by day, Chapter 8 of this book focuses on presenting a critical review of DL techniques implemented for this problem. Chest radiographs are one of the primary diagnostic medical imaging modalities in present clinical medicine. Compared to other medical imaging techniques, this noninvasive imaging modality is cost-effective. As a result, improving the radiography modality-based computer-aided diagnostic methods is a fruitful approach for obtaining reliable diagnostic results. In addition, it facilitates a wider clinical community around the globe, especially in low-income countries. Recently, DL has led to a promising performance in pathology detection in chest radiography used for the diagnosis of cancers, respiratory diseases, and some infectious diseases. As a result, various DL applications have been proposed for image enhancement, object detection and segmentation, localization, and image generation. A detailed discussion on this topic is provided in Chapter 8.

Computer vision and modern ML techniques for autonomous driving are discussed in Chapter 9. Human vision is one of the most important senses for receiving visual perception. When humans as the most intelligent living creatures look at a scene, they always perform a feature extraction from the information of that scene in order to understand its content. Using the extracted features, humans pay attention to the part of the scene that contains more valuable information and then turn their gaze to other parts of it, until they have analyzed all the relevant information. This is a natural and instinctive behavior of humans to gather information from the scenery and surrounding environment and it happens very quickly. Understanding the content of images in computer vision is not as fast as human understanding of the observer's scenery, but over many years, there has been an effort to increase the accuracy and speed of computer vision by imitating the behavior of human vision. In recent years, due to the significant advances in AI and the emergence of DL, we are witnessing increasing growth in computer vision and related areas, including autonomous driving. Recent works have demonstrated the incredible successes of computer vision and DL algorithms in various domains, including autonomous driving and robotics. Chapter 9 provides a detailed review of the state-of-the-art computer vision techniques for self-driving cars and some recent research advances in this field. After perceiving the challenges of autonomous driving, this chapter concentrates on five perspectives of autonomous driving from visual perception and computer vision viewpoints. These include (i) object detection, (ii) object tracking, (iii) segmentation, (iv) deep reinforcement learning, and (v) 3D scene analysis. A detailed discussion on this topic is provided in Chapter 9.

In order to demonstrate that dehazing techniques could be successfully used in actual practice, the Chapter 9 presents the study of the state-of-the-art dehazing approaches.

Poor visibility of outdoor images has drastically increased. Applications using computer vision such as surveillance systems and intelligent transportation systems are not able to function properly due to their limited visibility. Numerous image dehazing methods have been introduced as a solution to this problem, and they are crucial in enhancing the functionality of several computer vision systems. The dehazing approaches are intriguing to researchers as a consequence. A detailed study is presented in Chapter 10.

Agriculture is one of the potential parameters in the economic sector. Traditional modes of farming are not able to meet the growing need for food as the population is increasing hugely. Agricultural automation is very much essential to meet the supply–demand requirement of food and to minimize the employment issue and problems of food security. The introduction of AI in agricultural field has brought a revolution by improving the overall accuracy and harvest quality, detecting pests and diseases in plants using applications like drones, smart monitoring systems, and robots. Agricultural AI bots can harvest crops in a fast manner and in higher volume, which reduces the need for workers in higher numbers. ML, a subdomain under the umbrella of AI, is also used to capture the quality of seeds, pruning, parameters of soil, application of fertilizer, and environmental conditions. In addition, using AI and ML, farmers can solve other challenges like forecasting crop prices, market demand analysis, finding optimal time and conditions for harvesting and sowing, nutrient deficiencies in soil, and weight–diet balance using weight prediction systems. Using predictive analysis, ML techniques help to predict the right genes for different weather conditions and to reduce the chances of crop failures. As multimedia processing and computer vision also play a vital role in the domain of agriculture to achieve food security, Chapter 11 discusses the advancement in the domain of multimedia processing and computer vision for agricultural applications.

To date, surveillance systems are yielding the most critical and large volumes of data in the world from various sources. Hence, these data require proper management and analysis to produce relevant security information for modern security operations. However, it is still a challenge for humans to vigilantly monitor these large volumes of surveillance data for security assurance. Considering the upsurge in intelligent technologies, such as AI, ML, DL, and many more, the present security systems can be equipped with these technologies to radically increase the efficacy of surveillance systems. The self-learning capabilities of AI and ML technologies make a great impact on surveillance systems. Chapter 12 comprehensively discusses the possible amalgamation of AI and ML technologies with modern surveillance systems that will give them a technological edge. It also discusses about all new findings based on object detection, visual sentiment analysis, video analytics, vehicle analytics, and tracking people for potential crimes to ensure security for the society. Moreover, the specific types of AI and ML surveillance infrastructure being deployed is also discussed in Chapter 12.

Action recognition is a basic task in computer vision that focuses on identifying and understanding human activities from video stream. It is important for various applications, including video surveillance (static or dynamic), human–computer interaction (HCI), sports video analysis, and autonomous vehicles. Human action recognition covers an extremely large number of research topics in computer vision and has a wide range of applications in visual surveillance. Action recognition in visual surveillance refers to the process of automatically analyzing and understanding human actions and activities captured by surveillance cameras or video feeds. This plays a crucial role in various applications, such as security monitoring, anomaly detection, and behavior understanding. Chapter 13 presents a review of action recognition in visual surveillance, including its challenges, techniques, and recent advancements. Moreover, at the end of this chapter, future research directions are also presented.

Finally, conclusion, future perspectives, and research directions related to different topics discussed in this book are presented in Chapter 14.

Chapter 2

State-of-the-art analysis of deep learning techniques for image segmentation

Rini Smita Thakur[1], Shubhojeet Chatterjee[1], Ram Narayan Yadav[1] and Lalita Gupta[1]

Abstract

Image segmentation is an important computer vision problem that captures a particular region of interest by leveraging per-pixel image classification. It has significant applications in various fields, such as biomedical engineering, remote sensing, autonomous driving, etc. There has been a gradual evolution towards deep learning image segmentation methods, including convolutional neural networks, recurrent neural networks, encoder-decoder architectures, and generative adversarial networks. This chapter provides a description of deep learning image segmentation networks, offering insights into their architectural details, performance assessment metrics, advantages, and disadvantages.

2.1 Introduction

Image segmentation is the process of extracting set of desired pixels (objects, lines and curves) which render useful information for computer vision tasks. It often includes segregation of foreground from the background or clustering areas on the basis of the color, grey level, contrast, texture, brightness and shape similarity. It is used as the pre-processing step in many areas of computer vision and pattern recognition. The main applications are medical image analysis [1], automatic license plate recognition, video surveillance, hyperspectral image analysis, autonomous driving, etc. [2]. The epithelial and stroma segmentation from hematoxylin and eosin (H&E) stain images play a pivotal role in cancer diagnosis [3]. The detection of micro-calcification region in the mammogram is another important biomedical segmentation application [4]. In the remote sensing scenario, land use/land cover area classification is an important area of research. Face segmentation is key area of biometric research, which finds application in

[1]Department of Electronics and Communication Engineering, Maulana Azad National Institute of Technology, Bhopal, India

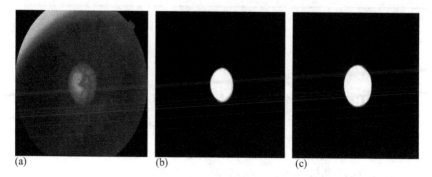

(a)   (b)   (c)

Figure 2.1   (a) Fundus image, (b) segmented optical cup and (c) segmented
            optical disk

sentiment analysis, facial pose and expression recognition, facial landmark detection, etc. Figure 2.1 depicts the fundus image along with ground-truth optical cup and optical disc masks.

The image segmentation task can be divided into three categories: semantic segmentation, instance segmentation and panoptic segmentation. Semantic segmentation assigns each pixel in an image to certain object category. It identifies pixel collection that forms different classes. For example, in case of automatic driving it labels foothpath, driveway, vehicles, and traffic sign. However, semantic segmentation cannot distinguish between different objects of the same class. So, the instance segmentation is further advancement of semantic segmentation. It is able to identify the instances of the particular class by creating segmentation map for each detected instance of an object. It treats the individual objects as distinct categories irrespective of the class. However, semantic segmentation treats all objects of the same class as the single entity. For example, in case of automatic driving, instance segmentation can identify instances of the vehicle class such as car, bike, truck, etc.

Panoptic segmentation combines the distinct function of semantic segmentation (class label assignment to each pixel) and instance segmentation (detection and segmentation of each object instance). It is widely used for real-world image segmentation applications. The goal of panoptic segmentation is to separate stuff and things. The stuff refers to the uncountable regions such as sky, ocean, etc., whereas things refer to the countable stuff such as people, car, etc. Panoptic segmentation is widely used for the video and LiDAR data [5].

Some classical approaches of image segmentation are thresholding-based methods, edge detection-based methods, clustering-based methods, region-based methods, watershed-based, sparsity-based methods, and machine learning-based methods [6]. Thresholding-based methods segments on the basis of the pixel intensity value using an appropriate threshold, ex histogram thresholding. In the edge detection-based methods, edges are segmented using certain filters or algorithms on image data such as Laplacian of Gaussian and Canny edge detection. Region growing is an example of bottom-up algorithm which starts from collection of pixels called seeds that belong to the area of interest. The goal is to grow connected and uniform region from each seed.

The sparsity-based methods are based on the concept of sparse representation of signal and dictionary learning. The selection of handcrafted features by genetic algorithm followed by machine learning models (support vector machines and artificial neural networks) is a common methodology for machine learning-based segmentation.

In recent years, there is a paradigm shift towards deep learning models, which offers improvement in accuracy on popular benchmark datasets. The deep learning networks provide high-dimensional hierarchical features for the precise image recognition [7]. The deep learning models commonly used for image segmentation are based on convolutional neural networks, generative adversarial networks, encoder–decoder networks, recurrent neural networks (RNNs) and long short-term memory. The following section gives overview of the deep learning models.

2.2 Outline of deep learning models

2.2.1 Convolutional neural networks

The convolutional neural networks (CNNs) are widely being used for various computer vision and pattern recognition tasks. It was adaptation of biological receptive fields based on the work of Hubel and Wessel on the visual cortex of the animal [8]. The first adaptation of concept of receptive field into the network is given in the Neocognitron model with two basic layers: convolutional and downsampling. The CNNs extract the image high-level image hierarchical features with the help of the convolutional operator. The convolutional filters are basically used for automated learning of image features such as edges, colour, texture, etc.

The basic CNN consists of input layer which is the basic image input data. The subsequent layers are hidden layers with convolution, activation and pooling operation. The convolution filter is slided over the entire input image and the output image termed as feature maps is obtained. The convolutional filter weights are the learnable parameters. The feature maps are then processed by the activation functions to facilitate non-linear functions modelling by the network. The pooling layer reduces spatial dimension by some statistical operation (min, max and average). The output layer usually comprises of the fully connected layer which yields the number of classes as the output nodes. The network optimization takes place by the stochastic gradient descent-based techniques and its variants (Adam, NAG), etc. on the basis of the value of the loss functions [9]. The layers receive the weighted inputs from the small regions of the previous layers known as receptive field. The multi-resolution pyramids are formed by stacking the layers. Subsequently, the higher-level layer learns the features from the incremental wider receptive fields. The advantage of the CNNs over ANNs is the concept of weight sharing which reduces the computational complexity. Figure 2.2 depicts basis CNN model.

There are some benchmark CNN-based image classification models such as Imagenet, ResNet, VGGNet, GoogleNet, etc. These image classification models can be adapted for the image segmentation tasks by the concept of transfer learning. The pre-trained models capture the semantic information required for segmentation enabling model to be trained by a smaller number of training samples.

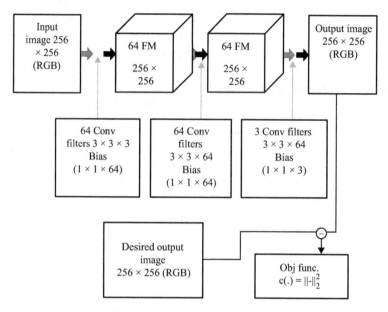

Figure 2.2   Basic CNN model

2.2.2   Recurrent neural network

The RNN is widely used in the tasks where previously stored information plays a key role in the prediction of the current output. For example, Google autocomplete feature predicts the rest of the words that user is typing. It is widely used for sequential data processing applications such as time-series, text, videos and speech. At each time instance, the network aggregates the input from current time and hidden state and produces two outputs (target value and new hidden state). The backpropagation in time algorithm computes gradient vector for training purpose.

A special RNN architecture termed as long short-term memory (LSTM) units overcome the vanishing and exploding gradient problem of simple RNN structure [10]. It has the capability to learn long-term dependencies and learning information over the large time interval. All the RNNs have the repeating modules of neural network. In the simple RNN, repeating module is tanh structure, whereas in LSTM the repeating module is made up of four interacting layers. The LSTM architecture comprises of the input gate, output gate and the forget gate which control the data/ information flow into and out from the memory cell.

2.2.3   Encoder–decoder architecture

The encoder–decoder architecture belongs to the category of two-stage representation (encoder and decoder) that maps input domain to an output domain [11]. The encoder and decoder units are made up of RNNs, CNNs depending upon the machine learning application. The encoder part (f) converts the input (x) into some intermediate latent space representation (z), given by function $z = f(x)$. The functionality of the decoder

(g) is to predict the output (y) from this latent representation ($y = g(z)$). The underlying semantic information of the input is being captured by the latent feature (vector) representation. The encoder–decoder architecture is widely used for the sequence-to-sequence prediction, image-to-image translation and neural machine translation. It is the core architecture used for the Google's translation services.

The training involves minimization of the reconstruction error loss $L(y, \hat{y})$, where L is mathematical formulation to measure difference between ground truth and estimated output. The output is basically the refined version of an image such as segmentation image, denoised image, deblurred image, high-resolution image, etc. The auto-encoders are special class of encoder–decoder architecture, which have the same input and output (Figure 2.3).

2.2.4 Generative adversarial networks

Generative adversarial networks (GANs) have harnessed lot of attention of the computer vision enthusiasts due to its ability to generate data without explicit modelling with the probability density function [12]. The generative modelling belongs to the unsupervised learning task category, that involves automatic learning of irregularities or patterns from the input data in order to generate new samples that plausibly could have been drawn from original dataset.

The GANs have the ability to translate unsupervised generative modelling task into the supervised problem with the help of two networks termed as the generator and the discriminator. The generator network $(G) = z \rightarrow y$ in the conventional GAN learns a mapping from noise z (with a prior distribution) to a target distribution y, which is similar to the 'real' samples. The task to the discriminator as its name implies is to 'discriminate' the real and fake input samples. The GAN's discriminator and generator work in collaboration to play a min–max game, i.e., loss function minimization by G and maximization by D. The GAN loss function may be written as

$$LGAN = E_{x \sim pdata(x)}[\log D(x)] + E_{Z \sim p(z)}\log[1 - D(G(z))] \qquad (2.1)$$

Figure 2.4 depicts a basic GAN architecture.

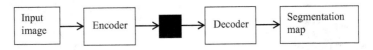

Figure 2.3   Basic encoder–decoder architecture

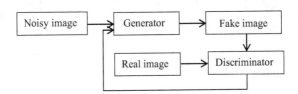

Figure 2.4   Basic generative adversarial network architecture

2.3   Types of semantic segmentation architectures

2.3.1   Convolutional neural network-based architecture

2.3.1.1   Fully convolutional neural-based networks

The fully convolutional neural networks for segmentation are derived from the benchmark image classification CNNs [13]. As it is evident, the simple image classifier network has the series for convolutional, activation and pooling units followed by the fully connected layers at the end. The fully connected layer at the outputs the probability or classification score for each class. However, in case of the image segmentation problems, the desired output is spatial segmentation map instead of the classification scores. Therefore, fully connected layers are converted into the fully convolutional layer to enhance the spatial dimension for segmentation map generation. The last fully connected retains the original resolution. The task of semantic segmentation assigns labels to every pixel. This is accomplished by the application of softmax cross-entropy between the pixel-wise predictions and actual segmentation ground-truth. Training is achieved by stochastic gradient descent and its variants with back-propagation. Figure 2.5 shows a fully convolutional neural network architecture.

The conversion of final feature maps into the original resolution is required for comparison with the ground-truth map. The spatial resolution of the network keeps reducing due to series of the convolution and pooling layers. The model reproduces the original resolution with the help of skip connections. Skip connections merge the output feature maps with the previous layer feature maps with adequate upsampling. The upsampling of output feature is done for proper addition of feature maps. Therefore, the segmentation mask can be predicted from either low level, middle level and high level features, as shown in Figure 2.6.

2.3.1.2   Convolutional models with graphical models

Convolutional deep learning image segmentation models integrate graphical models such as conditional random field (CRF) and Markov random field to include scene-level semantic context [14]. It performs better than fully connected

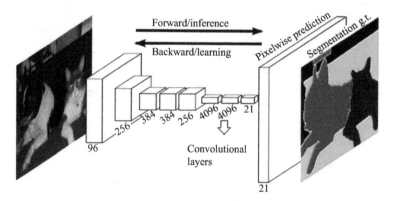

Figure 2.5   Fully convolutional neural network architecture

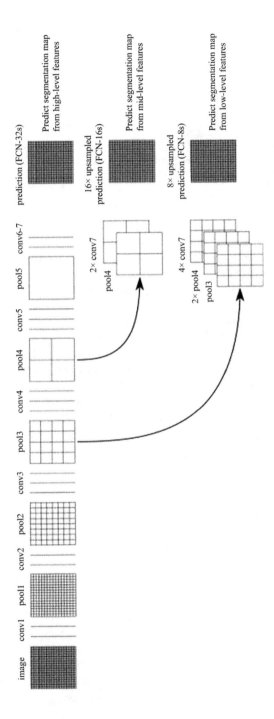

Figure 2.6 Fully convolutional neural network upsampling

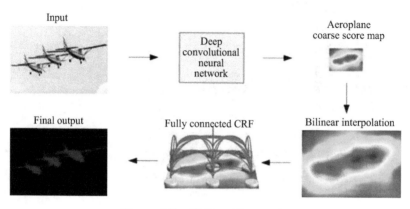

Figure 2.7   CNN + CRF model

convolutional neural networks. The invariance property of the CNN is good for classification task but it hinders localization for accurate semantic segmentation. Conditional random fields refine the coarse output segmentation map on the basis of label of each pixel along with neighbouring pixels labels and locations. The fully connected CRF is used in cascade connection with the CNN model as shown in Figure 2.7. It overcomes the disadvantage of poor localization of CNN. The CRF modifies the output of the pixel-based classifier on the basis of locations and labels of adjacent pixels. Fully connected pairwise connections imply that all pixels are connected in pairs with each other.

The core concept of CRF is based on the minimization of the energy function, i.e., minimization of the label assignment energy. The conditional probability distribution for the process of semantic segmentation of a label vector configuration is given by [15]:

$$p(y|,x) = \frac{1}{T(x)}\exp\{-E(y,x)\} \tag{2.2}$$

where x is the input image, y is the label vector configuration, $T(x)$ is the partition function and $E(y,x)$ is the energy function.

The energy function comprises the unary term and pairwise energy term. The unary energy term calculates the cost when label assignment disagreement is with the initial classifier. The pairwise energy term calculates the cost when there is variability in label identification of the two similar pixels.

$$E(x) = \sum_i \theta_i(x_i) + \sum_{i,j} \theta_{i,j}(x_i,x_j) \tag{2.3}$$

where $\theta_i(x_i)$ is the unary potential and $\theta_{i,j}(x_i,x_j)$ is the pairwise potential. A detailed literature review of segmentation with combination of modelling power of the CRF and the feature learning ability of the CNN is given in [16]. The similar image segmentation technique combining CRF with RNN is given in [17].

2.3.2   Encoder–decoder convolutional models

Encoder–decoder convolutional models are another category in which encoder portion traps the relevant features whereas decoder module maintains spatial resolution. The function of the decoder is to decode the segmentation information in the form of the desired segmentation map.

2.3.2.1   General segmentation

In [18], the encoder part extracts the feature vectors from VGG-16 network with the convolutional, ReLU units and pooling operation. The decoder part takes feature vectors as the input and generates the segmentation map with the help of multiple sections of deconvolution, rectification and unpooling operation. This network is applied on each proposal of the input image and produces the sematic segmentation map by aggregating the results of all proposals in a simplistic manner. The segmentation map contains pixel-wise class probabilities.

The SegNet [19] architecture consists of encoder module with 13 convolutional layers in the VGG-16 network as given in Figure 2.8. The pooling indices of two cross two max-pooling is stored to be used for decoding. The decoder module converts the output low resolution feature maps of the encoder into the input size resolution feature maps for pixel-wise classification. It upsamples the encoder feature maps with the stored pooling indices to generate the sparse feature maps and thereby eliminates the need of learning up-sampling. It is followed by convolutional operation with trainable filter kernels to further create dense feature maps. The k-class softmax classifier is employed in the final step to generate class-wise pixel probabilities. The SegNet model has been used in various applications, example semantic segmentation of plants [20]. The Bayesian version of the SegNet architecture is given in [21].

The residual learning-based encoder–decoder architecture has been used for autonomous driving with VGG-16 as encoder backbone. Residual learning restores the context information while reducing the feature maps size in the series of convolutional layers. It further restores the resolution by short-cut connections from the encoder module to the decoder module [22].

The other works based on the transposed convolutions are DT-CNN [23], CDTNet [24], stacked deconvolution network (SDN) [25], LinkNet and WNet.

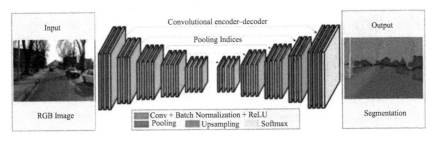

Figure 2.8   SegNet architecture

2.3.2.2   Bio-medical image segmentation

The U-Net architecture [26] and its variants are used for the biomedical image segmentation (Figure 2.9). It was first employed for segmentation of the neuronal structures and won ISBI cell tracking challenge 2015. In the U-Net architecture, the fully convolutional layers are used in the entire network. It intends to use the maximum information from the encoder layers at all levels during upsampling to maintain features of the context as well as localization. The U-net architecture consists of contracting path (context information) and the symmetric expanding path (localization). The encoder module or contracting path has the architecture resembling that of fully convolutional networks using four blocks. Each block has 3 × 3 convolutions with batch normalization, ReLU activation and max pooling. The decoder module or expansion path consists of four blocks. Each block has deconvolution with stride of two, concatenation module and two 3 × 3 convolutions plus ReLU activation and batch normalization. In the concatenation module, the feature maps from different stages of encoder are concatenated with the output of deconvolution layers using skip connection. At the final stage, the segmentation map with same size as that of the input image is generated with the help of 1 × 1 convolution. The detailed review of UNet and its variants for segmentation of different imaging modalities is given in [27].

There are various variants of the UNet architecture. The Half-UNet [28] architecture comprises of simplified architecture considering full-scale feature fusion, channel numbers unification and ghost modules. It has been used for both CT and MRI image segmentation. The UNet architecture is modified for semantic segmentation of the underwater images [29]. The Dense-UNet model is

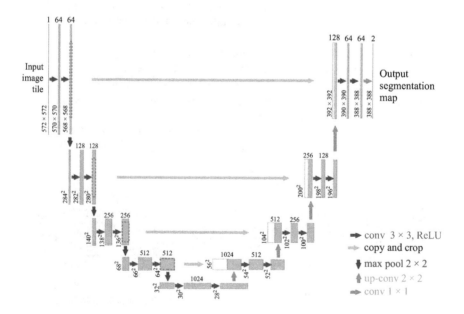

Figure 2.9   U-Net architecture

designed for multi-photon microscopy in vivo skin cells images. AM-UNet segments the human brain claustrum using 3D-MRI images [30]. U-Net and fully convolutional neural networks are also used for the fundus image segmentation on RIGA dataset [31].

However, the skip connections of the U-Net architecture fail to capture indistinct boundaries accurately. The high-resolution-multi-scale encoder–decoder network (HMEDN) [32] is designed with extra deeply supervised high-resolution pathways apart from the skip connections for 2D/3D semantic segmentation. These pathways along with difficulty guided cross-entropy loss function and contour regression task preserves the attribute of boundary detection. This network is used on cell segmentation dataset, CT image dataset and a multi-modal brain tumour dataset.

V-Net [33] is another architecture designed for 3D biomedical image segmentation. It is based on volumetric fully convolutional neural network with Dice coefficient-based loss function. The Dice coefficient-based loss function solves the class imbalance problem between background and foreground voxels. Data augmentation with histogram matching and random non-linear transformation withstand the effect of restricted number of samples availability at training time.

2.3.2.3   Deep lab versions (atrous convolutions)

The spatial resolution keeps on decreasing in the fully convolutional neural network architecture. The DeepLab family models preserve the spatial resolution with the help of dilated or atrous convolutions. The dilated convolutions introduce multiple field of views during feature extraction process. In dilated convolution, the zeroes are inserted between the elements on the convolution filter as per the dilation rate (r). The dilated convolution mathematical formula is given by:

$$y[i] = \sum_{k=1}^{K} x[i + rk]w[k] \qquad (2.4)$$

where r is the dilation rate that denotes the number of zeroes inserted between weights of the convolutional kernel. It keeps the output stride (input size/output size) of the feature maps constant without increasing computational complexity and number of parameters. For example, a 3×3 convolutional kernel with dilation rate of two has the same receptive field size as that of convolutional kernel of size (5×5). Therefore, dilated convolutions enhance receptive field with just nine parameters with no increment in the computational cost.

The DeepLab versions are based on the use of dilated convolutions and atrous spatial pyramid pooling. There are main three versions of DeepLab architecture for semantic segmentation with the following features:

(1) DeepLab v1: It maintains the image features resolution with the usage of atrous convolution and conditional random field.
(2) DeepLab v2: The information at multiple scales is extracted with atrous spatial pyramid pooling (ASSP). It is atrous version of the spatial pyramid pooling given in SPPNet.

(3) DeepLab v3+: It uses encoder–decoder module with multi-grid method, boot-strapping method, and atrous spatial pyramid pooling. The fully connected random fields of DeepLab v1 and DeepLab v2 are not used in this version.

The DeepLab v1 [34] just uses the backbone VGG-16 architecture and atrous convolutions to enhance the field of view (FOV). The atrous convolutions provide the trade-off between the accurate localization (small FOV) and context assimilation (large FOV). It captures the fine details from the segmented coarse map with the fully connected conditional random field and multi-scale prediction. It is basically a combination of convolutional neural network model with graphical probabilistic models for boundary refinement.

The DeepLab v2 [35] has additional atrous spatial pyramid pooling module (ASSP) for segmentation at the multiple scales. The input feature maps are con-volved with different dilation rates to capture effective field of views. The bi-linear interpolation is applied on the coarse map to increase the size same as that of the input image. The output of the bi-linear interpolation is fed as the input to the conditional random fields.

The DeepLab v3 [36] architecture uses the combination of the cascade of and parallel modules of the atrous convolutions (Figure 2.10). The batch normalization module from Inception-v2 and image pooling by the ParseNet is included in the ASSP. The ASSP module with multiple field of views augments with image level features. The final outputs of ASSP are concatenated by 1×1 convolution to generate the segmentation map with logits for every pixel. In the cascaded atrous convolution, dilation rate is doubled gradually.

The DeepLab v3+ [37] is the encoder–decoder-based architecture which utilize DeepLab v3 as the encoder part. In the decoder part of DeepLab v3+, concatenated feature maps from ASSP are bilinearly upsampled by the factor of four. It is then concatenated with the corresponding low-level feature maps. There is application of 1×1 convolution on the low-level features before concatenation to control the

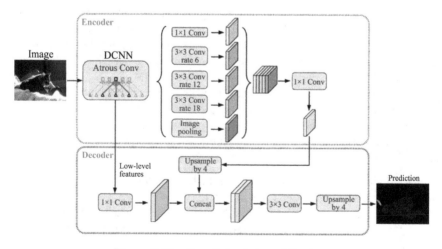

Figure 2.10   DeepLab v3 + architecture

number of channels. The concatenated (ASSP + low-level features) are passed through the 3 × 3 convolution for further feature refinement followed by the simple bilinear upsampling by a factor of four. It uses modified aligned Xception and ResNet as the backbone.

The DeepLab v3+ architecture has been used as the backbone in various other segmentation applications. It is used as the backbone network for the optic cup and disc segmentation in the fundus images by adversarial segmentation-based BEAL network [38].

2.3.2.4   Recurrent neural-based architectures

The RNNs capture the high level (long and short term) pixel dependencies of the similar pixels and it maintains spatial and appearance consistency of the segmentation labels. The RNNs comprise of the recurrent units and its gated variants. The sequential processing of the pixels with the RNNs improves the segmentation performance by capturing the global context. However, global context information is retrieved at the expense of computational complexity.

The image classification model ReNet is modified into the semantic segmentation model ReSeg [39]. The ReNet layer comprise of the four RNN sweeping the image horizontally and vertically (both upwards and downwards). This layer encodes the activations or patches in order to extract relevant global information. VGG-16 is used as the backbone network with the stacked ReNet layer. The feature maps extracted from the initial layers of the VGG-16 are fed into the ReNet layer. The consequent upsampling layer maintains the same resolution as that of the input image. The usage of gated recurrent units provide an optimum balance between the computational power and memory requirement.

The standard U-Net-based architecture is modified into the recurrent convolutional neural-based architecture termed as the R2AUNet [40]. It replaces the standard convolutional units of the U-Net architecture into the basic recurrent residual convolutional units. The original skip connections of the U-Net architecture are also replaced with the attention gates. The inclusion of attention gates utilizes deep features of the decoder module as the gating signal for shallow features modification and background feature response suppression. The other recurrent architectures based on the U-Net are recurrent CNN (RCNN) and the recurrent residual CNN (RRCNN) [41]. The recurrent convolutional layer and recurrent convolutional layer with residual units are added instead of the standard convolutional layers in both encoder and decoder. Residual units enhance the training efficiency of the deeper networks. The features accumulation with the residual units at different time steps improves segmentation results. Moreover, recurrent architecture-based models perform better than that of the UNet architecture with same number of the network parameters. The models are used for vessel segmentation from fundus images, lung lesion segmentation and skin cancer segmentation from the dermoscopic images.

RaceNet [42] architecture is based on level set-based deformable networks. The curve curvature velocities are estimated at the each time step. The normal and curvature of the level set function is formed by feed-forward neural network architecture at each time step. It overcomes the problems of CNN's such as over-fitting, memory requirements and region-based pixel labelling.

The combination of CNN and RNN termed as GRUU-net [43] has been used for the cell segmentation. It is the combination of the gated recurrent blocks and pooling blocks. The iterative refinement of the feature maps is done by the gated recurrent unit and the multi-scale feature aggregation is based on the U-Net architecture. The training includes normalized pixel-wise focal cross-entropy loss to deal with class imbalance and enforce object separation.

2.3.2.5   Generative adversarial network-based architectures

The GANs with the generative and discriminator sub-network has been used for various computer vision tasks including image segmentation [44]. In one of the first works of the GAN-based semantic segmentation, segmentor and adversarial network is connected in cascade manner (Figure 2.11). The convolutional segmentation network generates the segmentation map which is fed as the discriminator input [45]. The discriminator tries to discriminate between the ground-truth segmentation map and generated segmentation map. The impetus of this network design lies in detecting and correcting higher-order inconsistencies between ground truth segmentation maps and segmentor network segmentation maps.

SegGAN [46] uses a (a) pre-trained semantic segmentation network (DeepLab), (b) generator network for generating images from the segmentation network output, and (c) discriminator network for discriminating between fake images obtained from the generator and the original images of the datasets. The first step is to train the GAN with the ground-truth mask images as the input of the generator and try to reduce the loss between original images and the generated images. This step learns the relationship between the original images and ground-truth masks. Thereafter, the GAN network is combined with a pre-trained semantic segmentation network.

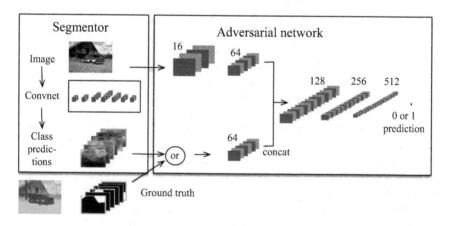

Figure 2.11   GAN architecture

2.4 Performance assessment metrics

The semantic segmentation model should be evaluated ideally on multiple parameters such as storage requirements, computational time and qualitative accuracy. However, most of the semantic segmentation performance assessment metrics focus on network accuracy. The commonly used performance metrics of the semantic segmentation are discussed below:

1) Pixel accuracy (PA): It denotes the number of correctly classified pixels (in percentage) for the task of the semantic segmentation. The PA of $K + 1$ classes (K foreground and background) is given by

$$PA = \frac{\sum_{i=0}^{K} p_{ii}}{\sum_{i=0}^{K} \sum_{j=0}^{K} p_{ij}} \tag{2.5}$$

where p_{ij} is the number of pixels of class i predicted as belonging to class j.

2) Mean pixel accuracy (MPA): It is used when ratio of corrected-pixels is computed in a per class manner and then averaging is done over the total number of classes.

$$\text{MPA} = \frac{1}{K+1} \sum_{i=0}^{K} \frac{p_{ii}}{\sum_{j=0}^{K} p_{ij}} \tag{2.6}$$

PA and MPA are the intuitive and interpretable semantic segmentation performance assessment metrics. It has been noticed that high PA does not directly imply good performance in case of the imbalanced datasets.

3) Intersection over Union (IoU): It is also termed as the Jaccard Index, and it is defined by area of intersection (predicted segmentation map, ground-truth) divided by the area of union (predicted segmentation map, ground-truth). It is given by:

$$IoU = J(A, B) = \frac{|A \cap B|}{|A \cup B|} = \frac{TP}{TP + FP + FN} \tag{2.7}$$

where A and B represent the ground-truth and predicted segmentation masks, respectively.

TP, FP and FN represent the true positive fraction, false positive fraction and false negative fraction, respectively.

4) Mean IoU: It is formulated by taking the mean over IoU over all the segmentation classes.

5) Precision/Recall/F1 score: They are common classification metrics which are used for segmentation as well. They can be defined for both class level and at the aggregate level. The formula of precision and recall is given by:

$$Precision = \frac{TP}{TP + FP} \tag{2.8}$$

$$Recall = \frac{TP}{TP + FN} \tag{2.9}$$

where *TP*, *TN*, *FP* and *FN* represent true positive fraction, true negative fraction, false positive fraction and false negative fraction, respectively.

The combined version of the combination of the precision and recall is given by *F*1 score, which is harmonic mean of precision and recall.

$$F1 \text{ score} = \frac{2 \times \text{Precision} \times \text{Recall}}{\text{Precision} + \text{Recall}} \tag{2.10}$$

6) Dice coefficient: It is denoted by the twice of the area overlapped by segmentation ground-truth and predicted segmentation masks divided by the number of pixels in both the images. It is given by the following formula:

$$\text{Dice} = \frac{2|A \cap B|}{|A| + |B|} \tag{2.11}$$

The Dice coefficient is identical to the *F*1 score in case of binary segmentation masks with the foreground as the positive class.

2.5   Performance analysis

The detailed performance analysis of the various models on the benchmark datasets such as PASCAL VOC, Cityscapes, MS COCO, ADE20k, e NYUD-v2 and SUN-RGBD datasets, etc. is given in [47]. It has been observed that there is significant performance improvement from the initial fully convolutional networks to the DeepLab family. The SegGaN network reports better performance than DeepLab on a Stanford Dataset. The U-Net architecture produce good segmentation results on the biomedical images. The exact comparative analysis between all models is hindrance due to usage of different datasets for training and testing, non-availability of source codes, missing details of experimental setup or the hyper parameters, etc. There is recent progress in image segmentation owing to the use of transformers, deep interactive image segmentation modules and design of the boundary sensitive loss functions.

2.6   Summary

This chapter gives overview of the deep learning-based image segmentation techniques with the basic architectural details. There is gradual evolution from conversion of convolutional neural network-based classification network into the fully convolutional segmentation network. The key concept involves conversion of the fully connected layers into the fully convolutional layers to retain the spatial resolution. The next series of models have encoder–decoder type architecture, where encoder entraps necessary features for segmentation, and decoder module use the information from the encoder to generate the original resolution segmentation maps. These models have additional connections from different parts of encoder to decoder (skip, copy and crop, concatenation, direct). The benchmark encoder–decoder network is U-Net, which is the basis of design of various other segmentation variants. DeepLabv3+ with backbone (MobileNet, VGGNet, ResNet and XceptionNet) has been used for many practical segmentation applications. RNN-based architectures tend to preserve regional homogeneity within and outside the boundary by explicitly modelling the high-level dependencies between the points on the object boundary. Recently, generative modelling-based generative adversarial networks with image synthesis power have further improved the segmentation results with different GAN variants such as Vanilla-GAN, Conditional-GAN, Cycle-GAN, DC-GAN, Wasserstein-GAN, etc. The future research directions are annotation of more challenging datasets, design of real-time and memory efficient models, design of 3D-cloud segmentation models, etc.

References

[1]   G. Makwana, R. N. Yadav, and L. Gupta, "Comparative analysis of image fusion techniques for medical image enhancement," in *Proc. Inter. Conf. Comput. Intell. Alg Intel. Sys*, 2022, pp. 241–252, doi: 10.1007/978-981-16-3802-2_20.

[2]   S. Patel, "Deep learning models for image segmentation," in *2021 8th Int. Conf. Compu. Sust. Global Dev. (INDIACom)*, 2021, pp. 149–154.

[3]   T. A. Azevedo Tosta, L. A. Neves, and M. Z. do Nascimento, "Segmentation methods of H&E-stained histological images of lymphoma: A review," *Informatics Med. Unlocked*, vol. 9, pp. 35–43, 2017, doi: 10.1016/J. IMU.2017.05.009.

[4]   G. Makwana, R. N. Yadav, and L. Gupta, "A comparative analysis of image enhancement techniques for detection of microcalcification in screening mammogram," *High Perform. Comput. Intell. Med. Syst.*, 2021, doi: 10.1088/978-0-7503-3815-8CH10.

[5]   X. Li and D. Chen, "A survey on deep learning-based panoptic segmentation," *Digit. Signal Process.*, vol. 120, p. 103283, 2022, doi: 10.1016/J. DSP.2021.103283.

[6]   R. Pal, S. Mukhopadhyay, D. Chakraborty, and P. N. Suganthan, "Very high-resolution satellite image segmentation using variable-length multi-objective genetic clustering for multi-class change detection," *J. King Saud Univ. – Comput. Inf. Sci.*, 2022, doi: 10.1016/J.JKSUCI.2021.12.023.

[7]   S. Masubuchi, E. Watanabe, Y. Seo, *et al.*, "Deep-learning-based image segmentation integrated with optical microscopy for automatically searching for two-dimensional materials," *NPJ 2D Mater. Appl.*, vol. 4, no. 1, pp. 1–9, 2020, doi: 10.1038/s41699-020-0137-z.

[8]   D. H. Hubel and T. Wiesel, "Receptive fields, binocular interaction and functional architecture in the cat's visual cortex," *J. Physiol.*, vol. 160, no. 1, pp. 106–154, 1962.

[9]   D. P. Kingma and J. L. Ba, "Adam: A method for stochastic optimization," in 3rd International Conference on Learning Representations, ICLR 2015 – *Conference Track Proceedings*, 2015.

[10]   B. Lindemann, T. Müller, H. Vietz, N. Jazdi, and M. Weyrich, "A survey on long short-term memory networks for time series prediction," *Procedia CIRP*, vol. 99, pp. 650–655, 2021, doi: 10.1016/J.PROCIR.2021.03.088.

[11]   H. Zhang, S. Li, Y. Chen, J. Dai, and Y. Yi, "A novel encoder-decoder model for multivariate time series forecasting," *Comput. Intell. Neurosci.*, vol. 2022, 2022, doi: 10.1155/2022/5596676.

[12]   A. Creswell, T. White, V. Dumoulin, K. Arulkumaran, B. Sengupta, and A. A. Bharath, "Generative adversarial networks: An overview," *IEEE Signal Process. Mag.*, vol. 35, no. 1, pp. 53–65, doi: 10.1109/MSP.2017.2765202.

[13]   J. Long, E. Shelhamer, and T. Darrell, "Fully convolutional networks for semantic segmentation," in *Proc. IEEE Comp. Soc. Conf. Comp. Vis. Pattern Recog.*, 2015, vol. 07–12 June, pp. 431–440, doi: 10.1109/CVPR.2015.7298965.

[14]   L.-C. Chen, G. Papandreou, I. Kokkinos, K. Murphy, and A. L. Yuille, "Semantic image segmentation with deep convolutional nets and fully connected CRFs," pp. 1–12, 2014, doi: 10.48550/arxiv.1412.7062.

[15]   L. Zhou, X. Kong, C. Gong, F. Zhang, and X. Zhang, "FC-RCCN: Fully convolutional residual continuous CRF network for semantic segmentation," *Pattern Recognit. Lett.*, vol. 130, pp. 54–63, doi: 10.1016/J.PATREC.2018.08.030.

[16]   A. Arnab, S. Zheng, S. Jayasumana, *et al.*, "Conditional random fields meet deep neural networks for semantic segmentation: Combining probabilistic graphical models with deep learning for structured prediction," *IEEE Signal Process. Mag.*, vol. 35, no. 1, pp. 37–52, doi: 10.1109/MSP.2017.2762355.

[17]   S. Zheng, S. Jayasumana, B. Romera-Paredes, *et al.*, "Conditional random fields as recurrent neural networks," *Proc. IEEE Int. Conf. Comput. Vis.*, vol. 2015 Inter, pp. 1529–1537, 2015, doi: 10.1109/ICCV.2015.179.

[18]   S. Hong, B. Han, and H. Noh, "Learning deconvolution network for semantic segmentation," in *IEEE Int. Conf. Comp. Vision (ICCV)*, 2015, pp. 1520–1528, doi: 10.1109/ICCV.2015.178.

[19]   V. Badrinarayanan, A. Kendall, and R. Cipolla, "SegNet: A deep convolutional encoder–decoder architecture for image segmentation," *IEEE Trans. Pattern Anal. Mach. Intell.*, vol. 39, no. 12, pp. 2481–2495, doi: 10.1109/TPAMI.2016.2644615.

[20]   S. Kolhar and J. Jagtap, "Convolutional neural network based encoder-decoder architectures for semantic segmentation of plants," *Ecol. Inform.*, vol. 64, p. 101373, doi: 10.1016/J.ECOINF.2021.101373.

[21]   A. Kendall, V. Badrinarayanan, and R. Cipolla, "Bayesian SegNet: Model uncertainty in deep convolutional encoder-decoder architectures for scene understanding."

[22]   Y. G. Naresh, S. Little, and N. E. O'Connor, "A residual encoder-decoder network for semantic segmentation in autonomous driving scenarios,"

Eur. Signal Process. Conf., vol. 2018, pp. 1052–1056, 2018, doi: 10.23919/EUSIPCO.2018.8553161.

[23] D. Im, D. Han, S. Choi, S. Kang, and H. J. Yoo, "DT-CNN: Dilated and transposed convolution neural network accelerator for real-time image segmentation on mobile devices," in *Proc. – IEEE Int. Symp. Circuits Sys.*, 2019, vol. 2019, doi: 10.1109/ISCAS.2019.8702243.

[24] Y. Zhou, H. Chang, Y. Lu, and X. Lu, "CDTNet: Improved image classification method using standard, dilated and transposed convolutions," *Appl. Sci. 2022*, vol. 12, no. 12, p. 5984, 2022, doi: 10.3390/APP12125984.

[25] J. Fu, J. Liu, Y. Wang, J. Zhou, C. Wang, and H. Lu, "Stacked deconvolutional network for semantic segmentation," *IEEE Trans. Image Process.*, pp. 1–1, 2019, doi: 10.1109/TIP.2019.2895460.

[26] O. Ronneberger, P. Fischer, and T. Brox, "U-net: Convolutional networks for biomedical image segmentation," in *Lect Notes Comp. Sci. (including subseries Lecture Notes in Artif. Intel. Lecture Notes Bioinf.)*, 2015, vol. 9351, pp. 234– 241, doi: 10.1007/978-3-319-24574-4_28/COVER.

[27] N. Siddique, S. Paheding, C. P. Elkin, and V. Devabhaktuni, "U-net and its variants for medical image segmentation: A review of theory and applications," *IEEE Access*, 2021, doi: 10.1109/ACCESS.2021.3086020.

[28] H. Lu, Y. She, J. Tie, and S. Xu, "Half-UNet: A simplified U-Net architecture for medical image segmentation," *Front. Neuroinform.*, vol. 16, p. 54, 2022, doi: 10.3389/FNINF.2022.911679/BIBTEX.

[29] N. A. Nezla, T. P. Mithun Haridas, and M. H. Supriya, "Semantic segmentation of underwater images using UNet architecture based deep convolutional encoder decoder model," *2021 7th Int. Conf. Adv. Comput. Commun. Syst. ICACCS 2021*, pp. 28–33, 2021, doi: 10.1109/ICACCS51430.2021.9441804.

[30] A. A. Albishri, S. J. H. Shah, S. S. Kang, and Y. Lee, "AM-UNet: Automated mini 3D end-to-end U-net based network for brain claustrum segmentation," *Multimed. Tools Appl.*, vol. 81, no. 25, pp. 36171–36194, 2022, doi: 10.1007/S11042-021-11568-7/FIGURES/13.

[31] J. Kim, L. Tran, E. Y. Chew, and S. Antani, "Optic disc and cup segmentation for glaucoma characterization using deep learning," in *Proc. – IEEE Symp. Computer-Based Med. Sys.*, 2019, vol. 2019, pp. 489–494, doi: 10.1109/CBMS.2019.00100.

[32] S. Zhou, D. Nie, E. Adeli, J. Yin, J. Lian, and D. Shen, "High-resolution encoder-decoder networks for low-contrast medical image segmentation," *IEEE Trans. Image Process.*, vol. 29, pp. 461–475, 2020, doi: 10.1109/TIP.2019.2919937.

[33] F. Milletari, N. Navab, and S. A. Ahmadi, "V-Net: Fully convolutional neural networks for volumetric medical image segmentation," in *2016 Fourth Int. Conf. 3D Vision (3DV)*, 2016, pp. 565–571, doi: 10.1109/3DV.2016.79.

[34]   L.-C. Chen, G. Papandreou, K. Murphy, and A. L. Yuille, "Semantic image segmentation with deep convolutional nets and fully connected CRFS," *arXiv preprint arXiv*:1412.7062, 2014.

[35]   L.-C. Chen, G. Papandreou, I. Kokkinos, K. Murphy, and A. L. Yuille, "DeepLab: Semantic image segmentation with deep convolutional nets, atrous convolution, and fully connected CRFs," *IEEE Trans. Pattern Anal. Mach. Intell.*, vol. 40, no. 4, pp. 834–848, 2018, doi: 10.1109/TPAMI.2017.2699184.

[36]   L.-C. Chen, G. Papandreou, F. Schroff, and H. Adam, "Rethinking atrous convolution for semantic image segmentation," *arXiv*:1706.*05587*, 2017, doi: 10.48550/arxiv.1706.05587.

[37]   L. C. Chen, Y. Zhu, G. Papandreou, F. Schroff, and H. Adam, "Encoder-decoder with atrous separable convolution for semantic image segmentation," *Lect. Notes Comput. Sci. (including Subser. Lect. Notes Artif. Intell. Lect. Notes Bioinformatics)*, vol. 11211 LNCS, pp. 833–851, 2018, doi: 10.1007/978-3-030-01234-2_49/TABLES/7.

[38]   S. Wang, L. Yu, K. Li, X. Yang, C. W. Fu, and P. A. Heng, "Boundary and entropy-driven adversarial learning for fundus image segmentation," in *Med. Image Comput. Comp. Assisted Intervention – MICCAI 2019: 22nd Int. Conf.*, 2019, vol. 11764 LNCS, pp. 102–110, doi: 10.1007/978-3-030-32239-7_12.

[39]   F. Visin, A. Romero, K. Cho, *et al.*, "ReSeg: A recurrent neural network-based model for semantic segmentation," *IEEE Comput. Soc. Conf. Comput. Vis. Pattern Recognit. Work.*, pp. 426–433, 2016, doi: 10.1109/CVPRW.2016.60.

[40]   Q. Zuo, S. Chen, and Z. Wang, "R2AU-Net: Attention recurrent residual convolutional neural network for multimodal medical image segmentation," *Secur. Commun. Networks*, vol. 2021, 2021, doi: 10.1155/2021/6625688.

[41]   M. Z. Alom, M. Hasan, C. Yakopcic, T. M. Taha, and V. K. Asari, "Recurrent residual convolutional neural network based on U-Net (R2U-Net) for medical image segmentation," *arXiv:1802.06955*, 2018, doi:10.48550/arxiv.1802.06955.

[42]   A. Chakravarty and J. Sivaswamy, "RACE-Net: A recurrent neural network for biomedical image segmentation," *IEEE J. Biomed. Heal. Informatics*, vol. 23, no. 3, pp. 1151–1162, 2019, doi: 10.1109/JBHI.2018.2852635.

[43]   T. Wollmann, M. Gunkel, I. Chung, H. Erfle, K. Rippe, and K. Rohr, "GRUU-Net: Integrated convolutional and gated recurrent neural network for cell segmentation," *Med. Image Anal.*, vol. 56, pp. 68–79, 2019, doi: 10.1016/J.MEDIA.2019.04.011.

[44]   S. Xun, D. Li, H. Zhu, *et al.*, "Generative adversarial networks in medical image segmentation: A review," *Comput. Biol. Med.*, vol. 140, p. 105063, 2022, doi: 10.1016/J.COMPBIOMED.2021.105063.

[45]   P. Luc, C. Couprie, S. Chintala, and J. Verbeek, "Semantic segmentation using adversarial networks," *arXiv*:1611.08408, 2016, doi: 10.48550/arxiv.1611.08408.

[46] X. Zhang, X. Zhu, X. Y. Zhang, N. Zhang, P. Li, and L. Wang, "SegGAN: Semantic segmentation with generative adversarial network," *2018 IEEE 4th Int. Conf. Multimed. Big Data, BigMM 2018*, 2018, doi: 10.1109/ BIGMM.2018.8499105.

[47] S. Minaee, Y. Boykov, F. Porikli, A. Plaza, N. Kehtarnavaz, and D. Terzopoulos, "Image segmentation using deep learning: A survey," *IEEE Trans. Pattern Anal. Mach. Intell.*, vol. 44, no. 7, pp. 3523–3542, 2022, doi: 10.1109/TPAMI.2021.3059968.

Chapter 3

Biometric-based computer vision for boundless possibilities: process, techniques, and challenges

Rinku Datta Rakshit[1], Deep Suman Dev[2], Nabanita Choudhury[1] and Dakshina Ranjan Kisku[3]

Abstract

Computer vision (CV) is a part of artificial intelligence (AI) that helps computers to interpret, understand and develop intuition about the real-world objects and scenes to annotate, classify and identify them with accurate precision. CV techniques have been gaining popularity since its inception and becoming a fundamental part of technological development and digital transformation. To enhance the domain knowledge of CV in the area of human identification and the use of the intrinsic properties of image interpretation and understanding biometrics systems have been proposed with several behavioral and physiological body evidences. Biometrics recognition employs various aspects of AI to enable a computer system to recognize a biometric pattern for identification purposes. It is an inevitable part of multiple applications, such as border control cyber security, 3D faces modeling and recognition, intelligent video surveillance, finger vein recognition, and forensic biometrics where vision techniques have been integrated with and instilled into the biometrics systems in order to perform the desired tasks. The main objective of this chapter is to introduce biometric-based CV and discuss the essential components of biometrics technologies for CV. The discussion also includes different processes, state-of-the-art techniques, challenges of biometric-based CV, application areas, the selection criteria of suitable biometrics, and the future of biometric-based CV applications.

[1]School of Computer Engineering, KIIT Deemed to be University, Bhubaneswar, India
[2]Department of Computer Science and Engineering, School of Science and Technology, The Neotia University, Kolkata, India
[3]Faculty of Computer Technology, Assam down town University, Guwahati, India
[4]Department of Computer Science and Engineering, National Institute of Technology Durgapur, Durgapur, India

3.1   Introduction

Nowadays biometric-based CV [1] is very significant for several fields such as health-care, border security, travel, finance, intelligent video surveillance, law enforcement and forensic biometrics for getting higher security and reliability. Biometric-based CV model can validate or ascertain [2,3] an individual with almost correct accuracy in less than a second. The area of CV has performed great progress toward becoming more extending in day-to-day life as an outcome of recent upliftment in fields like AI and computing capabilities. It is [4] expected that in the next 10 years the market for biometrics technologies, will rise at a compounded annual growth rate (CAGR) of a slightly over 17%, and will attain about $52.7 billion by 2025. The biometrics technologies are fast developing market section, which includes main geographical places across the world. This area is also noted by its variety and novelty. During the last three decades [4], the field of biometrics has experienced an outburst with the appearance of internet, cloud computing, and smart phones. Recently, biometric technologies are gaining dramatic improvements in terms of their robustness and reliability due to advancement in data processing capabilities, sensor technologies, data mining, and computational intelligence.

CV [5] is one of the areas of AI that trains and gives the capability to computers to realize the visual world. Computers can utilize digital images and videos to accurately classify and identify objects and respond to them. Biometric-based CV in AI is devoted to the promotion of automated systems that can explain visual data like digital images and motion pictures in the same way as human being do. The main concept behind CV is to train computers to explain and recognize images on a pixel-by-pixel basis. To perform the task assigned to a biometric-based CV system, computers need to extract visual data, manage it, and explore the outcomes using some sophisticated software.

Large volume of information is needed for CV. Periodical data analyses are carried out until the system is capable to distinguish between objects and identify visuals. CV is the integration of image processing and statistical pattern recognition. Biometrics acts to recognize persons by using their fingerprint, face, iris and hand geometry – physiological traits, or by using their gait, voice, and signature – behavioral traits. It integrates CV with knowledge of human behavior and physiology. Currently, biometrics [6–9] for border control, intelligent video surveillance, face recognition at a distance, 3D face modeling and recognition, finger vein recognition, and forensic biometrics are very demanding task. Important applications for biometrics comprise controlling physical access (entry to a building), authenticating a user to allow him/her to access some resource such as accessing a secure web site, and identifying a person among many people in a crowd such as looking for a terrorist at airports. There is no other spiffy option than biometrics for human identification, which is more invulnerable, safe, feasible, and affordable.

The primary goal of this chapter is to present biometric-based CV techniques. This chapter comprehends the necessity of biometric-based CV techniques, different biometric-based CV processes, techniques, challenges, application area, and selection criteria of suitable biometrics. Finally, this chapter discusses the future of biometric-based CV.

3.2 Need for biometric-based CV

In these days, a faultless security measure [10,11] is a basic need for a society. The security measure should be highly efficient, naturalistic, stable, and favorable at any cost. These needs can be fulfilled by biometric-based systems. Due to this reason, biometrics are flourishing as a leading layer to many individual and industry security systems. Individual and industries have used passwords and PINs to safe their data and assets for a long time. Passwords/PINs are not secure [12] as it can be presumed, shared, or stolen. Therefore, a more secure authentication technique is needed. Biometric is one such technique that works on the principle of "what you are." This technology removes the concern of remembering PIN, password or possessing of any ID card. The biometric is becoming a prime component to multifactor authentication and used for extensive variety of purposes such as attendance, passport verification, border control, and some other impressible places. Now, the entry and exit system of many companies are based on biometrics. Biometrics is a perplexing issue as there are various physical as well as behavioral characteristics (voice recognition/finger-print recognition/face recognition/iris recognition) to use this technique.

However, all biometric technologies are not suitable for all type of business environments. Also, the level of protection provided by different biometric traits are not same.

All authentication factors divided into the following three categories:

a) Something you know (passwords, PINS, etc.)
b) Something you have (token, certificate, ID card, etc.)
c) Something you are (biometrics: face, fingerprint, iris pattern, vein pattern, hand geometry, etc.)

Each category has its own advantages and disadvantages. Recently, across the world a wide range of companies are choosing biometric-based CV technology to provide the safeguard to their private and confidential data, protect identity theft and security holes, and enhance the entire experience of user.

The biometric-based CV is the need of various companies due its inherent characteristics. The inherent characteristics are:

- **Easy to use:** Biometric-based technology needs short time to check and verify a person.
- **Uniqueness:** Biometric traits are unique; they are capable of distinguishing one person from another uniquely.
- **Immutability:** There is no way to change or modify features of a biometric trait.
- **Performance:** Biological features perform robustness, accuracy, and speed.
- **Measurability:** Biological traits can be measured easily and do not need more time.

3.2.1 Benefits of biometric authentication

There are several benefits of biometric authentication which are discussed in the following sections.

3.3   Restricts access

Enterprises can enhance access control through biometric authentication. Giving entree only to a person with the true authorization is very critical. There is an added convenience of the collected data for biometrics not lending itself to being copied. For example, with a fingerprint scanner, unique data present on the fingers are collected along with the images of the fingerprint. This minimizes any chance for a violation of security and minimizes the need to update protective passwords continuously.

3.4   Records timeliness

Moreover, preventing access, biometric entree controls are a great way to ascertain timeliness within an organization. With fingerprint scanners, sign-ins and sign-outs of employees can be recorded in an organization. This supports in keeping exact log sheets as compared to any other conventional form of management and timekeeping.

3.5   Enhances security measures

Biometric authentication provides an extra layer to the security systems. It is very hard to replicate data in the forms of face image, voice, or fingerprint. Moreover, with these forms of authentication, the possibility of human error is decreased. For example, a lost or stolen key card can be used to steal data—but with biometric authentication, nobody does not have to worry about such things.

3.6   Replaces passwords

Passwords are not self-sufficient any longer, even if a two-factor password authentication method is used in an organization. Because, this is very common that people supposed to use the same combination of alphabets or numbers or even the similar passwords across the broad. Cracking this becomes very simple for hackers. Biometric authentication entirely replaces the necessity of conventional passwords forming it much easier for organizations with many employees. This type of systems is not attackable by hackers and removes the necessity of constantly updating passwords.

3.7   Minimizes the human error

Most conventional verification forms trust on employees—they are liable for storing passwords, key cards or codes. Conventional authentication system is prone to human error, which is very hard to monitor. Any person can share entry details through messages, via email or verbally—intentionally or unintentionally. Biometric authentication lessens the likelihoods of this significantly and helps organizations protect themselves. Today, biometric scanners are dependable and can establish the authorizations of a person from several stored templates.

3.8 Eases installation

Installing a biometric system like a fingerprint reader is fast and simple. It has enabled the process to come as close to plug and play as possible. Each day enterprises are adding more systems, devices, and products to their office to improve the authentication systems.

3.8.1 Offers reasonable costs

The initial investment cost is high in biometric readers. After that, only up-gradation is required to meet the company's requirements—be it an enlarging portfolio, a growth in the organization's volume, or its estimate.

3.9 Biometric-based CV: process, techniques, and challenges

Earlier biometrics was limited to the terra of science fiction. However, in the last decade, the uprising of biometrics has been seen in our day-to-day lives. Recently, biometric-based CV technology has developed fast. Nowadays, it is uncommon when we do not use several forms of biometric technology in a day. From unlocking a mobile phone to secure boarding a flight, biometric-based CV technology is all around us. The widely used first biometric technology is fingerprint recognition. Today, a wide range of biometric modalities like face, voice, iris, palm veins, and signature are all used alone or combined for different CV applications.

The biggest benefit of biometric authentication is the using something that is part of us, and there is no requirement of carrying it or retain it like PIN, ID card, or password. Biometric provides a means to gain quickly access to an online service or a physical building. The security is the biggest strength of biometric technologies as PINs and passwords can be stolen but stealing a biometric identifier such as a face or a fingerprint is extremely hard to steal. The combination of convenience means and the security will increase the adoption of biometric technologies in coming years.

Also, the necessities of biometric technology [13,14] has accelerated due to the COVID-19 pandemic. Accomplishment of contactless entree to a building and service, contactless payments and contactless ATM interactions is very demanding than ever before.

3.9.1 Biometric-based CV process

Biometric systems [1] are confided on various discrete processes: capture during enrollment/live capture, preprocessing, feature extraction (template generation), and matching (template comparison). Every biometric system comprises of four principal modules—sensor module (image acquisition), preprocessing module, feature extraction (template generation) module, and matching (template comparison) module.

1. **Sensor module:** A sensor is a machine that captures biometric data. For example, it could be a camera, voice analyzer, retina scanner, or fingerprint reader. This module is responsible for enrollment/live capture process. A person can interact with the biometric system through this module. This module is called as an image acquirement module. The enrollment/live capture process captures raw data for verification or identification.

2. **Preprocessing module:** Preprocessing module is responsible for image preprocessing process. Image preprocessing process performs the resizing, color correction, brightness enhancement, de-noising, filtering, and image normalization on raw images those are captured in sensor module.

3. **Feature extraction (template generation) module:** Feature extraction module is responsible for feature extraction and template generation process. The feature extraction process extracts discriminatory biometric features from preprocessed biometric data using some algorithms. Then extracted features are stored during enrollment to reduce processing time upon future comparisons.

4. **Matching (template comparison) module:** The matching module is responsible for template comparison process. The template comparison process compares two biometric templates using some algorithmic computations to measure their similarity. During comparison, a match score is generated. If the generated match score satisfies the specified threshold, then the test data is considered as a correct match.

Every biometrics system has two phases—enrollment (training) and testing. For first time when a person wants to use a biometric system, he/she need to enroll himself/herself by his/her biometric traits to train the system. In subsequent uses, biometric probe sample is collected from a person and compared with biometric templates present in gallery set, those are generated during the enrollment process.

To validate or ascertain an individual, biometric-based authentication system can be used. In person verification, to determine the identity of an individual, a biometric system assimilates a test (probe) sample with an appropriate biometric template that is present in the biometric database (1-to-1 matching). In person identification, a biometric system compares a test (probe) sample with all biometric templates present in the biometric database (1-to-M matching).

The block diagram of a biometric authentication system is shown in Figure 3.1.

3.9.2   Biometric-based CV techniques

Research on biometric-based CV has been in use for the last three decades and attracts a lot of public attention due to its increasing demand for deployment in real world applications. Till date, many research work has been reported on biometric-based CV and challenges need to be addressed in real world applications. An image of a biometric trait consists of several discriminatory features, which are very

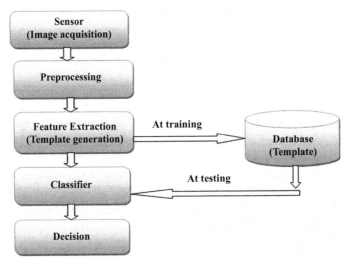

Figure 3.1 The block diagram of a biometrics authentication system [1]

complex in nature. The shape of the biometric trait, texture of the overlying surface, and the overlying reflectance function at each point on the surface varies from person to person. The complicated nature of the information in a biometric sample (images) makes discriminatory feature extraction a challenging task. Based on biometric feature extraction, the biometric-based CV techniques can be classified into several approaches, viz. feature-based method, holistic method, model-based method, learning-based method, hybrid method, and sparse representation-based method.

3.9.2.1 Holistic methods

Holistic method [15] is one of the earliest approaches to biometric-based authentication. This method exploits global information from images of a biometric trait to recognize an individual. The whole image of a biometric trait is considered as a single feature and used as input; therefore, each image is illustrated as a high-dimensional vector by linking all pixels of the gray scale image of the input face image. In this method, individual features (nose, eyes, mouth, etc.) of an image are not considered for comparison during the matching phase of a biometric authentication system. Holistic methods are also known as subspace methods as these methods project a feature space onto a smaller subspace and it results in a reduced set of features. Some examples of subspace methods are PCA [16], linear discriminant analysis (LDA) [17], independent component analysis (ICA) [18], Fisher linear discriminant analysis (FLDA) [19], etc.

3.9.2.2 Feature-based methods

Feature-based biometric authentication system [20–24] extract discriminatory features from the raw image irrespective of their structure. It uses geometric relationships between major features, invariant interest points and local regions of an image to obtain discriminatory features for authentication. Feature-based methods can extract local as well as global description of a biometric sample. In local description, an image is partitioned into many small sub-regions, and then distinctive local features are extracted. Further, concatenation of all distinctive local features is made to form a global description of the biometric sample. Already, feature-based methods showed robustness in biometric authentication system compared to holistic methods; because feature-based methods are more stable to local variations. Some examples of feature-based methods are scale-invariant feature transform (SIFT) [21], histograms of oriented gradients (HOG) [23], speeded-up robust features (SURF) [22], elastic bunch graph matching (EBGM) [24], local binary pattern (LBP) [25], multi-scale local binary pattern (MS-LBP) [26], modified local binary pattern [27], local derivative pattern (LDP) [28], local tetra pattern (LTrP) [29] , local vector pattern (LVP) [30], local gradient hexa pattern [31], local graph structure (LGS) [32], symmetric local graph structure (SLGS) [33], etc.

3.9.2.3   Model-based methods

Model-based methods are mainly founded on statistical models of the appearance of the objects or the shape of the objects. The models are designed in such a way that they are found to be robust to locate and recognize an individual in the presence of clutter, noise, and occlusion. Two well-known model-based methods are active shape model (ASM) [34] and active appearance model (AAM) [35].

3.9.2.4   Learning-based methods

Learning-based biometric authentication system extract discriminatory features automatically from an image of a biometric sample by using different types of learning methods. Learning-based methods include deep neural networks (DNNs) [36,37] and convolutional neural network (CNN) [38]. A more advanced deep learning method is known as generative adversarial nets [39]. Besides these basic learning techniques, several advanced deep learning techniques such as deep residual network [40], recurrent neural network [41], and deep belief network [42] have been developed to strengthen biometric authentication system performance further while large numbers of samples are used for training.

3.9.2.5   Hybrid methods

Hybrid methods [43–45] are special kinds of biometric authentication methods which combine different biometric authentication approaches in either parallelly or serially to surpass the weaknesses of individual methods. Holistic methods and feature-based methods are two principal classes of biometric authentication methods. These two methods have their relative advantages and disadvantages; and, their way of feature extraction is different. Generally, these two methods are combined to form the hybrid recognition methods.

3.9.2.6   Sparse representation-based methods

The sparse representation-based biometric image representation techniques have received a lot of attention. The work presented by [46] sparse representation (SR) technique is employed effectively for robust face recognition [46]. Sparse representation represents an image of a test sample as a sparse linear combination of images of all training samples, and then classifies the probe image of a biometric sample by computing which class generates the least representation error. The biometric-based authentication based on sparse representation is limited to the frontal view of any biometric sample. Although sparse representation-based authentication [46] has shown captivating outcomes and extensively practiced by researchers, the working mechanism of it is found to be partly unpredictable for other constrictions and image features.

3.9.3 Different biometric traits

Varied biometric traits can be used for secure automated person authentication [80–90]. Widely used biometric traits are face, fingerprint, ear, voice, iris, hand-writing, and finger vein, etc. Apart from these biometric traits some other biometric traits—palmprint, tongue print, retinal scan, hand geometry, footprint, gait, and ECG, etc. are also used for authentication. Different techniques for face recognition are introduced in [15–46,47–49]. Different fingerprint recognition techniques are introduced in [50–52]. Different palmprint techniques are introduced in [53–57]. Different tongue print techniques are proposed and introduced in [58–62]. Different finger vein recognition techniques are proposed in [63–72]. Different palm print recognition techniques are proposed in [73–75]. Different hand geometry recognition techniques are proposed in [76–78]. Different footprint recognition techniques are proposed in [79–82]. Different ear recognition techniques are proposed in [88–94]. Different voice recognition techniques are proposed in [95–99]. Different iris recognition techniques are proposed in [100–103]. Different gait recognition techniques are proposed in [104,105–118]. Different hand vein recognition techniques are proposed in [119–125]. Different signature recognition techniques are proposed in [126–130]. Different ECG recognition techniques are introduced in [131–135]. Sometimes using a single biometric is not enough for secure authentication. Use of multiple biometric is useful in those cases. Different multi-biometric systems are introduced in [136–139].

Authentication using some biometric traits is discussed briefly in the above section.

3.9.3.1 Face recognition

The human face is one of the commonly used biometric traits. The authentication is facilitated with static or video face images. During the process, AI maps out an individual's facial features, such as the location, shape, and spatial relationships of their nose, eyes, lips, and so on. This technology can determine if two different images represent the same person and helps locate a face image among a large collection of existing face images.

A human has a set of facial characteristics that can be used to authenticate the identity of a person. Face biometric-based CV approaches accept image or video of faces as input. The main underlying technique that is used in face biometrics-based CV is face recognition. To verify or identify the identity of an individual by images/videos of their face, automated/semi-automated face recognition technique is used. Face recognition is very important in the field of border security, healthcare, and law enforcement. In routine policing, face recognition is used more frequently by law enforcement agencies.

3.9.3.2   Benefits of facial recognition

Facial recognition systems have the edge over other biometric trait-based authentication system. When this biometric modality paired with other technologies like liveness detection, thermal imagery, this biometric modality exhibits a highest level of security.

Facial recognition technology allows the detection of various spoof artifacts, such as photos, screens, masks, etc., making the process a fast and effective way to authenticate users.

Additionally, face recognition is very easy to use. Since cameras have become an essential part of our lives, the face recognition can be performed with the help of a user's phone. For this reason, the face is the most preferred biometric trait for authentication.

Common challenges of facial recognition

There are different issues users may envisage during facial recognition-based authentication. The first one is the inappropriate background of the image or a video. An inappropriate background can create difficulties in a person's face recognition, preventing successful authentication. Another challenge is illumination/lighting condition. Poor illumination can also prevent the authentication process. A face can alter drastically over time due to illness, aging, cosmetic surgery, and accidents, and illness.

3.9.3.3   Fingerprints

Fingerprints are no longer used exclusively in forensics. These days, fingerprint biometrics is used most widely. Since it can be easily deployed in any device, such as a laptop or a mobile phone, to safeguard these devices owner of these devices can use their fingerprint.

Benefits of fingerprint recognition

The main advantage of fingerprint scanning is that fingerprints are unique to every person. Even twins have varied fingerprint patterns and ridges.

Another benefit is the ease of use and availability. Fingerprint-based authentication are widely implemented and generally used in consumer devices, from door locks to laptops, a standalone fingerprint scanner is easy to obtain, too.

Common challenges of fingerprint recognition

Despite its benefits, fingerprint-based biometric authentication systems have downsides. Fraudsters have devised ways to falsify fingerprints and use them for illicit activities. While the process of bypassing fingerprint-based security is challenging, it is possible with enough effort. Also, it is possible to perform unauthorized authentication while a person is asleep or unconscious.

3.9.3.4 Ear recognition

Biometric security systems, also known as modalities, are built to recognize different biometric traits during authentication. Each biometric system involves unique biological and behavioral aspects. The biometric traits implemented in a system impact its performance. Thus, it is important to get familiar with the most common types.

Voice recognition

Voice is a biometric attribute that assemble both biological and behavioral traits. The sound of a person's voice is determined by many physical properties, such as the shape and size of their tongue, mouth, vocal cords, or nose. Also, it can be significantly affected by their language, emotions, or medical issues.

Voice or speaker recognition identifies an individual based on his/her voice. It works by assigning a speaker simple speaking duties to make a unique profile of their voice. The system then cross-matches the profile with test voice samples used to authenticate the speaker.

Benefits of voice recognition

A person's voice is unique and extremely hard to falsify. Additionally, voice recognition is simple to implement. Users are not required to possess any additional devices and typically use their phones.

Common challenges of voice recognition

There are some important parts that can make a voice recognition system fail. Any respiratory sickness, such as a common cold, can spontaneously alter the user's voice preventing the authentication. The noise may also interfere with the process.

Like face or fingerprint voice is an inherent feature of each person. Nowadays, many companies are using phones for communication offers an excellent convenience for the use of this biometric authentication method. Moreover, voice recognition is very beneficial for users and requires less effort on their side.

Voice biometric-based authentication technology is extensively used in several areas which process users' voices, such as in call centers. Acceptance of this technology allows for speeding up of the service. It makes the work of agents easier, and help them in more efficient way. This technology may have wide deployment area such as credit card verification, security systems, teleconferencing, and forensic analysis, etc. To protect confidential information in a more secure way, voice identification can be integrated with another authentication method such as fingerprint scanning.

Advantages of voice recognition:

- Voice is a naturalistic way of interaction and communication between people.
- It reduces time for both agents and users and agents.
- The voice is an unmatchable biometric feature that is very hard to falsify.
- It is a broadly used process that is familiar to users.

Disadvantages of voice recognition:

- Users may not realize that how their data is stored and have secrecy-related disquiet.
- The authentication accuracy may be affected in noisy places due to noise.
- The authentication accuracy may be also affected by severe respiratory illness.

3.9.3.5 Iris recognition

Iris, a colored, circular membrane surrounding the pupil of the human eye, is another unique trait. The complex structure of the iris is extremely hard to replicate. Also, it is used in biometric systems.

Benefits of iris recognition
Iris is an externally visible organ. It is very easy to access and set up for authentication. Moreover, changing pupil size can be beneficial for ensuring liveness.

Challenges of iris recognition
Despite its benefits, the iris scanners are still under development. Even though it seems promising, a high false nonmatch rate has been generated by current systems.

In this technology, at first, the pupil is located, followed by detecting the iris and eyelids. Next, redundant parts such as eyelashes and eyelids are cropped to keep the iris part. Then iris part is partitioned into multiple blocks and converted into some numerical values which represents the image. Finally, matching with gallery data is performed to verify the identity.

Advantages of iris recognition:

- Iris is an optical organ that is well protected.
- The iris has unique features which are large enough to identify an individual.

Disadvantages of iris recognition:

- This a new technology which is still under improvements.
- The distance between the device and the user's eye must be less during authentication.
- The accuracy of iris recognition is less in poor lighting condition.

3.9.3.6 Handwriting

Similarly, to optical character recognition, handwriting recognition is capable of using pattern matching for converting handwritten letters into computer text. However, handwriting is more or less unique to a person, so it can also be used as a behavioral biometric system.

The technology can be dynamic and static. The static process simply compares the handwriting. On the other hand, the dynamic process analyzes pen pressure, stroke, shape writing speed, and some other characteristics to verify an individual's identity. If the text is imputed digitally, typing recognition aids the process.

Benefits of handwriting recognition
Handwriting recognition is simple to understand and intuitive enough for users. When the process is dynamic, the possibility of falsified handwriting is minimized, increasing its security.

Challenges of handwriting recognition
While our handwriting is unique, it is also highly inconsistent. Many factors can lead to change in a person's writing; the most common examples are fatigue, stress, emotional state, or injury. For this reason, this technology provides low-level security.

In banking or judicial systems, dynamic signature verification can be applied for workflow automation.

Advantages of handwriting recognition:

- To confirm identities for centuries signatures have been used. Thus, this technology addresses the belief.
- There is no need to use advanced devices to work for this technology (touchscreen devices are very common in these days).

Disadvantages of handwriting recognition:

- Many individuals have inconsistent signatures.
- It is impracticable to use this technology in case of injuries like broken arms or fingers may make.
- This method is appropriate only for low-level security.

3.9.3.7 Finger vein

The finger vein recognition technology captures images of the veins by glowing near-infrared light on fingers of a person. It is very hard to be forged.

Finger vein recognition technology is founded on the images of the inimitable veins under the skin of a person's hands. To record the image, an attester terminal bearing a near-infrared light-emitting diode (LED) light and a monochrome charge-coupled device (CCD) camera is exploited. The hemoglobin in the blood imbibes the light, which prepares the veins exhibit as a pattern of lines. To store data, camera captures the image and the raw data is digitized.

It is more accurate than a fingerprint as it is based on the vein patterns under the skin surface, which have been very difficult to fake. The finger veins authentication process provides proof of the liveness of the person whose identity is being verified.

Currently, this technology is applied for extensive range of applications such as employee attendance, credit card authentication, network authentication, time tracking, automobile security, end-point security, and at ATMs.

3.9.4 Challenges of biometric-based CV techniques

The applications of biometric systems and technologies are extending significantly within the private and public sectors. Biometric technologies are becoming inexpensive, more accurate, and more advanced. Due to these advancements, this technology has integrated with people's daily life. Designing and deploying a robust person authentication system is a difficult task. Different biometrics samples of similar biometrics traits of an individual may vary due to multiple factors. Moreover, two biometrics samples of similar biometrics trait of two different individual may seems to be same (face images of look-alikes or twins). There are various risk and challenges that are associated with a biometrics-based authentication system. These are summarized as follows:

- **Challenges**

  Variation within persons: Inputs of a biometrics-based authentication system is a biometric sample. These inputs may be affected by multiple factors like, age, variations in environment, diseases, tension, socio-cultural perspective of the circumstance, occupational factors, variations in interface of human with the system, and so on. Therefore, each time an individual may provide different biometric information to the biometric authentication system during his/her interaction. This intra-class variations in biometric samples may leads ambiguity in biometrics authentication systems.

  Sensors: Sensors play a vital role in perfection of biometrics-based authentication system. Age of the sensor, the sensibility factor of the sensor, and interface provided by a sensor stimulate the performance level of a biometrics authentication system.

  Feature extraction and matching algorithms: Sample of biometrics traits cannot be considered as an input for an authentication process directly. Therefore, it is an inevitable part of any biometric authentication process to design or develop a robust feature extraction algorithm to extract discriminatory features from a biometric sample. This task is very much challenging.

  Data integrity: Biometric information may be altered through manipulation, transformation, inappropriate compression, mismanagement, or some other mean.

- **Risks**

  Being hackable: Biometrics samples can also be hacked. Governments and businesses organizations that collect and store users' personal data in the form of biometric sample are under constant threat from hackers. However, they are a victim of a data infringement. Biometric data are irreplaceable; therefore, organizations require to treat users' biometrics sample with care and alertness.

  Partial matches: Maximum biometric-based authentication methods confide on partial information to validate an individual's identity. For example, during the enrolment process of registering your fingerprint, it will take data from your entire print and change it into data. During future authentication however, it will only take partial fingerprint data to verify your identity so it is quicker and faster.

  Fail to recognize a valid user: When you register for facial recognition, you are registering a specific angle, and expression to your face. However, because the system only has the data from the enrolment process, anytime a user wears glasses, makeup, or even smiling, the facial recognition has a hard time recognizing the user, which could make the login process difficult.

Bias: Facial recognition systems may fail to verify/identify a person of color or non-cisgender people as exactly. Various biometric authentication systems may be trained initially using white or white male photos. This type of biometric authentication systems may lead to an inherent bias. The inherent bias of any biometric authentication system causes difficulty in recognizing people of other color and gender.

Fears of sharing biometric data: selling or providing biometric data to others, such as immigration enforcement, law enforcement, or repressive foreign governments by a company is not acceptable. These secrecy disquiets have caused many US states to decree biometric information privacy laws. When biometrics samples are changed into data and stored, especially in countries or places that have main surveillance measures, a user runs the danger of giving up a stable digital record that can be possibly tracked by crooked actors.

Data storage: Wherever biometric data is captured; it must be kept securely in the database. Biometric data cannot be changed/reset like a password. There is really nothing a user can do if biometric data is hacked.

Which type of biometric authentication is best?

Each biometric authentication method varies in its applications and security.

However, this does not mean that the unsecure options are worthless. It all comes down to the purpose and usability. For example, replacing voice recognition with facial recognition in a home assistant would prevent the ability for them to give commands. On the other hand, facial recognition technology, implemented into a banking app can aid to authenticate a client swiftly and safely.

What is liveness detection?

Biometric systems often employ additional technology to improve security. The most common choice is liveness detection.

Liveness detection is a process of verifying that a person is alive by using their body parts as an identifier. For example, the technology can verify that a person has placed a finger on an infrared sensor. During an iris scan, this technology looks for the movement in a person's eye. When paired with facial recognition-based biometrics modality, liveness is detected by asking a person to perform simple movements to ensure an authentic presence.

3.10 Application areas

One field of machine learning where primary conceptions are comprised in mainstream products is CV. Biometrics is a competent mode to empower access to services or assets. The security method includes some common use cases – user authentication, access control, preventing fraud, online browsing control, payment method, and presence control. Biometrics have extensive range of uses. Nowadays many industries like healthcare providers, government agencies, hotel chains, retailers, and airlines are using benefits of biometric security. Biometric technology is becoming the part of our daily life to carry out different tasks [140]. In near future the use of biometric technology will grow and will become the most popular technology to access varied range of products. The applications include:

- **Facial recognition at a distance**
  Face recognition systems use CV to recognize individuals in photographs or videos. Face recognition is very important in the field of border security, healthcare and law enforcement. In routine policing face recognition are used more frequently by law enforcement agencies.
- **Healthcare**
  CV has provided significantly to the development of health tech. Recently, the biometric-based CV is gaining popularity in healthcare to provide the safeguard to their patients. Recognizing a patient correctly and protecting file of a patient is a difficult task in a healthcare system. In some cases, patients may lose their life due to improper identification. A senseless patient cannot produce his/her ID in front of the healthcare personnel. The conventional patient tagging or disparity within hospital records and patient tag are not free from fault due to clerical error. This form of mistakes can increase danger of a patient's life by improper patient identification, incorrect blood transfusion or insidious medicine dispensation. Therefore, there is a need of biometric-based CV in healthcare system.
- **Border control**
  A key application area for biometric-based system is at the border. In border control, manual process of body searching and passport-stamping cannot ensure the security. Border control officers can use biometric technology to verify passengers' identities. Recently, the smart border control technology is very demanding to get touchless and secure travel experience.
- **Airport security**
  Already biometric-based technology has installed in airports throughout the worlds. Making the secure journey via airports is a target take part by airports around the world. For several years to verify traveler's identity, biometric-based technology has been used in some of the major airports around the globe and now use of this technology becoming more expansive.
  Airports are one of the chief adopters of biometric-based security systems and it is anticipated that parallel systems will be rolled out across a much wider range of industries.
- **Intelligent video surveillance**
  The intelligent video surveillance is an significant technology to provide safety and security in different public places like railway stations, markets, shopping malls, etc. CCTV offers the power to look on, respond and report to dangers and threats in an area without the human intervention. Face recognition upgrade the abilities of CCTV.

- **3D face modeling and recognition**
  3D face modeling and recognition has the potent to attain higher accuracy than its 2D complement. 3D face recognition measures the geometry of rigid features on the face or use the 3D model of the face to improve accuracy.
- **Biometrics in forensic identification**
  Due to varieties of criminal activities, correct identification has become an essential need for forensic applications. Recently, in forensic science biometric-based CV techniques is replacing manual identification approaches. The rise of forensic biometrics covers an extensive range of applications for cybercrime detection.
- **Blood banks**
  In blood banks, identity of an individual is very important in case of giving the blood. The use of biometric technology can overcome the risk of replication, issues related with data entry, and increase the overall security of the customers.
- **Public transport**
  To increase the security of passengers during their travel public transportation can adopt biometric technology. In this sector, still this technology is in its early stages. The cameras with face recognition technology can be used in public transport to keep the track of different activities of passengers throughout the travel. Biometrics technology can also be used for smart ID cards, smart ticketing and passenger management.
- **Schools**
  Already different countries in world implement biometric-based technology on school premises. Biometric is a rising technology in the US education section. Biometric-based technology increase the safety within a school premises and make the enrolment procedure more proficient.
  Using this technology, we can ensure that only authorized persons will get entry to school buildings. In school, biometrics is also used for attendance recording, monitoring of examination, paying for meals or checking out library books.
  The widely used biometric technology in school is fingerprint recognition. However, to identify "unknowns" who is roaming in school premises or on school grounds, face recognition can be used.
- **Building access**
  Now biometric technology is the common means of giving access to a home/ workplace or specific areas within a building. The biometric technology (face recognition/iris recognition/fingerprint) can give a smooth and secure entry experience within a building or a restricted area.
- **Home assistants**
  Voice recognition is one of the most important significant identifiers which is already used by Alexa, Google Home, and Siri. Google Assistant on Android devices is suitable with varied range of Internet of Things devices like door locks, light bulbs, security lights, security cameras, and more.

When we link our home assistant devices with any connectable devices (door locks/light bulbs/security lights/security cameras), security is compulsory. We would not want those limited by just anyone. Therefore, recognizing the voice of authorized users is very troublesome for Google Assistant.

- **Banking**

The banking sector is a such kind of field where delivering security across a range of services is very important. Currently, biometrics technology adds an extra level of security in banking services.

Face recognition can be used as an extra layer of security to authenticate that the owner of the ATM card is the individual using the card.

Nowadays, varied banking services are more digitally based. Therefore, to enhance the employee and customer identity management, to counteract deception, to increase customer convenience, and to tighten the transaction security, banks are also implementing biometric-based technologies.

Customers are more concerned about identity stealing and the difficulty associated with continuously having to assert their identities. Therefore, more and more customers are searching for banks that have integration with biometric-based authentication system.

- **Mobile access**

Obviously one of the most general uses of biometric technology is security of smartphone. Face recognition, voice recognition, fingerprint recognition, and iris recognition are widely used technology in mobile phone security.

Now, to secure the smartphone devices or to secure some special applications such as banking apps or payment related apps all new smartphones are integrating some form of biometric modality with conventional PIN and password. The integration of biometric technology with conventional PIN/password provides two-factor authentication for our smartphone devices as well as some special apps.

- **Law enforcement**

Law enforcement uses face recognition software to track down convicts using surveillance footage. Biometrics is extensively used across law enforcement agencies and Interpol exploiting biometrics in criminal inquisitions.

3.11   Selection criteria of suitable biometrics

The selection criteria [1] of suitable biometrics for CV depends on the application and the ground in which the process of recognition is accomplished. The properties those are very significant while selecting a biometric trait for CV technique are accuracy, robustness to spoofing, the overall system cost, long term maintenance cost, throughput, complexity, social and cultural exposures that could affect the acceptance of user.

The principal measure in the choice of favorable biometric technology is its excellence. In a biometric-based CV technique, when the test biometric sample is compared to the biometric templates stored in the biometric database for either

Table 3.1   Comparative study of some biometrics traits [1]

Biometrics technology	Accuracy	Cost	Equipment used	Social acceptance	Use	Interference
Fingerprint	High	Medium	Scanner	Medium	Person identification	Cut or wound on finger, dirtiness, and roughness of finger.
Face recognition	Medium	Medium	Camera	High		Illumination, facial expression, pose, and occlusion
Retinal scan	High	High	Camera	Low		Irritation
Iris recognition	High	High	Camera	Medium		Glasses
Hand geometry recognition	Medium	Low	Scanner	High		Rheumatism and arthritis
DNA	High	High	Test equipment	Low		Multiple samples are required, complex
Signature recognition	Low	Medium	Touch panel, optic pen	High		Changeable
Voice recognition	Medium	Medium	Microphone	High		Cold, noise

identification or verification process, a match score is generated. The generated match score is exploited to ensure the identity of an individual. In case of verification process, a threshold of the matching score is determined by the system developer to ensure the desired level of precision for the system. Generally, the level of perfection is ascertained by the False Rejection Rate (FRR) and False Acceptance rate (FAR). The FRR and FAR can be adjusted to get the desired level of perfection. The probability that an imposter is verified or accepted by a biometric system is known as FAR. The possibility that a genuine person is rejected by a biometric system is known as FRR. A comparative study of widely used biometric traits is shown in Table 3.1.

3.12   Future of biometric-based CV

Nowadays, in the technology savvy world, it is really very important to recognize the tools and techniques which naturalize the true person identification. Current research works reveal that the main reason for using biometric-based technology is high security. This prospect is approved by policy makers and governments to recognize criminals, immigrants at border crossing or to fight against terrorism.

The biometric-based solutions are best solutions for automated person identification in all circumstances. Biometrics scanners are currently used in offices, homes, computers, smartphones, machines, different devices, etc. to attain the security. In near future the biometric-based CV will be the main technology in the market which will be deployed in all respects. However, for the maximum segment, the usage of this technology will take the place of existing access control and user authentication methods, providing increased amenities and security. The biometric-based CV technologies will dispel the burden of carrying identity cards, keys, personal documents or remembering passwords. The biometric-based CV will offer new approaches and attributes towards security solutions.

The integration of CV technology with biometrics in companies and startups is getting special attraction from venture capitalists. Some of the future trends for biometric-based CV are:

- **Physical identity verification:** The deployment of AI-driven biometrics will fuel new mode of real-time physical authentication through on-premises cameras.
- **Advanced biometric authentication:** The emerging technologies are directing on more progressive biometric authentication to provide hard-to-spoof services. The advanced biometric authentication can include heartbeat pattern recognition, hand geometry recognition, odor recognition and DNA signature interpretation.
- **Identity proofing:** One of the biggest potencies of biometric-based authentication is that the user must appear physically to give biometric sample during authentication process.
- **Continuous authentication:** Continuous authentication uses behavioral Authentication usually occurs once, during login process, or several times grounded on user access to various resources. Continuous authentication uses behavioral biometric patterns or other biometric markers to keep authentication to guarantee continual user verification over time.

3.13 Summary

The field of biometric-based CV has currently become fully trendy in the reign of cutting-edge technology. This technology is a novel approach due to its data analysis capability. Furthermore, this technological progression gives an instance of stride forward in the upliftment of AI on par with that of human beings. This chapter has attempted to give an overview of CV-based biometric technologies.

References

[1]   Rakshit RD and Kisku DR. Biometric technologies in healthcare biometrics. *In Research Anthology on Securing Medical Systems and Records 2022* (pp. 31–58). IGI Global.

[2]   Rakshit RD and Kisku DR. Face identification via strategic combination of local features. *In Computational Intelligence in Pattern Recognition: Proceedings of CIPR 2019–2020* (pp. 207–217). Springer Singapore.

[3]   Datta Rakshit R, Rattani A, and Kisku DR. An LDOP approach for face identification under unconstrained scenarios. *Journal of Experimental & Theoretical Artificial Intelligence*. 2023 2:1–49.

[4]   Obaidat MS, Traore I, and Woungang I (eds.). *Biometric-based physical and cybersecurity systems*. Cham: Springer International Publishing; 2019.

[5]   Szeliski R. Computer vision: Algorithms and applications. Springer Nature; 2022 January 3.

[6]   Jain AK, Ross A, and Pankanti S. Biometrics: A tool for information security. *IEEE Trans Inf Forensics Security*. 2006;1(2):125–143

[7]   Jain AK, Flynn PJ, and Ross A (eds.). *Handbook of Biometrics*. Springer, 2007.

[8]   Jain AK and Kumar A. Biometrics of next generation: An overview. *Second Generation Biometrics*. 2010;12(1):2–3.

[9]   Nixon MS, Bouchrika I, Arbab-Zavar B, and Carter JN. On use of biometrics in forensics: Gait and ear. In *2010 18th European Signal Processing Conference 2010 Aug 23* (pp. 1655–1659). IEEE.

[10]   Georgiadou A, Mouzakitis S, Bounas K, and Askounis D. A cyber-security culture framework for assessing organization readiness. *Journal of Computer Information Systems*. 2022;62(3):452–62.

[11]   Papaioannou M, Karageorgou M, Mantas G, *et al.* A survey on security threats and countermeasures in internet of medical things (IoMT). *Transactions on Emerging Telecommunications Technologies*. 2022;33(6): e4049.

[12]   Shahzad M, Liu AX, and Samuel A. Secure unlocking of mobile touch screen devices by simple gestures: You can see it but you can not do it. *In Proceedings of the 19th Annual International Conference on Mobile Computing & Networking 2013 September 30* (pp. 39–50).

[13]   Carlaw S. Impact on biometrics of Covid-19. Biometric Technology Today. 2020;2020(4):8–9.

[14]   Liébana-Cabanillas F, Muñoz-Leiva F, Molinillo S, and Higueras-Castillo E. Do biometric payment systems work during the COVID-19 pandemic? Insights from the Spanish users' viewpoint. *Financial Innovation*. 2022;8 (1):1–25.

[15]   Zafaruddin GM and Fadewar HS. Face recognition: A holistic approach review, In *2014 International Conference on Contemporary Computing and Informatics (IC3I)*, IEEE, 2014, November, pp. 175–178.

[16]   Sirovich L and Kirby M. Low-dimensional procedure for the characterization of human faces. *JOSA A*, 1987;4(3):519–524.

[17]   Etemad K and Chellappa R. Discriminant analysis for recognition of human face images. *JOSA A*, 1997;14(8):1724–1733.

[18]   Bartlett MS, Movellan JR, and Sejnowski TJ. Face recognition by indepen-
         dent component analysis. *IEEE Transactions on Neural Networks*, 2002;13(6):
         1450–1464.

[19]   Welling M. Fisher linear discriminant analysis, *Department of Computer
         Science*. University of Toronto, 2005, 3, pp.1–4.

[20]   Campadelli P, Lanzarotti R, and Savazzi C, A feature-based face recognition
         system, In *12th International Conference on Image Analysis and Processing*,
         2003, IEEE, Proceedings, 2003, September, pp. 68–73.

[21]   Kisku DR, Tistarelli M, Sing JK, and Gupta P. Face recognition by fusion of
         local and global matching scores using DS theory: An evaluation with uni-
         classifier and multi-classifier paradigm, *In Computer Vision and Pattern
         Recognition Workshops*, 2009, June.

[22]   Du G, Su F, and Cai A. Face recognition using SURF features, *In Sixth
         International Symposium on Multispectral Image Processing and Pattern
         Recognition, International Society for Optics and Photonics*, 2009, October,
         v. 7496, pp.749628.

[23]   Déniz O, Bueno G, Salido J, and De la Torre F. Face recognition using
         histograms of oriented gradients. *Pattern Recognition Letters*, 2011;32(12):
         1598–1603.

[24]   Wiskott L, Krüger N, Kuiger N, and Von Der Malsburg C. Face recognition
         by elastic bunch graph matching. *IEEE Transactions on Pattern Analysis
         and Machine Intelligence*, 1997;19(7):775–779.

[25]   Maturana D, Mery D, and Soto A. Face recognition with local binary pat-
         terns, spatial pyramid histograms and naive Bayes nearest neighbor classi-
         fication, *In 2009 International Conference of the Chilean Computer Science
         Society*, IEEE, 2009, pp. 125–132.

[26]   Chan H, Kittler J, and Messer K. Multi-scale local binary pattern histograms
         for face recognition, In: *International Conference on Biometrics*, Springer,
         Berlin, Heidelberg, 2007, pp. 809–818.

[27]   O'Connor B and Roy K. Facial recognition using modified local binary
         pattern and random forest. *International Journal of Artificial Intelligence &
         Applications*, 2013;4(6):25.

[28]   Zhang B, Gao Y, Zhao S, and Liu J. Local derivative pattern versus local
         binary pattern: Face recognition with high-order local pattern descriptor.
         IEEE Transactions on Image Processing, 2010;19(2):533–544.

[29]   Murala S, Maheshwari RP, and Balasubramanian R. Local tetra patterns: A
         new feature descriptor for content-based image retrieval. *IEEE Transactions
         on Image Processing*, 2012;21(5):2874–2886.

[30]   Fan KC and Hung TY. A novel local pattern descriptor—local vector pattern
         in high-order derivative space for face recognition. *IEEE Transactions on
         Image Processing*, 2014;23(7):2877–2891.

[31]   Chakraborty S, Singh SK, and Chakraborty P. Local gradient hexa pattern: A
         descriptor for face recognition and retrieval. *IEEE Transactions on Circuits
         and Systems for Video Technology*, 2016;28(1):171–180.

[32] Abusham EE and Bashir HK. Face recognition using local graph structure (LGS), In *International Conference on Human-Computer Interaction*, Springer, Berlin, Heidelberg, 2011, July, pp. 169–175.

[33] Abdullah MFA, Sayeed MS, Muthu KS, Bashier HK, Azman A, and Ibrahim SZ. Face recognition with symmetric local graph structure (slgs). *Expert Systems with Applications*, 2014;41(14):6131–6137.

[34] Cootes TF, Taylor CJ, Cooper DH, and Graham J. Active shape models-their training and application. *Computer Vision and Image Understanding*, 1995; 61(1):38–59.

[35] Edwards GJ, Cootes TF, and Taylor CJ. Face recognition using active appearance models, In *European Conference on Computer Vision*, Springer, Berlin, Heidelberg, 1998, pp. 581–595.

[36] Gupta P, Saxena N, Sharma M, and Tripathi J. Deep neural network for human face recognition. *International Journal of Engineering and Manufacturing (IJEM)*, 2018;8(1):63–71.

[37] Best-Rowden L, Han H, Otto C, Klare BF, and Jain AK. Unconstrained face recognition: Identifying a person of interest from a media collection. *IEEE Transactions on Information Forensics and Security*, 2014;9(12):2144–2157.

[38] Parkhi OM, Vedaldi A, and Zisserman A. Deep face recognition, In: *BMVC* 2015, pp. 41.1–41.12.

[39] Goodfellow I, Pouget-Abadie J, Mirza M, *et al.* Generative adversarial networks. *Advances in Neural Information Processing Systems*, 2014, 27.

[40] He K, Zhang X, Ren S, and Sun J. Deep residual learning for image recognition, *In Proceedings of the IEEE Conference on Computer Vision and Pattern Recognition*, 2016, pp. 770–778.

[41] Medsker LR and Jain LC. Recurrent neural networks design and applications, 2001.

[42] Hinton GE. Deep belief networks. *Scholarpedia*, 2009;4(5):129–135.

[43] Mian A, Bennamoun M, and Owens R. An efficient multimodal 2D-3D hybrid approach to automatic face recognition. *IEEE Transactions on Pattern Analysis and Machine Intelligence*, 2007;29(11):1927–1943.

[44] Hsieh PC and Tung PC. A novel hybrid approach based on sub-pattern technique and whitened PCA for face recognition. *Pattern Recognition*, 2009;42(5):978–984.

[45] Dargham JA, Chekima A, Moung EG, and Hamdan M. Hybrid face recognition system based on linear discriminant analysis and voting: Artificial intelligence in robotics and imaging. *International Journal of Imaging and Robotics*, 2014;12(1):106–116.

[46] Wright J, Yang AY, Ganesh A, Sastry SS, and Ma Y. Robust face recognition via sparse representation. *IEEE Transactions on Pattern Analysis and Machine Intelligence*, 2008;31(2):210–227.

[47] Jain AK and Li SZ. *Handbook of Face Recognition*. New York: Springer; 2011.

[48]   Adjabi I, Ouahabi A, Benzaoui A, and Taleb-Ahmed A. Past, present, and future of face recognition: A review. *Electronics*. 2020;9(8):1188.

[49]   Parkhi OM, Vedaldi A, and Zisserman A. Deep face recognition.

[50]   Fathel WR. Fingerprint recognition using principal component analysis. Near East University, 2014.

[51]   Shuping N and Feng W. The research on fingerprint recognition algorithm fused with deep learning. *In 2020 IEEE International Conference on Information Technology, Big Data and Artificial Intelligence (ICIBA) 2020 Nov 6* (Vol. 1, pp. 1044–1047). IEEE.

[52]   Kundu S and Sarker G. A modified LBP network using Malsburg learning for rotation and location invariant fingerprint recognition and localization with and without occlusion. *In 2014 Seventh International Conference on Contemporary Computing (IC3) 2014 Aug 7* (pp. 617–623). IEEE.

[53]   Yang Z, Leng L, and Min W. Extreme downsampling and joint feature for coding-based palmprint recognition. *IEEE Transactions on Instrumentation and Measurement*. 2020;70:1

[54]   Zhao S and Zhang B. Joint constrained least-square regression with deep convolutional feature for palmprint recognition. *IEEE Transactions on Systems, Man, and Cybernetics: Systems*. 2020;52(1):511–22.

[55]   Zhao S and Zhang B. Learning complete and discriminative direction pattern for robust palmprint recognition. *IEEE Transactions on Image Processing*. 2020;30:1001–14.

[56]   Ungureanu AS, Salahuddin S, and Corcoran P. Toward unconstrained palmprint recognition on consumer devices: A literature review. *IEEE Access*. 2020;8:86130–48.

[57]   Fei L, Zhao S, Jia W, Zhang B, Wen J, and Xu Y. Toward efficient palmprint feature extraction by learning a single-layer convolution network. *IEEE Transactions on Neural Networks and Learning Systems*. 2022.

[58]   Caya MV, Durias JP, Linsangan NB, and Chung WY. Recognition of tongue print biometrie using binary robust independent elementary features. In *2017 IEEE 9th International Conference on Humanoid, Nanotechnology, Information Technology, Communication and Control, Environment and Management (HNICEM)*, 2017 December 1 (pp. 1–4), IEEE.

[59]   Sadasivan S, Sivakumar TT, Joseph AP, Zacharias GC, and Nair MS. Tongue print identification using deep CNN for forensic analysis. *Journal of Intelligent & Fuzzy Systems*. 2020;38(5):6415–22.

[60]   Diwakar M and Maharshi M. An extraction and recognition of tongue-print images for biometrics authentication system. *International Journal of Computer Applications*. 2013;61(3).

[61]   Sivakumar TT, Nair SS, Zacharias GC, Nair MS, and Joseph AP. Identification of tongue print images for forensic science and biometric authentication. *Journal of Intelligent & Fuzzy Systems*. 2018;34(3):1421–6.

[62]   Kannan S, Vinod KD, Murali G, and Baskar D. Tongue print image recognition and authentication using convolutional neural networks. In *2022 7th*

International Conference on Communication and Electronics Systems (ICCES) 2022 Jun 22 (pp. 1301–1305). IEEE.

[63] Yang L, Yang G, Wang K, Hao F, and Yin Y. Finger vein recognition via sparse reconstruction error constrained low-rank representation. *IEEE Transactions on Information Forensics and Security.* 2021;16:4869–81.

[64] Shaheed K, Mao A, Qureshi I, *et al.* DS-CNN: A pre-trained Xception model based on depth-wise separable convolutional neural network for finger vein recognition. *Expert Systems with Applications.* 2022;191:116288.

[65] Wang Y, Lu H, Qin X, and Guo J. Residual Gabor convolutional network and FV-Mix exponential level data augmentation strategy for finger vein recognition. *Expert Systems with Applications.* 2023;223:119874.

[66] Yang L, Liu X, Yang G, Wang J, and Yin Y. Small-area finger vein recognition. *IEEE Transactions on Information Forensics and Security.* 2023;18:1914–25.

[67] Zheng L and Hao C. Finger vein recognition based on PCA and sparse representation. In *2022 IEEE 5th International Conference on Information Systems and Computer Aided Education (ICISCAE) 2022*, September 23 (pp. 363–367). IEEE.

[68] Yang W, Luo W, Kang W, Huang Z, and Wu Q. FVRAS-net: An embedded finger-vein recognition and antispoofing system using a unified CNN. *IEEE Transactions on Instrumentation and Measurement.* 2020;69(11):8690–701.

[69] Noh KJ, Choi J, Hong JS, and Park KR. Finger-vein recognition based on densely connected convolutional network using score-level fusion with shape and texture images. *IEEE Access.* 2020;8:96748–66.

[70] Meng X, Xi X, Li Z, and Zhang Q. Finger vein recognition based on fusion of deformation information. *IEEE Access.* 2020;8:50519–30.

[71] Weng L, Li X, and Wang W. Finger vein recognition based on deep convolutional neural networks. In *2020 13th International Congress on Image and Signal Processing, BioMedical Engineering and Informatics (CISP-BMEI) 2020 Oct 17* (pp. 266–269). IEEE.

[72] Shen J, Liu N, Xu C, *et al.* Finger vein recognition algorithm based on lightweight deep convolutional neural network. *IEEE Transactions on Instrumentation and Measurement.* 2021;71:1–3.

[73] Ma S, Hu Q, Zhao S, Wu W, and Wu J. Multiscale multidirection binary pattern learning for discriminant palmprint identification. *IEEE Transactions on Instrumentation and Measurement.* 2023;72:1–2.

[74] Fei L, Wong WK, Zhao S, Wen J, Zhu J, and Xu Y. Learning spectrum-invariance representation for cross-spectral palmprint recognition. *IEEE Transactions on Systems, Man, and Cybernetics: Systems.* 2023.

[75] Yang Z, Leng L, Wu T, Li M, and Chu J. Multi-order texture features for palmprint recognition. *Artificial Intelligence Review.* 2023;56(2):995–1011.

[76] Vora RA, Bharadi VA, and Kekre HB. Retinal scan recognition using wavelet energy entropy. In *2012 International Conference on Communication, Information & Computing Technology (ICCICT) 2012 Oct 19* (pp. 1–6). IEEE.

[77]   Shaydyuk NK and Cleland T. Biometric identification via retina scanning with liveness detection using speckle contrast imaging. *In 2016 IEEE International Carnahan Conference on Security Technology (ICCST) 2016 Oct 24* (pp. 1–5). IEEE.

[78]   Sultan S and Faris Ghanim M. Human retina based identification system using Gabor filters and GDA technique. *Journal of Communications Software and Systems.* 2020;16(3):243–53.

[79]   Sidlauskas DP and Tamer S. Hand geometry recognition. *Handbook of Biometrics.* 2008:91–107.

[80]   Tyagi A and Bansal S. Recognition of Indian sign language using hand geometry and neural network. *In 2022 International Conference on Computing, Communication, and Intelligent Systems (ICCCIS) 2022 Nov 4* (pp. 817–822). IEEE.

[81]   Pititeeraphab Y and Pintavirooj C. Identity verification using geometry of human hands. In *2018 11th Biomedical Engineering International Conference (BMEiCON) 2018 Nov 21* (pp. 1–4). IEEE.

[82]   Oldal LG and Kovács A. Hand geometry and palmprint-based authentication using image processing. *In 2020 IEEE 18th International Symposium on Intelligent Systems and Informatics (SISY) 2020 Sep 17* (pp. 125–130). IEEE.

[83]   Liu E. Infant footprint recognition. *In Proceedings of the IEEE International Conference on Computer Vision 2017* (pp. 1653–1660).

[84]   Cao H, Zhang H, Liu Z, and Lai J. Footprint recognition and feature extraction method based on artificial intelligence. In *2020 5th International Conference on Mechanical, Control and Computer Engineering (ICMCCE)* 2020, December 25 (pp. 1302–1305). IEEE.

[85]   Kamble V and Dale M. Deep learning for biometric recognition of children using footprints. In *2022 International Conference on Emerging Smart Computing and Informatics (ESCI)* 2022, March 9 (pp. 1–6). IEEE.

[86]   Keatsamarn T and Pintavirooj C. Footprint identification using deep learning. *In 2018 11th Biomedical Engineering International Conference (BMEiCON) 2018, November 21* (pp. 1–4). IEEE.

[87]   Kushwaha R, Singal G, and Nain N. A texture feature based approach for person verification using footprint bio-metric. *Artificial Intelligence Review.* 2021;54(2):1581–611.

[88]   Benzaoui A, Hadid A, and Boukrouche A. Ear biometric recognition using local texture descriptors. *Journal of Electronic Imaging.* 2014;23(5):053008-.

[89]   Emeršič Ž, Štruc V, and Peer P. Ear recognition: More than a survey.

[90]   Ganapathi II, Ali SS, Prakash S, Vu NS, and Werghi N. A survey of 3D ear recognition techniques. *ACM Computing Surveys.* 2023;55(10):1–36.

[91]   Galdámez PL, Raveane W, and Arrieta AG. A brief review of the ear recognition process using deep neural networks. *Journal of Applied Logic.* 2017;24:62–70.

[92]   Anwar AS, Ghany KK, and Elmahdy H. Human ear recognition using geometrical features extraction. *Procedia Computer Science.* 2015;65:529–37.

[93] Guo Y and Xu Z. Ear recognition using a new local matching approach. In *2008 15th IEEE International Conference on Image Processing 2008 Oct 12* (pp. 289–292). IEEE.

[94] Ross A and Abaza A. Human ear recognition. *Computer.* 2011;44(11):79–81.

[95] Ali AT, Abdullah HS, and Fadhil MN. Voice recognition system using machine learning techniques. *Materials Today: Proceedings.* 2021:1–7.

[96] Yamazaki Y, Tamaki M, Premachandra C, Perera CJ, Sumathipala S, and Sudantha BH. Victim detection using UAV with on-board voice recognition system. *In 2019 Third IEEE International Conference on Robotic Computing (IRC) 2019 Feb 25* (pp. 555–559). IEEE.

[97] Cui B and Xue T. Design and realization of an intelligent access control system based on voice recognition. In *2009 ISECS International Colloquium on Computing, Communication, Control, and Management, 2009 August 8* (vol. 1, pp. 229–232). IEEE.

[98] Barbu T. Comparing various voice recognition techniques. *In 2009 Proceedings of the 5th Conference on Speech Technology and Human-Computer Dialogue,* 2009 June 18 (pp. 1–6). IEEE.

[99] Azarang A, Hansen J, and Kehtarnavaz N. Combining data augmentations for CNN-based voice command recognition. *In 2019 12th International Conference on Human System Interaction (HSI),* 2019 June 25 (pp. 17–21). IEEE.

[100] Bowyer KW and Burge MJ (eds.). *Handbook of Iris Recognition.* Springer London; 2016.

[101] Nguyen K, Fookes C, Jillela R, Sridharan S, and Ross A. Long range iris recognition: A survey. *Pattern Recognition.* 2017;72:123–43.

[102] Daugman J. New methods in iris recognition. *IEEE Transactions on Systems, Man, and Cybernetics, Part B (Cybernetics).* 2007;37(5):1167–75.

[103] Xu Y, Chuang TC, and Lai SH. Deep neural networks for accurate iris recognition. *In 2017 4th IAPR Asian Conference on Pattern Recognition (ACPR), 2017 November 26* (pp. 664–669). IEEE.

[104] Boulgouris NV and Chi ZX. Gait recognition using radon transform and linear discriminant analysis. *IEEE Transactions on Image Processing.* 2007;16(3):731–40.

[105] Singh JP, Jain S, Arora S, and Singh UP. Vision-based gait recognition: A survey. *IEEE Access.* 2018;6:70497–527.

[106] Zou Q, Wang Y, Wang Q, Zhao Y, and Li Q. Deep learning-based gait recognition using smartphones in the wild. *IEEE Transactions on Information Forensics and Security.* 2020;15:3197–212.

[107] Arora P, Srivastava S, and Singhal S. Analysis of gait flow image and gait Gaussian image using extension neural network for gait recognition. *In Deep Learning and Neural Networks: Concepts, Methodologies, Tools, and Applications 2020* (pp. 429–449). IGI Global.

[108] Fan C, Peng Y, Cao C, *et al.* Gaitpart: Temporal part-based model for gait recognition. In *Proceedings of the IEEE/CVF Conference on Computer Vision and Pattern Recognition 2020* (pp. 14225–14233).

[109]   Hou S, Cao C, Liu X, and Huang Y. Gait lateral network: Learning discriminative and compact representations for gait recognition. In *Computer Vision–ECCV 2020: 16th European Conference, Glasgow, UK, August 23–28, 2020, Proceedings, Part IX 2020 Nov 5* (pp. 382–398). Cham: Springer International Publishing.

[110]   Li X, Makihara Y, Xu C, Yagi Y, Yu S, and Ren M. End-to-end model-based gait recognition. In *Proceedings of the Asian Conference on Computer Vision*, 2020.

[111]   Elharrouss O, Almaadeed N, Al-Maadeed S, and Bouridane A. Gait recognition for person re-identification. *The Journal of Supercomputing.* 2021;77:3653–72.

[112]   Chen X, Luo X, Weng J, Luo W, Li H, and Tian Q. Multi-view gait image generation for cross-view gait recognition. *IEEE Transactions on Image Processing.* 2021;30:3041–55.

[113]   Chao H, Wang K, He Y, Zhang J, and Feng J. GaitSet: Cross-view gait recognition through utilizing gait as a deep set. *IEEE Transactions on Pattern Analysis and Machine Intelligence.* 2021;44(7):3467–78.

[114]   Sepas-Moghaddam A and Etemad A. Deep gait recognition: A survey. *IEEE Transactions on Pattern Analysis and Machine Intelligence.* 2022;45 (1):264–84.

[115]   Chen Y, Xia S, Zhao J, *et al.* Adversarial learning-based skeleton synthesis with spatial-channel attention for robust gait recognition. *Multimedia Tools and Applications.* 2023;82(1):1489–504.

[116]   Li G, Guo L, Zhang R, Qian J, and Gao S. TransGait: Multimodal-based gait recognition with set transformer. *Applied Intelligence.* 2023;53 (2):1535–47.

[117]   Maqsood M, Yasmin S, Gillani S, *et al.* An autonomous decision-making framework for gait recognition systems against adversarial attack using reinforcement learning. *ISA Transactions.* 2023;132:80–93.

[118]   Khan MA, Arshad H, Khan WZ, *et al.* HGRBOL2: Human gait recognition for biometric application using Bayesian optimization and extreme learning machine. *Future Generation Computer Systems.* 2023;143:337–48.

[119]   Alashik KM and Yildirim R. Human identity verification from biometric dorsal hand vein images using the DL-GAN method. *IEEE Access.* 2021;9:74194–208.

[120]   Alshayeji MH, Al-Roomi SA, and Abed SE. Efficient hand vein recognition using local keypoint descriptors and directional gradients. *Multimedia Tools and Applications.* 2022;81(11):15687–705.

[121]   Aberni Y, Boubchir L, and Daachi B. Palm vein recognition based on competitive coding scheme using multi-scale local binary pattern with ant colony optimization. *Pattern Recognition Letters.* 2020;136:101–10.

[122]   Kumar R, Singh RC, and Kant S. Dorsal hand vein-biometric recognition using convolution neural network. *In International Conference on Innovative Computing and Communications: Proceedings of ICICC 2020, Volume 1, 2021* (pp. 1087–1107). Springer Singapore.

[123]   Alshayeji MH, Al-Roomi SA, and Abed SE. Efficient hand vein recognition using local keypoint descriptors and directional gradients. *Multimedia Tools and Applications.* 2022;81(11):15687–705.

[124]   Shaheed K, Mao A, Qureshi I, Kumar M, Hussain S, and Zhang X. Recent advancements in finger vein recognition technology: Methodology, challenges and opportunities. *Information Fusion.* 2022;79:84–109.

[125]   Zhang Z and Wang M. Multi-feature fusion partitioned local binary pattern method for finger vein recognition. *Signal, Image and Video Processing.* 2022;16(4):1091–9.

[126]   Soelistio EA, Kusumo RE, Martan ZV, and Irwansyah E. A Review of Signature Recognition Using Machine Learning. *In 2021 1st International Conference on Computer Science and Artificial Intelligence (ICCSAI),* 2021 October 28 (Vol. 1, pp. 219–223). IEEE.

[127]   Ghosh S, Ghosh S, Kumar P, Scheme E, and Roy PP. A novel spatio-temporal Siamese network for 3D signature recognition. *Pattern Recognition Letters.* 2021;144:13–20.

[128]   Ghosh R. A recurrent neural network based deep learning model for offline signature verification and recognition system. *Expert Systems with Applications.* 2021;168:114249.

[129]   Li W, Xu X, Aysa A, and Ubul K. A simple convolutional neural network for small sample multi-lingual offline handwritten signature recognition. In *Biometric Recognition: 16th Chinese Conference, CCBR 2022, Beijing, China, November 11–13, 2022, Proceedings 2022 November 3* (pp. 393–403). Cham: Springer Nature Switzerland.

[130]   Naz S, Bibi K, and Ahmad R. DeepSignature: Fine-tuned transfer learning based signature verification system. *Multimedia Tools and Applications.* 2022;81(26):38113–22.

[131]   Labati RD, Muñoz E, Piuri V, Sassi R, and Scotti F. Deep-ECG: Convolutional neural networks for ECG biometric recognition. *Pattern Recognition Letters.* 2019;126:78–85.

[132]   Meltzer D and Luengo D. An efficient clustering-based non-fiducial approach for ECG biometric recognition. *In 2022 30th European Signal Processing Conference (EUSIPCO) 2022 Aug 29* (pp. 623–627). IEEE.

[133]   Zhang Y, Zhao Z, Deng Y, Zhang X, and Zhang Y. Human identification driven by deep CNN and transfer learning based on multiview feature representations of ECG. *Biomedical Signal Processing and Control.* 2021;68:102689.

[134]   Ibrahim AE, Abdel-Mageid S, Nada N, and Elshahed MA. Human identification using electrocardiogram signal as a biometric trait. *International Journal of System Dynamics Applications (IJSDA).* 2022;11(3):1–7.

[135]   Patro KK, Jaya Prakash A, Jayamanmadha Rao M, and Rajesh Kumar P. An efficient optimized feature selection with machine learning approach for ECG biometric recognition. *IETE Journal of Research.* 2022;68 (4):2743–54.

[136] Hezil N and Boukrouche A. Multimodal biometric recognition using human ear and palmprint. *IET Biometrics.* 2017;6(5):351–9.

[137] Zhou C, Huang J, Yang F and Liu Y. A hybrid fusion model of iris, palm vein and finger vein for multi-biometric recognition system. *Multimedia Tools and Applications.* 2020;79:29021–42.

[138] Khodadoust J, Medina-Pérez MA, Monroy R, Khodadoust AM, and Mirkamali SS. A multibiometric system based on the fusion of fingerprint, finger-vein, and finger-knuckle-print. *Expert Systems with Applications.* 2021;176:114687.

[139] Attia A, Mazaa S, Akhtar Z, and Chahir Y. Deep learning-driven palmprint and finger knuckle pattern-based multimodal person recognition system. *Multimedia Tools and Applications.* 2022;81(8):10961–80.

[140] Grünenberg K, Møhl P, Olwig KF, and Simonsen A. Issue introduction: Identities and identity: Biometric technologies, borders and migration. *Ethnos.* 2022;87(2):211–22.

Chapter 4

Channel refinement of fingerprint pre-processing models

Indu Joshi[1,2], Ayush Utkarsh[3], Tashvik Dhamija[4], Pravendra Singh[5], Antitza Dantcheva[1], Sumantra Dutta Roy[2] and Prem Kumar Kalra[2]

Abstract

Deep models are the state-of-the-art models for fingerprint pre-processing. However, these models have very high number of parameters, usually in millions. As a result, redundancy is observed among the features learnt by deep learning-based fingerprint pre-processing models. A popular technique to help deep models learn distinct and informative features is channel refinement. A recent study has illustrated the capability of channel refinement to improve generalization of fingerprint enhancement models. Motivated by the above-mentioned study, this chapter delves into presenting a detailed study illustrating the usefulness of channel refinement in reducing redundancy and imparting generalization ability to fingerprint enhancement models. Furthermore, we extend this study to assess whether channel refinement generalizes on fingerprint region of interest (ROI) segmentation. Extensive experiments on 14 challenging publicly available fingerprint databases and a private database of fingerprints of the rural Indian population are conducted to assess the potential of channel refinement on fingerprint pre-processing models.

4.1 Introduction

The robustness of fingerprints has long established it as a tool for facilitating person identification. Subsequently, consequently, fingerprints have emerged as one of the most widely used biometrics modalities. These are used in a wide range of

[1]STARS team, Inria Sophia Antipolis, France
[2]Indian Institute of Technology Delhi, New Delhi, India
[3]Independent Researcher, India
[4]Department of Electronics and Communication, Delhi Technological University, New Delhi, India
[5]Computer Science department, Indian Institute of Technology Roorkee, Uttarakhand, India

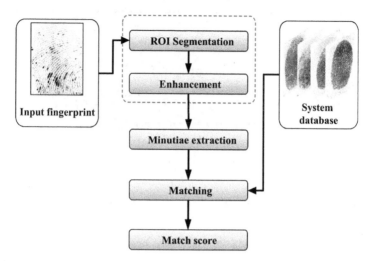

Figure 4.1   Schematic diagram of an AFRS. This chapter discusses the impact of channel refinement on deep learning-based fingerprint pre-processing models. For understanding, fingerprint pre-processing blocks constituting of fingerprint ROI segmentation *and* fingerprint enhancement *are marked using the red box.*

applications, including law enforcement, border security and civilian applications. An automated fingerprint recognition system (AFRS) constitutes various steps which can be broadly categorized as: fingerprint acquisition, pre-processing, feature extraction and matching. A fingerprint pre-processing model is a term used to jointly refer to the fingerprint ROI segmentation and fingerprint enhancement (see Figure 4.1).

Fingerprint pre-processing initiates with the fingerprint ROI segmentation step. This step separates the background and the foreground fingerprint region in a given fingerprint image [1]. Formally, the foreground fingerprint region can be described as the fingerprint image region constituting of fingerprint ridges and valleys. On the other hand, background region in a fingerprint image typically constitutes unnecessary textured patterns such as overlapping text, or noise observed to the presence of oil and dirt on sensor surface or wearing of fingerprint sensing device. Subsequent to fingerprint ROI segmentation, what follows is the fingerprint enhancement step. This step improves the quality of fingerprint images. In particular, fingerprint enhancement refines the ridge structure of a fingerprint image by improving ridge-valley contrast, removing noise observed in background and predicting the ridge details in unclear regions [2]. Both the fingerprint pre-processing steps are crucial for appropriately extracting features and achieve satisfactory comparison results. The need for pre-processing models is even more profound for poor-quality fingerprints with visibly low contrast and missing ridge details (see Figure 4.2).

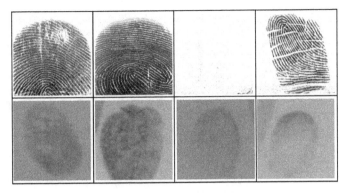

Figure 4.2   Sample poor-quality fingerprints used to study the impact of channel refinement on fingerprint pre-processing models

Deep convolutional neural networks (CNNs) dominate modern fingerprint pre-processing models for fingerprint recognition. These networks have a very large number of layers and model parameters. Although, an effective deep model is expected to learn distinct and useful features, however, with such a high model capacity, it is often observed that the learnt features have high correlation. A cutting-edge method to lessen redundancy among channel weights (features) learnt by CNNs is through channel refinement. Recently, Joshi *et al.* [3] demonstrate that channel weights learnt by fingerprint enhancement models have redundant information and propose channel refinement of fingerprint enhancement models and demonstrate its effectiveness to reduce redundancy among channel weights (see Figure 4.3).

4.1.1   Research contributions

Following research contributions are made in this chapter:

- A recently conducted study by Joshi *et al.* [3] demonstrates the ability of channel refinement to improve the generalization ability of fingerprint enhancement models. This chapter delves into evaluating whether channel refinement generalizes for fingerprint ROI segmentation.
- The performance of channel refinement on several varying fingerprint pre-processing models is studied.
- Additionally, study is done on how channel refining applies to various cutting-edge deep learning models.
- Visualization of the feature correlation matrix is provided to understand redundancy among features.
- Relevant ablation studies and comparisons with cutting-edge techniques of channel attention are provided.
- Rigorous experimentation on 15 fingerprint databases is conducted to understand the generalization ability of channel refinement.

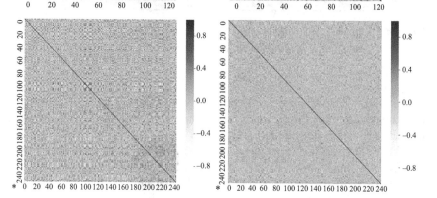

Figure 4.3   Left-correlation matrix demonstrating high redundancy among features learnt by cutting-edge CNN-based fingerprint pre-processing model. Right-redundancy among features is significantly reduced after incorporating proposed channel refinement.

4.2   Related work

4.2.1   Fingerprint enhancement

Several factors make fingerprint enhancement a highly challenging problem. Some of these factors include presence of smudged ridge patterns, poor contrast between ridges and valleys due to wet or dry fingertips, presence of sensor noise, oil and dirt on sensing surface or structured background noise due to overlapping text or fingerprint patterns. Several algorithms have been proposed to address these challenges. However, the design of a generalizable fingerprint enhancement algorithm is still an open challenge. We proceed to describe the literature on fingerprint enhancement.

4.2.1.1   Classical image processing techniques for fingerprint enhancement

Filtering in spatial or Fourier domain constitutes the most widely used classical image processing-based fingerprint enhancement methods. These methods utilize ridge information, e.g., ridge continuity or ridge orientations to predict missing ridge information in poor-quality regions [4–11]. The contribution of Hong *et al.* [4] is one of the introductory and seminal contributions in the field. To approximate the frequency and orientation of the ridge, the authors simulate a sinusoid wave in a direction perpendicular to the ridge orientation. The enhanced fingerprint image is computed via using Gabor filters that are set in accordance with the approximated frequency and orientation. Yoon *et al.* [12] approximate fingerprint ridge orientation using zero-pole method based on singular points as well as fingerprint skin distortion and rotation model. Gottschlich and Schönlieb [5] exploit anisotropic filtering to propose a locally adaptive fingerprint enhancement algorithm. Filtering is applied with respect to the ridge orientations in the local fingerprint region. Turroni *et al.* [6] as well utilize context. The context in their approach is approximated through local fingerprint quality, frequency and orientation. The local context is used for adapting the filter accordingly. The authors suggest iterative application of contextual filtering. Filtering begins from regions with high fingerprint quality to the ones with low fingerprint quality. Ramos *et al.* [7] propose adaptive Gabor filtering that is tuned to the signal frequency. Wang *et al.* [8] overcame the limited bandwidth challenge of Gabor filter by proposing log-Gabor filters. For filtering, the authors utilize curvature, ridge frequency and the orientation information. Similarly, Gottschlich [9] exploit curvature information by proposing filtering using curved Gabor filters. The contribution of Chikkerur *et al.* [10] is among the first few approaches that that exploit frequency domain to study fingerprints. The authors approximate ridge frequency and orientation using short-time Fourier transform (STFT). Ghafoor *et al.* [11] propose fingerprint enhancement through filtering in both spatial and frequency domains.

Hsieh *et al.* [13] proposed the utilization of both local and global contextual information. The authors execute wavelet decomposition to extract global information. The enhanced fingerprint is generated using wavelet reconstruction. Jirachaweng and Areekul [14] note the limitations of Gabor filters in generating fingerprints with blocking artefacts and poor ridge continuity around high curvature fingerprint regions. The authors exploit filtering on the discrete cosine transform domain to address the limitations of Gabor filters. We note that since the classical image processing-based fingerprint enhancement methods directly exploit contextual information, ridges in poor-quality fingerprint regions with unreliable contextual information are often incorrectly enhanced. Learning-based fingerprint enhancement methods are proposed to address these limitations of classical image processing-based methods.

4.2.1.2   Learning-based algorithms for fingerprint enhancement

Several notable works in fingerprint enhancement utilize learnable dictionaries to estimate fingerprint ridge orientations [15–19]. Feng *et al.* [15] propose a dictionary-based fingerprint enhancement method that exploits compatibility between orientations in neighbouring fingerprint image patches to estimate fingerprint ridge orientations. Yang *et al.* [16] observe that only certain orientations exist in a specific fingerprint region. The authors exploit this information by proposing location-specific dictionaries for quicker dictionary look-ups and lower orientation estimation errors. Chen *et al.* [17] observe that dictionary with larger patches are better suited for poor-quality fingerprint regions. Motivated by this observation, the authors propose multi-scale dictionaries to account for varying amount of noise in different fingerprint regions. Liu *et al.* [18] learnt efficient dictionaries for fingerprint enhancement by sparse coding the fingerprint ridge orientation dictionaries. Chaidee *et al.* [19] exploit information from both Gabor and curved filters. The response of both these filters are combined to construct a frequency domain dictionary which is subsequently to estimate orientations and generate the enhanced image.

A standard practice for dictionary-based fingerprint enhancement approaches is that the orientation dictionaries are computed from good-quality fingerprint regions. Thus, dictionary-based methods often perform poorly on low-quality fingerprint regions. This shortcoming of dictionary-based approaches is addressed by *orientation prediction networks* [20,21]. Cao and Jain [20] formulated fingerprint ridge orientation approximation to be a classification task. The authors propose a CNN to perform the orientation classification. Qu *et al.* [21] posed an orientation angle prediction as a regression problem and exploit a deep model estimate the direction of the fingerprint ridge. Driven by the accomplishments of deep models in orientation estimation, researchers argued to directly generate the enhanced fingerprint as opposed to predicting orientation [2,22–27].

Sahasrabudhe and Namboodiri [22] suggested enhancing fingerprint using a deep belief network. Schuch *et al.* [23] exploited a deconvolutional autoencoder (DeConvNet) for enhancing fingerprints. Svoboda *et al.* [25] introduce domain knowledge into the fingerprint enhancement domain by introducing an gradient and orientation optimizing autoencoder model. Qian *et al.* [26] proposed to enhance fingerprint patches using DenseUnet-based fingerprint enhancement model. Li *et al.* [2] and Wong and Lai [27] demonstrated that multitasking using an orientation correction task facilitates improved fingerprint enhancement performance. Joshi *et al.* [28,29] demonstrated that generative adversarial network is an effective model for fingerprint enhancement. Later, the authors demonstrate that Monte Carlo Dropout [30] imparts interpretability to fingerprint enhancement models while estimating data uncertainty facilitates noise-aware fingerprint enhancement [31]. The most recent works in fingerprint enhancement domain include cross-domain consistency [32] and context-aware enhancement by solving jigsaw puzzles [33]. For a comprehensive survey on fingerprint enhancement methods, the readers are referred to the survey by Schuch *et al.* [34]. To summarize, we note that existing state-of-the-art fingerprint approaches are autoencoder or generative adversarial network-based approaches. However, designing a generalizable fingerprint enhancement model is still an open challenge in the domain.

4.2.2 *Fingerprint ROI segmentation*

Similar intensities of foreground and background pixels around fingerprint boundaries make Fingerprint ROI segmentation a challenging problem. Many algorithms are proposed to address the challenges posed by fingerprint ROI segmentation. However, generalization on disparate sensing technologies is an existing challenge. We now describe the literature on fingerprint ROI segmentation which can be broadly categorized as follows:

4.2.2.1   Classical image-processing techniques for fingerprint ROI segmentation

Hu *et al.* [35] and Hai *et al.* [36] suggest frequency domain filtering to differentiate between foreground and background. A fusion-based segmentation technique is recommended by Hu *et al.* [35] that combines information from the frequency domain and domain knowledge of orientations. At first, they apply log-Gabor filtering on the fingerprint image followed by adaptive thresholding to obtain the first segmentation mask. The second mask is obtained using the orientation reliability metric defined by the authors. Both these masks are fused followed by post-processing to obtain the segmented ROI. Thai *et al.* [36] argue that the frequencies of ridge patterns observed in the foreground fingerprint image region lie only in a specific band of the Fourier spectrum. They suggest Fourier domain filtering using factorized directional bandpass filter. The aforementioned technique attenuates frequencies occurring due to artefacts and only preserve the relevant frequencies pertaining to the true fingerprint region. The reconstructed image is then followed by morphological operations to obtain the segmented fingerprint image.

Some approaches use only morphological operations for fingerprint ROI segmentation [37,38]. To separate the noise and fingerprint region, Thai and Gottschlich [37] suggest a three-part decomposition approach. To create the segmented image, morphological techniques are applied to the binarized fingerprint image. For the input fingerprint image, Fahmy and Thabet [38] compute the range image. Subsequently, adaptive thresholding is used to transform the range image into a binary image. To create the segmented image, morphological techniques and contour smoothing are used to the binary image. Another prominent direction explored by researchers to approach fingerprint ROI segmentation is through making use of ridge orientation information [39,40]. Teixeira and Leite [39] suggest a multi-scale pyramidal structuring element for monotonic filtering of image extrema while a multi-scale directional operator is used to determine the orientation of each pixel. The computed directional field is used to estimate the background. The segmented image is obtained using after subtracting the estimated background followed by post-processing. da Silva Vasconcelos and Pedrini *et al.* [40] pointed out that the ridges and valleys can be identified as pixels parallel and normal to the ridge orientation, respectively. Further, the authors use orientation information to assess the quality of ridge and valleys and compute directional images. Clustering on the directional image followed by post-processing is performed to find the segmented image. Different from the above-mentioned approaches, Wu *et al.* [41] observed that the strength of Harris corner points in the background is lower compared to the foreground. The high corner strength possessed by ridge boundaries helps to distinguish between foreground and background.

A significant limitation of traditional image processing-based fingerprint ROI segmentation approaches is that these approaches do not perform well when the intensity of background pixels is similar to the intensity of foreground fingerprint pixels. Furthermore, the segmentation performance of these approaches is heavily dependent on the post-processing step. Therefore, to improve the segmentation performance, learning-based approaches are proposed, which are described next.

4.2.2.2   Learning-based algorithms for fingerprint ROI segmentation

Initial approaches to learning-based ROI segmentation algorithms propose to cluster image pixels to identify foreground and background [42–45]. Yang *et al.* [42] calculated the coherence, mean and variance features from non-overlapping blocks of the fingerprint image. These features are then clustered through K-means clustering. The clusters are then classified into foreground or background using voting of neighbours. Morphological post-processing is performed to obtain the final segmented image. Ferreira *et al.* [43] apply block-wise range filter to enhance the ridges of the fingerprint image. The output range image that results is clustered and binarized. Later, the ROI segmentation mask is attained by conducting post-processing. Lei and Lin *et al.* [44] propose to apply a range filter to enhance fingerprint ridge boundaries. The clusters created by the range filter are then combined. To create the ROI mask, morphological operations are used. Ferreira *et al.* [45] apply filtering through the range, entropy and variance filters. Three different clustering methods are evaluated. The decision is re-evaluated through different classifiers. The final image is obtained after post-processing of the binarized image. However, a common shortcoming of clustering-based approaches is that these require prior knowledge of the number of clusters and their performance is heavily dependent on this parameter. This adversely affects the generalization ability of clustering-based approaches.

Some learning-based methods work on a patch-level and classify a given patch as foreground or background [1,46–51]. Stojanović *et al.* [1] proposed to divide each image into patches and classify each patch using off-the-shelf CNN model, AlexNet. Predictions for each block are combined for achieving ROI mask. This mask is smoother by post-processing to obtain the segmented ROI mask. Liu *et al.* [46] extracted handcrafted texture and intensity features from patches of a fingerprint image. The foreground or background label for each patch is obtained using an Adaboost classifier. Later, post-processing is applied to obtain a smooth ROI mask. Zhu *et al.* [47] extracted multi-sized overlapping patches and classify them using three different neural networks. Predictions from the three networks are combined to generate a prediction score for each patch. The prediction scores are thresholded, followed by post-processing to generate the segmentation mask. Ezeobiejesi and Bhanu [48] proposed a two-phased method for ROI segmentation where in the first phase model learns representative fingerprint features by training a hierarchy of restricted Boltzmann machines to learn an identity mapping of image patches. In the second phase, the network is trained to predict foreground or background class for each patch. Predictions of all the patches are merged to obtain the ROI mask. Serafim *et al.* [49] suggested classifying image patches through

AlexNet and apply smoothing and hole filling post-processing techniques on the combined predictions for achieving ROI mask. Sankaran *et al.* [50] extracted saliency, intensity, gradient, ridge and quality-based features for each patch and perform feature selection to find the most discriminative features. Each patch is classified as either foreground or background using a random forest classifier trained on the chosen features. Khan and Wani [51] exploit CNN for classifying a patch as background or foreground. Furthermore, they take a majority of neighbours to decide whether a patch is misclassified and change the label of a misclassified patch.

The patch-based classification approaches for ROI segmentation suffer from many limitations. The first being the high computational time since the network has to make a prediction for each patch. Second, the segmented ROI obtained through these approaches suffer from block-effect around boundaries and needs post-processing. Joshi *et al.* [30,31] demonstrated that recurrent Unet (RUnet) [52] is a promising CNN architecture for fingerprint ROI segmentation. However, designing a generalizable fingerprint ROI segmentation is still an open challenge in fingerprint ROI segmentation domain.

4.2.3   Attention mechanisms

The attention mechanism is a technique for directing the viewer's attention on an image's most crucial components and ignoring unimportant aspects. The attention mechanism of the human visual system is used to examine [53,54] and comprehend complicated pictures effectively and efficiently. This has motivated researchers to enhance computer vision systems' functionality by adding attention methods. A visual system's attention mechanism can be conceptualized as a dynamic process for selection that is implemented through adaptively weighing features in line with the significance of the input. We can classify existing attention methods into six categories: channel attention, spatial attention, temporal attention, branch attention, channel and spatial attention, and spatial and temporal attention. Channel attention [55–61] creates a channel-wide attention mask and uses it to identify the most crucial channels. Spatial attention [62–67] creates attention masks across spatial domains and employs them to either directly predict or pick out important spatial locations. By creating an attention mask in real-time, temporal attention [68,69] chooses key frames. Branch attention [70–73] creates an attention mask over all of the branches and uses it to identify the most significant ones. In order to choose key characteristics, channel and spatial attention [74–78] either directly produce a joint 3-D channel, width, and height attention mask, or individually forecast channel and spatial attention masks. In order to focus attention on informative locations, spatial and temporal [79–82] attention computes temporal and spatial attention masks individually or generates a joint spatiotemporal attention mask.

4.2.3.1   Channel attention

In deep CNNs, distinct channels of various feature maps typically signify distinct objects [83]. Channel attention is comparable to a mechanism of choosing an object to decide what to focus on by adaptively recalibrating [84] the weight of each channel. Hu *et al.* [55] introduced SENet and originally put out the idea of channel attention. A squeeze-and-excitation (SE) block, which is the core element of SENet, is utilized to gathering global data, record associations between channels, and enhances representational capacity. Squeeze modules and excitation modules are the two components that make up SE blocks. Global average pooling is used in the squeeze module to collect spatial data on a global scale. Utilizing fully connected layers, the excitation module collects channel-wise relationships and generates an attention vector. The relevant component of the attention vector is multiplied to scale each channel of the input feature [85].

In order to enhance the squeeze module, Gao *et al.* [56] suggested utilizing a global second-order pooling block for representing high-order statistics while accumulating global information. It is not practical to employ a SE block post each convolution block because of the computation complexity and a large number of parameters in the fully connected layer in the excitation module. Additionally, an implicit approach for modelling channel relationships is to use fully connected layers. Yang *et al.* [57] suggested using gated channel transformation to efficiently capture information while explicitly describing channel-wise interactions in order to solve the aforementioned issues. SENet decreases the number of channels to avoid having a complex model. However, this approach fails to accurately simulate the relationship between the weight vectors and the inputs, which lowers the quality of the output. Wang *et al.* [58] suggested the efficient channel attention block to get around this problem by determining the interaction between channels using a 1D convolution rather than dimensionality reduction. The squeeze module can only use global average pooling, which has representational limitations. Qin *et al.* [86] exploited frequency domain information for applying global average pooling operation so as to get a more potent representation capability. In order to describe the link between probabilities of object categories and scene context, Zhang *et al.* [87] suggested the semantic encoding loss pertaining to a context encoding module. For semantic segmentation, this approach makes advantage of contextual information present in a global scene.

4.2.3.2   Spatial attention

One way to think of spatial attention is as an adaptive mechanism for choosing which spatial region to focus on. Particularly for big inputs, CNNs require a significant computing cost. Mnih *et al.* [62] introduced the recurrent attention model, which uses reinforcement learning [88] and recurrent neural networks (RNNs) [89] to instruct the network where to focus its attention for concentrating scarce computational assets on critical areas. Ba *et al.* [63] suggested a deep recurrent network, similar to [62], that can process an image glimpse for tasks involving several objects. Here glimpse refers to an image cropping at several different resolutions. To be specific, the suggested model uses a glimpse as an input to update its hidden state, and at each step predicts both the location of the subsequent glimpse and a new object. The network's computational efficiency is enhanced by the fact that the glimpse is typically substantially smaller compared to entire image. Xu *et al.* [64]

suggested to exploit both soft and hard attention to help an image caption generation model visualize where and what it ought to concentrate. By enabling the user to discern the model's emphasis, the application of suggested attention model enhances the interpretability of the procedure of creating image captions. Additionally, it aids in enhancing the network's capacity for better representation. Hu *et al.* [65] developed GENet, which draws inspiration from SENet, with the goal of offering a spatial domain recalibration function for gathering long-range dependencies present in spatial domain. Part gathering and excitation procedures are combined in GENet. It combines input features over broad neighbourhoods in the first stage and simulates the relationship between various spatial locations. The second stage begins by utilizing interpolation to create an attention map whose dimensions are similar to the dimensions of feature that is provided as the input. The next step is to scale the input feature map by multiplying each point by the matching element in the attention map.

4.2.3.3 Temporal attention

Video processing typically makes use of temporal attention, which may be regarded of as a dynamic means for choosing the time when the model must be attentive. In research on video representation learning, temporal pooling and RNNs have been frequently utilized to capture interaction among different frames. However, such techniques suffer from limited ability to model temporal relationship. In order to get around these, Li *et al.* [68] suggested to learn global–local temporal representation to take advantage of many scales of temporal information present in a video clip. The suggested attention model consisted of a temporal self-attention module that helps to capture temporal dependencies on a global scale. Additionally, the model proposed to learn temporal dependencies on a local scale through employing dilated convolutions that span a variety of temporal ranges with progressively increasing dilatation rates. Different outputs are concatenated to merge multi-scale information. Liu *et al.* [69] introduced a temporal adaptive module to efficiently and adaptably capture complicated temporal interactions. In order to collect context at a global scale, however, in lesser time than [68], it utilized an adaptive kernel as opposed to self-attention.

4.2.3.4 Branch attention

When employed with a multi-branch structure, branch attention may be regarded of as a dynamic means for choosing the branch on which the module must focus. In order to solve the issue of training very deep networks, Srivastava *et al.* [70] suggested highway networks, which use adaptive gating techniques to facilitate information flows across layers. Using straightforward gradient descent techniques, very deep highway networks may be immediately trained. This is made possible by the gating mechanism and skip-connection structure. Information is routed through layers due to the gating mechanism, which, in contrast to fixed skip-connections, adapts to the input. According to the studies conducted in the field of neuroscience, in response to the input signal, visual cortical neurons adaptively modify the dimensions pertaining to receptive fields [90]. Inspired by this, Li *et al.* [71]

proposed the selective kernel (SK) convolution using the automatic selection method. Three operations are used to implement SK convolution: split, fuse, and select. The feature map is subjected to transformations with various kernel sizes during split to produce various sizes RFs. Then, to compute the gate vector, element-wise summation is used to merge information available from the different branches. By doing this, the information flow from the various branches is regulated. The final feature map is then created via combining all branch feature maps under the guidance of the gate vector.

Convolution kernel uniformity is a fundamental presumption in CNNs. In light of this, increasing a network's depth or width is typically the best approach to improve its ability to represent information, but doing so comes with a high additional cost to computation. Yang *et al.* [72] suggested a multi-branch convolution referred as CondConv for boosting the capability of CNNs. Leveraging a computationally less expensive means for branch attention, CondConv fully exploits the benefits of the multi-branch structure. It offers an innovative way to effectively improve networks' capacity. The model's width and depth are constrained by lightweight CNNs' incredibly low computational cost, thus lowering the representational power of the networks. In order to solve the aforementioned issue, dynamic convolution was suggested by Chen *et al.* [73], that in addition to CondConv [72], boosts representational power at a small additional computational cost without altering the network's width or depth.

4.2.3.5   Channel and spatial attention

The benefits of both channel and spatial attention are combined in channel and spatial attention. It chooses important objects and regions in an adaptive manner. Residual attention network [74] highlighted the significance of relevant elements in both the dimensions: spatial and channel. Subsequently, the authors [74] established the channel spatial attention domain. It uses numerous convolutions in a bottom-up framework to build a 3D (channel, breadth and height) attention map. Woo *et al.* [75] suggested to serially stack channel and spatial attention and referred it as a convolutional block attention module. The proposed method improved both informative channels and important regions. Decoupling channel and spatial attention enables increased computational efficiency. Global pooling is then used to make use of global spatial information. In addition to [75], Park *et al.* [76] also put out the bottleneck attention module (BAM), which sought to effectively increase networks' representational capacity. The spatial attention sub-receptive module's field is expanded using dilated convolution, and to reduce computational costs, a bottleneck structure is built in accordance with ResNet's suggestions. The feature map is subjected to global pooling by a SE block, which combines global spatial data. However, it disregards the spatial information at the pixel level, which is crucial for dense prediction problems. Roy *et al.* [77] thus suggested spatial and channel SE blocks. In a manner similar to BAM, spatial SE blocks are utilized in addition to SE blocks for enabling concentration on salient input regions through weights pertaining to spatial dimensions. Both convolution block attention module [75] and BAM [76] individually estimated separately in

CBAM and BAM, neglecting the connections between these two domains. Triplet attention, a straightforward but effective attention method to model cross-domain interaction, was first described by Misra *et al.* [78].

4.2.3.6 Spatial and temporal attention

The benefits of both spatial attention and temporal attention are combined in spatial and temporal attention, which adaptively chooses both salient regions and crucial frames. Each type of action in human action recognition often only depends on a small number of distinct kinematic joints. Multiple actions might also be carried out across time. These findings led Song *et al.* [79] to propose a hybrid LSTM model [89] for spatial and temporal attention. Suggested model helps to adaptively identify keyframes and discriminative features. A spatial attention sub-network that selects significant areas and a temporal attention sub-network that selects critical frames are its key modules for learning attention weights. In order to choose important aspects globally and adaptively in order to capture spatial and temporal information that exists in video frames, Du *et al.* [80] introduced spatiotemporal attention. The sequential application of spatial attention component followed by a temporal attention component constitutes the framework for spatiotemporal attention in [80]. Prior attention models to re-identify individuals in videos merely gave each frame a weighted attention value; they were unable to recognize joint spatial and temporal relationships. Fu *et al.* [81] presented a novel spatiotemporal attention method to address this problem, which rates attention in every spatial location in various frames with the use of no additional parameters. In order to understand the spatial dependencies inside a frame and the temporal links among different frames, Yang *et al.* [82] introduced a spatiotemporal graph convolutional network. The network is trained to learn discriminative features from a video. Pairwise similarity is used to build a patch graph. Subsequently, combines data using graph convolution.

To summarize, depending upon the nature of application, different kinds of attention mechanisms can be introduced in a deep neural network. For a deep fingerprint pre-processing model, we hypothesize that its huge model capacity makes it prone to poor generalization. In order to ensure learning of distinct features that generalize over different databases, for fingerprint pre-processing models, we propose to exploit channel-level attention.

4.3 Proposed method

This subject of this research is to study the significance of channel-level dependencies in a deep learning-based model fingerprint pre-processing. We propose a method to effectively refine the features learnt by a fingerprint pre-processing model such that redundancy among features is reduced and improved generalization is obtained. We now proceed to describe channel refinement unit (CRU) to refine the features of fingerprint pre-processing models.

4.3.1   Channel refinement unit

A CRU is designed to transform the features such that redundancy among channels is reduced. For an input feature $X \in R^{L \times H \times C}$, CRU transforms it into $X_{new} \in R^{L \times H \times C}$ such that X_{new} has lesser channel level redundancy and more informative features are learnt by the fingerprint pre-processing model (see Figure 4.4). Convolution is a local operation due to its limited receptive field. As a result, standard convolution operation cannot successfully extract the global information from fingerprint images. CRU exploits global information derived using the activation maps to evaluate the significance of each channel towards fingerprint processing. Therefore, as its very first step, CRU computes the global representation corresponding to each channel of a given convolution layer. To compute the global representation, CRU leverages a global average pooling (gap) layer. This (gap) layer averages activations across channels, to output a C dimensional vector, corresponding to each input channel.

Next operation in the CRU is aimed towards understanding the significance of each of the C channels. To achieve this, the CRU executes C depth-wise convolution (dwc) (1×1). This provides an output vector $W = [w_i, w_2, \ldots, w_c]$, where $w_i \in R$. The operations that follow on Vector W are batch normalization (bn) and sigmoid activation (a). These operations output a refinement vector (A) that represents how much each channel must be refined to obtain the optimal fingerprint pre-processing performance. $A = [a_i, a_2, \ldots a_c]$ ($a_i \in R$), this vector contains a refinement weight for each of the input channel. The refined feature X_{new} is obtained through conducting element-wise product between input feature X and the

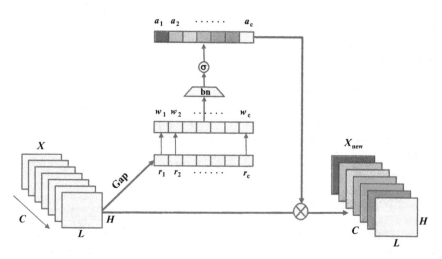

Figure 4.4   CRU transforms X to X_{new} such that redundancy among channels is reduced and the fingerprint pre-processing model is enabled to learn more informative features, leading to improved fingerprint pre-processing performance

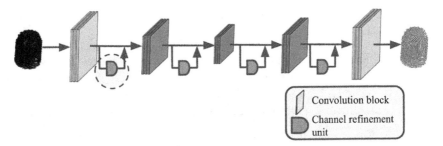

Figure 4.5   Flowchart depicting introduction of the CRU into an existing fingerprint pre-processing model. CRU transforms the features learnt by the baseline fingerprint pre-processing model such that redundancy among channels is reduced. Thus, the CRU helps to learn more informative features, facilitating improved fingerprint pre-processing performance.

corresponding refinement weight pertaining to its channels.

$$A = \sigma(bn(dwc(gap(X))))$$
$$X_{new} = [x_1 \cdot a_1, x_2 \cdot a_2, \ldots x_C \cdot a_C]$$

Instead of X, after exploiting CRU the refined feature X_{new} is used for computation at the following layers to generate the improved pre-processed fingerprints.

4.3.2   Introducing channel refinement unit into a fingerprint pre-processing model

The incorporation of CRU does not need much change in the network design of the backbone deep model for fingerprint pre-processing. CRU is included after each convolution layer. As a result, refined features after each convolution layer and these refined features are forwarded to the next convolution layer for generating the pre-processed fingerprint image at the output layer (see Figure 4.5). The refined features have lesser redundancy and therefore capture distinct and more informative characteristics from input fingerprints. Learning of more informative features facilitates improved fingerprint pre-processing performance.

4.4   Experimental set-up

We rigorously assess the impact of channel refinement by introducing CRU into different fingerprint pre-processing models conducting different fingerprint pre-processing tasks (fingerprint ROI segmentation and fingerprint enhancement).

4.4.1   Databases

For evaluating this research, we used 14 challenging and publicly available fingerprints databases, and a challenging private dataset of poor-quality fingerprints, resulting in a total of 15 databases for experimental evaluation of the proposed CRU.

4.4.1.1   Fingerprint enhancement

As suggested in the literature [28,29,91], fingerprint enhancement models are trained in a supervised manner using synthetic data. For evaluating the fingerprint processing performance on the enhancement task, we use the following databases:

1. *Multi-sensor optical and latent fingerprint (MOLF) database* [92]: MOLF is the largest publicly available latent fingerprint database. This database constitutes 4 400 poor-quality latent fingerprints acquired from 100 volunteers. The volunteers press their fingertips on ceramic tiles. The latent fingerprints are captured via exploiting the standard black powder dusting process.
2. *Rural Indian fingerprint database* [93]: This is a challenging open access dataset of poor-quality fingerprints. These fingerprints are collected from rural Indian volunteers rigorously involved with physical activity requiring extensive use of fingers, such as farming. In total, this dataset has 1 631 poor-quality fingerprints obtained from an optical sensor.
3. A private rural Indian fingerprint database [94] with samples from aging and the subjects engaged with rigorous manual work. This dataset has 1 000 poor-quality fingerprint samples obtained from an optical sensor.

4.4.1.2   Fingerprint ROI segmentation

To evaluate the fingerprint processing performance on the ROI segmentation task, we use the fingerprint verification challenge (FVC) databases. We evaluate the fingerprint ROI segmentation on different series of FVC competitions, FVC2000, FVC2002 and FVC2004. The fingerprints in these databases are acquired from different fingerprint sensing technologies, i.e. optical, capacitive, thermal and even synthetic fingerprints [95]. Each series has four databases, each with 80 training samples and 800 testing samples. Therefore, in total, we train the fingerprint ROI segmentation model on 960 images and evaluate the fingerprint ROI segmentation performance on 9 600 fingerprints. The authors of [37] prepared the ground truth annotations of ROI. The information about the FVC databases is presented in Table 4.1.

4.4.2   Assessment criteria

We proceed to describe the different assessment criteria used to judge the fingerprint pre-processing performance.

4.4.2.1   Fingerprint enhancement

We exploit the following metrics to evaluate the fingerprint enhancement performance:

1. Ridge structure preservation ability: Ridge details in a fingerprint image entail the identity information. Therefore, it is crucial that the fingerprint details are preserved while enhancing the fingerprint images. To measure the fingerprint enhancement model's capacity to preserve ridge structure, we calculate common

Table 4.1 *Details about FVC databases exploited to assess the fingerprint ROI segmentation performance*

Database	Resolution	Sensor name	Sensing tech.
2000 DB1	300 × 300	S.D. scanner	Optical
2000 DB2	256 × 364	Touch chip	Capacitive
2000 DB3	448 × 478	DF-90	Optical
2000 DB4	240 × 320	Synthetic generator	NA
2002 DB1	388 × 374	Touch View II	Optical
2002 DB2	296 × 560	FX2000	Optical
2002 DB3	300 × 300	100 SC	Capacitive
2002 DB4	288 × 384	Synthetic generator	NA
2004 DB1	640 × 480	V300	Optical
2004 DB2	328 × 364	U.are.U 4000	Optical
2004 DB3	300 × 480	Finger chip	Thermal
2004 DB4	288 × 384	Synthetic generator	NA

measures such as SSIM [96], Jaccard similarity score [97], PSNR [98], and Dice score [99] between ground truth binarization and the enhanced fingerprint.

2. Fingerprint quality assessment: A fingerprint enhancement algorithm is meant to improve the quality of the input fingerprint image. Using the publicly available tool NFIQ [100], we compute fingerprint quality scores for measuring the improvement in quality of fingerprints. This tool assess a given input fingerprint on various parameters such as ridge-valley clarity, number of minutiae and ridge smoothness.

3. Fingerprint matching performance: We also quantify the improved matching performance on enhanced images. Matching performance on latent fingerprints is analysed in identification mode of fingerprint recognition. As a result, for latent fingerprints, the matching performance is analysed by calculating rank-50 accuracy and plotting the corresponding cumulative matching curve (CMC). On the other hand, the matching performance on the rural Indian fingerprints is analysed in verification mode of fingerprint recognition. Subsequently, for rural Indian fingerprints, the matching performance is analysed by presenting the detection error trade-off (DET) curve that corresponds to the average equal error rate (EER).

4.4.2.2 Fingerprint ROI segmentation

We evaluate the finger ROI segmentation performance by computing the standard metrics for assessing segmentation performance: Dice score [99] and Jaccard score [97].

4.5 Results: fingerprint enhancement

4.5.1 Enhancement of latent fingerprints

We begin the analysis of impact of introducing CRU into a fingerprint enhancement model by assessing its performance on latent fingerprints. Figure 4.6 depicts samples enhanced before (FP-E-GAN) and after introducing CRU (CR-GAN). We find that introduction of CRU enables improved enhancement performance quantified by improved fingerprint quality scores and improved rank-50 accuracy on both Bozorth and MCC fingerprint matching tools (see Tables 4.2 and 4.3). The corresponding histogram comparing fingerprint quality scores and CMC curves corresponding to both the matching tools are presented in Figure 4.7. We also find

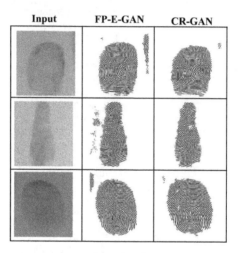

Figure 4.6   Examples presenting latent fingerprints [93] enhanced by CR-GAN and baseline FP-E-GAN

Table 4.2   An analysis of the latent fingerprints' [93] average quality scores computed through NFIQ

Enhancement algorithm	Quality score
Raw image	4.96
FP-E-GAN [28]	1.91
CR-GAN	**1.77**

Table 4.3   An analysis of the latent fingerprints' [93] identification results when compared against the gallery of the Lumidigm sensor

Enhancement algorithm	Bozorth	MCC
Raw image	5.45	6.06
Svoboda *et al.* [25]	NA	22.36
FP-E-GAN [28]	28.52	34.43
CR-GAN	**29.30**	**35.25**

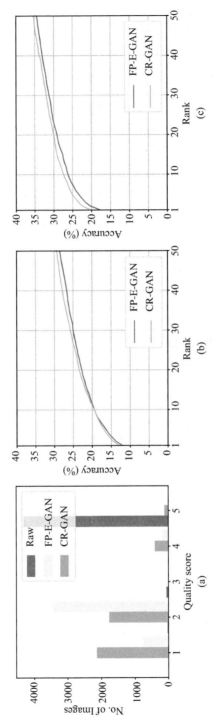

Figure 4.7   Enhancement performance before (FP-E-GAN [28]) and after introduction of CRU (CR-GAN): (a) histogram presenting the distribution of quality scores of fingerprints, CMC curves obtained using (b) Bozorth and (c) MCC

that introducing CRU enables improved ridge preservation ability to FP-E-GAN [28], quantified by higher SSIM scores after introducing CRU (CR-GAN) compared to FP-E-GAN (see Figure 4.8). Having successfully demonstrated improved fingerprint enhancement of latent fingerprints, we proceed with analysis of fingerprint enhancement performance on rural Indian fingerprints.

4.5.2   Enhancement of rural Indian fingerprints

Subsequently, we assess the enhancement results obtained by CR-GAN on two rural Indian fingerprint databases. We contrast the enhancement results obtained by CR-GAN with the cutting-edge models for fingerprint enhancement: STFT [10], DeConvNet [23], FP-E-GAN [28] and Hong [4]. Tables 4.4 and 4.5 reflect on the improved performance of fingerprint matching as measured by average EER and the corresponding DET curves are presented in Figure 4.9(b) and (c). Regardless of the fingerprint matching algorithm chosen, the average EER is much lower in both rural fingerprint databases. This demonstrates how the suggested CRU enhances FP-E-GAN's performance [28]. As a result, on both datasets, CR-GAN performs better than state-of-the-art. These findings support the assertion that FP-E-GAN does indeed learn some redundant channel weights during training, and that channel weight refinement aids in enhancing FP-E-GAN's performance. Then, we

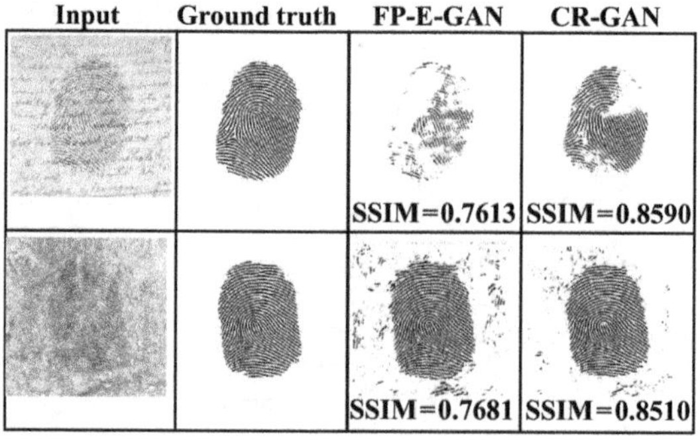

Figure 4.8   Examples demonstrating improved ridge preservation ability after the introduction of CRU

Table 4.4   An analysis of verification results obtained in [92] quantified by the average EER

Enhancement algorithm	Bozorth	MCC
Raw image	16.36	13.23
STFT [10]	18.13	14.52
Hong *et al.* [4]	11.01	11.46
DeConvNet [23]	10.93	10.86
FP-E-GAN [28]	7.30	5.96
CR-GAN	**5.72**	**4.45**

Table 4.5   An analysis of verification results obtained on the
private fingerprint database quantified by the
average EER

Enhancement algorithm	Bozorth	MCC
DeconvNet [23]	28.75	26.80
FP-E-GAN [28]	17.06	15.85
CR-GAN	**13.23**	**11.52**

contrast the CR-GAN fingerprint quality ratings with cutting-edge algorithms for fingerprint enhancement. We display distribution of NFIQ values through a histogram in Figure 4.9(a), while Table 4.6 displays the average NFIQ score. The results demonstrate that while matching performance is greatly increased, the quality of enhanced fingerprints that CR-GAN produces is comparable to that of FP-E-GAN.

The example restored fingerprint pictures in Figure 4.10 are created using both the proposed CR-GAN and the most recent cutting-edge algorithms for fingerprint enhancement. When compared to the currently available fingerprint enhancement algorithms, CR-GAN produces the most continuous ridge patterns for all of the sample inputs. The scenario of high pressure when taking a fingerprint impression is shown in the first row. As a result, valleys are obscured and very thick ridges are produced. The fingerprint image produced by CR-GAN has the highest ridge-valley clarity and performs the best at predicting ridges and valleys. The issue of low ridge clarity caused by uneven pressure is seen in the second row. While many of the most cutting-edge enhancement algorithms produce fictitious ridge features, CR-GAN properly predicts any ridge details that are obscure in the input fingerprint image. In addition, in the third and fourth rows, where there are creases, the ridge features that are missing are more accurately predicted by CR-GAN than by other techniques.

4.5.3   Contrasting CRU with squeeze and excitation block

Now, we contrast the suggested CRU's performance to that of the squeeze and excitation (SE) block [55], a cutting-edge channel attention model. Inside CR-GAN's design, the SE block is used to substitute the suggested CRU, and the resulting model is named SE-GAN. Table 4.7 shows a comparison of parameter counts, and we find that CR-GAN has fewer parameters than SE-GAN. This observation demonstrates that the SE-block introduces more parameters into the architecture of a fingerprint pre-processing model than the suggested CRU (Figure 4.11).

Quality scores of the enhanced fingerprints generated by CR-GAN and SE-GAN are compared in Table 4.8. The matching distribution of NFIQ scores represented through a histogram is shown in Figure 4.12(a). Results reveal that when compared to CR-GAN, SE-GAN generates inferior quality enhanced fingerprints. The average EER is presented in Table 4.9 in order to compare matching

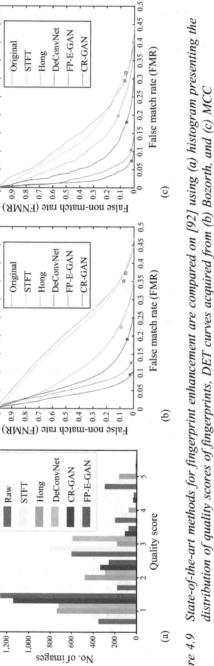

Figure 4.9 State-of-the-art methods for fingerprint enhancement are compared on [92] using (a) histogram presenting the distribution of quality scores of fingerprints, DET curves acquired from (b) Bozorth, and (c) MCC

*Table 4.6 An analysis of the openly accessible rural Indian
fingerprints' [92] average quality scores computed
through NFIQ*

Enhancement algorithm	Quality score
Raw image	2.94
STFT [10]	2.86
Hong *et al.* [4]	2.05
DeconvNet [23]	1.95
CR-GAN	1.42
FP-E-GAN [28]	**1.31**

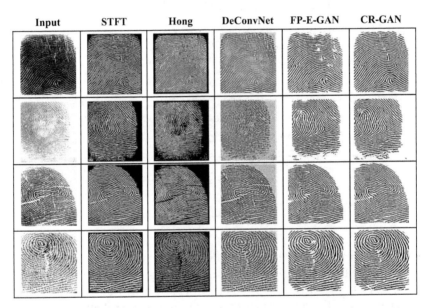

*Figure 4.10 Examples presenting effective fingerprint enhancement obtained
through CR-GAN and comparisons with cutting-edge algorithms*

*Table 4.7 Comparison of the CRU's introduced model
parameters with model parameters introduced by the
SE-block [55]*

Network	Generator	Discriminator	Total
FP-E-GAN [28]	11376129	2765505	14141634
CR-GAN	11383041	2768193	14151234
SE-GAN [55]	12072081	3165177	15237258

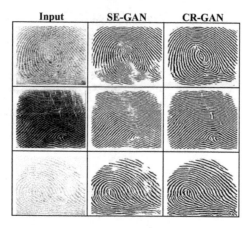

Figure 4.11   Comparison of enhanced fingerprints generated from the fingerprint enhancement model with CRU (CR-GAN) and the fingerprint enhancement model with SE block (SE-GAN)

Table 4.8   An analysis of average quality scores (computed through NFIQ) achieved for the proposed CRU and SE block

Enhancement algorithm	Quality score
SE-GAN [55]	1.76
CR-GAN	**1.42**

performance. In Figure 4.12(b) and (c), the relevant DET curves are provided. In comparison to SE-GAN, the verification error for fingerprints enhanced using CR-GAN is much lower for both Bozorth and MCC matchers. Due to the inferior verification results of SE-GAN in comparison to the FP-E-GAN baseline, these findings demonstrate that SE-block is inappropriate for fingerprint enhancement. The performance of CR-GAN, on the other hand, with the suggested CRU, surpasses that of SE-GAN and FP-E-GAN, showing that it is a good candidate to introduce channel attention into a pre-processing model enhancing fingerprints. These findings further show that the CR-GAN's enhanced performance cannot be only explained by an increase in model capacity as a result of CR-GAN's higher parameter space than FP-E-GAN. SE-GAN performs substantially worse than FP-E-GAN despite having larger parameter space than CR-GAN. In Figure 4.13, we present the matrices of correlations between different layers' learnt channel weights. We study correlation matrices pertaining to different enhancement models: FP-E-GAN, SE-GAN and CR-GAN, to examine the impact of introduction of their respective channel attention on the features the model learns in contrast to the features learnt by the backbone model (low correlation values signify less redundant features).

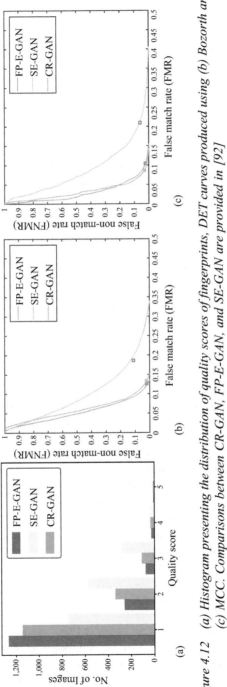

Figure 4.12 (a) Histogram presenting the distribution of quality scores of fingerprints, DET curves produced using (b) Bozorth and (c) MCC. Comparisons between CR-GAN, FP-E-GAN, and SE-GAN are provided in [92]

Table 4.9   Comparison of verification results obtained after introducing CRU and SE-block quantified by the average EER

Enhancement algorithm	Bozorth	MCC
SE-GAN [55]	12.34	10.50
CR-GAN	**5.72**	**4.45**

In theory, a channel-level attention mechanism is introduced to lessen redundancy in the backbone network's channel weights. In contrast to the FP-E-GAN backbone, we discover that SE-GAN exhibits stronger channel correlation rather than decreased correlation among channel weights. This demonstrates how the SE-block introduces redundant features. Conversely, the correlation values for CR-GAN are the lowest. This shows that the suggested CRU lowers feature redundancy and aids in learning robust features. CR-GAN outperforms both FP-E-GAN and SE-GAN due to its learning of more robust features than both these enhancement models. The representative cases presenting the recovered fingerprint images produced using the proposed CR-GAN and SE-GAN are provided in Figure 4.11. CR-GAN performs better than SE-GAN in every situation. CR-GAN outputs fingerprints with greater clarity between ridges and valleys, smoother ridges, and less erroneous ridge details, when contrasted to SE-GAN.

4.5.4   Application of CRU to various deep models for fingerprint enhancement

As of now, we can see that the suggested CRU enhances the reconstruction ability of a fingerprint enhancement model leveraging a GAN framework at its core. We then examine the proposed CRU's generalizability for various network architecture options for fingerprint enhancement. As the foundational network designs for our experiment, we use Unet [101] and DeConvNet [23], a autoencoder model for enhancing low-quality fingerprints. We create new architectures on both of these designs named CR-Unet and CR-DeConvNet by adding CRU after each convolution block, like done for CR-GAN. To see if the suggested CRU improves the performance of these networks, we contrast the verification error obtained using CR-Unet with that of Unet and likewise of CR-DeConvNet to DeConvNet. Additionally, we contrast CR-Unet's verification error to that of the Attention Unet (Att-Unet), which is based on spatial attention. Baseline Unet and Att-Unet implementation is taken from the source provided in [3].

First, we evaluate the enhanced fingerprint images produced by various models over fingerprint quality ratings. The histogram presenting the distribution of quality scores of fingerprints is presented in Figure 4.15(a), while Table 4.10 reports the average NFIQ score. The results back up the assertion that the proposed CRU enhances performance. When reconstructing fingerprints, CR-DeConvNet outperforms DeConvNet, in terms of quality scores. Similar observation holds for CR-Unet and Unet. Table 4.11 reports the average verification error obtained by all

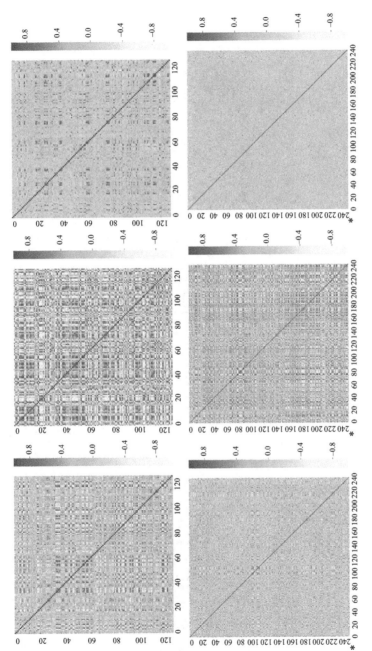

Figure 4.13   FP-E-GAN, SE-GAN, and CR-GAN channel weights correlation matrices (from left to right). The first, second, and third rows in all three columns correspond to layers 3, 16, and 21, respectively, of the corresponding fingerprint enhancement model.

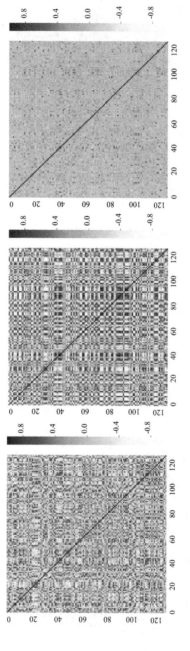

Figure 4.13 (Continued)

*Table 4.10   An analysis of average quality scores (computed
through NFIQ) achieved by cutting-edge deep models*

Enhancement algorithm	Quality score
Deconv Net [23]	1.95
CR-DeConvNet	*1.78*
Unet [101]	1.45
Att-Unet [102]	1.51
CR-Unet	*1.45*
CR-GAN	**1.42**

*Table 4.11   An analysis of verification results obtained by
several cutting-edge deep models in [92]*

Enhancement algorithm	Bozorth	MCC
Unet [101]	11.35	10.58
DeConvNet [23]	10.93	10.86
Att-Unet [102]	9.50	9.08
FP-E-GAN [28]	7.30	5.96
CR-DeConvNet	*6.53*	*5.45*
CR-Unet	*5.99*	*5.55*
CR-GAN	**5.72**	**4.45**

Note: Performance is quantified by the average EER.

cutting-edge deep models, while Figure 4.15(b) and (c) illustrates the related DET curves. Average EER is dramatically decreased for both fingerprint matchers. These findings show how cutting-edge deep models trained to learn fingerprint enhancement may learn redundant features. The suggested CRU helps learn robust features by reducing feature redundancy. Subsequently, the enhancement performance of CR-DeConvNet turns out significantly better than DeConvNet. Likewise, results are reported for CR-Unet and Unet. The claim that the suggested CRU generalizes to several cutting-edge deep models is verified by all of these results.

Additionally, we see that CR-Unet performs noticeably better than Att-Unet [102]. While CR-Unet makes use of channel-level attention, Att-Unet makes use of spatial attention. Because CR-Unet surpasses Att-Unet both in terms of matching performance and fingerprint quality score, we conclude that spatial attention is less useful for fingerprint enhancement than channel attention. It is also interesting to note that both the deep models: CR-DeConvNet and CR-Unet, that were suggested in this subsection perform better than FP-E-GAN. However, FP-E-GAN performs much better than Unet and DeConvNet at baseline compared to those two networks. The suggested CR-GAN hence performs better than CR-Unet and CR-DeConvNet. We contrast the sample reconstructed fingerprints produced by Unet, Att-Unet, and

CR-Unet in Figure 4.14(a). We discover that CR-Unet's produced fingerprints have superior clarity between ridges and valleys and fewer false ridge characteristics than those created by Unet and Att-Unet. When CR-DeConvNet and DeConvNet are compared, similar findings are found (see Figure 4.14(b)).

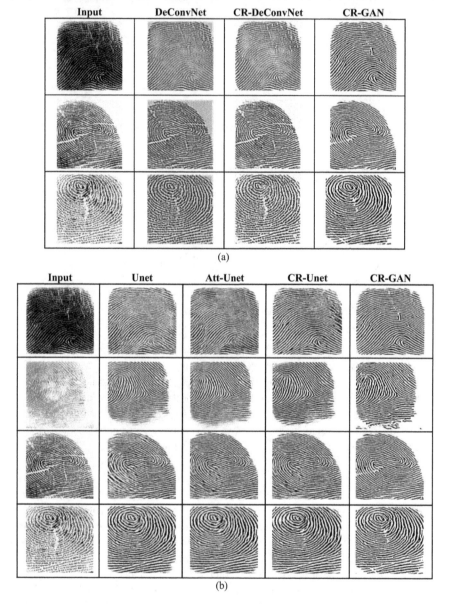

Figure 4.14   Examples showing the suggested CRU's generalizability on (a) DeConvNet and (b) Unet designs, while contrasting with the suggested CR-GAN

4.6   Contrasting CR-GAN with cutting-edge fingerprint enhancement methods leveraging GAN framework

This section contrasts the Cycle-GAN [103] and DU-GAN [31], two cutting-edge generative adversarial network-based fingerprint enhancement models, in terms of performance with the proposed CR-GAN (Figure 4.15). Figure 4.16(a) and Table 4.12 compare the average fingerprint quality scores obtained on enhanced fingerprints obtained by Cycle-GAN, DU-GAN, and the proposed CR-GAN. In comparison to Cycle-GAN and DU-GAN, we discover that the fingerprint quality of photos produced by CR-GAN is substantially higher. The average EER derived by each model is shown in Figure 4.16(b) and (c) and Table 4.13. We discover that Cycle-GAN performs poorly because it is unable to maintain ridge structure throughout improvement. In contrast to the other two enhancement models leveraging GAN framework, suggested CR-GAN achieves the most satisfactory enhanced fingerprints, as evidenced by the lowest verification error rate.

4.7   Impact of CRU on fingerprint enhancement

4.7.1   Ridge structure preservation

A poor input fingerprint may be accompanied by many types of noise patterns. In order to measure the suggested CR-GAN's capacity to preserve ridges over a variety of noise patterns observed in real poor quality fingerprints, we compute SSIM similarity scores between the ground truth binarized image and the output corresponding to the input. A high similarity score means the model keeps ridge details, i.e., while enhancing them, the fingerprint picture input preserves the type of fingerprint pattern, the direction of the ridges, and minutiae details. Sample degraded fingerprints are shown in the first column from the left in Figure 4.17 along with enhanced pictures produced by CR-GAN (rightmost column). The related ground truth binarized fingerprint images are shown in the second column. High similarity scores between CR-GAN's output and ground truth are attained, proving that the suggested method preserves the input fingerprint's ridge structure while enhancing it.

4.7.2   Ablation study

In order to more precisely measure the effects on the generator and discriminator networks by incorporating the suggested CRU, we analyse CR-GAN's enhancement results on different variants of CR-GAN. When using the suggested CRU, we investigate three alternative variants: using just the generator, just the discriminator, and using both the generator and the discriminator. Table 4.14 reports the verification error rate for all three versions, and Figure 4.18(a) and (b) illustrates the related DET curves. Figures 4.17 and 4.19 display sample reconstructions produced by each of the three variations.

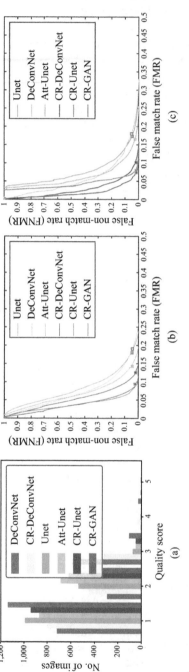

Figure 4.15   Evaluation of the suggested CRU's generalizability over cutting-edge deep architectures: (a) histogram presenting the distribution of quality scores of fingerprints; DET curves generated using (b) Bozorth; and (c) MCC

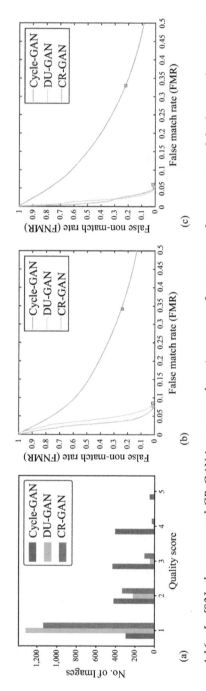

Figure 4.16   In [92], the suggested CR-GAN is compared against recent fingerprint enhancement models that employ a GAN framework: cycle-GAN and DU-GAN: (a) histogram presenting the distribution of quality scores of fingerprints; DET curves derived using (b) Bozorth and (c)MCC

Table 4.12   An analysis of average quality scores (computed through NFIQ) achieved by several enhancement models leveraging GAN framework

Enhancement algorithm	Quality score
Cycle-GAN [103]	1.76
DU-GAN [31]	**1.26**
CR-GAN	1.42

Table 4.13   An analysis of verification results obtained in [92] by several models leveraging GAN framework for enhancement

Enhancement algorithm	Bozorth	MCC
Cycle-GAN [103]	29.52	27.96
DU-GAN [31]	7.13	5.13
CR-GAN	**5.72**	**4.45**

Note: Performance is quantified by the average EER.

4.7.3   Successful scenarios

Few samples in which the suggested CR-GAN achieves satisfactory enhancement results are illustrated in Figure 4.20. The two left-most columns are latent fingerprints that are acquired using dusting with a chemical powder which sometimes lead to non-uniform amount of powder at different fingerprint regions. As a result, latent fingerprints may possess unclear ridge structure. However, interestingly, with decent ridge-valley clarity, CR-GAN successfully reconstructs fingerprints for both the samples. The scenario of indistinct valleys caused by thick ridges arising due to moist finger or excessive pressure is depicted in the third column. Once more, the suggested CR-GAN properly predicts details about ridges and valleys and produces a fingerprint with significantly improved ridge information. The lost ridge details owing to warts or creases is shown in the two rightmost columns. CR-GAN accurately approximates the otherwise missing ridge features at fingerprint image pixels with creases and cuts.

4.7.4   Challenging scenarios

The effectiveness of CR-GAN on few difficult instances is shown in Figure 4.21. CR-GAN produces erroneous ridge patterns close to the distorted region, in the top row. The input fingerprint's ridges in the middle row, close to the area of excessive pressure, are either invisible or very dark. Subsequently, CR-GAN produces ridges that are not smooth or erroneous ridge features. Nonetheless, CR-GAN consistently beats the backbone FP-E-GAN (in addition to several cutting-edge models for

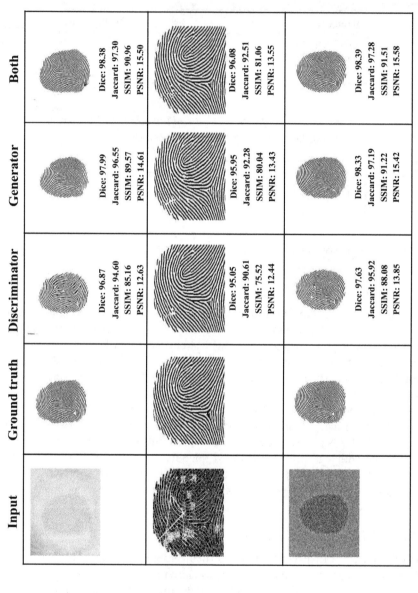

Figure 4.17 Example scenarios that show the ridge preservation capabilities of the CR-GAN and its variations (analysed during ablation) to keep the ridge details intact

Table 4.14 *An analysis of verification results obtained on [92] by GAN variants curated by introducing the suggested CRU into its different sub-networks*

Refinement	Bozorth	MCC
Discriminator	7.68	5.81
Generator	6.79	4.73
Both	**5.72**	**4.45**

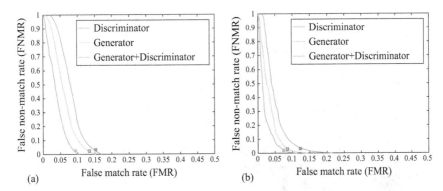

Figure 4.18 *DET curves utilizing (a) Bozorth and (b) MCC to illustrate the importance of the suggested channel refinement*

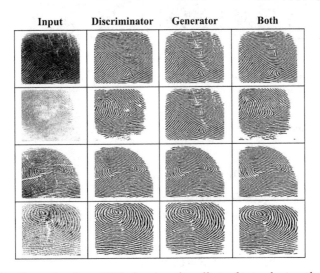

Figure 4.19 *Examples from [92] showing the effect of introducing the suggested CRU into FP-E-GAN's [28] different sub-networks*

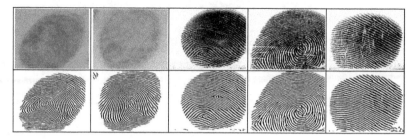

*Figure 4.20   Examples of effective enhancement results obtained using the
suggested CR-GAN*

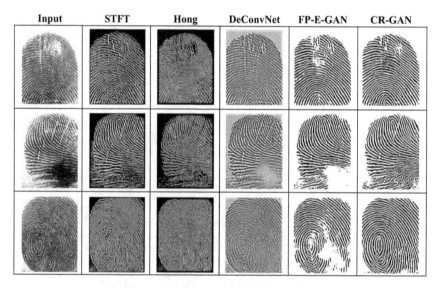

*Figure 4.21   Examples illustrating difficult instances and contrasting cutting-edge
algorithms for fingerprint enhancement*

fingerprint enhancement). This confirms the idea that refining channel weights enhances the model performance in terms of both quality and subsequent match scores.

4.7.5   Fingerprint ROI segmentation

Lastly, we study the generalization ability of the proposed CRU on fingerprint pre-processing tasks by evaluating the fingerprint ROI segmentation task. For this experiment, we take RUnet [52], a state-of-art deep model for fingerprint pre-processing [30,104–106] as the backbone network. Subsequently, we introduce CRU into RUnet and design CR-RUnet. Later, CR-RUnet is trained in a fully supervised manner to learn to segment foreground and background fingerprint regions. As any channel level attention model increases the model parameters (see

Table 4.15), which under limited availability of training data, can deteriorate the model performance. Table 4.16 compares the fingerprint ROI segmentation performance with (CR-RUnet) and without (RUnet) the introduction of CRU. We find that fingerprint ROI segmentation ability of the model after introducing CRU is competitive to RUnet, with RUnet performing better on the majority of datasets. We hypothesize that better ROI segmentation performance of RUnet in contrast to CRUnet is observed due to potential overfitting by CRUnet as a result of more model parameters. However, as the increase in model parameters is not so significant, the performance doesn't drop significantly.

To validate the above-mentioned hypothesis, we perform an additional experiment. We compare CRU with the SE block. The fingerprint ROI segmentation model designed after introducing the SE block into RUnet is named SE-RUnet (Figure 4.22). Table 4.17 compares the fingerprint ROI segmentation performance after the introduction of CRU (CR-RUnet) and SE block (SE-RUnet). The fingerprint ROI segmentation performance of SE-RUnet drops significantly compared to CR-RUnet. These results signify that although the fingerprint ROI segmentation performance does not improve significantly after introducing channel level

Table 4.15   Comparison of the CRUs introduced model parameters with model parameters introduced by the SE-block [55]

Model	Total
RUnet	3104178
CR-RUnet	3110586
SE-RUnet	3643599

Table 4.16   Fingerprint ROI segmentation performance degrades after incorporating CRU into the RUnet architecture

Database	Jaccard similarity (↑) CR-RU net	SE-RU net	Dice score (↑) CR-RU net	SE-RUnet
2000DB1	**88.15**	86.97	**93.34**	92.71
2000DB2	**86.40**	84.87	**92.39**	91.55
2000DB3	**93.74**	93.04	**96.50**	96.16
2000DB4	**94.28**	88.68	**97.04**	93.94
2002DB1	**96.95**	96.65	**98.44**	98.29
2002DB2	**94.88**	93.93	**97.28**	96.73
2002DB3	91.83	**92.75**	95.53	**96.11**
2002DB4	**91.17**	88.67	**95.32**	93.93
2004DB1	**98.78**	98.64	**99.38**	99.31
2004DB2	93.94	**95.46**	96.69	**97.65**
2004DB3	94.62	**94.90**	97.17	**97.35**
2004DB4	94.73	**95.17**	97.21	**97.48**

| Input | RUnet | SE-RUnet | CR-RUnet | Ground truth |

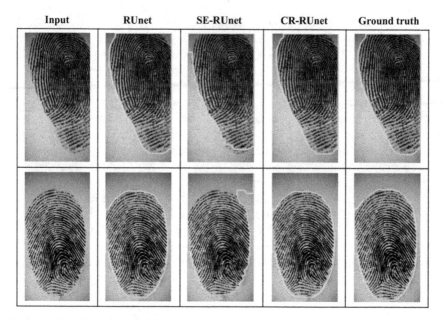

Figure 4.22   Fingerprint ROI segmentation performance after incorporating both CRU and SE block into the RUnet architecture

Table 4.17   Fingerprint ROI segmentation performance degrades after incorporating both CRU and SE block into RUnet architecture

Database	Jaccard similarity (↑) CR-RUnet	SE-RU net	Dice score (↑) CR-RUnet	SE-RUnet
2000DB1	86.97	49.66	92.71	34.82
2000DB2	84.87	61.69	91.55	49.08
2000DB3	93.04	86.81	96.16	78.47
2000DB4	88.68	86.65	93.94	78.44
2002DB1	96.65	94.66	98.29	90.41
2002DB2	93.93	69.22	96.73	57.73
2002DB3	92.75	60.07	96.11	43.91
2002DB4	88.67	66.23	93.93	51.38
2004DB1	98.64	96.72	99.31	93.94
2004DB2	95.46	84.85	97.65	75.94
2004DB3	94.90	84.93	97.35	76.95
2004DB4	95.17	61.58	97.48	46.79

Note: However, CRU performs significantly better than the SE block.

attention, however, CRU significantly outperforms the cutting-edge channel attention method SE block. These findings support the assertion that the suggested CRU is a better-suited channel-level attention mechanism for fingerprint pre-processing compared to the state-of-the-art.

4.8 Conclusion

This research presents a CRU, a channel-level attention mechanism for deep fingerprint pre-processing models. Extensive experimentation confirms that CRU generalizes on different choices of deep architectures for fingerprint pre-processing. Visualization of correlation matrix indicates that CRU reduces correlation among features, explaining the improved generalization ability. However, as CRU introduces additional parameters into the fingerprint pre-processing models, CRU is better suited for applications with enough training data. In the future, several other applications in the domain, such as presentation attack detection, as well as deep models for fingerprint feature extraction and matching, can benefit from the proposed CRU.

References

[1] Stojanović, B., Marques, O., Nešković, A. and Puzovic, S.: 'Fingerprint ROI Segmentation Based on Deep Learning'. *Proceedings of the Telecommunications Forum*, 2016. pp. 1–4.

[2] Li, J., Feng, J. and Kuo, C.C.J.: 'Deep Convolutional Neural Network for Latent Fingerprint Enhancement', *Signal Processing: Image Communication*, 2018, 60, pp. 52–63.

[3] Joshi, I., Utkarsh, A., Singh, P., Dantcheva, A., Dutta Roy, S. and Kalra, P. K.: 'On Restoration of Degraded Fingerprints', *Multimedia Tools and Applications*, 2022, 81, (24), pp. 35349–35377.

[4] Hong, L., Wan, Y. and Jain, A.: 'Fingerprint Image Enhancement: Algorithm and Performance Evaluation', *IEEE Transactions on Pattern Analysis and Machine Intelligence*, 1998, 20, (8), pp. 777–789.

[5] Gottschlich, C. and Schönlieb, C.B.: 'Oriented Diffusion Filtering for Enhancing Low-Quality Fingerprint Images', *IET Biometrics*, 2012, 1, (2), pp. 105–113.

[6] Turroni, F., Cappelli, R. and Maltoni, D.: 'Fingerprint Enhancement Using Contextual Iterative Filtering'. *Proceedings of the International Conference on Biometrics (ICB)*, 2012. pp. 152–157.

[7] Ramos, R.C., de Lima Borges, E.V.C., Andrezza, I.L.P., Primo, J.J.B., Batista, L.V. and Gomes, H.M.: 'Analysis and Improvements of Fingerprint Enhancement from Gabor Iterative Filtering'. *SIBGRAPI Conference on Graphics, Patterns and Images*, 2018. pp. 266–273.

[8] Wang, W., Li, J., Huang, F. and Feng, H.: 'Design and Implementation of Log-Gabor Filter in Fingerprint Image Enhancement', *Pattern Recognition Letters*, 2008, 29, (3), pp. 301–308.

[9] Gottschlich, C.: 'Curved-Region-Based Ridge Frequency Estimation and Curved Gabor Filters for Fingerprint Image Enhancement', *IEEE Transactions on Image Processing*, 2011, 21, (4), pp. 2220–2227.

[10] Chikkerur, S., Cartwright, A.N. and Govindaraju, V.: 'Fingerprint Enhancement Using STFT Analysis', *Pattern Recognition*, 2007, 40, (1), pp. 198–211.

[11] Ghafoor, M., Taj, I.A., Ahmad, W. and Jafri, N.M.: 'Efficient 2-Fold Contextual Filtering Approach for Fingerprint Enhancement', *IET Image Processing*, 2014, 8, (7), pp. 417–425.

[12] Yoon, S., Feng, J. and Jain, A.K.: 'On Latent Fingerprint Enhancement'. *Biometric Technology for Human Identification VII.* 7667, 2010. pp. 766707–766716.

[13] Hsieh, C.T., Lai, E. and Wang, Y.C.: 'An Effective Algorithm for Fingerprint Image Enhancement Based on Wavelet Transform', *Pattern Recognition*, 2003, 36, (2), pp. 303–312.

[14] Jirachaweng, S. and Areekul, V.: 'Fingerprint Enhancement Based on Discrete Cosine Transform'. *Proceedings of the International Conference on Biometrics (ICB)*, 2007. pp. 96–105.

[15] Feng, J., Zhou, J. and Jain, A.K.: 'Orientation Field Estimation for Latent Fingerprint Enhancement', *IEEE Transactions on Pattern Analysis and Machine Intelligence*, 2013, 35, (4), pp. 925–940.

[16] Yang, X., Feng, J. and Zhou, J.: 'Localized Dictionaries Based Orientation Field Estimation for Latent Fingerprints', *IEEE Transactions on Pattern Analysis and Machine Intelligence*, 2014, 36, (5), pp. 955–969.

[17] Chen, C., Feng, J. and Zhou, J.: 'Multi-Scale Dictionaries Based Fingerprint Orientation Field Estimation'. *Proceedings of the International Conference on Biometrics (ICB)*, 2016. pp. 1–8.

[18] Liu, S., Liu, M. and Yang, Z.: 'Sparse Coding Based Orientation Estimation for Latent Fingerprints', *Pattern Recognition*, 2017, 67, pp. 164–176.

[19] Chaidee, W., Horapong,K. and Areekul, V.: 'Filter Design Basedon Spectral Dictionary for Latent Fingerprint Pre-Enhancement'. *Proceedings of the International Conference on Biometrics(ICB)*, 2018. pp. 23–30.

[20] Cao, K. and Jain, A.K.: 'Latent Orientation Field Estimation via Convolutional Neural Network'. *Proceedings of the International Conference on Biometrics (ICB)*, 2015. pp. 349–356.

[21] Qu, Z., Liu, J., Liu, Y., Guan, Q., Yang, C. and Zhang, Y.: 'Orienet: A Regression System for Latent Fingerprint Orientation Field Extraction'. *Proceedings of the International Conference on Artificial Neural Networks*, 2018. pp. 436–446.

[22] Sahasrabudhe, M. and Namboodiri, A.M.: 'Fingerprint Enhancement using Unsupervised Hierarchical Feature Learning'. *Proceedings of the IAPR-and ACM-sponsored Indian Conference on Computer Vision, Graphics and Image Processing (ICVGIP)*, 2014. pp. 1–8.

[23] Schuch, P., Schulz, S. and Busch, C.: 'De-Convolutional Auto-encoder for Enhancement of Fingerprint Samples'. *Proceedings of the International Conference on Image Processing Theory, Tools and Applications (IPTA)*, 2016. pp. 1–7.

[24] Rama, R.K. and Namboodiri, A.M.: 'Fingerprint Enhancement using Hierarchical Markov Random Fields'. *Proceedings of the IEEE International Joint Conference on Biometrics (IJCB)*, 2011. pp. 1–8.

[25] Svoboda, J., Monti, F. and Bronstein, M.M.: 'Generative Convolutional Networks for Latent Fingerprint Reconstruction'. *Proceedings of the IEEE International Joint Conference on Biometrics (IJCB)*, 2017. pp. 429–436.

[26] Qian, P., Li, A. and Liu, M.: 'Latent Fingerprint Enhancement Based on Dense-UNet'. *Proceedings of the International Conference on Biometrics (ICB)*, 2019. pp. 1–6.

[27] Wong, W.J. and Lai, S.H.: 'Multi-Task CNN for Restoring Corrupted Fingerprint Images', *Pattern Recognition*, 2020, 101, pp. 107203–107213.

[28] Joshi, I., Anand, A., Vatsa, M., Singh, R., Dutta. Roy, S. and Kalra, P.: 'Latent Fingerprint Enhancement using Generative Adversarial Networks'. *IEEE Winter Conference on Applications of Computer Vision (WACV)*, 2019. pp. 895–903.

[29] Joshi, I., Anand, A., Dutta. Roy, S. and Kalra, P.K. 'On Training Generative Adversarial Network for Enhancement of Latent Fingerprints'. In: *AI and Deep Learning in Biometric Security*. 2021. pp. 51–79.

[30] Joshi, I., Kothari, R., Utkarsh, A., *et al.*: 'Explainable Fingerprint ROI Segmentation using Monte Carlo Dropout'. *IEEE Winter Conference on Applications of Computer Vision Workshops (WACVW)*, 2021. pp. 60–69.

[31] Joshi, I., Utkarsh, A., Kothari, R., *et al.*: 'Data Uncertainty Guided Noise-Aware Preprocessing of Fingerprints'. *International Joint Conference on Neural Networks (IJCNN)*, 2021. pp. 1–8.

[32] Joshi, I., Dhamija, T., Kumar, R., Dantcheva, A., Roy, S.D. and Kalra, P.K.: 'Cross-Domain Consistent Fingerprint Denoising', *IEEE Sensors Letters*, 2022.

[33] Joshi, I., Prakash, T., Jaiswal, B.S., *et al.*: 'Context-aware Restoration of Noisy Fingerprints', *IEEE Sensors Letters*, 2022.

[34] Schuch, P., Schulz, S. and Busch, C.: 'Survey on the Impact of Fingerprint Image Enhancement', *IET Biometrics*, 2017, pp. 102–115.

[35] Hu, C., Yin, J., Zhu, E., Chen, H. and Li, Y.: 'A Composite Fingerprint Segmentation Based on Log-Gabor Filter and Orientation Reliability'. *Proceedings of the IEEE International Conference on Image Processing (ICIP)*, 2010. pp. 3097–3100.

[36] Thai, D.H., Huckemann, S. and Gottschlich, C.: 'Filter Design and Performance Evaluation for Fingerprint Image Segmentation', *PloS One*, 2016, 11, (5), pp. 1–31.

[37] Thai, D.H. and Gottschlich, C.: 'Global Variational Method for Fingerprint Segmentation by Three-Part Decomposition', *IET Biometrics*, 2016, 5, (2), pp. 120–130.

[38] Fahmy, M.F. and Thabet, M.: 'A Fingerprint Segmentation Technique Based on Morphological Processing'. *Proceedings of the International Symposium on Signal Processing and Information Technology*, 2013. pp. 215–220.

[39] Teixeira, R.F. and Leite, N.J.: 'Unsupervised Fingerprint Segmentation Based on Multiscale Directional Information'. *Proceedings of the IberoAmerican Congress on Pattern Recognition*, 2011. pp. 38–46.

[40]   da Silva Vasconcelos, R.C. and Pedrini, H.: 'Fingerprint Image Segmentation Based on Oriented Pattern Analysis'. *Proceedings of the 14th International Joint Conference on Computer Vision, Imaging and Computer Graphics Theory and Applications (VISIGRAPP 2019)*, 2019. pp. 405–412.

[41]   Wu, C., Tulyakov, S. and Govindaraju, V.: 'Robust Point-Based Feature Fingerprint Segmentation Algorithm'. *Proceedings of the International Conference on Biometrics (ICB)*, 2007. pp. 1095–1103.

[42]   Yang, G., Zhou, G.T., Yin, Y. and Yang, X.: 'K-Means Based Fingerprint Segmentation with Sensor Interoperability', *EURASIP Journal on Advances in Signal Processing*, 2010, 2010, (1), pp. 1–12.

[43]   Ferreira, P.M., Sequeira, A.F. and Rebelo, A.: 'A Fuzzy C-Means Algorithm for Fingerprint Segmentation'. *Proceedings of the Iberian Conference on Pattern Recognition and Image Analysis*, 2015. pp. 245–252.

[44]   Lei, W. and Lin, Y.: 'A Novel Dynamic Fingerprint Segmentation Method Based on Fuzzy C-means and Genetic Algorithm', *IEEE Access*, 2020, 8, pp. 132694–132702.

[45]   Ferreira, P.M., Sequeira, A.F., Cardoso, J.S. and Rebelo, A.: 'Robust Clustering-Based Segmentation Methods for Fingerprint Recognition'. *Proceedings of the International Conference of the Biometrics Special Interest Group (BIOSIG)*, 2018. pp. 1–5.

[46]   Liu, E., Zhao, H., Guo, F., Liang, J. and Tian, J.: 'Fingerprint Segmentation Based on An Adaboost Classifier', *Frontiers of Computer Science in China*, 2011, 5, (2), pp. 148–157.

[47]   Zhu, Y., Yin, X., Jia, X. and Hu, J.: 'Latent Fingerprint Segmentation Based on Convolutional Neural Networks'. *IEEE Workshop on Information Forensics and Security (WIFS)*, 2017. pp. 1–6.

[48]   Ezeobiejesi, J. and Bhanu, B. 'Latent Fingerprint Image Segmentation Using Deep Neural Network'. In: *Deep Learning for Biometrics*. (Springer, 2017. pp. 83–107).

[49]   Serafim, P.B.S., Medeiros, A.G., *et al.*: 'A Method Based on Convolutional Neural Networks for Fingerprint Segmentation'. *International Joint Conference on Neural Networks (IJCNN)*, 2019. pp. 1–8.

[50]   Sankaran, A., Jain, A., Vashisth, T., Vatsa, M. and Singh, R.: 'Adaptive Latent Fingerprint Segmentation Using Feature Selection and Random Decision Forest Classification', *Information Fusion*, 2017, 34, pp. 1–15.

[51]   Khan, A.I. and Wani, M.A.: 'Patch-Based Segmentation of Latent Fingerprint Images Using Convolutional Neural Network', *Applied Artificial Intelligence*, 2019, 33, (1), pp. 87–100.

[52]   Wang, W., Yu, K., Hugonot, J., Fua, P. and Salzmann, M.: 'Recurrent U-Net for Resource-Constrained Segmentation'. *Proceedings of the IEEE International Conference on Computer Vision (ICCV)*, 2019. pp. 2142–2151.

[53]   Itti, L., Koch, C. and Niebur, E.: 'A Model of Saliency-Based Visual Attention for Rapid Scene Analysis', *IEEE Transactions on Pattern Analysis and Machine Intelligence*, 1998, 20, (11), pp. 1254–1259.

[54] Corbetta, M. and Shulman, G.L.: 'Control of Goal-directed and Stimulus-Driven Attention in the Brain', *Nature Reviews Neuroscience*, 2002, 3, (3), pp. 201–215.

[55] Hu, J., Shen, L. and Sun, G.: 'Squeeze-and-Excitation Networks'. *Proceedings of the IEEE Conference on Computer Vision and Pattern Recognition*, 2018. pp. 7132–7141.

[56] Gao, Z., Xie, J., Wang, Q. and Li, P.: 'Global Second-Order Pooling Convolutional Networks'. *Proceedings of the IEEE/CVF Conference on Computer Vision and Pattern Recognition*, 2019. pp. 3024–3033.

[57] Yang, Z., Zhu, L., Wu, Y. and Yang, Y.: 'Gated Channel Transformation for Visual Recognition'. *Proceedings of the IEEE/CVF Conference on Computer Vision and Pattern Recognition*, 2020. pp. 11794–11803.

[58] Wang, Q., Wu, B., Zhu, P., *et al.*: 'ECA-net: Efficient Channel Attention for Deep Convolutional Neural Networks'. *The IEEE Conference on Computer Vision and Pattern Recognition (CVPR)*, 2020.

[59] Singh, P., Verma, V.K., Mazumder, P., Carin, L. and Rai, P.: 'Calibrating CNNS for Lifelong Learning', *Advances in Neural Information Processing Systems*, 2020, 33, pp. 15579–15590.

[60] Singh, P., Mazumder, P. and Namboodiri, V.: 'Accuracy Booster: Performance Boosting Using Feature Map Re-calibration'. *Proceedings of the IEEE/CVF Winter Conference on Applications of Computer Vision (WACV)*, 2020.

[61] Verma, V.K., Singh, P., Namboodri, V. and Rai, P.: 'A "Network Pruning Network" Approach to Deep Model Compression'. *Proceedings of the IEEE/CVF Winter Conference on Applications of Computer Vision (WACV)*, 2020.

[62] Mnih, V., Heess, N., Graves, A., *et al.*: 'Recurrent Models of Visual Attention', *Proceedings of the 27th International Conference on Neural Information Processing Systems*, 2014, pp. 2204–2212.

[63] Ba, J., Mnih, V. and Kavukcuoglu, K.: 'Multiple Object Recognition with Visual Attention', arXiv preprint arXiv.14127755, 2014.

[64] Xu, K., Ba, J., Kiros, R., *et al.*: 'Show, Attend and Tell: Neural Image Caption Generation with Visual Attention'. *International Conference on Machine Learning*, 2015. pp. 2048–2057.

[65] Hu, J., Shen, L., Albanie, S., Sun, G. and Vedaldi, A.: 'Gather-Excite: Exploiting Feature Context in Convolutional Neural Networks', *Advances in Neural Information Processing Systems*, 2018, 31.

[66] Singh, P., Mazumder, P., Rai, P. and Namboodiri, V.P.: 'Rectification-Based Knowledge Retention for Continual Learning'. *Proceedings of the IEEE/CVF Conference on Computer Vision and Pattern Recognition (CVPR)*, 2021. pp. 15282–15291.

[67] Singh, P., Mazumder, P. and Namboodiri, V.P.: 'Context Extraction Module for Deep Convolutional Neural Networks', *Pattern Recognition*, 2022, 122, pp. 108284.

[68]   Li, J., Wang, J., Tian, Q., Gao, W. and Zhang, S.: 'Global-Local Temporal Representations for Video Person Re-identification'. *Proceedings of the IEEE/CVF International Conference on Computer Vision*, 2019. pp. 3958–3967.

[69]   Liu, Z., Wang, L., Wu, W., Qian, C. and Lu, T.: 'TAM: Temporal Adaptive Module for Video Recognition'. *Proceedings of the IEEE/CVF International Conference on Computer Vision*, 2021. pp. 13708–13718.

[70]   Srivastava, R.K., Greff, K. and Schmidhuber, J.: 'Training Very Deep Networks'. *Proceedings of the 28th International Conference on Neural Information Processing Systems*, 2015, pp. 2377–2385.

[71]   Li, X., Wang, W., Hu, X. and Yang, J.: 'Selective Kernel Networks'. *Proceedings of the IEEE/CVF Conference on Computer Vision and Pattern Recognition*, 2019. pp. 510–519.

[72]   Yang, B., Bender, G., Le, Q.V. and Ngiam, J.: 'Condconv: Conditionally Parameterized Convolutions for Efficient Inference'. *Proceedings of the 33rd International Conference on Neural Information Processing Systems*, 2019. pp. 1307–1318.

[73]   Chen, Y., Dai, X., Liu, M., Chen, D., Yuan, L. and Liu, Z.: 'Dynamic Convolution: Attention Over Convolution Kernels'. *Proceedings of the IEEE/CVF Conference on Computer Vision and Pattern Recognition*, 2020. pp. 11030–11039.

[74]   Wang, F., Jiang, M., Qian, C., *et al.*: 'Residual Attention Network for Image Classification'. *Proceedings of the IEEE Conference on Computer Vision and Pattern Recognition*, 2017. pp. 3156–3164.

[75]   Woo, S., Park, J., Lee, J.Y. and Kweon, I.S.: 'CBAM: Convolutional Block Attention Module'. *Proceedings of the European Conference on Computer Vision (ECCV)*, 2018. pp. 3–19.

[76]   Park, J., Woo, S., Lee, J.Y. and Kweon, I.S.: 'BAM: Bottleneck Attention Module', arXiv preprint arXiv:180706514, 2018.

[77]   Roy, A.G., Navab, N. and Wachinger, C.: 'Recalibrating Fully Convolutional Networks with Spatial and Channel "Squeeze and Excitation" Blocks', *IEEE Transactions on Medical Imaging*, 2018, 38, (2), pp. 540–549.

[78]   Misra, D., Nalamada, T., Arasanipalai, A.U. and Hou, Q.: 'Rotate to Attend: Convolutional Triplet Attention Module'. *Proceedings of the IEEE/CVF Winter Conference on Applications of Computer Vision*, 2021. pp. 3139–3148.

[79]   Song, S., Lan, C., Xing, J., Zeng, W. and Liu, J.: 'An End-to-End Spatio-temporal Attention Model for Human Action Recognition from Skeleton Data'. *Proceedings of the AAAI Conference on Artificial Intelligence*. vol. 31, 2017.

[80]   Du, W., Wang, Y. and Qiao, Y.: 'Recurrent Spatial-Temporal Attention Network for Action Recognition in Videos', *IEEE Transactions on Image Processing*, 2017, 27, (3), pp. 1347–1360.

[81] Fu, Y., Wang, X., Wei, Y. and Huang, T.: 'STA: Spatial-Temporal Attention for Large-Scale Video-Based Person Re-identification'. *Proceedings of the AAAI Conference on Artificial Intelligence*. vol. 33, 2019. pp. 8287–8294.

[82] Yang, J., Zheng, W.S., Yang, Q., Chen, Y.C. and Tian, Q.: 'Spatial-Temporal Graph Convolutional Network for Video-Based Person Re-identification'. *Proceedings of the IEEE/CVF Conference on Computer Vision and Pattern Recognition*, 2020. pp. 3289–3299.

[83] Chen, L., Zhang, H., Xiao, J., *et al.*: 'SCA-CNN: Spatial and Channel-Wise Attention in Convolutional Networks for Image Captioning'. *Proceedings of the IEEE Conference on Computer Vision and Pattern Recognition*, 2017. pp. 5659–5667.

[84] Singh, P., Mazumder, P., Karim, M.A. and Namboodiri, V.P.: 'Calibrating Feature Maps for Deep CNNS', *Neurocomputing*, 2021, 438, pp. 235–247.

[85] Roy, R., Joshi, I., Das, A. and Dantcheva, A. '3D CNN Architectures and Attention Mechanisms for Deepfake Detection'. In: *Handbook of Digital Face Manipulation and Detection*. 2022. pp. 213–234.

[86] Qin, Z., Zhang, P., Wu, F. and Li, X.: 'FcaNet: Frequency Channel Attention Networks'. *Proceedings of the IEEE/CVF International Conference on Computer Vision*, 2021. pp. 783–792.

[87] Zhang, H., Dana, K., Shi, J., *et al.*: 'Context Encoding for Semantic Segmentation'. *Proceedings of the IEEE Conference on Computer Vision and Pattern Recognition*, 2018. pp. 7151–7160.

[88] Sutton, R.S., McAllester, D., Singh, S. and Mansour, Y.: 'Policy Gradient Methods for Reinforcement Learning with Function Approximation'. *Proceedings of the 12th International Conference on Neural Information Processing Systems*, 1999. pp. 1057–1063.

[89] Hochreiter, S. and Schmidhuber, J.: 'Long Short-Term Memory', *Neural Computation*, 1997, 9, (8), pp. 1735–1780.

[90] Spillmann, L., Dresp-Langley, B. and Tseng, C.H.: 'Beyond the Classical Receptive Field: The Effect of Contextual Stimuli', *Journal of Vision*, 2015, 15, (9), doi: https://doi.org/10.1167/15.9.7.

[91] Joshi, I., Grimmer, M., Rathgeb, C., Busch, C., Bremond, F. and Dantcheva, A.: 'Synthetic Data in Human Analysis: A Survey', arXiv preprint arXiv: 220809191, 2022.

[92] Puri, C., Narang, K., Tiwari, A., Vatsa, M. and Singh, R.: 'On Analysis of Rural and Urban Indian Fingerprint Images'. *Proceedings of the International Conference on Ethics and Policy of Biometrics*, 2010. pp. 55–61.

[93] Sankaran, A., Vatsa, M. and Singh, R.: 'Multisensor Optical and Latent Fingerprint Database', *IEEE Access*, 2015, 3, pp. 653–665.

[94] Tiwari, K. and Gupta, P.: 'Fingerprint Quality of Rural Population and Impact of Multiple Scanners on Recognition'. *Proceedings of the Chinese Conference on Biometric Recognition*, 2014. pp. 199–207.

[95] Maltoni, D., Maio, D., Jain, A.K. and Prabhakar, S.: 'Handbook of Fingerprint Recognition'. (2009).

[96]   Wang, Z., Bovik, A.C., Sheikh, H.R. and Simoncelli, E.P.: 'Image Quality Assessment: From Error Visibility to Structural Similarity', *IEEE Transactions on Image Processing*, 2004, 13, (4), 600–612.

[97]   Choi, S.S., Cha, S.H. and Tappert, C.C.: 'A Survey of Binary Similarity and Distance Measures', *Journal of Systemics, Cybernetics and Informatics*, 2010, 8, (1), pp. 43–48.

[98]   Ndajah, P., Kikuchi, H., Yukawa, M., Watanabe, H. and Muramatsu, S.: 'An Investigation on the Quality of Denoised Images', *International Journal of Circuit, Systems, and Signal Processing*, 2011, 5, (4), pp. 423–434.

[99]   Dice, L.R.: 'Measures of the Amount of Ecologic Association Between Species', *Ecology*, 1945, 26, (3), pp. 297–302.

[100]   NIST. 'NBIS-NIST Biometric Image Software'. (http://biometrics.idealt-est.org/).

[101]   Ronneberger, O., Fischer, P. and Brox, T.: 'U-Net: Convolutional Networks for Biomedical Image Segmentation'. *Proceedings of the International Conference on Medical Image Computing and Computer-Assisted Intervention (MICCAI)*, 2015. pp. 234–241.

[102]   Oktay, O., Schlemper, J., Folgoc, L.L., *et al.*: 'Attention U-Net: Learning Where to Look for the Pancreas', arXiv preprint arXiv:180403999, 2018.

[103]   Karabulut, D., Tertychnyi, P., Arslan, H.S., *et al.*: 'Cycle-Consistent Generative Adversarial Neural Networks based Low Quality Fingerprint Enhancement', *Multimedia Tools and Applications*, 2020, 79, (25), pp. 18569–18589.

[104]   Joshi, I., Utkarsh, A., Kothari, R., *et al.*: 'Sensor-Invariant Fingerprint ROI Segmentation Using Recurrent Adversarial Learning'. *International Joint Conference on Neural Networks (IJCNN)*, 2021. pp. 1–8.

[105]   Joshi, I. 'Advanced Deep Learning Techniques for Fingerprint Preprocessing'. IIT Delhi, 2021.

[106]   Joshi, I., Utkarsh, A., Kothari, R., *et al.* 'On Estimating Uncertainty of Fingerprint Enhancement Models'. In: *Digital Image Enhancement and Reconstruction*, (2022).

Chapter 5

A review of deep learning approaches for video-based crowd anomaly detection

Santosh Kumar Tripathy[1] and Rajeev Srivastava[1]

Abstract

In recent years, the video surveillance system has gained huge demand in public and private places to provide security and safety. Video-based crowd anomaly detection (VCAD) is one of the crucial applications of a surveillance system whose timely detection and localization can prevent massive loss of public or private properties and the lives of many people. Crowd anomalies or abnormal activities can be defined as irregular activities that deviate from normal crowd behavior patterns. Some abnormal activities in crowd scenes are panic, fights, stampedes, congestion, riots, and abandoned luggage, whose real-time detection is paramount. The crowd anomaly detection (CAD) becomes a more challenging task due to the dynamic nature of the crowd, the effect of the cluttered background, daylight changes, shape variation due to perspective distortion, and lack of large-scale ground-truth crowd datasets. Both conventional machine learning and deep learning approaches have been explored to provide different solutions for CAD. The current research trend shows the vast development of deep-learning approaches for CAD. However, state-of-the-art reviews still need to address the comprehensive analysis of deep models, performance evaluation methodologies, open issues, and challenges for VCAD. Therefore, the main objective of this review is to provide an insightful analysis of several deep models for VCAD, their comparative analysis on different datasets based on various performance metrics, and to discuss future research scope for VCAD.

5.1   Introduction

Nowadays, a considerable demand for installing video surveillance systems can be observed worldwide to provide safety and security. A recent statistic [1] shows that the gross revenues of the global video surveillance market in 2022 accounted for $48.70

[1]Computing and Vision Lab, Department of Computer Science and Engineering, Indian Institute of Technology (BHU), Banaras Hindu University, Varanasi, India

billion and will reach $76.4 billion by 2027 at a Compound Annual Growth Rate (CAGR) of 9.4%. The reason for such an increase in demand is due to increased violence, vandalism, security, and life theft incidents in the places like shopping malls, hospitals, restaurants, public transport areas, streets, highways, playgrounds, and pilgrim places. Such incidents in the crowd are also known as crowd anomalies or abnormal activities. These situations require an automated security surveillance system for VCAD which not only minimize the revenue invested for human employment but also increase the safety of people. The VCAD does not define a single type of event in the crowd. For saying an anomaly could be a violent activity, nonpedestrian activity in restricted areas, vandalism, theft or terrorist attacks, or stampede. Figure 5.1 shows different types of anomalies generally happen in the crowd.

The most frequent crowd disaster happens due to stampede and violence. Stampede occurs due to panic caused by unwanted surprises or rumors in crowd-gathering scenarios in stadiums, shops, and religious festivals like Hajj or Kumbha-mela. According to Wikipedia [2], many human life losses occurred in the twenty-first century, and Figure 5.2 shows an average loss of human life every year around the world due to stampedes since 2001.

So, to avoid such calamities, early detection of crowd anomalies and management of the crowd are highly required. Detection of crowd anomalies with the help of human resources costs substantial financial investment, and the limitation of human expertise can lead to erroneous results. The limitations mentioned earlier can be avoided by developing an artificial intelligence (AI) VCAD, which is independent of bias and requires tiny human interference. However, the complex nature of crowd

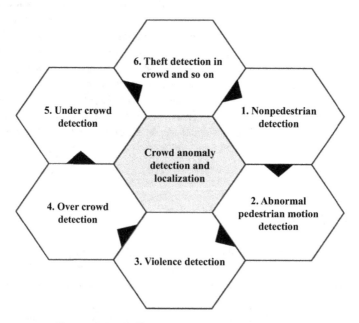

Figure 5.1   Different types of crowd anomalies

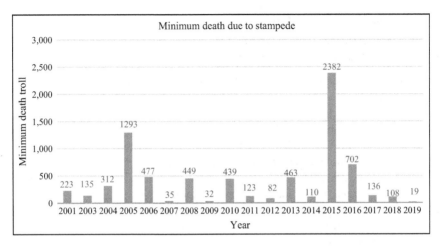

Figure 5.2   Statistics on human death due to stampede [2]

scenes, challenging situations like occlusions, illumination changes, and lack of well-annotated datasets influences the performance of AI-based VCAD.

The VCAD can be achieved using conventional feature-engineering approaches or deep learning-based approaches. The conventional approaches rely on accurate feature engineering efforts to capture required features representing normal and abnormal scenes. However, due to the lack of ground truth abnormal sequences and the complex nature of crowd scenes, capturing accurate features representing crowd dynamics would take much work. Another area for improvement with the conventional approach is real-time implementation. Studies showed that most of the conventional approaches rely on many matrix operations, which is very time-consuming. So, real-time implementation of VCAD cannot be achieved. Nevertheless, Lu *et al.* [22] developed a real-time implementation of VCAD by achieving 150 fps but failed to locate crowd anomalies in the scene. So, there is a need to maintain a trade-off between accuracy and real-time implementation, which is very difficult to observe in conventional approaches. However, the deep learning-based VCAD maintains this trade-off.

The current research trends show that many works for VCAD using deep-learning techniques have emerged. So, a brief review of such approaches is highly required for a reader. In addition, reviewing the existing datasets and identifying possible future scopes for the VCAD using deep learning approaches can help the reader to a large extent. It can make the proposed review paper unique compared to other review papers [3,4].

5.2   Challenges and taxonomy of VCAD

In this section, the challenges and a generalized taxonomy of VCAD are discussed in the following sections.

5.2.1   Challenges of VCAD

Several researchers [66] have identified the issues and challenges of VCAD. The following list shows the significant challenges of VCAD.

- The dynamic nature and shape of crowd behavior highly influence the performance of VCAD.
- Occlusion, low lighting situations, and varying viewing angles influence the detection of crowd anomalies.
- Video anomalies are highly contextual; for example, running in the playground is not abnormal, whereas running in the shopping mall is abnormal. Hence, the diversity of different types of anomalies and the misleading nature of abnormal behavior makes it challenging to detect anomalous events in the video.
- The definition of anomaly is ambiguous and vague; for example, if a man roaming around a subway platform is normal, some may think it suspicious. These challenges made it difficult for machine learning approaches to generate feature patterns that will be used for real-time scenarios for abnormality detection.
- The deep learning techniques require a large-scale crowd of anomaly datasets to understand their behavior pattern clearly. However, the available ground-truth video footage or datasets are insufficient to capture all types of abnormal activities.
- Most available datasets are of low resolution, unclear and noisy, making the model less generalizable.

5.2.2   Taxonomy of video-based CAD

Figure 5.3 shows the taxonomy of the CAD system. We derived this taxonomy by understanding the existing state-of-the-art approaches and reviews on VCAD.

According to Figure 5.3, the VCAD approaches are broadly categorized into object-centric and nonobject-centric approaches.

5.2.2.1   Object-centric approaches

Under this category, the VCAD approaches depend on identifying the objects of interest by segmenting the anomalous objects from the crowd scene or by tracking the trajectories of the crowd. In the literature, we can find that only traditional approaches have been proposed for the object-centric categories. This category has vastly explored approaches based on tracking and trajectory classification or clustering techniques [7–14]. However, the performance of such models has been affected by occlusion.

5.2.2.2   Nonobject-centric approaches

The nonobject-centric approaches do not depend on the trajectory or segmentation but rely on extracting patch-level or scene-level features. These features may be obtained using handcrafted [15–18] or automatic feature extraction [19,20] manner. Both approaches rely on spatial or spatial-temporal features from the crowd scenes. Most existing techniques adopt one class classification (OC)-based approach, only trying to

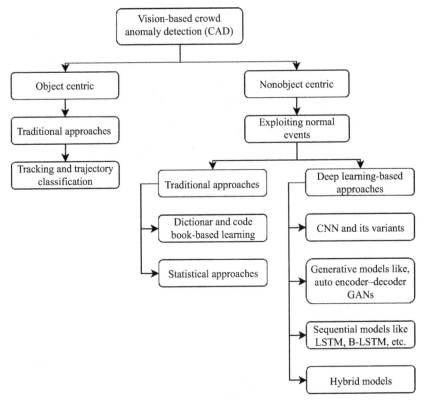

Figure 5.3   Taxonomy of VCAD

learn the normal scenes, and the outliers are the anomalies. Based on the processes adopted by the researchers, we can categorize the nonobject-centric approaches into two parts: traditional and deep-learning-based techniques. The traditional approaches are further classified into dictionary-based and statistical-based techniques.

The Sparse coding and dictionary-based learning approach consist of two things. One is a dictionary formed by learning from the training dataset (normal events only), and the second is finding the reconstruction error. It is assumed that anomaly events possess large reconstruction errors. Based on this intuition, several state-of-the-art approaches have been proposed to solve the objective. Another assumption of this model is that it is impossible to reconstruct anomalous events from the normal dictionary. The dictionary is developed by extracting features from the video at the patch or frame levels. Different features are extracted to build a dictionary for normal events. Zhao *et al.* [21] adopted dictionary-based learning for CAD. The authors extracted the histogram of optical flow (HoF) and histogram of oriented gradients (HoG) from the patches to build the dictionary. Lu *et al.* [22] formed a dictionary basis vectors containing 3D gradient features of the volume of patches. The dictionary is built to model normal events; the outliers are the anomalies. Cong *et al.* [23] proposed a variant of normal dictionary-based learning. The authors introduced a sparse reconstruction cost to define the normalness in order to detect anomalies. The authors proposed both local as well as global anomaly detection. The authors extracted multi-scale histograms of optical flow (MHoF) features from the scene to build the dictionary. Cong *et al.* [24] utilize the spatial-temporal features from the patches of the normal scenes.

On the other hand, the statistical-based approaches extract statistical properties like mean, variance, standard deviation, kurtosis, etc., from the crowd scene and are used for CAD. Recently, Bansod *et al.* [25] extracted statistical features from the histogram of magnitude and momentum (HOMM) for frame-level CAD.

Apart from the traditional approaches, the current research trend focuses on exploiting deep models for CAD. In the following section, we will briefly review the deep learning-based VCAD techniques.

5.3   Deep learning techniques for VCAD

A generalized structure of any deep learning-based VCAD is shown in Figure 5.4. The input samples are in the form of video sequences, which are pre-processed according to the requirement of the designed deep model. The pre-processing may be video-to-frame conversion, color conversion, noise removal, contrast enhancement or brightness enhancement, or resizing. The feature extract followed by classification has been done using an end-to-end model or transfer learning-based approaches. The deep model classifies frames or videos into normal or abnormal crowd behaviors. The current research trends show a vast utilization of several deep models to learn normal scenes and the outliers are treated as anomalies or abnormal activities. Models like CNN [19,20,26–30], sequential models (long short-term memory (LSTM)), and generative models like autoencoders, encoder–decoders, GANs, and hybrid models [31] have been vastly explored for VCAD. Table 5.1 illustrates a basic comparison of several VCAD approaches. The following sub-section presents a brief review of VCAD using each type.

5.3.1   CNN-based VCAD

The CNN-based VCAD models extract spatial-temporal features from crowd videos. Most of these models have utilized CNN as a backbone for modeling

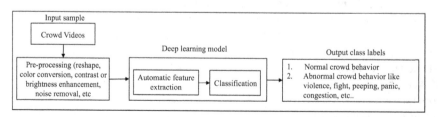

Figure 5.4   A generalized deep learning framework for VCAD

Table 5.1 Comparison of deep models for vision-based CAD

Ref.	Model type				Model details	Feature type	Anomaly detection at	
	CNN or its variants	Sequential model	Generative model	Hybrid model			Patch-level	Frame-level
[19]	✓	×	×	×	3D-CNN	Spatial–temporal	×	✓
[31]	×	×	×	✓	CNN-LSTM	Spatial–temporal	×	✓
[6]	×	×	×	✓	Encoders and decoders and convolutional LSTM	Spatial–temporal	×	✓
[42]	×	×	✓	×	GANs	Spatial–temporal	✓	✓
[20]	✓	×	×	×	CNN + OCSVM	Spatial–temporal	×	✓
[43]	×	×	✓	×	Auto-encoder + OCSVM	Spatial–temporal	×	✓
[44]	×	×	✓	×	SDAE	Spatial–temporal	×	✓
[26]	✓	×	×	×	CNN + OCSVM	Spatial–temporal	×	✓
[45]	×	×	×	✓	3D-SAE and 3D-CNN	Spatial–temporal	✓	×
[46]	×	×	✓	×	SAE + Gaussian	Spatial–temporal	✓	×
[47]	×	×	×	✓	FCN + SAE + Gaussian	Spatial–temporal	✓	✓
[48]	×	×	×	✓	PCA-Net + deep-Gaussian Net	Spatial–temporal	✓	✓
[27]	✓	×	×	×	FCN	Spatial–temporal	✓	✓
[49]	×	×	×	✓	AE + Conv. LSTM	Spatial–temporal	✓	×
[50]	×	×	×	✓	Generator (Conv. LSTM) + discriminator (CNN)	Spatial–temporal	✓	×
[28]	✓	×	×	×	3DCNN + OCSVM	Spatial–temporal	✓	✓
[51]	×	×	✓	×	Stacked variational AE	Spatial–temporal	✓	✓
[52]	×	×	✓	×	GANs	Spatial–temporal	✓	✓
[53]	×	×	×	✓	CAE + Conv. LSTM	Spatial–temporal	×	✓
[54]	×	×	✓	×	CAE + OCSVM	Spatial–temporal	×	✓
[55]	×	×	✓	×	CAE + k-mean SVM	Spatial–temporal	✓	×
[29]	✓	×	×	×	CNN + two GMM	Spatial–temporal	✓	×

(Continues)

Table 5.1 (Continued)

Ref.	Model type				Model details	Feature type	Anomaly detection at	
	CNN or its variants	Sequential model	Generative model	Hybrid model			Patch-level	Frame-level
[40]	×	×	✓	×	BLSTM	Spatial–temporal	×	✓
[30]	✓	×	×	×	3D-CNN	Spatial–temporal	×	✓
[32]	✓	×	×	×	3D atrous CNN	Spatial–temporal	×	✓
[36]	✓	×	×	×	2D CNN	Spatial	×	✓
[32]	✓	×	×	×	2D CNN	Spatial	×	✓
[37]	✓	×	×	×	2D CNN	Spatial	×	✓
[34]	✓	×	×	×	CNN	Spatial–temporal	×	✓
[38]	✓	✓	×	×	CNN	Spatial–temporal	×	✓
[39]	×	✓	×	×	LSTM	Spatial–temporal	×	✓
[41]	×	✓	×	✓	Vision transformer	Spatial–temporal	×	✓
[56]	×	×	×	✓	CNN + LSTM	Temporal	×	✓
[56]	×	×	×	✓	CNN + SRU	Spatial–temporal	×	✓

spatial-temporal features followed by one-class classifiers (OC) to learn the crowd's normal behavior patterns. During testing, the outliers are treated as abnormal crowd activities. Mentioning some of the state-of-the-art, Smeureanu *et al.* [26] proposed a transfer learning-based approach to extract appearance features using a pre-trained CNN architecture (VGG-f) and detected crowd anomalies using a one-class support vector machine (O-SVM). Such a model processes 20 frames per second and can exhibit in real-time. A similar approach has been proposed by Bouindour *et al.* [20] for VCAD where the authors extracted features from a pre-trained CNN architecture. The extracted features are given to an OC, such as a one-class support vector machine (O-SVM), for crowd abnormal behavior detection. Chen *et al.* [29] proposed a multi-feature fusion model for CAD. The authors fused multiscale optical and CNN-based appearance features and inputted them into a Gaussian mixture model (GMM) for CAD. Recently, Tripathy *et al.* [32] proposed a crowd panic-like anomaly detection model using a two-stream-based 3D Atrous CNN. The authors extracted multi-scale appearance and temporal features from the normal crowd scenes and reduced the dimension of the fused features using PCA. Authors adopted O-SVM to detect crowd anomalies such as Panic behaviors from the reduced feature sets. Mehmood *et al.* [33] detected VCAD using a 2D CNN structure. The author argued that 2D-CNN has less computational complexity than 3D-CNN. Other than the OC-based approaches, VCAD using reconstruction error-based techniques have also been proposed in the literature. Recently, Alafif *et al.* [34] proposed a ConvNet architecture for CAD. The authors exploited motion attributes to solve the objective. Table 5.1 briefly compares the deep models used for video-based CAD.

Only some models are available that solve the CNN-based VCAD as a binary or multiclass classification problem. Mentioning a few Zhou *et al.* [19] proposed a CNN architecture to extract spatial-temporal features to classify normal or abnormal crowd behaviors. The authors achieved better performance as compared with the conventional machine learning approaches. Ravanbakhsh *et al.* [27] proposed a plug-and-play CNN to exploit low-level motion features from the crowd scenes for VCAD. Authors achieved better performance than the state-of-the-art. On the other hand, Song *et al.* [30] proposed a 3D CNN architecture to exploit spatial-temporal features from crowd video sequences to detect crowd anomaly of violence type. Singh *et al.* [35] proposed a novel framework for VCAD using ensembled ConvNets. Authors have used VGGNet, AlexNet, and GoogLeNet for the ensemble purpose and achieved better performance than the state-of-the-art. Lalit *et al.* [36] proposed a simple CNN-based network for the VCAD. The CNN structure proposed by the authors exploits spatial features from the gray-scale frames and achieves better performance regarding anomaly detection. Similarly, Khan *et al.* [37] proposed an AlexNet-based CNN architecture for the VCAD. The model only exploits spatial features. However, the temporal features should be included as they can improve the model's performance. Singh and Kumar [38] proposed a deep CNN structure for crowd panic detection. The authors exploited motion attributes from the crowd videos and optimized the objective function using chronological ant lion optimizer.

5.3.2   Sequence-to-sequence models for VCAD

In sequence-to-sequence model-based CAD, we can find the use of LSTM [39] and its variant, i.e., bidirectional LSTM [40], in the literature. Such models extract spatial-temporal features from the normal crowd scene and train the model by solving it as OC problem. Ammar and Cherif [39] proposed an LSTM model to detect crowd panic-like anomaly behaviors in real-time. On the other hand, Dinesh Jackson *et al.* [40] proposed VCAD using bidirectional LSTM architecture. The proposed model processes the frames in real time. Other than LSTM, vision-transformers have also been used for the VCAD. Recently, Ullah *et al.* [41] proposed a vision-transformer-based CAD model where the authors achieved tremendous success regarding anomaly detection. In the literature, it is very hard to find models that use only single sequence-to-sequence models as they are used in a hybrid manner, which will be discussed in the forthcoming section.

5.3.3   Generative models for VCAD

We can find the use of generative models such as Auto-Encoder-decoders(AE) [47,52,55,58] and generative adversarial network (GAN) [58] for the VCAD. We can find the use of variants of AEs such as sparse autoencoders (SAE) [46], variational autoencoders (VAE) [52,60], sparse denoised AE (SDAE) [44] for the VCAD. Gutoski *et al.* [54] designed a CNN-based AE for feature modeling followed by O-SVM for CAD. The authors claimed that the model outperforms the existing state-of-the-art. Sabokrou *et al.* [46] proposed SAE and Gaussian classifiers for the VCAD in real-time. Narasimhan and Kamath [44] proposed a unified model using the SDAE model for dynamic VCAD. Wang *et al.* [51] proposed a VAE-based model to detect anomalous crowd events locally and globally. Similarly, Xu *et al.* [59] proposed a VAE-based model for the VCAD and achieved better performance. Li *et al.* [60] proposed two streams of deep spatial and temporal AE for the VCAD. Recently, Hu *et al.* [57] developed a 3D CNN-based AE for the VCAD. The model can exploit appearance and motion attributes from the crowd videos and outperform the state-of-the-art.

On the other hand, Generative adversarial networks (GAN) [42,52,58,61] are also explored in this area. Ravanbakhsh *et al.* [42] developed a GAN architecture for the VCAD. The authors used CNN as a generator and discriminator. The anomalous crowd events are determined by using a semantic difference-based approach. Similarly, in another work by Ravanbakhsh *et al.* [52], the authors proposed a crows channel crowd abnormality detection using GAN. The model can exploit optical flow-based motion attributes from the crowd video and detect anomalies using a normalized score-based approach. Li *et al.* [61] proposed a two-stream generator-based GAN structure to exploit motion and appearance properties from the crowd videos for the VCAD. The authors achieved better performance as compared with the state-of-the-art. Alafif *et al.* [58] recently proposed a GAN architecture for CAD. Authors have also taken a case study of Hajj to show the efficacy of their proposed architecture. Authors have used U-Net as a generator and achieved better accuracy than the state-of-the-art approaches. Although these models are state-of-the-art, there is ample scope to design more sophisticated models using graph-neural networks, transformers, etc. Another aspect of CAD is available to be explored, content-based CAD.

5.3.4   Hybrid models for VCAD

In the literature, we can find a huge number of hybrid models [7,46,48,50,51,54,57,63] for the VCAD. Most of these models were used to extract spatial-temporal features from the crowd scene and solve it as an OC problem. Chong and Tay [6] exploited spatial-temporal features from AE-guided LSTM architecture. Sabokrou *et al.* [45] proposed a deep cascaded architecture for the VCAD. The authors used 3D CNN and AE to fulfill the objective function and achieve better accuracy. In another work by Sabokrou *et al.* [47], authors proposed FCN and SAE to model crowd videos for anomaly detection Authors have used Gaussian classifier for the VCAD. Li *et al.* [50] proposed a spatial-temporal deep architecture using GAN for the VCAD. The authors have used Conv. LSTM and CNN architectures for the generator and discriminator, respectively. Sabih and Vishwakarma [56] proposed a combination of CNN and LSTM for the VCAD. The authors used the optical flow of the video as far as the input to the model is concerned. Authors achieved better performance than the state-of-the-art approaches. Qasim and Verdu [62] proposed a CNN and simple recurrent unit-based hybrid model for the VCAD, which outper-forms the state-of-the-art approach model. Although those mentioned above are some of the state-of-the-art hybrid models for the VCAD, there is a huge scope for developing better generalizable capability-guided deep models for the VCAD.

5.4   Review of the datasets

This section will review some of the available crowd anomaly datasets.

- UCSD Anomaly Detection Dataset [63]
  - This dataset was captured from a static camera with two scenes such as Ped1 and Ped2. The camera is mounted at an elevation. Each scene has both training and testing clips. The training clip consists of normal pedestrians only, and the testing clip consists of anomalies like bikers, small carts, skaters, and people walking across the sidewalk or grass. The crowd density in the walkways varies from sparse to very crowded. The clips of Ped1 consist of people walking away and toward the camera. Ped1 has 34 training samples and 36 testing samples. The clips of Ped2 consist of people's walkways parallel to the camera, with 16 training video clips and 12 testing video clips. The dataset contains the ground truth of anomalous events. The dataset contains TIF frames.

- UMN [64]
  - The UMN dataset provides benchmark datasets for tracking, surveillance, human activity detection, motion recognition, etc. The unusual crowd activity detection is one such dataset. The dataset is recorded from a surveillance

camera in three different scenarios containing eleven sequences. Each scene contains two types of events for a group of people, such as normal walkways and abnormal or sudden walkways or escape of a group of people.

- AVENUE or CUHK [65]
  - ○ The avenue dataset contains video clips (.avi) of both normal and abnormal events which are captured on the CUHK campus. The dataset consists of 16 training clips (15 328 frames) which capture normal events, and 21 testing video clips (15 324 frames), which capture both normal and abnormal scenes. Some challenging situations are included in the dataset, such as the appearance of normal patterns in the training data, outliers in the training data, and slight camera shake. The abnormal events include strange actions, walking in the wrong direction, and abnormal objects. It also contains the ground truth of abnormal events.

- VIOLENT FLOW [66]
  - ○ The dataset contains 246 real-world video clips (.avi) downloaded from YouTube. It provides benchmark protocols for classifying violent or nonviolence crowd activities and violence outbreak detection. The shortest and longest clips are 1.04 s and 6.52 s. The dataset contains five sets, each containing violence and nonviolence crowd datasets.

- PETS 2009 BENCHMARK DATASET [67]
  - ○ It contains multisensory crowd activity sequences. This dataset contains four datasets, namely S0, S1, S2, and S3. S0 is the training dataset. S1 is for the human count and crowd density estimation. S2 is for people tracking. S3 is for crowd flow analysis and crowd event detection. The challenging situations included in the dataset are varying crowd density (sparse, medium, and dense), bright sunshine and shadow, overcast, and running.

- SUBWAY DATASET [68]
  - ○ The dataset consists of two video clips named Subway-Entrance and Subway-Exit, recorded from passengers entering and exiting a subway station, respectively. The lengths of the subway entrance and subway-exit clips are 1:36 h (144 249 frames) and 43 min (64 900) frames, respectively. Each clip contains an alternation of normal and abnormal behaviors. The abnormal events include avoiding payments and moving in the wrong direction.

- U-TURN DATASET
  - ○ It contains a clip of sparse traffic sequences captured at a road intersection point. It consists of 6 117 frames, each of size 360×240. It also provides frame-level ground truth.

- TRAIN DATASET [69]
  - ○ The Train dataset contains normal and abnormal people's movements inside the train. The dataset includes challenging situations such as extreme lighting changes and camera jitter. The authors provided the video clip (.avi) and the ground truth (.png). It contains 19 218 frames.

Table 5.2 Quantitative comparison of several deep models

Ref.	Dataset	EER				AUC				F1-Measure	P/R/S	Accuracy	Run time (FPS in ms)
		Frame-level	Pixel-Level	Dual Pixel Level	Patch-Level	Frame-level	Pixel-level	Dual pixel level	Patch-level				
[71]	UCSD Ped1	16	40.1	×	×	92.1	67.2	×	×	×	×	×	5.2
	UCSD Ped2	17	×	×	×	90.8	×	×	×	×	×	×	7.5
	Subway-Exit	6.80	×	×	×	87.90	×	×	×	×	×	×	6.30
	Train	×	×	×	×	×	×	×	×	×	×	×	8.80
[19]	U-Turn	×	×	×	×	95.20	×	×	×	×	×	×	×
	Subway-Entrance	×	×	×	×	92.70	×	×	×	×	×	×	×
	Subway-Exit	×	×	×	×	91.9	×	×	×	×	×	×	×
	UCSD Ped1	24.00	×	×	×	×	×	×	×	×	×	81.3	×
	UCSD Ped2	24.20	×	×	×	×	×	×	×	×	×	81.9	×
	UMN	×	×	×	×	99.63	×	×	×	×	×	×	×
[31]	Violent Flow	×	×	×	×	×	×	×	×	×	×	93.59	×
	CUHK	×	×	×	×	×	×	×	×	×	×	80.33	×
[42]	UCSD-Ped1	8.00	35	×	×	97.4	70.3	×	×	×	×	×	×
	UCSD-Ped2	14.00	×	×	×	93.5	×	×	×	×	×	×	×
	UMN	×	×	×	×	0.99	×	×	×	×	×	×	×
[6]	UCSD-Ped1	12.50	NA	NA	×	89.9	×	×	×	×	×	×	0.007
	UCSD-Ped2	12.00	×	×	×	87.4	×	×	×	×	×	×	×
	Avenue (CUHK)	20.70	×	×	×	80.3	×	×	×	×	×	×	×
	Subway-Entrance	23.70	×	×	×	84.7	×	×	×	×	×	×	×
	Subway-Exit	9.50	×	×	×	94.0	×	×	×	×	×	×	×
[43]	UCSD-Ped1	15.90	11.2	×	×	91.9	92.8	×	×	×	×	×	×
	UCSD-Ped2	35.70	22.2	×	×	68.7	80.9	×	×	×	×	×	×
	Avenue (CUHK)	24.20	45.2	×	×	82.1	55	×	×	×	×	×	×

(Continues)

Table 5.2 (Continued)

Ref.	Dataset	EER				AUC				F1-Measure	P/R/S	Accuracy	Run time (FPS in ms)
		Frame-level	Pixel-Level	Dual Pixel Level	Patch Level	Frame-level	Pixel-level	Dual pixel level	Patch-level				
[26]	Avenue	×	×	×	×	84.6	93.5	×	×	×	×	×	0.05
	UMN	×	×	×	×	97.1	×	×	×	×	×	×	
[45],	UCSD-Ped1	9.10	15.8	24.5	×	×	×	×	×	×	×	×	0.06
	UCSD-Ped2	8.20	19	23.8	×	×	×	×	×	×	×	×	0.08
	UMN	2.50	×	×	×	99.6	×	×	×	×	×	×	×
[72]	UCSD-Ped2	11	15	×	×	×	×	×	×	×	×	×	×
	Subway (Entrance/Exit)	17/16	×	×	×	90.4/90.2	×	×	×	×	×	×	0.0027
[27]	UCSD-Ped1	8	40.8	×	×	95.7	64.5	×	×	×	×	×	×
	UCSD-Ped2	18	×	×	×	88.4	×	×	×	×	×	×	×
	UMN	×	×	×	×	0.988	×	×	×	×	×	×	×
[49]	UCSD-Ped1	8	×	×	×	87.2	×	×	×	×	×	×	×
	UCSD-Ped1	12	×	×	×	89.1	×	×	×	×	×	×	×
[73]	Avenue	×	×	×	×	94.8	0.78	×	×	×	×	×	34.85
	UCSD Ped-1	×	29.49	×	×	×	0.91	×	×	×	×	×	66.47
	UCSD Ped-2	×	15.78	×	×	×	×	×	×	×	×	×	17.08
	UMN	×	×	×	×	×	×	×	×	×	×	×	15.26
	Subway-Entrance	×	22.68	×	×	×	0.84	×	×	×	×	×	
[74]	Subway-Exit	×	19.58	×	×	×	0.86	×	×	×	×	×	32.85
	UCSD-Ped1	×	14.82	×	×	×	×	×	×	×	×	×	5.80
	UCSD-Ped2	×	11.1	×	×	×	×	×	×	×	×	×	5.40
	Avenue	7.40	×	×	×	×	×	×	×	×	×	×	4.20
	LV Dataset	14.60	×	×	×	×	×	×	×	×	×	×	5.30
[75]	UCSD- Ped1	11.20	38.70	×	×	92.60	69.71	×	×	×	×	62.80	×
	Avenue	×	×	×	×	×	×	×	×	×	×	×	×

Ref	Dataset										
[76]	UCSD-Ped1	15.80	×	×	86.70	×	×	×	×	×	×
	UCSD-Ped2	18.10	×	×	92.50	×	×	×	×	×	×
	Avenue	22.10	×	×	79.10	×	×	×	×	×	×
[50]	UCSD Ped1	×	×	×	82.10	×	×	×	92.50	×	×
	UCSD Ped2	×	×	×	96.50	×	×	×	100	×	×
	AVENUE				87.20						×
[77]	UCSD Ped1	19.10	19.4	×	89.70	88.90	×	×	×	×	×
	UCSD Ped2	15.90	16.8	×	89.60	91.30	×	×	×	×	×
	UMN	2.400	×	×	99.70	×	×	×	×	×	×
[28]	UCSD Ped2 (SC1, SC2)	6.25, 7.45	9.82, 9.63	×	×	×	×	×	×	×	0.15
[78]	CUHK Avenue	22.00	×	×	86.10	94.10	×	×	95.6/91.6	×	×
	UCSD Ped1	25.20	×	×	83.50	45.20	×	×	88.9/100	×	×
	UCSD Ped2	10.3	×	×	94.9	52.8	×	×	92.3/100	×	×
[51]	UMN	×	×	×	99.6	×	×	×	×	×	×
	UCSD Ped1	14.3	×	×	87.6	94.25	×	×	×	87.4	×
	Avenue	×	×	×	100.00,99.92, 99.51		×	×	×	×	×
	UMN (L, I, P)	×	×	×			×	×	×	×	×
	PETS (14:17, 14:31)	×	×	×			×	×	×	(99.3 98.8)	×
[52]	UCSD Ped1	7	34	×	96.80	70.8	×	×	×	×	×
	UCSD Ped2	11	×	×	95.50	×	×	×	×	×	×
	UMN	×	×	×	0.99	×	×	×	×	×	×
[53]	Avenue	14.5	×	×	90.70	×	×	×	×	×	×
	UCSD Ped1	0.75	×	×	98.40	×	×	×	×	×	×
	UCSD Ped2	0.92	×	×	98.50	×	×	×	×	×	×
Ionescu et al. [55]	Avenue	90.4	×	×	×	×	×	×	×	×	×
	UCSD-Ped1	97.8	×	×	×	×	×	×	×	×	×
	UCSD-Ped2	99.6	×	×	×	×	×	×	×	×	×
	UMN		×	×	×	×	×	×	×	×	×

(Continues)

Table 5.2 (Continued)

Ref.	Dataset	EER				AUC				F1-Measure	P/R/S	Accuracy	Run time (FPS in ms)
		Frame-level	Pixel-Level	Dual Pixel Level	Patch-Level	Frame-level	Pixel-level	Dual pixel level	Patch-level				
[29]	SanghaiTech	84.9	×	×	×	×	×	×	×	×	×	×	×
	UCSD Ped1	15.8	18.6	×	×	90.80	86.7	×	×	×	×	×	×
	UCSD Ped2	5.9	9.3	×	×	97.80	94.8	×	×	×	×	×	×
[79]	UCSD Ped1	11.3	36.3	×	×	94.90	71.4	×	×	×	×	×	×
	UCSD Ped2	12.6	19.2	×	×	92.20	78.2	×	×	×	×	×	×
[80]	UMN	×	×	×	×	98.20	×	×	×	×	×	×	×
	UCSD Ped1	22	×	×	×	88.20	×	×	×	×	×	×	217
	UCSD Ped2	13	×	×	×	94.20	×	×	×	×	×	×	325
	Avenue	×	×	×	×	80.99	×	×	×	×	×	×	×
[81]	SanghaiTech	×	×	×	×	76.80	×	×	×	×	×	×	×
	UCSD Ped1	×	×	×	×	×	×	×	×	×	85.1/1	×	×
	UCSD Ped2	×	×	×	×	×	×	×	×	×	92.3/1	×	×
	Avenue	×	×	×	×	×	×	×	×	×	95.2/ 92.3	×	×
	Subway Entrance	×	×	×	×	×	×	×	×	×	81.6/ 93.9	×	×
	Subway Exit	×	×	×	×	×	×	×	×	×	49.90/ 98.30	×	×
[82]	UMN	12.80	×	×	×	99.00	×	×	×	×	×	×	×
	UCSD Ped1	11.10	31.00	×	×	94.40	76.10	×	×	×	×	×	×
	UCSD Ped2	×	×	×	×	94.80	×	×	×	×	×	×	×
	Subway	×	×	×	×	×	×	×	×	×	×	×	×
[35]	UCSD Ped1	×	×	×	×	94.60	×	×	×	×	×	×	×
	UCSD Ped1	×	×	×	×	95.90	×	×	×	×	×	×	×
	Avenue	×	×	×	×	98.30	×	×	×	×	×	×	×
[36]	UCSD Ped1	×	×	×	×	98.50	×	×	×	×	×	×	×
	UCSD Ped1	×	×	×	×	97.90	×	×	×	×	×	×	×
	Avenue	×	×	×	×	95.10	×	×	×	×	×	×	×

- THE LV DATASET [70]
  - The dataset contains videos for both training and testing purposes. It includes challenging situations such as different lighting conditions and camera movement situations.

A quantitative analysis of several deep models is performed and illustrated in Table 5.2. The performance measures such as equal error rate (EER), area under ROC-curve (AUC), F1-score, precision (P), recall (R), specificity (S), accuracy, and run time, i.e., frames per second (FPS) are considered.

It can be observed from Table 5.2 that there is still huge scope available to develop better deep model techniques for the VCAD.

5.5   Future research scope

Although a good number of works can be identified in the literature for the VCAD, there is ample scope for developing an improved video-based CAD. For this, the following things need to be considered.

- Development of large-scale dataset: The existing anomaly crowd videos are limited in sequence length. In addition, most existing solutions adopt OC approach because the existing datasets have two types of crowd behaviors, i.e., normal and abnormal. However, the abnormal behavior could be violence, Panic, Congestion, or Fight, which could have different motion and behavior patterns. So, treating different anomalous events in one class is not good. This all happens because of the need for more availability of large-scale multiclass crowd anomaly datasets. So, there is a scope that still exists in this direction.
- Developing a real-time CAD: The models we reviewed in Section 5.3 are state-of-the-art approaches regarding the current research direction. Some process the frames in real-time and are very suitable for real-time applications. However, the performance of these models needs to be improved. So, there is ample scope to develop a much improved real-time CAD model.
- AI drones for VCAD: Still, there is a lack of availability of AI-enabled drones for the VCAD. Using drones for VCAD will have huge application as far as a smart city is concerned. One of the applications could be Drone Patrolling.
- Scenario-invariant VCAD: The meaning of anomaly varies under several scenarios. For example, riding a bike on the road is normal, but when the same incident happens in a restricted area, it is abnormal. So, the VCAD should perform scenario invariant manner.
- Development of lightweight VCAD is still a challenging task to perform the frames in real time.
- Domain generalization of VCAD is still an open research scope.

5.6   Conclusions

In this chapter, we reviewed VCAD approaches using deep learning techniques. We discussed the motivation behind the VCAD, in which we provided some real-time statistics, which will motivate us to develop a video-based CAD. We also identified the challenges faced by a VCAD system and also discussed the taxonomy of VCAD. In Section 5.3, we briefly reviewed the current research trends in this area. More specifically, we reviewed deep learning approaches for VCAD. We also reviewed the datasets used for the VCAD. In addition, we also performed a quantitative analysis of several approaches on different datasets, showing a huge scope for developing new and improved models. We also listed some prominent future research scopes for the VCAD, which will help the reader in their future research work.

References

[1]   "No Title." [Online]. Available: https://www.marketsandmarkets.com/Market-Reports/video-surveillance-market-645.html?gclid=CjwKCAjw_YShBhAiEiw AMomsEG9TXrPuP7iRlH2Fj1P-nzvDr1jHv_R0XCwt6tyxttfbedPo7-V1KBo C0-cQAvD_BwE. [Accessed: 27-Mar-2023].

[2]   Wikipedia, "List of human stampedes." [Online]. Available: https://en. wikipedia.org/wiki/List_of_human_stampedes#2019.

[3]   R. Raja, P. C. Sharma, R. Mahmood, and D. K. Saini, "Analysis of anomaly detection in surveillance video: recent trends and future vision," *Multimed. Tools Appl.*, vol. 82, pp. 12635–12651, 2023.

[4]   G. Tripathi, K. Singh, and D. K. Vishwakarma, "Violence recognition using convolutional neural network: A survey," *J. Intell. Fuzzy Syst.*, vol. 39, pp. 7931–7952, 2020.

[5]   Y. Huang, X. Hu, H. Zhang, H. Wu, and S. Hu, "Video anomaly detection using deep incremental slow feature analysis network," *IET Comput. Vis.*, vol. 10, no. 4, pp. 258–267, 2016.

[6]   Y. S. Chong and Y. H. Tay, "Abnormal event detection in videos using spatiotemporal autoencoder," *Lect. Notes Comput. Sci. (including Subser. Lect. Notes Artif. Intell. Lect. Notes Bioinformatics)*, vol. 10262 LNCS, pp. 189–196, 2017.

[7]   F. Abdullah and A. Jalal, "Semantic segmentation based crowd tracking and anomaly detection via neuro-fuzzy classifier in smart surveillance system," *Arab. J. Sci. Eng.*, vol. 48, no. 2, pp. 2173–2190, 2023.

[8]   S. Wu, B. E. Moore, and M. Shah, "Chaotic invariants of Lagrangian particle trajectories for anomaly detection in crowded scenes," *Proc. IEEE Comput. Soc. Conf. Comput. Vis. Pattern Recognit.*, pp. 2054–2060, 2010.

[9]   S. Calderara, U. Heinemann, A. Prati, R. Cucchiara, and N. Tishby, "Detecting anomalies in people's trajectories using spectral graph analysis," *Comput. Vis. Image Underst.*, vol. 115, no. 8, pp. 1099–1111, 2011.

[10] F. Tung, J. S. Zelek, and D. A. Clausi, "Goal-based trajectory analysis for unusual behaviour detection in intelligent surveillance," *Image Vis. Comput.*, vol. 29, no. 4, pp. 230–240, 2011.

[11] C. Piciarelli and G. L. Foresti, "On-line trajectory clustering for anomalous events detection," *Pattern Recognit. Lett.*, vol. 27, no. 15, pp. 1835–1842, 2006.

[12] B. T. Morris and M. M. Trivedi, "Trajectory learning for activity under-standing: Unsupervised, multilevel, and long-term adaptive approach," *IEEE Trans. Pattern Anal. Mach. Intell.*, vol. 33, no. 11, pp. 2287–2301, 2011.

[13] C. Piciarelli, C. Micheloni, and G. L. Foresti, "Trajectory-based anomalous event detection," *IEEE Trans. Circuits Syst. Video Technol.*, vol. 18, no. 11, pp. 1544–1554, 2008.

[14] S. Lamba and N. Nain, "Detecting anomalous crowd scenes by oriented Tracklets' approach in active contour region," *Multimed. Tools Appl.*, vol. 78, no. 22, pp. 31101–31120, 2019.

[15] S. Xie, X. Zhang, and J. Cai, "Video crowd detection and abnormal behavior model detection based on machine learning method," *Neural Comput. Appl.*, vol. 31, no. s1, pp. 175–184, 2019.

[16] J. Wang and Z. Xu, "Spatio-temporal texture modelling for real-time crowd anomaly detection," *Comput. Vis. Image Underst.*, vol. 144, pp. 177–187, 2016.

[17] R. Lalit and R. K. Purwar, "Crowd abnormality detection using optical flow and GLCM-based texture features," *J. Inf. Technol. Res.*, vol. 15, no. 1, pp. 1–15, 2022.

[18] A. A. Mohamed, F. Alqahtani, A. Shalaby, and A. Tolba, "Texture classification-based feature processing for violence-based anomaly detection in crowded environments," *Image Vis. Comput.*, vol. 124, p. 104488, 2022.

[19] S. Zhou, W. Shen, D. Zeng, M. Fang, Y. Wei, and Z. Zhang, "Spatial-temporal convolutional neural networks for anomaly detection and locali-zation in crowded scenes," *Signal Process. Image Commun.*, vol. 47, pp. 358–368, 2016.

[20] S. Bouindour, M. M. Hittawe, S. Mahfouz, and H. Snoussi, "Abnormal event detection using convolutional neural networks and 1-class SVM classifier," *8th International Conference on Imaging for Crime Detection and Prevention (ICDP 2017)*, pp. 1–6, 2018.

[21] B. Zhao, L. Fei-Fei, and E. P. Xing, "Online detection of unusual events in videos via dynamic sparse coding," *Proc. IEEE Comput. Soc. Conf. Comput. Vis. Pattern Recognit.*, pp. 3313–3320, 2011.

[22] C. Lu, J. Shi, and J. Jia, "Abnormal event detection at 150 FPS in MATLAB," *Proc. IEEE Int. Conf. Comput. Vis.*, pp. 2720–2727, 2013.

[23] Y. Cong, J. Yuan, and J. Liu, "Sparse reconstruction cost for abnormal event detection," *Proc. IEEE Comput. Soc. Conf. Comput. Vis. Pattern Recognit.*, pp. 3449–3456, 2011.

[24] Y. Cong, J. Yuan, and Y. Tang, "Video anomaly search in crowded scenes via spatio-temporal motion context," *IEEE Trans. Inf. Forensics Secur.*, vol. 8, no. 10, pp. 1590–1599, 2013.

[25] S. D. Bansod and A. V. Nandedkar, "Crowd anomaly detection and locali-zation using histogram of magnitude and momentum," *Vis. Comput.*, vol. 36, no. 3, pp. 609–620, 2020.

[26]   S. Smeureanu, R. T. Ionescu, M. Popescu, and B. Alexe, "Deep appearance features for abnormal behavior detection in video," in *Image Analysis and Processing – ICIAP 2017*, 2017, vol. 10484, no. October.

[27]   M. Ravanbakhsh, M. Nabi, H. Mousavi, E. Sangineto, and N. Sebe, "Plug-and-play CNN for crowd motion analysis: An application in abnormal event detection," *Proc. – 2018 IEEE Winter Conf. Appl. Comput. Vision, WACV 2018*, vol. 2018, pp. 1689–1698, 2018.

[28]   S. Bouindour, H. Snoussi, M. Hittawe, N. Tazi, and T. Wang, "An on-line and adaptive method for detecting abnormal events in videos using spatio-temporal ConvNet," *Appl. Sci.*, vol. 9, no. 4, p. 757, 2019.

[29]   Z. Chen, W. Li, C. Fei, B. Liu, and N. Yu, "Robust anomaly detection via fusion of appearance and motion features," *VCIP 2018 – IEEE Int. Conf. Vis. Commun. Image Process.*, pp. 1–4, 2019.

[30]   W. Song, D. Zhang, X. Zhao, J. Yu, R. Zheng, and A. Wang, "A novel violent video detection scheme based on modified 3D convolutional neural networks," *IEEE Access*, vol. 7, pp. 39172–39179, 2019.

[31]   N. Zhuang, "Convolutional DLSTM for crowd scene understanding," 2017.

[32]   R. Tripathy, S. K., Sudhamsh, R., Srivastava, S., and Srivastava, "MuST-POS: Multiscale spatial-temporal 3D atrous-net and PCA guided OC-SVM for crowd panic detection.," *J. Intell. Fuzzy Syst.*, pp. 1–16, 2022.

[33]   A. Mehmood, "Efficient anomaly detection in crowd videos using pre-trained 2D convolutional neural networks," *IEEE Access*, vol. 9, pp. 138283–138295, 2021.

[34]   T. Alafif, A. Hadi, M. Allahyani, *et al.*, "Hybrid classifiers for spatio-temporal abnormal behavior detection, tracking, and recognition in massive Hajj crowds," *Electronics*, vol. 12, no. 5, p. 1165, 2023.

[35]   K. Singh, S. Rajora, D. K. Vishwakarma, G. Tripathi, S. Kumar, and G. S. Walia, "Crowd anomaly detection using aggregation of ensembles of fine-tuned ConvNets," *Neurocomputing*, vol. 371, pp. 188–198, 2020.

[36]   L. Ruchika, R. K. Purwar, S. Verma, and A. Jain, "Crowd abnormality detection in video sequences using supervised convolutional neural network," *Multimed. Tools Appl.*, vol. 81, no. 4, pp. 5259–5277, 2022.

[37]   A. A. Khan, M. A. Nauman, M. Shoaib, *et al.*, "Crowd anomaly detection in video frames using fine-tuned AlexNet model," 2022.

[38]   J. P. Singh and M. Kumar, "Chronological ant lion optimizer-based deep convolutional neural network for panic behavior detection in crowded scenes," 2023.

[39]   H. Ammar and A. Cherif, "DeepROD: a deep learning approach for real-time and online detection of a panic behavior in human crowds," *Mach. Vis. Appl.*, vol. 32, no. 3, 2021.

[40]   S. R. Dinesh Jackson, E. Fenil, G. Manogaran, *et al.*, "Real time violence detection framework for football stadium comprising of big data analysis and deep learning through bidirectional LSTM," *Comput. Networks*, vol. 151, pp. 191–200, 2019.

[41] W. Ullah, T. Hussain, and S. Wook, "Vision transformer attention with multi-reservoir echo state network for anomaly recognition," *Inf. Process. Manag.*, vol. 60, no. 3, p. 103289, 2023.

[42] M. Ravanbakhsh, M. Nabi, E. Sangineto, L. Marcenaro, C. Regazzoni, and N. Sebe, "Abnormal event detection in videos using generative adversarial nets," *Icip*, pp. 1577–1581, 2017.

[43] H. T. M. Tran and D. Hogg, "Anomaly Detection using a Convolutional Autoencoder, Winner-take-all," 2017.

[44] M. G. Narasimhan and S. Kamath, "Dynamic video anomaly detection and localization using sparse denoising autoencoders," *Multimed. Tools Appl.*, vol. 77, pp. 13173–13195, 2018.

[45] M. Sabokrou, M. Fayyaz, M. Fathy, and R. Klette, "Deep-cascade: Cascading 3D deep neural networks for fast anomaly detection and localization in crowded scenes," *IEEE Trans. Image Process.*, vol. 26, no. 4, pp. 1992–2004, 2017.

[46] M. Sabokrou, M. Fathy, M. Hoseini, and R. Klette, "Real-time anomaly detection and localization in crowded scenes," *IEEE Comput. Soc. Conf. Comput. Vis. Pattern Recognit. Work.*, vol. 2015, pp. 56–62, 2015.

[47] M. Sabokrou, M. Fayyaz, M. Fathy, Z. Moayed, and R. Klette, "Deep-anomaly: Fully convolutional neural network for fast anomaly detection in crowded scenes," *Comput. Vis. Image Underst.*, vol. 172, pp. 88–97, 2018.

[48] Y. Feng, Y. Yuan, and X. Lu, "Learning deep event models for crowd anomaly detection," *Neurocomputing*, vol. 219, no. 2016, pp. 548–556, 2017.

[49] B. Yang, J. Cao, N. Wang, and X. Liu, "Anomalous behaviors detection in moving crowds based on a weighted convolutional autoencoder-long short-term memory network," *IEEE Trans. Cogn. Dev. Syst.*, vol. 14, no. 8, 2018.

[50] S. Lee, H. G. Kim, and Y. M. Ro, "Stan: Spatio- temporal adversarial networks for abnormal event detection," *ICASSP, IEEE Int. Conf. Acoust. Speech Signal Process. – Proc.*, vol. 2018-April, pp. 1323–1327, 2018.

[51] T. Wang, M. Qiao, Z. Lin, *et al.*, "Generative neural networks for anomaly detection in crowded scenes," *IEEE Trans. Inf. Forensics Secur.*, vol. 14, no. 5, pp. 1390–1399, 2019.

[52] M. Ravanbakhsh, E. Sangineto, M. Nabi, and N. Sebe, "Training adversarial discriminators for cross-channel abnormal event detection in crowds," *Proc. – 2019 IEEE Winter Conf. Appl. Comput. Vision, WACV 2019*, pp. 1896–1904, 2019.

[53] A. Ramchandran and A. K. Sangaiah, "Unsupervised deep learning system for local anomaly event detection in crowded scenes," *Multimed. Tools Appl.*, 2019.

[54] M. Gutoski, N. Marcelo, R. Aquino, M. Ribeiro, A. E. Lazzaretti, and S. Lopes, "Detection of video anomalies using convolutional autoencoders and one-class support vector machines," *XIII Brazilian Congr. Comput. Intell. 2017*, 2017.

[55] R. T. Ionescu, F. S. Khan, M.-I. Georgescu, and L. Shao, "Object-centric auto-encoders and dummy anomalies for abnormal event detection in

video," *In Proc. IEEE Conf. Comput. Vis. Pattern Recognit.* 2019, pp. 7842–7851, 2019.

[56] M. Sabih and D. K. Vishwakarma, "Crowd anomaly detection with LSTMs using optical features and domain knowledge for improved inferring," *Vis. Comput.*, vol. 38, no. 5, pp. 1719–1730, 2021.

[57] X. Hu, J. Lian, D. Zhang, X. Gao, L. Jiang, and W. Chen, "Video anomaly detection based on 3D convolutional auto-encoder," *Signal, Image Video Process.*, vol. 16, no. 7, pp. 1885–1893, 2022.

[58] T. Alafif, B. Alzahrani, Y. Cao, R. Alotaibi, A. Barnawi, and M. Chen, "Generative adversarial network based abnormal behavior detection in massive crowd videos: a Hajj case study," *J. Ambient Intell. Humaniz. Comput.*, vol. 13, no. 8, pp. 4077–4088, 2022.

[59] M. Xu, X. Yu, D. Chen, C. Wu, and Y. Jiang, "Applied sciences: An efficient anomaly detection system for crowded scenes using variational auto-encoders," *Appl. Sci.*, vol. 9, no. 16, p. 3337, 2019.

[60] T. Li, X. Chen, F. Zhu, Z. Zhang, and H. Yan, "Two-stream deep spatial-temporal auto-encoder for surveillance video abnormal event detection," *Neurocomputing*, vol. 439, pp. 256–270, 2021.

[61] D. Li, X. Nie, X. Li, Y. Zhang, and Y. Yin, "Context-related video anomaly detection via generative adversarial," *Pattern Recognit. Lett.*, vol. 156, pp. 183–189, 2022.

[62] M. Qasim and E. Verdu, "Results in engineering video anomaly detection system using deep convolutional and recurrent models," *Results Eng.*, vol. 18, p. 101026, 2023.

[63] Statistical Visual Computing Laboratory (SVCL) at UC SanDiego (UCSD), "UCSD anomaly detection dataset." [Online]. Available: http://www.svcl. ucsd.edu/projects/anomaly/dataset.htm.

[64] "The UMN Dataset." [Online]. Available: http://mha.cs.umn.edu/proj_ events.shtml#crowd. [Accessed: 31-Jul-2019].

[65] "The Avenue Dataset." [Online]. Available: http://www.cse.cuhk.edu.hk/ leojia/projects/detectabnormal/dataset.html. [Accessed: 31-Jul-2019].

[66] "The Violent Flow Dataset." [Online]. Available: http://www.cslab.openu. ac.il/download/violentflow/. [Accessed: 31-Jul-2019].

[67] "PETS-2009 BENCHMARK DATASET," 2009. [Online]. Available: http:// cs.binghamton.edu/~mrldata/pets2009. [Accessed: 31-Jul-2019].

[68] A. Adam, E. Rivlin, I. Shimshoni, and D. Reinitz, "Robust real-time unusual event detection using multiple fixed-location monitors," *IEEE Trans. Pattern Anal. Mach. Intell.*, vol. 30, no. 3, pp. 555–560, 2008.

[69] Andrei Zaharescu and Richard P. Wildes, "The Train Dataset," 2010. [Online]. Available: http://vision.eecs.yorku.ca/research/anomalous-behaviour-data/. [Accessed: 02-Aug-2019].

[70] R. Leyva, V. Sanchez, and C. T. Li, "The LV dataset: A realistic surveillance video dataset for abnormal event detection," *Proc. – 2017 5th Int. Work. Biometrics Forensics, IWBF 2017*, pp. 1–6, 2017.

[71] D. Xu, Y. Yan, E. Ricci, and N. Sebe, "Detecting anomalous events in videos by learning deep representations of appearance and motion," *Comput. Vis. Image Underst.*, vol. 156, pp. 117–127, 2017.

[72] M. Sabokrou, M. Fayyaz, M. Fathy, Z. Moayed, and R. Klette, "Deep-anomaly: Fully convolutional neural network for fast anomaly detection in crowded scenes," *Comput. Vis. Image Underst.*, vol. 172, no. October 2017, pp. 88–97, 2018.

[73] M. George, B. R. Jose, J. Mathew, and P. Kokare, "Autoencoder-based abnormal activity detection using parallelepiped spatio-temporal region," *IET Comput. Vis.*, vol. 13, no. 1, pp. 23–30, 2018.

[74] K. Gunale and P. Mukherji, "Deep learning with a spatiotemporal descriptor of appearance and motion estimation for video anomaly detection," *J. Imaging*, vol. 4, no. 6, p. 79, 2018.

[75] S. Huang, D. Huang, and X. Zhou, "Learning multimodal deep representations for crowd anomaly event detection," *Math. Probl. Eng.*, vol. 2018, 2018.

[76] X. Wang, W. Xie, and J. Song, "Learning spatiotemporal features with 3DCNN and ConvGRU for video anomaly detection," *Int. Conf. Signal Process. Proceedings, ICSP*, vol. 2018, pp. 474–479, 2019.

[77] T. Wang, Z. Miao, Y. Chen, Y. Zhou, G. Shan, and H. Snoussi, "AED-Net: An abnormal event detection network," *Engineering*, 2019.

[78] J. T. Zhou, J. Du, H. Zhu, X. Peng, Y. Liu, and R. S. M. Goh, "AnomalyNet: An anomaly detection network for video surveillance," *IEEE Trans. Inf. Forensics Secur.*, vol. 14, no. 10, pp. 2537–2550, 2019.

[79] D. P. Kingma and J. Ba, "Adam: A method for stochastic optimization," pp. 1–15, 2014.

[80] A. Sikdar and A. S. Chowdhury, "An adaptive trainingless system for anomaly detection in crowd scenes," *arXiv Prepr. arXiv1906.00705*, pp. 1–29, 2019.

[81] J. R. Medel and A. Savakis, "Anomaly detection in video using predictive convolutional long short-term memory networks," *arXiv Prepr. arXiv1612.00390*, 2016.

[82] J. Yu, K. C. Yow, and M. Jeon, "Joint representation learning of appearance and motion for abnormal event detection," *Mach. Vis. Appl.*, vol. 29, no. 7, pp. 1157–1170, 2018.

Chapter 6

Natural language and mathematical reasoning

Daniela López De Luise[1]

Abstract

Every natural language presents certain regularities that have been studied for years. From statistical approaches to machine learning, many authors have found that automatic processing is far more complex than any other brain production. Despite the current status in the field, many applications like chatter-bots, speech recognition, and sentiment analysis, show that there is still an interesting gap between analysis and production of sentences. Despite the solutions used nowadays, the deep essence of linguistic reasoning dynamics keeps mostly not revealed, and many of the current approaches involve the conception of restricted patterns for human linguistic reactions, usage, and interpretation. This chapter presents a perspective of this problem centered in the idea followed by many authors that considers the brain as a complex device working under some kind of fractal rules, and deeply related to entropy. As part of the scope, there is a short review of some of the most paradigmatic proposals of language mathematical descriptions related to entropy and fractals, the relationship between them in this context and a summary of previous publications of the author that aim to reveal the deep nature of natural language, modeling linguistics-related brain activity.

6.1 Introduction

According to Friesen, people believe that reality is composed of space and time because the mind thinks in terms of space and time [1], there are thinking patterns. The scientific method is intended to be rigorous. To acquire that goal it systematically intends to avoid any kind of mental bias and to gain a clearer understanding of what is being under analysis. But when the subject under the magnifying glass is the cognition mechanism, the brain as an abstract engine that produces reasoning, then the approach needs to be conversely, to erase specific information and to retain the essence of the mental process, the brain bias in the process needs to be isolated.

[1]CI2S Labs, Buenos Aires, Argentina

The mathematical expression of linguistic reasoning, and any of the rules presented in this chapter fall in this field where it matters finding authors that have an attentive depiction of the intrinsic skeleton of thinking processes on certain topics. In this work, the subject is the reasoning that produces natural language communications. Therefore, a proper study must include a wide range of analysis on thought productions, game strategies, or even Zen Buddhism [1].

The strategy to be used here is framed in Friesen, Gentner and many other scientists. It consists in minimizing concrete data, finding shared elements among different applications of thought on diverse fields, and looking for patterns.

As Friesen expressed, it is different from the standard approach in science where empirical data gives the strength of a hypothesized statement. But for cognition there is a requirement for the opposite, to clear noisy "images" of how the mind functions could be improved by restoring the original image from a different perspective. The methodology to build a reasonably detailed cognitive model is the "theory of mental symmetry" developed by Gentner [2].

Mental symmetry, as a meta-theory of cognition, is an excellent framework for more specific theories, and the thermodynamic rules of natural language is one of them. Cognitive mechanisms, this acquires its rigor by "image stacking," that is by comparing different paradigms. As Friesen declares, the problem is resulting in papers that are too long and too interdisciplinary to be published. The consequence is that the scientific community lacks many valuable contributions that do not have the opportunity to be presented since they mostly lay out of the traditionally covered topics in the relevant publications.

It is important to note that mental symmetry must follow the principles described by Gentner.

The cognitive analysis has two steps. The first consists in determining which cognitive modules are being activated in a given situation. The second is the examination of how these cognitive modules are interacting within the situation or book (for more information, see Gentner [2]). In order to gain more impartiality, this cognitive analysis should then be repeated within many different contexts. In summary, the method for developing and clarifying a cognitive model needs to compare thinking in different fields in order to uncover cognitive mechanisms [1].

Regarding natural language and its mathematical models, there are many publications with dialectical Background [3–5], biological clues [6–8], and practical considerations [9,10] showing chaos and entropy as a way to regulate language and its productions. From the technical perspective, many authors explored mathematical models related to fractals [11–14], chaos and thermodynamics considerations [15–20].

For years now, in academic contexts, there has been the conception that chance is a manifestation of the complexity of nontrivial systems. The scientists Kolmogorov and Shaitin were probably the firsts to relate complexity to chance and this to the level of information, or ignorance.

But contingency does not imply indeterminacy, as Prigogine suggests, but a type of behavior characterized by a subtle relationship between randomness and determinism, where the laws of chaos are associated with chaotic systems but with a measurable statistical level. Based on this, academics such as Dr. Sanchez Medina, a specialist in psychiatry and mental health, proposed the concept of "deterministic chance" [21]. In his work he associates the conscious and unconscious system of our mind and fields such as wave physics, particle physics and other areas of science. For this paradigm it is possible to know its equilibrium state following this principle that combines determinism and chance. If chance allows us to explain natural processes, coincidences and principles of causality, "deterministic chance" allows us to designate facts or factors that operate and configure everyday psycho-physical behavior. It unites the unpredictable with the predictable and determined (with a principle of causality). In this range also, fall phenomena linked to the unconscious system, the paraverbal and extra-verbal. Sanchez Medina in his work declares that they are not extrasensory but physical sensory and that there are even measurable cases. He also dares to go a step further, stating that these "paranormal" phenomena have not been covered correctly by traditional science until now, but that "they are typical of the sensory-perceptual apparatus of man and even of the animal." He also believes that ignorance often plays in the middle and therefore, although they would correspond to the field of science, they still remain labeled as occultism and magical phenomena.

Academics generally consider something is science when all theory becomes testable laws, but it must be recognized that the testability of scientists has to do with time. So the current laws such as those of thermodynamics are science now but with this same criterion before their first verification they were speculation. Currently it can be postulated, for example, that the second and third principles of thermodynamics tend to entropy and equilibrium, but that is not contradictory, it does not mean that there is a propensity to reach the static, but rather the movement to go from equilibrium to imbalance and vice versa.

6.2   Language, communication, and time

Language implies communication. Given a linguistic production of any kind, there is a sequence for its generation that sets a sort of words. There is a time before, during and after the stream of linguistic tokens used. To be able to analyze and understand it, both producer and receiver must play in a defined temporal and spatial direction with a perception of time. But getting rid of this time–space postulate, the composition loses the direction and thus the before, the in and the after of the message. In that condition it is not possible to share concepts of any kind.

At this stage, Prigogine [22] postulated that it is possible to eliminate the notion of time, specially to approach the theological concepts of God, in which it is conceived as "everything is given" and therefore there is no temporality. Then, communication is time dependent and even requires the existence of a certain order.

Mathematician Pierre Simon Laplace introduced in 1814 in his book, *A Philosophical Essay on Probabilities*, a controversial experiment, known as Laplace's Demon [23], testing determinism as a fact where a being that knows the present, could also devise the past and future. The mathematical philosopher writes:

"time has no defined direction and it does not matter if time advances or recedes"; here are the concepts of irreversibility and reversibility of time. On the contrary, another well-known scientist called Albert Einstein wrote in a letter a line that is now famously condensed into "God does not play dice with the universe." It was not anything spiritual; Einstein was expressing that there is order in the universe, as a way of rejecting randomness. But the deterministic model of the universe is far from widely accepted, especially by current scientists.

6.3   Linear time and determinism as condition for language

Albert Einstein wrote in a letter a line that is now famously condensed into "God does not play dice with the universe." It was not anything spiritual; Einstein was expressing that there is order in the universe, as a way of rejecting randomness.

This brings us to determinism, which gives us the picture of the entire universe as just an infinite series of dominoes that have been set up to fall and cannot be disrupted. It is an idea that has interested both philosophers and physicists alike. Laplace's Demon has through time come to represent determinism.

Laplace's Demon could be considered as the starting root for experimental determinism, by describing how a being knows the present, and therefore is able to determine past and future. Just as Einstein, postulates that there is an order in the universe, where randomness is out of scene. Universe would be an unlimited and incorruptible chain of facts.

This conception is known as Causal Determinism. Postulates that everything that happens is caused by everything that happened before it. In other words, any current event result from past ones. In the same way, events of the present cause the events of the future. It then follows that everything has been predetermined since the beginning of time. That is, cause and effect determines everything that we do.

Note that Laplace's Demon, the imaginary being with universal knowledge at a certain moment, has a computational capability to embrace, understand and analyze it. Of course, language productions are also part of the set. Then it arises a question on how it is possible that every communication, every linguistic creation from every individual is known (even predetermined), so it is perfectly reasonable to have success in knowledge administration between counterparts.

But that omniscience conception has many detractors. Probably the strongest counterargument comes from quantum mechanics: which has the Heisenberg's uncertainty principle as a keystone, defines a universe that is essentially non-deterministic. Subatomic particles break classical mechanics rules. It is not possible to determine their behavior precisely but through probabilities. Furthermore, it is not possible to precise both the position and velocity of a particle at the same time. Heisenberg's uncertainty principle is mathematically expressed as follows:

$$\Delta p . \Delta x \geq \frac{h}{4\pi} \tag{6.1}$$

where h stands for the Planck's constant, Δp for the uncertainty in position and Δx for the uncertainty of momentum. Keeping this in mind, the explanation of language success as a deterministic effect goes down. How is it possible for two or more people to communicate using just a basic agreement called grammar, on how to articulate thousands of words with many possible combinations, exceptions and personal adaptations.

6.4   Entropy and synergic dissipative structures

The second and third principles of thermodynamics explain the relationship between entropy and equilibrium. They describe a dynamic behavior where there is an alternation between balance and imbalance rather than a trend to a static equilibrium. This applies to any subsystem as a replica of the universe, including human beings and their brain productions. Therefore biological, psychological, social, political and many other procedural effects of their systems evolve. They pass through transitional or stationary states, sometimes preserving a certain balance with no movement or dynamics.

From the same thermodynamics law derives the entropy concept. It could be thought of as a disorder degree of a system, which is in permanent increase in the universe. As the disorder level grows, it becomes more unpredictable. Figure 6.1 shows the Chareley schema for entropy [24] in relation to life forms in time.

Note that thermodynamic irreversibility collides with Laplace's Demon conception where it is supposed to determine the past by reverse-engineering the present. Then, the sole existence of one system that cannot be restored to the initial state makes it impossible to infer its initial state by just examining the present state.

Wolfgang Wildgen explains the second law from the linguistic perspective [25]. The entropy of an isolated system never decreases, in nature this results from the aggregated entropy of many thermodynamic interacting subsystems. But in

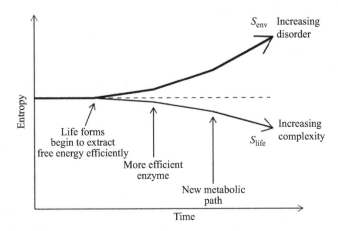

Figure 6.1   Schema for entropy in life (Credits: Chareley, 1970)

linguistics, the system is producing entropy as an expansion not a deterioration. The author understands it as an entropy multiplication, an increase that results in something newly created. He also explains that many systems in biology, chemistry and physics working under specific conditions get their balance and at the same time increase their information level. That means that the system reached a balance far from thermodynamic equilibrium. According to Wildgen, this process is evident in the loss of words in all the languages, and in the loss of accent of certain syllables. The change is compensated by a lexical and grammatical innovation effect.

From that duality in modern languages emerges the *theory of synergic dissipative structures*. It can be summarized with following principles:

1. There is a flow of information of type S → environment, in the form of energy
2. There is an immutable catalyst that changes the input to output
3. Every process is synergic. There is a self-organization approach between dominant and dominated modes of expressions, which flow according to a kind of selection of best suited and discard of unnecessary modes.

Note the relevance given to the synergic concept here, since human beings are considered as a complex entity that produces language which is also complicated, in fact more than the communication approach of the rest of animals in nature. Abstraction, which underlies the global dynamics of linguistic production, is a collective competence with inter-individual meaning. As a consequence, communication using textual or vocal tokens is also a synergic process.

6.5 Chaos in psycholinguistics

In Chaos theory, one of the most paradigmatic components is the butterfly effect. It represents the impact of every small action in the rest of the universe. The complexity of the aggregated effect of everything, in practical words, turns unpredictable any consequence both in size and characteristics.

Note that from Laplace's Demon perspective any prediction is only possible from within the system (with at least a slightest interaction), otherwise it will be only an approximation.

Prigogine [26] explains that unstable dynamical systems work on a time following Joseph Liouville's conception of time. The French mathematician created a theorem asserting that there is a probabilistic density function of system points in the vicinity of a given system point traveling through phase–space with constant time.

This density, time independent, is the known "a priori probability" of statistical mechanics. One of its consequences is that human life, as known in the present, is just one among infinite being modalities of life.

Following that probabilistic conception, a system consisting in numbers, letters, and other linguistic special tokens can be considered at any state of its energy performance as a dot within a current function density. Wolfgang Wildgen introduced in the *Origin of Fractals in Linguistics* [22] the idea of numbers and letters as symbols representing a certain amount of energy.

It is possible to observe syntagmas working in the context of grammars, how apparently very different symbols and symbolic systems can nevertheless be identical in their content. Wildgen conceived symbols acting within the consciousness of those who open themselves to it, producing order and understanding. Human beings perform deep interactions at an abstract level, using a symbolic language as a guide for the human faculties from perception to vision. It leads to brain performance ranging from the ability to find relationships in the context, through the ability to see deep equivalences reaching to the complexity of analogical thinking.

There is an analogy to a wave behavior vibrating in harmony with several frequencies, resonating at two or more levels. It is a kind of link that gives entity at each component and to the union of them, resulting in a synergetic and most complete element that outperforms the mere union of its terms.

A symbol pushes away a close ontology, and approaches what is far away, so that the subjective appreciation is able to observe and grasp both of them at any time.

According to the Argentine poet, essayist, and short-story writer Jorge Luis Borges, linguistic symbols have their unique and secret algebra, and in whose ambiguous territory one thing can be many.

Regarding spoken language, context moves expressions to specific meaning in such a subtle way that Wildgen denotes "collective personality", setting a locus, a trace to eventual prevailing designation according to social and specific circumstances. But in societies where writing dominates, language expressions can perform out of that social operation. Consequently, individualism is increasingly imposed as a determining attitude of human behavior and relationships [25].

There is a question that emerges: could that collective personality be a kind of expression of the Maximum Entropy Production (MEP) principle? Lineweaver is one of the researchers working on MEP applicability to biological and cosmological processes [24]. As many others like Paltridge [26,27] and Lorenz [28] extends the Boltzmann's derivation of the second law of thermodynamics: $S = k \log W$, and adopts Dewar's interpretation of W [29] not as the number of microstates of a macro-state in a system but as the number of paths to it. This way he breaks down the equilibrium requirement wall and shifts the problem to a reproducibility one. His work focused on the analogy of the dissipative structures of the original MEP, and the ones in cosmology and biology.

6.6   Fractals and language

Probably the first step for explaining language with fractals and thermodynamics was performed in 1998 by Wolfgang Wildgen [25]. Previously, language was considered as a phenomena framed within certain predefined well-formed structures. The XX century brought a set of new paradigms commonly known as nonlinear, dropping the generative conception. A new chaos perspective of the topic did not fully replace the deterministic ideas, but combined with them. Far from instability, the new chaotic formulation relies on probabilistic determination of inferring evolution of the performance. An interesting phenomenon is the change over time of language. Wildgen explains this by a mechanism called "copy", where the receiver of a communication performs a kind of reception activity that may distort the original version of the message. The accumulative effect produces the known mutation of the praxis.

Another consequence of chaos consideration of language is that abstractions become a structure independent of any individual production (input). Paradoxically, the systematic control on inputs represents and limits them. Therefore, a concept expresses a collective competence, an inter-individual construction. In humans, in contrast to any other animal the control is very complex.

6.6.1   Fractal patterns and categories

It is possible to aggregate words and sayings in categories that function as smart containers providing context. Sometimes a word exceeds its original meaning delimitation. If this happens according to [25], the new acquired scope represents a fraction that Wildgen calls fractal. In general, linguistic boundaries are fractals (in the sense of fraction of the original scope).

Nominal composition moves in such a field with chaotic attractors determining the dominant interpretation. According to the author something similar happens with semantic organization and with expressions that do not conform sentences.

Wilgen was a prolific author with a long list of quite diverse and interesting contributions, among them there is a Dynamical linguistic model based on Catastrophe theory, from 1982. From this theory language expressions are predicates located in a space of morphosyntactic constructs. They are meaning-attractors fighting for giving an interpretation to the statements. This constitutes also some kind of approximation to chaos theory.

There are other models that are just as original as that of Wilgen's. One of them relates human olfactory system with an analogy between organs and language elements, while the other relies on Petri nets to analyze the evolution of certain schematized cases.

6.6.2   Fractal patterns in language

Lakoff was the first defining the container metaphor for describing categories in language. As mentioned previously, he considers that categories do not have a rigid container but a limit that gradually expands with linguistic performance with a kind of fractality. Note that the fractal conception of Wilgen does not correspond to Mandelbrot's fractals. It mainly refers to a portion of the whole but without a rigorous mathematical explanation. It was the Polish mathematician Benoir Mandelbrot who explicitly added the possibility of a fractal behavior in linguistic boundaries when he adjusted the original Zipfian distribution of words.

There are other perspectives that explain dynamical models of linguistics-related elements like functions, phrases, predicates, linguistic levels considerations, etc. They conform part of the evolution from the old structuralism [15] to nonlinear paradigms, best suited to the real practice of natural language. This road traversed corresponds not only to a formal but also a philosophical shift prevailing in the XXI century, a new era mainly described by chaos dynamics, fractals, wavelets and synergetic considerations.

6.7   Fuzzy considerations of language

In 1965, the mathematician Lofti Zadeh introduced the fuzzy logic, a type of logic that introduces the imprecision of people managing nonnumerical information. This covers, among others, language semantical articulation. Its strength allows it to systematically evaluate vague and incomplete data. The fuzzy interpretation of texts could be considered as the counterpart of chaos perspective of meaning-attractors theory.

The key concept here is the truth value as a function ranging from zero (false) to one (true) [30], with complete coherence with Boolean and multivariate logic. However, it represents vagueness and possibility of facts more than mere probability of truth.

Zadeh worked on it his whole life, creating a big community that keeps working in the extension of the seminal work. There are many fuzzy operators, meaning strength adapters (called edges), labels for defining expected fuzzy values, and a metric variable to match with a numeric assessment.

In language processing, it is a very valued tool that allows one to handle natural language, for example to interpret experts recommendations, users opinion, subjective evaluation of complex events, etc.

Technically, its application could be performed using set theory, ruled artificial systems, matrix operation or analytical functions. This flexibility helps to process textual information by combining more than one in order to make the implementation more efficient.

Type-2 fuzzy sets and systems (T2FS) are a peculiar derivation of Zadeh fuzzy modeling (Type-1 fuzzy sets, or T1FS). While the original applies to a wide range of problems, this is best suited for textual processing. Unlike T1FS, its membership functions are also fluctuating. A fuzzy set typically determines the way input becomes a fuzzy variable [31].

Note that in this fuzzy modeling approach, the information is provided in the operators, membership functions, and edges. Chaos considerations of the previous sections are precondition to this pragmatic tool that expresses its manifestation.

6.8   Cognitive linguistics

Tom De Smedt performs an interesting compilation on what is considered creativity in systems performing artwork, from 2008 to 2012 [17]. His approach includes a number of short pieces of Python and covers art from visual and linguistic perspectives. Although there are some new contributions like the ability to turn any character into flesh and blood using AI [32], to create 3D Scenes, or many other View Synthesis [33–35].

The cases shown by De Smedt are a typical expression on the question if and how machines can be creative and intelligent in those years and sets an interesting set of underlying concepts:

1. Generative art, computational creativity and computational linguistics have a common ground in creativity.
2. As artistic creativity is the result of nonrandom thought processes and social consensus it could not yet be established if the result of such a system is art.
3. Artificial creativity relays on a more or less formal set of methods.
4. The creativity process in general involves a cycle of an idea selected from a pool, a work (art) interpreting the idea, and an evaluation by the author (with an eventual delivery to the community). The cycle restarts after some kind of adaptation.
5. Creativity is the result of a multitude of underlying, interacting processes.

Among the models revised are evolution by natural selection, rule-based, self-organization, generative art responsive to brain activity, artificial consciousness (as a search space), rudimentary analogy to perceptions (samplings), semantic networks, vector space model and some kind of sentiment analysis.

Cognitive linguistics (CL) is a multidimensional field that traditionally roots in biology, psychology and linguistics. Early research was dominated in the 1970s and early 1980s by a relatively small number of scholars, primarily (although not exclusively) situated on the western seaboard of the United States. But in the eighties it expanded to other countries and started a really pioneer CL [15]. It is clear that language also has important concepts from many other fields like philosophy, psychology, neuroscience and computer science. Of course there are many other fields that are involved in natural language performance like mathematics, anthropology, sociology, physics, etc.

The main aim of CL is to seek the broadest generalizations possible of language as a product. In contrast, other approaches study language with specific perspectives such as phonology (sound), semantics (word and sentence meaning), pragmatics (meaning in discourse context), morphology (word structure), syntax (sentence structure), and so on. Linguistic reasoning focuses on reasoning and its components articulated in order to understand and produce using certain language.

In general, there is a little basis for generalization across these aspects of language, or for study of their interrelations. This is particularly true of formal linguistics. For that reason, there are many authors that intend to find mathematical models for linguistic reasoning instead of modeling language cases.

There are two main branches of CL: cognitive semantics (that looks for the broadest generalizations possible) and cognitive approaches to grammar. The first covers the classical structuring principles for phonology (sound), semantics (word and sentence meaning), pragmatics (meaning in discourse context), morphology (word structure), syntax (sentence structure), etc. formal linguistics is also part of it, and considers mechanical procedures in order to produce grammatical sentences of a given language. The second perspective is named Cognitive Commitment, explaining how different models concrete linguistic brain performances.

6.8.1   Cognitive semantics

Semantics in this context could be defined by the following characteristics [15]:

- Conceptual structure is embodied, due to a species-specific view of the world.
- Semantic structure is conceptual structure, as language refers to concepts in the mind of the speaker rather than, directly, to entities which inherits in an objectively real external world.
- Meaning representation is encyclopedic, in other words lexical concepts do not represent neatly packaged bundles of meaning. Rather, they serve as a reference to vast repositories of knowledge relating to a particular concept or conceptual domain
- Meaning construction is conceptualization, language itself does not encode meaning. Linguistic units (like words) are prompts that guide the meaning construction. In this way, meaning construction becomes conceptualization, a type of arrangement of those units, conceptual operations and background knowledge. Then meaning is a process and not a static concept.

The rest of this subsection explains some of the main theories and approaches in semantics.

6.8.1.1   Image schema theory

According to this theory of the mid-1980s, cognition is a set of image schema. From sensory-perceptual experience derive image-schematic concepts that keep linked to them. Some authors consider them to serve to structure more complex concepts and ideas, and for semantics. But other researchers found that it under-specifies certain spatial categories that children acquire.

6.8.1.2   Encyclopedic theory

This holds that any meaning derives from dictionaries: for word formulation (lexical semantics) and for linguistics. But it lacks application to world knowledge that involves other aspects like pragmatics (in fact it is considered the same as semantics), unstructured knowledge, and disruptive knowledge (that does not emerge from direct context). Though this perspective is very used due to the possibilities it provides in computational linguistics.

6.8.1.3   Human categorization models

The models express that knowledge is built around prototypes acting as reference points with fuzzy boundaries. This explains certain ambiguities but provides a weak explanation of the origin of the prototypes and their life cycles (if any). Many authors provide different theories about fuzziness, real world and their relationship with prototype management in the brain.

6.8.1.4   Lexical semantics

Here, words (lexical items) are the leading attractors, the key for conceptual categories. Thus they are manifestations of semantic groups that do not follow probabilistic rules. This explains polysemy as a kind of degree between prototypical and peripheral concepts. Of course, it also lacks a complete explanation of language dynamics like the handling of senses proliferation, the low performance of empirical approaches using corpora and statistical analysis, and words conceptual migrations according to intention.

6.8.1.5   Metaphor theory

It is one of the seminal theories and has many limitations. The main idea is that thought is metaphorical: a sort of mapping between pre-conceptual experiences concepts and new ones. There are extensions to culture-specific sets of metaphors.

6.8.1.6   Metonymy-based theory

It works in a similar way to metaphor based theory, but it centers the trope in metonymy. Many scientists hold that it fits for explaining conceptual organization and others think it subsumes metaphor explanation.

6.8.1.7   Mental spaces theory

It intends to explain some hidden conceptual phenomena in meaning construction. For conceptualization, there is an initial step of building mental spaces. The next step is centered in mappings between them. It is led by local discourse context. The is not encoding but a building process following linguistic expressions directives working under discourse context. There is a navigation of the attention between such spaces, and the linking process.

6.8.1.8   Spaces blending

From this perspective cognition is a process of synergetic integration of mental spaces. The emergent structure is more than the simple aggregation of its spaces. This theory accounts for linguistic structure and some creative processes in meaning construction. Some authors argue that this is not a privative behavior of linguistics but a characteristic for most of the advanced human behaviors.

6.8.1.9   Morphosyntactic linguistic wavelets

It is a mathematical perspective for modeling language. Wavelets refers to an approach that describes information with progressive degree of precision. The main idea is to consider a mother wave (initial oscillation) that changes in frequency. There are many wavelets proposed, with different number and direction of pulses in the mother function. They have been broadly used to process signals, since some of them are very well suited for compressing images, and many types of signals. This happens when there is a close correlation between the wavelet definition and a portion of the target entity to be modeled.

From the information perspective, it constitutes a strong tool, to collect information from data, and the complementary wavelets (father functions) could be used to decompose a signal without gaps or overlaps, which is in fact a reversible process. Thus, wavelets proved to be excellent tools for compression/decompression algorithms with minimal loss and high accuracy.

In the linguistic field, there is an extension called Morphosyntactic Linguistic Wavelets (MLW) [cb1] that aim to replace mother function with a reduced set of features named "descriptors", that describe several morphology and syntactic specific values of a textual information. The increase or decrease of them constitutes the analogy to changes in frequency and location of a mother function is interpreted as the location in the text. This section introduces it briefly. For detailed information please refer to [36–40].

(i) Concept of distance

In MLW, distance is an important concept since it determines the structure of a word, its syntactic functioning, position, part of its semantic administration, how it relates with its close neighborhood, and some other information. In order to get that, the approach must migrate from characters and punctuation in a way that every word turns to be a numerical vector (namely an HBE, or homogenized basic element).

As a consequence of the change in the language representation, now sentences are vectors that in order to retain the meaning have a structure that follows a precise heuristics. The structure (called inner composition structure, E_{ci}) represents certain simple combinations of punctuation, type and number of words. It is important to note here that HBE does not contain every word, since there is a filtering out of tails after a lower and upper predefined threshold in the spectrum of frequencies. Punctuation is also removed and not included as HBE. In spite of the fact that those words and punctuations are removed at an early stage of processing, they are considered and somehow represented in the numeric calculation.

Paragraphs are represented as superstructures of E_{ci} units called E_{ce} (external composition structure), retaining just the relationships between sentences behind (E_{ci}).

Next subsections are a short summary of how textual information is changed to numbers, weighting considerations of words, and how MLW could be used to represent semantic regions (just as an alternate approach of Kohonen's self-organizing maps [41]).

(ii) Mathematical features of words

Textual information is not well suited for metrical considerations, MLW is a basic language dependent translation that considers a set of steps adopted as a set of rules in order to obtain meta-data called *descriptors*. The building blocks here are HBE vectors, containing mostly numerical meta-data useful for further processing, while nominal meta-data are preserved just as reference for a human that could be interested in it.

Table 6.1 has some of the rules. As mentioned earlier, words are converted into a vector named HBE, that represents a structure with some metadata automatically derived from the word. Some of them are numeric features converted to categorical descriptors. Table 6.2 shows the heuristic taken for texts in Spanish websites.

The number of categories in every case is determined by data mining analysis (see [36–40]). There are other meta-data representing nonmetric and subtle features. The rule-based heuristic entries for the same texts (Spanish websites) are presented in Table 6.2.

Table 6.1   Rules for nominalization of meta-data and data

Meta-data	Rule	Output
Web deep page: integer ϵ [0, n]	Determine x in one of the five categories for the metric value	$x \epsilon$ [0, 4]
Occurrences of word w in the web-page integer ϵ [0, n]	Determine x in one of the three categories for the metric value	$x \epsilon$ [0, 2]
Length of word w integer ϵ [0, n]	n = len(word) Determine x in one of the five categories for l	$n \epsilon$ [1, 32]*x ϵ [0, 4]*
Number of strong vowels in the word w integer ϵ [0, n]	n = number of instances of "a", "e", "o" in w Determine x in one of the three categories for l	$n \epsilon$ [0, 32]*x ϵ [0, 4]*
Number of weak vowels in the word w integer ϵ [0, n]	n = number of instances of "i", "u" in w Determine x in one of the three categories for l	$n \epsilon$ [0, 32]*x ϵ [0, 4]*
Length (number of words) of the sentence containing word w integer ϵ [0, n]	Determine x in one of the five categories for the metric value	$x \epsilon$ [0, 4]
Amount of numbers in the sentence containing word w integer ϵ [0, n]	Determine x in one of the five categories for the metric value	$x \epsilon$ [0, 4]
Number of special characters** in the sentence containing word w integer ϵ [0, n]	Determine x in one of the five categories for the metric value	$x \epsilon$ [0, 4]

*According to RAE, the largest word in Spanish [42].
**A special character for Spanish in this context is any character out of {A–Z, 0-9, ' '} or any valid punctuation sign.

A final set of numeric meta-data just remains as numbers (see Table 6.3). In these cases, the MLW does not require rules associated, since the range of the fields do not bias the information goal of the wavelet.

(iii) Words weighting

From the MLW perspective, a word is a clue to build HBEs which holds many of its morphological and syntactic features. They can be also used to derive the weighting p_0, an analogous of the relevance with some extra-verbal information, more related to its semantic functioning in the current context. It is also possible to evaluate a p_0 for any E_{ci}, but with different meaning since it is a certain function of the location, number and weighting of HBEs corresponding to the words that conform the paragraph. Any case, (6.2) expresses the formula to calculate values p_0 [43].

$$p_0 = \sum_{i=1}^{n} \frac{(p_i + p_{i-1})}{2} \tag{6.2}$$

Table 6.2   Rules for nonmetric and subtle features

Meta-data	Rule	Output
Internal unique ID of the word w: currently the entire word w	Split w as a vector such that: $\forall c_i \in w = \{c_1' c_2' \ldots c_n'\} \cup \{null_{n+1} \ldots null_{32}\}$ $x = [ASCII(c_1), ASCII(c_2), \ldots, ASCII(c_n)]$	$x = \langle a_1, a_2, \ldots, a_n \rangle$ $n \in [0..32]^* a_i \in [0 \ldots 255]$
Topic: First noun t in the title. If not: null	Split t as a vector such that: $\forall c_i \in t = \{c_1' c_2' \ldots c_n'\} \cup \{null_{n+1} \ldots null_{32}\}$ $x = [ASCII(c_1), ASCII(c_2), \ldots, ASCII(c_n)]$	$x = \langle a_1, a_2, \ldots, a_n \rangle$ $n \in [0..32]^* a_i \in [0 \ldots 255]$
Syntactic category of w	$x' = f_{148}(w)^{**}$ $x = \{0 if x' = noun \, 1 if x' = verb \, 2 if x' = other\}$	$x \in [0..2]$
Previous word: Word w_{t-1} located on the left of w in the sentence or null.	If $w_{t-1} = null$: $x = <0, \ldots, 0>$ else $\forall c_i \in w = \{c_1' c_2' \ldots c_n'\} \cup \{null_{n+1} \ldots null_{32}\}$ $x = [ASCII(c_1), ASCII(c_2), \ldots, ASCII(c_n)]$	$x = \langle a_1, a_2, \ldots, a_n \rangle$ $n \in [0..32]^* a_i \in [0 \ldots 255]$
Syntactic category of previous word w_{t-1}	$x' = f_{148}(w_{t-1})^{**}$ $x = \{0 if x' = noun \, 1 if x' = verb \, 2 if x' = other\}$	$x \in [0..2]$
Type of web page	$x = \{0 if page is index \, 1 if page is other\}$	$x \in [0..1]$
Country	$x = \frac{i}{x_i}; i \in \{A\}; i \in [0 \ldots len(A) - 1]$ $A = \{$a country in List of Country Code Top Level Domains$\}$	$x \in [0..241]$
Suffix of word w	$x = \frac{i}{x_i} \in \{A\}; i \in [0..len(A) - 1]$ $A = \{$'ar', 'er', 'ir', 'or', 'ur', 'ra', 're', 'ri', 'ro', 'ru', 's', 'm', 'sa', 'se', 'si', 'so', 'su', 'an', 'en', 'in', 'on', 'un', 'cion', 'ciones', null$\}$	$x \in [0..24]$
Punctuation	$x = \{1 if w_{i-1} \in A \, 0 if w_{i-1} \notin A\}$ $A = \{$'.', ',', ';', ':', '?', '!'$\}$	$x \in [0..1]$
Upper-case	$x = \{1 if isUpperCase(c_0) = true \, 0 if isUpperCase(c_0) = false\}$ $w_i = \{c_0 c_1 \ldots c_m\} c_j$ a character of w_i	$x \in [0..1]$
Entity type	$x = \frac{i}{x_i} \in \{A\}; i \in [0..len(A) - 1]$	$x \in [0..3]$

(Continues)

Table 6.2 (Continued)

Meta-data	Rule	Output
	$A = \{\text{org, com, net, other}\}$	
Emphasized word w_i	$x = \{1 \, if \, betweenQuotationMarks(w_i) \\ = true \, 1 \, if \, isCapitalized(w_i) = true \, 0 \, othercase\}$	$x \in [0 \ldots 1]$
Title	$x = \{1 \, if \, isInTitle(w_i) \\ = true \, 1 \, if \, isFirstWordOfText(w_i) = true \, 0 \, othercase\}$	$x \in [0 \ldots 1]$
Special sentence	$x = \left\{ 1 \, if \, enclosedWith \frac{(w_{i-1,p})}{p} \in A0 \, if \, not \right\}$	$x \in [0 \ldots 1]$
	$A = \{``;!", ``¿?", ``<>", ``()", ``[]", ``\{ \}", ``\ll \gg"\}$	
Stem w_i	$s = \text{stemPorter}(w_i)$	$s \in \{``a" - ``z", ``A" - ``Z", ``\ ", ``\ "\}$

*According to RAE, the largest word in Spanish [42].
**Use trained J48 on w, see induction tree of [44].

Table 6.3   Rules for metric features

Meta-data	Rule	Output
Occurrences w_i in the WEB page	$x = count(page.html, w_i)$	$x \in N$
Occurrences w_i, for any word i in the WEB page	$x = \sum_i count(page.html, w_i)$	$x \in N$
Length in characters of w_i	$x = len(w_i)$	$x \in N$
Occurrences of strong vowels in w_i	$x = \sum_{c \in \{a,e,o\}} count(c, w_i)$	$x \in N$
Occurrences of weak vowels in w_i	$x = \sum_{c \in \{i,u\}} count(c, w_i)$	$x \in N$
Length of sentence s_j in words	$x = \sum_i count(s_j, w_i), w_i \in s_j$	$x \in N$
Number of digits in s_j	$x = \sum_k count(s_j, n_k) : isNumber(n_k) = true$	$x \in N$
Number of special characters in s_j	$x = \sum_k count(s_j, sp_k) : isSpecialCharacter(sp_k) = true$	$x \in N$

with n being the number of words in the sentence, p_i, p_{i-1} derived using the heuristic in [37,38]. The properties of p_0 are [36]:

- independency from the document length
- independency from the context
- is a good indicator of writer's profile. It can be used to distinguish plain text, from an index, blog, forum, etc.
- is a good indicator of the relevance of the related sentence in the text.

  An alternate formulation of p_0, p'_0 is derived using (6.3).

$$p'_0 = \frac{p_0}{(w_0)} 2^n + \sum_{i=1}^{n} \frac{p_0}{(w_i)} 2^{(n+1-i)} \tag{6.3}$$

  Here:

n: the number of words in the current sentence
w: HBE (vector modeling word w_i)
$p_0(w_i)$: weight of a word w

  p'_0 has the following properties [39]:

- Expresses morphosyntactic features of a portion of the text
- It ranges from -2 to $+2$.
- $p(w_i)$ lies between 0 and 1.
- Many values are null since the related HBE has a value only if it is closely related to the main topic of the document.
- Higher values of $p(w_i)$ does not imply relevance in the document.

(iv) Biasing and semantic regions

Any textual document has at least a main topic that constitutes the concept to be presented in it. There is a set of tables that are used by a MLW heuristic in order to express the semantics. The heuristic uses the tables to delete words that are not expressing the meaning of the document. The process is very similar to declaring a set of attractors in the word's field and to let the entire set of words interact with it [40]. The bias determines which words are not relevant and need to be eliminated, which ones have negative/positive/neutral bias, and where is the relevant expression [38].

(v) Creation of semantic regions to allow self-expansion

Another tool that belongs to MLW is an heuristic **M** that uses the set of words {W}, descriptors and meta-data. The main idea here is to find subtle semantic patterns by replacing a subset of words from the original text with a similarity criterion.

A self-organized map with the entire lexical of the document Δ, is extended with meta-data derived to express the pragmatics of the discourse. This works as an automatically derived pragmatic context, and has shown to be a good model to detect the closest new words and documents.

6.9 Language and grammar

The approach that the human brain follows during the generation of expressions in natural language is commonly denoted under the term "Grammar". As a subject of study there are many properties and principles that govern the process. As a tool it consists of building blocks called linguistic units, that can be part of several structures [15]. In any case, Grammar runs under certain conditions that have been considered as a biological premise of the brain functioning:

- Cognition is prior to its expression in any language formalization (grammar).
- The symbolic thesis. Performance in natural language has three components: a sign (the manifestation in a concrete set of tokens), an abstract entity behind the sign (concept), a way of expressing the sign (utterance). The triplet are deeply related, being concept and utterance units running within the psychological field, the mental system of the speaker. From this perspective sign, concept and utterance relationship is the main part of the study.
- Pragmatic thesis. Since language is being used by individuals, it is important to know the internal approach to communication using the elements declared in the symbolic perspective. Every performance is a case, a guide to understand how a speaker understands the language as a tool for expression. From this perspective the analysis focuses on a systematic explanation of language change and acquisition.

The following is a short introduction of some of the proposed studies in the field.

6.9.1 Qualitative distinction of elements

In this conception of the language, the elements of a grammar are categorized as open or closed. The first type of units corresponds to a lexical order while the second one is part of a grammatical subsystem. Lexicon is focused on how the meanings are administered while grammatical is concerned mainly with structures. From a general perspective, it could be said that in essence both perspectives are just different levels of encoding certain concept. Note that in closed category there is a predetermined and restricted scope of functioning while the open category can expands with no limits.

6.9.2   Cognitive grammar

In this conception, grammar consists, like in the previous case, of units expressing a defined concept. They are used to perform a cognitive process, to produce expressions. Here, there could be many degrees of complexity during the sentence formulation. Sometimes the symbolic units evolve and change the way it is used, becoming a relatively formal new unit. But the process of change does not stop as the usage reinforces the way the expressions work in the language. This perspective focuses on formalization through phonology, semantics and symbolics.

6.9.3   Dynamic approaches

Under this category fall many models that try to explain the building mechanism of Grammar. This perspective is intended to explain derivations like idioms and how they articulate with the standard consideration of meaning. The weakness of this set of proposals is the fact that there should be a kind of stock of expressions, and the entire interpretation depends on its completeness and quality. As a counter side, the strength resides in the possibility of manipulating constructions with highly changing meaning, of semantic consideration out of simple subset analysis.

6.9.4   Cognitive approaches to grammaticalization

In this type of approach units evolve from open to closed class, where the evolution relates to the historical grammaticalization process in linguistics.

6.9.5   Pragmatic-driven approaches

These are based on empiric perspective of cognition to lexical semantics. Some of the proposals use a specific corpus, others simulations of mental processes, brain scanning techniques, etc. They shift from a predictive model conception to an evidence-based description model.

6.10   Applications of cognitive linguistics

Cognition at language level is used in medical and practical fields of human activity. Among them phonology, academia, sales, security, creativity studies, evaluation of the evolution of knowledge evolution and many fields of health, education, security, etc.

In 1966, Lakov expressed that sociolinguistics has suffered an important evolution from its original consideration of how natural language emerges and is used by native speakers. There are many models, where dominant relies on sets of rules, logical considerations, analytical formulations analogous to signal fields and several structuralism alternate models [15]. One of the more productive paradigms within a dynamic premise is known as nonlinear modeling. Although there is not a clear boundary of this type of conceptions, many of them consider neural nets, swarm computing, chaos theory, synergetics, etc. There is a strong bias to concentrate the essence in mathematical explanation of the core process, with a systemic generative formulation mostly working but not limited to: thermodynamics, synergetic processes and fractal principles.

6.11   Chaos and linguistics

There is a line of work that considers life as a structure that works under certain rules analogous to thermodynamics. This perspective was first introduced by Lineweaver [24]. He interpreted that there is a cosmological reproducibility that governs life and the living beings in the universe. In order to explain how the mechanism is and how the entropy evolves despite the life entity's behavior being chaotic, he identifies life with dissipative structures. Furthermore, the starting point of life should be lowest entropy, and the history and the acts performed increases it permanently. In this conception there are macro-states that are connected by certain bridges which are gravitational potential energy paths. Life increases the entropy production rate, mainly due to the complexity of its reasoning, that generates constantly new things and very diverse events. As a consequence the entropy of the system containing that life increases, c.t. "more efficient metabolisms should be equivalent to the evolution of larger entropy production" [24]. Here the concept of external constraint becomes dynamic for living beings. According to the author, entropy should have a stable maxima (for nonliving dissipative structures) and a transient local maxima (for life).

The explanation of linguistics from the chaos perspective could be a field with attractors that work on units of the language, changing the meanings and structures systematically but not avoiding the possibility of a disruptive event.

One important thing to consider is the fact that chaotic behavior does not imply complete unpredictability, since there is still a probability explanation that covers the process. Then, it is possible to compute in advance the changes of state with a reasonable degree of precision. This means that the covered process could be thought as deterministic. But there remains uncovered the disruptive events mentioned previously.

The disruptions are the result of a progressive aggregation of perturbations in the communication, a shifting in the semantics due to the fussiness of the copy process in the receiver of the expressions. After a certain degree of perturbation, the syntactics and/or semantics suffer a permanent change.

Wildgen [15] explained the long-term effect as describing a fractal pattern: a very small change respecting the entity under specific control. After several fractals, the resulting expression is quite away from its original conception and becomes independent from the original input. The initial construct converts into something else, with its own characteristics. The process is disruptive since it is not possible to derive the new structure using the logic of derivation in the current organization of the linguistic system. In fact the original concept is lost, and a new pattern emerges with an unpredictable set of features, hence the outcome is considered chaotic.

Note that perturbations are possible because there is an initial assumption that every individual behaves as a chaotic linguistic unit working under a field determined by the specific language community where it belongs. In this system there are many specific features given by the dialect or sociolect area. The rest of this section explains how thermodynamics explain linguistics as an analogy of other fields using this concept.

6.11.1 Thermodynamics: diffusive and synergetic processes

Thermodynamics can be defined as a part of physics that describes and relates the physical properties of systems, studying the heat exchanges that take place in bodies that are heated. Here entropy is a key concept. The word derives from $\theta\tau\rho\omega\pi\eta$, which in Greek means evolution or transformation. It is frequently understood as a degree of chaos. The bigger the entropy the greater the disorder.

Entropy as a term was first introduced by the German physicist and mathematician Rudolf Clausius. His work focused on heat interchanges, their effects and the relationship between heat and energy. The curiosity led him to discover the deep connection between them and the existence of a rule of interchange among them. He called this finding the *principle of equivalence of energy transformations*. Under this principle lower heat levels cannot promote a hot body by itself, there must be some source of energy to produce the state change.

Clausius explained the word chosen as follows: "*... I propose to call the quantity S the entropy of the body by taking the Greek word transformation. The design that I have put together with the word entropy was made in such a way that it resembled the word energy as much as possible.*" (quote from [16]).

The term entropy is not specific to physics, it is also used in chemistry, and other fields more close to human centered sciences like psychology, philosophy, business, etc. In any case, entropy is used to express some kind of *state property*, where typically only the initial and final states matter, no matter the path taken between them. Note that another characteristic is the consideration of its magnitude not by itself, but as a tool to measure differences or changes (like positive or negative increments Δ) between two states.

As might be expected, entropy expresses a concrete feature, sometimes from nature and sometimes from other ontology systems. For instance it, represents the disorder of molecules in chemistry, the heat in physics, lack of information in information systems, etc. As a global concept it relates to an amount of something not used but able to produce an effect: let say in physical words the unused energy that is capable of producing physical work. From the perspective of Computational Linguistic reasoning, which is the main focus of this chapter, it expresses the number of potential alternate ontologies liable to be articulated with some current semantics and communication, through linguistic levels (which is the *work* produced).

6.11.2   The linguistic reasoning laws

In the computational linguistic field, deep administration of natural language expressions appeals to some kind of uncovered mental device. For that reason many scientists have been working on the conception of theories like the ones presented in previous sections. They explain with more or less success the language production, evolution and manipulation at an individual or collective level, from perspectives social, psychological, physiological, cognitive, among others. This chapter performs another point of view, a kind of thermodynamic explanation of the marvelous internal device within every human that is responsible for linguistic reasoning. Hopefully it will help to understand some of the dimensions covering the complexity involved in linguistic interchanges. This subsection introduces briefly the framework and justification of the work presented in the last section, which is part of the current work of the author.

The main idea behind a linguistic thermodynamic conception is to be able to gain some knowledge about the hidden gear governing language essence, how it works and its basic rules of functioning. To start with, there are four known thermodynamic laws that change their phrasing according to the specific field of study, and describe the same phenomena from different perspectives (i.e. different fields of application). They define basically two main concepts: possibilities (P), current effects (E) and entropy (H) as a measure of how stable is P. The physical interpret them as energy and work. The laws determine that there is a total quantity of P that is predetermined and cannot be changed, but can mutate (first law), that under certain conditions it could evolve to a stability point called equilibrium with maximum amount of H (second law), the source of E goes back to P so the stability is obtained by means of it (third law) and the precondition of everything is the existence of a transference possibilities of the equilibrium status between systems under certain conditions (law 0).

In the consideration of those laws, Wildgen takes the second law as the most important. He conceives the amount of information within an expression as the degree of negentropy. There is a universal trend toward a loss of information (increase of disorder). Note that a system can reach the equilibrium state even being away from the thermodynamic equilibrium. The gap is covered by language innovation, that is here represented by changes in the socially accepted and recognized constitution of grammar and/or vocabulary. The innovation is called disruptive, as mentioned in previous sections, since the change could not be explained by performing linguistic derivations. The reason for the deviation is out of the current system, and comes from humans during its practical usage of vocal and written interchanges. They are associated with the concept of *dissipative structures* and *synergetics* that alter the flow of information between the system and its environment. As a consequence, part of the process of communication fails, the conversion of message received by the target has a failure and the input (the original communication) departs from its initial formulation. The output (the

Table 6.4   Comparison between traditional and linguistic reasoning thermodynamics

Law	Traditional	Linguistic
L1	There is a fixed total amount of energy (S_T) in the universe can change its manifestation	Rule 1
L2	S_T cannot be created/destroyed. An isolated sub-system has S'_T that can increase until an equilibrium status	Rule 2
L3	There is a unique force that leads S'_T to equilibrium	Rule 4
L0	The equilibrium has a transient property for sub-systems (A in equilibrium with C, B in equilibrium with C, then A in equilibrium with C)	Rule 3

interpretation and usage) persists in a changed output, the new output information now replaces the original one.

Wildgen submits that a consistent persistence in the biased relation input–output is supported by an extra process that performs a self-organization process where certain modes are eliminated in favor of other ones. The result of this evolution is the loss of entropy (the information that remains uncovered at destination). For that reason humans are the *dissipative structures* in systems with any type of linguistic performance (or *synergetic process*). Note that there are levels of such structures like starting with the brain, to face to face and vocal communication, where the loss presents different characteristics.

Follow-up these conceptions there is a possibility to go a step forward and determine a set of rules that precise how dissipative structures could be able to practice the synergetic process. The next section introduces four from a complete set of seven rules that the author encompassed as *Linguistic Reasoning Thermodynamic*. Table 6.4 presents a summary that matches each rule with traditional thermodynamic laws.

There are three more rules that are out of the scope of this chapter, not shown here.

6.12   Thermodynamic rules for linguistic reasoning

From the practical point of view, the analysis of linguistic rules need to be tested with real language performance in concrete communications. The proposal in this section is framed in the work of Lineweaver, Wildgen, Spinadel, Rebolledo and Widyarto among others. As mentioned in previous sections, Friesen, Gentner and many other scientists worked that way in order to get around the variations of the language and gain cognition of the subtle process underlying the process. The approach here is to generate cases in a very controlled context, as follows:

- Evaluating dialogs not isolated sentences. The complete word performance requires context at several levels (sentence, dialog and pragmatics), therefore, any validation needs to be able to access them properly. For that reason any test is performed here with dialogs in a game called 20Q [45]. The game used is an online version (see Figure 6.2). It asks gender, country and age in order to select the neural networks trained with similar conditions. The game starts asking the user to think a secret word. Then the system has 20 opportunities to perform yes/no questions in order to guess the word.

- Limiting the ability of creating expressions to one of both ends of the communication. The communication needs two ends, one for originating the communication (M), and a receiver (F). In the controlled framework M is a neural network trained with interchanges with humans using the same language. The cases presented in this chapter correspond to Spanish.
- Verifying that the interchange has a concrete semantic goal to cover. This is because it is important to evaluate if the communication succeeds. In the case of 20Q, when the system wins the communication is complete.
- Determining the universe of expressions available. The restriction in the case of the game selected consists in Spanish nouns or noun sentences. No other restriction has been imposed.

The following introduces the first four rules published by the author previously. There remain three that are under research and publication. For that reason, they are not detailed here nor included in the explanation of the fundamentals. Just to mention them: Rule 5 expresses the relationship between time and knowledge, and a sort of stratified behavior in cognition, Rule 6 connects time and speed of communication, and finally Rule 7 expresses something called observation capability.

Figure 6.2   20Q game from http://www.20q.net/

6.12.1   *Working hypothesis derivations and rules*

Beyond the conditions, approach and framework, there are a set of hypotheses that can be summarized as:

1.   There is a universe O, of available concepts and E is the one chosen to be communicated.
2.   As any concept, E expresses an ontology e. The communication makes it part of the process using it in an indirect way through E.
3.   E is an abstract expression not encoded in any language. For practical reasons, tests consider E to be the encoded version in Spanish.
4.   There is E even before the moment of every linguistic interchange. Furthermore, E is not altered by it.
5.   The information emerges from the evolution of the communication process, as an offspring that remains within O.
6.   The timing of the information is associated with the evolution of the communication.
7.   Any E from e inserts itself in a time-dependent process and can be understood as a kind of information movement, a time t dependent thought.
8.   Reasoning is a movement in t that accumulates information sent by sender (M) to receiver (F). M and F storage is not identical but analogous since they relate with previous communications at each end. That accumulation is a context or specific awareness of the phenomenon e.

6.12.2   *Rules and findings*

In order to determine the general rules of linguistic reasoning, *Linguistic Thermodynamics* evaluates the meaning in specific language experiences. It aims to be a novel interpretation and scoping of textual processing, giving a sort of thermodynamics of language practical usage [46]. The model intends to reveal conditions and biases of the brain during the production and manipulation of expressions in a concrete language (in this case Spanish). Deep behind the rules there is a conception of reasoning as a sort of entropy and fractals mix-up [20].

Table 6.5 is a summary of four rules that have been tested, analyzed, evaluated and published. This work does not cover the remaining rules from the total of seven.

There are three more rules that have no equivalence here.

Note that context in every test here is a dialog using 20Q. The rule R1 express how a message (denoted as a C communication) succeeds in the semantical transmission from M to F, R2 articulates expressions with a sequence of messages along time t, R3 is a metric D that could be used to evaluate the Shannon entropy dynamics in a dialog, and finally Rule R4 reveals that there is a kind of spatial locality of the symbolic representations by Hilbert fractals (and the characteristics of this locality).

Table 6.6 presents a summary of the properties of the language usage after every rule, based on the findings in a previous work.

Table 6.5   Summary of rules 1–4

Rule	Summary	Characteristic
R1	Rule of the main behavior Timeline balance *Ex post facto* the entire process is timeless A communication C succeeds if there is a complete transference of entropy.	Space of concepts O exists before time
R2	Dimension and rhythm The relationship between elements in *E* (for instance, verbs and nouns) is one of balance *C* expresses *E* in a behavior in *t* with a specific rhythm and cycle.	Time $t \in [-\infty, +\infty]$ determines C dynamics
R3	Action When the entropy of elements in *C* is expressed with a fractal dimension *D*: there is an evolution of *D* in *t*, which means that $D(t + 1)$ depends on $D(t)$ so that always $D(t + 1) >= D(t)$	Language is a combination (space, *t*) => is movement
R4	*Duality* Message M communicates with a counterpart *F*. The locality of its symbolic representation in a language can be modeled by Hilbert fractals. Zone presents clouds representing both: temporality and content (meanings)	$H(t)$ preserves space in *x*, *y*, *z* *x*, *y*, *z*, *h* represent both *t* and meaning

Table 6.6   Summary of the rules 1–4

Rule	Explanation	Properties
R1	A communication C succeeds if it is composed of sentences able to transfer entropy in a proper way	1. Global entropy does not change: equilibrium 2. All the entropy remains within the system 3. No entropy is transferred out of the system but held as local entropy
R2	There is a complement between nouns and verbs, though not perfect they balance each other and the entropy flows as information and has a certain rhythm and cycle	1. Timing $t [-\infty, +\infty]$ holds the entire activity (sequence of sentences) in a lapse $[t_1; t_2]$ 2. There are no changes in H out of $[t_1; t_2]$ 3. H presents breakouts in C 4. H is cyclical in C
R3	Any communication C is an activity with a triplet (O, E, C) composed of cause, effect and evolution in *t*	1. Language relates to a tuple (space, *t*) => it involves movement 2. Causality: cause and effect 3. Fractal dimension *D* evolves with $t => D(t + 1)$ depends on $D(t)$

(Continues)

Table 6.6   (Continued)

Rule	Explanation	Properties
R4	The communication C from M to F is the result of a dual and balanced process combining $f(e, t) + f(e, -t)$	1. M runs under a tuple (O, E, C) with $t \rightarrow +\infty$, while F runs $t \rightarrow -\infty$ 2. $e(t)$ is the specific option that becomes evident in the physical world. 3. Dimension n, $e(t)$ becomes a Hilbert in an n-dimensional parallelepiped representation. 4. For $f/(O, E, C)$: $f(e, t) + f(e, -t) \;\forall\; t$. 5. When there is a communication $C \sim f(e, t)$ When there is no communication C, there is an infinite number of possible canvas e: $\Sigma_{i \,\epsilon\, [1 \ldots \infty)} \, e_i(t)$

The rule R4 is the first that performs a relationship between the instances in a communication and a spatial conception of the conceptualization. Note that it is a Hilbert fractal that guides the organization along *t*, in a way to preserve space.

6.13   Conclusions and final remarks

There is an important set of background and publications that indicate a fractal and entropic conception and language are not separated. Many of the studies tend to be practical and are focused on direct usage of factual features that can be found with simple models. But a deeper understanding of the genesis of the entire process, the reasoning production, requires a complete set of new conceptual tools. Some of them were provided here, but it remains a lot of work to be able to understand and model in detail the complexity of the hidden internal device responsible for linguistics in human beings.

References

[1] Friesen L. Using mental bias to construct a model of cognition. Academia Letters, Article 1681. https://doi.org/10.20935/AL1681. 2021.

[2] Friesen L. A cognitive model of science and theology. DOI: 10.13140/RG.2.2.27653.17122/1. 2020.

[3] Von Bertalanffy L. General system theory foundations, development, applications (Teoría general de los sistemas; fundamentos, aplicaciones). Fondo de Cultura Económica. 1984.

[4] Rodríguez Duch M. F. Chaos, entropy and public health: Legal analysis from a multidimensional perspective (caos, entropía y salud pública: Análisis desde una perspectiva jurídica multidimensional). Argentina Association of Administrative law Magazine. N 1. 2016.

[5]   Esteva Fabregat C. Follow-up for a complexity theory (Acompañamientos a una teoría de la complejidad). *Desacatos.* 12(28). 2008.

[6]   Siegler R. S., Booth J. L. Development of numerical estimation in young children. *Child Development.* 2(75) N 2, pp. 428–444. 2004.

[7]   Wynn K. Addition and subtraction by human infants. Letters to nature. *Nature.* Vol. 358. 1992.

[8]   Rodriguez Santos A. Epswiclas. I.E.S. San Cristóbal de los Ángeles de Madrid. 2011.

[9]   Jencks C. El nuevo paradigma en arquitectura. Architectural review. Trad. Sebastián D'Andrea. 2003.

[10]   Sulbarán Sandoval J. A. Fractal as architectural paradigm: Deconstruction vs vivid patterns language (El fractal como paradigma arquitectónico: deconstrucción vs lenguaje de patrones vivientes). *Procesos Urbanos.* N 3, pp. 79–88. 2016.

[11]   Widyarto S., Syafrullah M., Sharif M. W., Budaya G. A. Fractals study and its application. *6th International Conference on Electrical Engineering, Computer Science and Informatics (EECSI)*, pp. 200–204, DOI:10.23919/ EECSI48112.2019.8977124. 2019.

[12]   Spinadel V. M. Fractals (Fractales). Second International Congress of Mathematics in Engineering and Architecture, pp. 113 – 123. 2008.

[13]   Mandelbrot B. Information theory and psycholinguistics. B.B. Wolman and E. Nagel (ed). *Scientific Psychology.* 1965.

[14]   Spinadel V. W. Fractal geometry and Euclidean thermodynamics (Geometría fractal y geometría euclidiana). *Magazine Education and Pedagogy. Univ. Antioquia*, vol. XV, N 1(35), pp. 85–91. 2003.

[15]   Evans V., Bergen B.K., Zinken J. Chaos, Fractals and dissipative structures. Systems, new paradigms for the human sciences. *The Cognitive Linguistic Reader.* 2007.

[16]   López De Luise D. Linguistic intelligence as a root for computing reasoning. Advances in Selected Artificial Intelligence Areas: World Outstanding Women in Artificial Intelligence (Learning and de Maria Virvou (Editor), George A. Tsihrintzis (Editor), Lakhmi C. Jain (Editor) Analytics in Intelligent Systems, 24) 1st ed. 2022.

[17]   de Smedt T. Modelling creativity case studies. University Press Antwerpen (UPA). 201

[18]   Rebolledo, R. Complexity and chance (Complejidad y azar). *Humanities Journal of Valparaiso.* https://doi.org/10.22370/rhv.2018.12.1322. 2018.

[19]   Shannon, C.E. A mathematical theory of communication. *Bell System Technical Journal* 3(27), pp. 379–423 and 623–656. 1948.

[20]   López De Luise D. Language and reasoning by entropy fractals. Signals. MDPI. 2021.

[21]   Sánchez Medina G. The deterministic chance (El Azar Determinista). Available online: Encolombia.com. 2022.

[22]   Prigogine I. The end of certainties (La fin des certitudes). Editions O. Jacob. 1996.

[23]   Nambiar K. What Is Laplace's demon? Does this Mat Soc. demon know everything? In Science ABC. 2022.

[24]   Lineweaver C.H. Cosmological and biological reproducibility: Limits on the maximum entropy production principle. School of Physics, University of New South Wales, Sydney, Australia. DOI:10.1007/11672906_6. 1970.

[25]   Peano G. On a curve, which fills an entire flat area (Sur une courbe, qui remplit toute une aire plane). *Mathematische Annalen* 36, 157–160. 1890.

[26]   Paltridge G.W. Global dynamics and climate – a system of minimum entropy exchange, *Q J R Meteorol Soc* 101: 475–484. 1975.

[27]   Paltridge G.W. Climate and thermodynamic systems of maximum dissipation. *Nature* 279: 630–631. 1979.

[28]   Lorenz R. Full steam ahead-probably. *Science* 299:837–838. 2003.

[29]   Dewar R.C. Information theory explanation of the fluctuation theorem, maximum entropy production and self-organized criticality in non-equilibrium stationary states. *J Phys A* 36: 631. also at http://arxiv.org/abs/condsmat/0005382. 2003.

[30]   Novák V., Perfilieva I., Močkoř J. *Mathematical Principles of Fuzzy Logic.* Dordrecht: Kluwer Academic. ISBN 978-0-7923-8595-0. 1999.

[31]   Mendel J., Hagras H., Woei-Wan T. *Introduction to Type-2 Fuzzy Logic Control: Theory and Applications.* Wiley. ISBN 978-1-118-90144-1. 2014.

[32]   López De Luise D. An artist uses AI to flesh characters (Un artista usa IA para darle carne a personajes). National Academy of Sciences in Buenos Aires (Academia Nacional de Ciencias de Buenos Aires). https://r9.ieee.org/argentina-cis. 2021.

[33]   Xie J., Girshick R.B., Farhadiand A. Deep3D: Fully automatic 2D-to-3D video conversion with Deep Conv. N networks. In ECCV. 2016.

[34]   Yao S., Wang L., Li D., Zhang M. A Real-time full HD 2D-to-3D video conversion system based on FPGA. 7th ICIG & Graph. 2013.

[35]   Mildenhall B., Srinivasan P.P., Tancik M., Barron J.T., Ramamoorthi R., Ng R. Representing scenes as neural radiance fields for view synthesis. In *Proceedings ECCV*. 2020.

[36]   Hisgen D., López De Luise D. Dialog structure automatic modeling. *MICAI* 2010. DOI: 10.1007/978-3-642-16761-4_7. 2010.

[37]   López De Luise D. A morphosyntactical complementary structure for searching and browsing. SCSS 2005. Springer. 2005.

[38]   López De Luise D. A metric for automatic word categorization. SCSS 2007. Springer. 2007.

[39]   Soffer M., López De Luise D. Automatic text processing for Spanish texts. ANDESCON 2008. 2008.

[40]   López De Luise D. Web usability by means of a meta structure. PhD thesis. 2007.

[41]   López De Luise D., Pascal A., Álvarez C., Pankrac C., Santa Cruz J. M., Tournoud M. Chatbots: Autoexpansion approach to improve natural language automatic dialogs. 2020 IEEE Congreso Bienal de Argentina

(ARGENCON), pp. 1–9, doi: 10.1109/ARGENCON49523.2020.9505504. 2020.

[42]   Royal Academy of Spain (RAE). Rae.es. 2022.

[43]   Kohonen T. Automatic formation of topological maps of patterns in a self-organizing system. *Scand. Conf. on Image Analysis.* 1981.

[44]   López De Luise D., Soffer M. Improved induction tree training for automatic lexical categorization. *International Joint Conferences on Computer, Information, and Systems Sciences, and Engineering.* CISSE 2008.

[45]   20Q. http://www.20q.net/. Taken on July 12th, 2021.

[46]   López De Luise D. Entropy, chaos and language. IGI Global. 2021.

Chapter 7

AI and machine learning in medical data processing

Deba Prasad Dash[1] and Maheshkumar H Kolekar[2]

Abstract

A seizure is defined as a sudden synchronous activity of group of neurons causing sudden movement of the body. Nearly 10 million people from India are suffering from epilepsy. Electroencephalogram (EEG) is a non-invasive technique to measure the neural activity of brain. EEG signal processing and speech signal processing have applications in seizure detection. Sudden neural activity in the brain is reflected in the EEG signal and is processed using machine learning and deep learning techniques for efficient seizure detection. This chapter gives an overview of different speech processing and signal processing techniques for seizure detection. Deep learning and machine learning techniques are implemented and the results are discussed in this chapter. Different techniques are compared to give a future direction to the researcher to work in this field. Long short-term memory (LSTM) network model is applied for seizure detection and the results are discussed in this chapter.

7.1 Introduction

EEG is a non-invasive method to measure the brain activity. Apart from EEG, there are various medical signals that are used to diagnose a particular disease. Electromyogram (EMG) gives the muscle activity information, Electrocardiogram (ECG) gives the heart activity information and electro-neurogram (ENG) gives the measure of neuron activity. Apart from biomedical signals, medical images are used for the diagnosis of a disease. Magnetic resonance images can be used in detecting diseases like COVID-19. Other imaging modalities such as CT scan and X-ray are also used in the diagnosis of diseases. Machine learning and artificial intelligence (AI) are currently used for designing a disease diagnosis model. The machine learning models are dependent on the types of features extracted from the data. The deep learning model, on the other hand, is not dependent on feature

---

[1]Thapar Institute of Engineering and Technology, Patiala, India
[2]Indian Institute of Technology Patna, Bihar, India

selection. The major advantage of the use of machine learning and AI model is the increase in accuracy of disease detection and faster processing of the information.

In this chapter, we will discuss about seizure, how it can be detected automatically using machine learning and deep learning techniques? How the speech signal-processing techniques can be used in seizure detection? A detailed state-of-the-art methods comparison is given in this chapter. The support vector machine (SVM) classifier and LSTM classifier are implemented for seizure detection and the results are presented and discussed in this chapter.

7.2   Literature review

Johnson *et al.* [1] proposed a Gaussian mixture model and the minimum classification error training approach for EEG-based seizure detection. Recurrent neural network has vast application in signal classification. Johnson *et al.* [1] evaluated the LSTM and gated recurrent unit (GRU) model efficiency in seizure detection. TUH EEG Corpus was used for evaluating the model and convolutional LSTM was found to perform better compared to convolutional GRU network. Discrete wavelet transforms (DWTs) are widely applied in biomedical signal analysis. Omidvar *et al.* [2] proposed DWT-based seizure detection. In the research, authors have used genetic algorithm for feature selection and used both artificial neural network and SVM classifier for seizure classification. The model achieved 100% accuracy in healthy-seizure classification. Akut *et al.* [3] proposed wavelet and CNN-based epileptic seizure detection. CNN-based approach achieved 100% accuracy in healthy-seizure EEG signal classification. Hussain [4] compared the classification accuracy for both wavelet- and empirical mode decomposition (EMD)-based approach for epileptic seizure detection. EMD-based approach achieved the highest accuracy. Jana *et al.* [5] proposed DWT–EMD feature-level fusion approach for multi- and single-channel EEG-based seizure detection. Different time domain features were extracted from DWT coefficients such as the mean, variance, standard deviation, curve length, skewness, kurtosis and minima. Different time domain features were also extracted from the intrinsic mode functions such as the variance, RMS, standard deviation, curve length, skewness and kurtosis. SVM classifier along with RBF kernel achieved good classification accuracy compared to other state-of-the-art methods. Apart from DWT and EMD approaches, different modified versions of it were also utilized to develop a seizure detection algorithm. Dual-tree complex wavelet transform (DTCWT) along with KNN classifier was used for seizure detection [6]. Fourier transform features were extracted from the wavelet coefficients and the proposed approach achieved 100% classification accuracy. DTCWT along with least square-SVM classifier was proposed for seizure detection by Al-Salman *et al.* [7]. The method achieved average 97% accuracy in seizure detection for different seizure databases. A new tree-based wavelet transform and directed acyclic graph SVM classifier were proposed for epileptic seizure detection by Murugavel and Ramakrishnan [8]. DAG SVM achieved 97% accuracy in seizure detection.

Apart from epileptic seizure detection, a lot of research studies were also conducted in predicting the seizure. Deep convolutional auto-encoder and bi-LSTM model were proposed for seizure prediction using EEG signals [9]. Different types of models were compared in those research studies such as multilayer perceptron network, CNN-MLP network and CNN-Bi-LSTM. Kiral-Kornek *et al.* [10] proposed a deep learning-based wearable seizure prediction system. In a multi-channel EEG signal-based seizure prediction approach, there is a need to select the EEG channel having seizure event. A CNN and EEG channel optimization technique-based seizure detection approach was proposed by Jana *et al.* [11]. In [11], the classification-based channel selection approach was proposed. In this approach, initially the average accuracy by taking each channel was considered and gradually by removing the channel one by one and the important channel was selected for achieving final classification. But this approach of channel selection is time-consuming and is valid only for one set of database. Ra *et al.* [12] proposed permutation entropy, while K-nearest neighbour classifier and genetic algorithms were used to select the significant channel in seizure detection.

In recent years, EMG- and ECG-based systems have been proposed for designing wearable seizure detection system. The ratio of high-frequency to low-frequency component of EMG signal gives the measure of tonic–clonic seizure as proposed by Beniczky *et al.* [13]. The proposed approach achieved a sensitivity of maximum 100%. The heart rate variability evaluated from the ECG signal acts as an indicator of seizure and achieved 70% sensitivity [14].

A multi-parameter seizure detection approach was evaluated by Dong *et al.* [15]. In [15], three different sensors EMG, accelerometer and gyrometer were used together for seizure detection in night during sleep. The data were recorded wirelessly and analysed for variation during seizure. The model overall achieved 75.92% sensitivity in seizure detection.

This chapter discusses different machine learning and deep learning algorithms in seizure detection. The role of speech signal processing is also discussed and in the last section all the state-of-the-art methods are discussed. In conclusion, the chapter discusses the future scope.

7.3 What is seizure?

Seizure is defined as a sudden synchronous activity of group of neurons. Seizure can be of various types. Usually seizures are detected by acquiring the surface EEG signals and analysing the signal. Signal recording has to be done continuously to capture the seizure activity. The seizure activity can occur for maximum 5 min in 24 h. So, analysing the signal manually is very difficult and often time consuming. In another approach, seizure activity can be stimulated by a physician and EEG of the person was recorded to confirm the seizure activity. Apart from detecting seizure, a lot of work has been done in predicting seizure using ECG, EMG or EEG signals. It is also important to detect the brain lobe affected from seizure so that surgery can be performed to remove the part of brain affected from seizure so that patient can be cured.

Based on the symptoms, seizure can be of the following types.

A. Absence seizure
B. Tonic seizure
C. Clonic seizure
D. Tonic–clonic seizure
E. Myoclonic seizure
F. Atonic seizure
G. Focal and non-focal seizure

Focal seizure is the seizure where only one area of the brain is affected. In non-focal seizure, multiple brain areas are affected by seizure. In non-focal seizure, seizure is treated by using drugs.

In the absence seizure, the patient stairs into space for 10 min continuously. Tonic seizure results in the stiffening of muscles. Atonic seizure results in the loss of muscle control which causes sudden collapse of the body. Clonic seizure results in repeated rhythmic and jerking muscle movement. Tonic–clonic seizure results in body jerk and loss of consciousness.

Different types of EEG patterns are observed during seizure. Triphasic waveforms are non-specific, high amplitude, sharply contoured waves with a unique morphology. Other types of waveforms are interictal epileptic discharges, which include spike waves, sharp waves, rolandic spikes, ploy-spikes, generalized periodic discharge and generalized spikes waves. The spike waveforms are recognized as small duration pointed waveform. Generalized periodic discharge is the repetitive discharges at regular intervals. These patterns are identified automatically using the machine learning and deep learning algorithm for real-time seizure detection.

7.4   Role of EEG and speech signal in seizure detection

EEG gives the neuron activity with high temporal resolution. Because of non-invasiveness and the ease to record, EEG has found vast applications in disease diagnosis and rehabilitation. Many neuron-related disorders such as dementia and epilepsy, can be detected by processing the EEG signal. There are different steps that are followed for EEG signal processing. In any signal processing, the first step is to remove noises from the signal. EEG signals can be said to have five different bands representing different brain activities. The delta band represents sleep condition with frequency ranges between 0.5 and 4 Hz. The theta band represents the drowsy condition with a frequency range between 4.1 and 8 Hz. The alpha and beta bands represent active state with a frequency range between 8.1 and 13 Hz and 13.1 and 30 Hz. The gamma band represents the high active state of the brain with a frequency range between 30.1 and 60 Hz. Some of the papers utilize band pass filter and wavelet decomposition to select the desired band from the EEG signal. Infinite impulse response notch filter and independent component analysis (ICA) are widely used for filtering EEG signals. A variable Gaussian filter was used for removing noises from the EEG signals as reported by Harishvijey and Raja [16]. Adaptive filters and signal averaging technique were explored for effectiveness in real-time seizure detection [17]. In [18], Malekzadeh *et al.* have used band-pass filters to filter the EEG data between 0.5 and 40 Hz before decomposing the data into various bands using tunable Q-wavelet transform (TQWT). ICA was used to identify the ripple effects from the iEEG signals as reported in [19]. ICA decomposes into various independent components, and each component can be analysed separately and the noise component can be removed to get the denoised signal.

The next step in EEG signal processing is feature extraction. In order to extract features, the signal can be decomposed into various bands and features can be extracted from each bands. In some of the research studies, features were extracted directly from the EEG signals. The features can be divided into time domain features, frequency domain features and time–frequency domain features. The time domain features are extracted from the bands directly such as the mean amplitude, maximum amplitude, variance, standard deviation, entropy, etc. The frequency domain features were extracted after converting time series data into frequency domain by using fast Fourier transform. The frequency domain features include frequency band skewness and kurtosis, maximum and minimum frequency, etc. The features extracted from wavelet coefficients are the time–frequency domain features. Sharmila and Geethanjali [20] extracted time domain features from the EEG signals for seizure classification. The different time domain features are the wavelet length, number of zero crossings, mean absolute value, average power, standard deviation and the number of slope sign changes. Naïve Bayes classifier and SVM classifier were implemented for detecting seizure automatically and achieved 97.9% accuracy. Shanir *et al.* [21] used simple line length and energy features for seizure detection and KNN classifier achieved better accuracy compared to other approaches. The widely used frequency features are peak frequency and power spectral density and extracted from the EEG signals for seizure detection [6].

The next step in the signal processing is feature selection. The features were selected using different statistical tests such as the analysis of variance (ANOVA) test, Student's *t*-test, etc. Other approaches include classification accuracy-based feature selection. In some research studies, features were extracted from different domains and feature fusion approach was used to convert the input into machine learning or deep learning algorithms as one feature vector. The features can be directly added or can be normalized using algorithms like min–max normalization technique. A discriminant correlation algorithm was applied for feature fusion as reported by Haghighat *et al.* [22].

Speech recognition techniques have also found applications in seizure detection. Yavuz *et al.* [23] had proposed cepstral analysis and generalized regression neural network in seizure detection and achieved 98.78% accuracy in seizure–non-seizure EEG signal classification. Higher-order spectral analysis used for the speech signal analysis was applied to detect seizure along with SVM classifier by Mahmoodian *et al.* [24] and it achieved 96.84% accuracy.

The fused features were given as input to the different machine learning and deep learning techniques.

7.5   Machine learning techniques in seizure detection

The machine learning algorithms can be divided into unsupervised, supervised and semi-supervised learning algorithms. This section discusses the application of SVM classifier in seizure detection. A free online database [25] was used to evaluate the proposed algorithm. Both time and frequency domain features were extracted from the EEG signals and the accuracy is compared. The selected features were used for evaluating the final classification accuracy.

7.5.1   Database used

In this research, an online seizure database was used to check the accuracy of different time and frequency domain features in seizure detection. The database consists of healthy, seizure and inter-seizure EEG signals. There are five different set of EEG signals in the database, Sets A and B consist of healthy EEG signals recorded from volunteers using surface electrodes. A total of 100 EEG signals are included in each set. Set A contains healthy EEG data in eye open and set B contains EEG data in eye-closed conditions. Set C and set D contain the interictal EEG signal. Set E contains seizure EEG signals. All signals have a length of 4096 samples. The sampling frequency of the data was 173.81 Hz. Initially the data were filtered up to 40 Hz. In this research (A), healthy EEG signals, inter-seizure (D) and seizure (E) EEG signals were used to evaluate the models for seizure detection.

7.5.2   Methodology

In this work, time domain features, such as the maximum amplitude, minimum amplitude, mean amplitude, standard deviation and variance of the amplitude, were calculated directly from the EEG signals. Different moment features such as skewness and kurtosis were verified for accuracy in seizure detection. Shannon entropy was extracted from the EEG signals. Mathematically, the features are defined as:

1. Max (X)
2. Min (X)
3. Standard deviation: $\sigma = \sqrt{\dfrac{\sum_{i=1}^{n}(X_i - \mu)^2}{n}}$

4. Variance: $\sigma^2 = \dfrac{\sum (X_i - \mu)^2}{n-1}$

5. Skewness: $\dfrac{\sum_{i=1}^{n}(X_i - \mu)^3}{(n-1)*\sigma^3}$

6. Kurtosis: $\dfrac{\sum_{i=1}^{n}(X - \mu)^4}{(n-1)\sigma^4}$

where n is the number of observations, X is the time series data value, μ is the mean of time series and σ is the standard deviation.

7.5.3   Shannon entropy

Entropy measures the randomness of a signal. It represents the quantity of information in a signal. Mathematically, it can be represented as:

$$H(x) = -\sum_{i=0}^{N-1} P_i(X) * \log_2(P_i(X)) \qquad (7.1)$$

Here, X is the time series data and $P(X)$ is the probability distribution function.

Algorithm 1: Proposed algorithm

1. Input signal X.
2. Extract all time domain features from the EEG signal: $f_t(x)$.
3. Find the fast Fourier transform of the signal and extract frequency domain features from the EEG signal. $f_f(x)$.

$$f_f(x) = Features(FFT(x))$$

1. Apply SVM classifier and evaluate the classification accuracy for each feature vector.
2. The best features were selected based on the classification accuracy.
3. The selected features were used to get the final classification accuracy.

7.5.4   SVM classifier

SVM classifier [26] is a binary classifier based on the regression analysis. The SVM model tries to find a separating hyperplane between the feature vectors of two classes. The aim is to optimize the margin of separation of two support vectors. Support vectors are the vectors consisting of the features closer to the separating hyperplane. The equation governing the model can be mathematically written as:

$$y = w * X + b \qquad (7.2)$$

$$W = \sum a_i X_i y_i \qquad (7.3)$$

where w is the weight matrix and b is the bias factor to design an SVM model. Here, α is the Lagrange multiplier and y_i is the class label. The feature vectors which are away from the separating hyperplane have zero Lagrange multiplier. The Lagrange multiplier is calculated using the following equation.

$$L = \frac{1}{2}|w|^2 - \sum_i a_i y_i * (w_i * x_i + b) + a_i \qquad (7.4)$$

The radial basis function (RBF) kernel and polynomial kernel were used in this research. Mathematically, both the kernels are defined as follows:

$$K(X_1, X_2) = \exp\left(-\frac{||X_1 - X_2||^2}{2\sigma^2}\right) \qquad (7.5)$$

$$K(X_1, X_2) = (1 + X^t{}_1 * X_2)^d \qquad (7.6)$$

where X_1 and X_2 are the two feature values, d is the degree of polynomial kernel and σ is a free parameter.

7.6 Results

Table 7.1 shows the classification result of seizure and inter-seizure EEG signal for different time domain features used in this research. The accuracy of each feature vector was compared and it has been observed that the standard deviation, minimum amplitude and Shannon entropy achieved higher accuracy compared to other feature vectors.

Table 7.2 shows the classification accuracy of seizure and inter-seizure EEG signal using frequency domain features. A maximum accuracy was achieved by the mean amplitude. The mean amplitude features achieved the lowest accuracy in time domain features. Standard deviation achieved a good accuracy. The SVM classifier with RBF kernel achieved the highest accuracy, i.e. 95% using the mean amplitude.

Tables 7.3 and 7.4 represent the classification accuracy between healthy-seizure EEG signals. Time domain standard deviation and Shannon entropy features achieved 100% accuracy. The frequency domain-based feature standard deviation achieved 100% accuracy.

Table 7.1   Time domain feature-based classification accuracy (%) between seizure (E) and inter-seizure (D) EEG signal

SVM kernel	Max. amp.	Min. amp.	Mean amp.	Std. deviation	Var.	Shannon entropy	Skewness	Kurtosis
RBF	89.0	91.5	50.0	92.5	89.0	93	66.5	62.0
Linear	88.5	90.5	52.5	92	89.5	93.5	73.5	65.5
Polynomial Order 3	87.5	89.0	49.0	89.0	87.0	93.5	44.5	53.0

Table 7.2   Frequency domain feature-based classification accuracy (%) between seizure (E) and inter-seizure (D) EEG signal

SVM kernel	Max. amp.	Min. amp.	Mean amp.	Std. deviation	Var.	Skewness	Kurtosis
RBF	76.5	76.5	95	93	88.5	71.0	64.5
Linear	79.5	76.0	94.5	90.5	88.0	68.0	65.0
Polynomial order 3	79.5	78.0	94	88.5	86.5	66.5	64.5

Tables 7.5 and 7.6 tabulate the accuracy achieved by the SVM model using different kernel functions. The time domain minimum amplitude, standard deviation and Shannon entropy features achieved good accuracy in classifying non-seizure and seizure EEG signals. The frequency domain mean amplitude feature

Table 7.3   Time domain feature-based classification accuracy (%) between seizure (E) and healthy (A) EEG signal

SVM kernel	Max. amp.	Min. amp.	Mean amp.	Std. deviation	Var.	Shannon entropy	Skewness	Kurtosis
RBF	98	98	54.5	100	99.5	100	90	77.5
Linear	97.5	97.5	65.5	100	94	100	88.5	81.5
Polynomial order 3	97.5	97.5	44.5	100	92.5	100	63.0	59.0

Table 7.4   Frequency domain feature-based classification accuracy (%) between seizure (E) and healthy (A) EEG signal

SVM kernel	Max. amp.	Min. amp.	Mean amp.	Std. deviation	Var.	Skewness	Kurtosis
RBF	85.5	78.5	99.5	100	99	61.5	61.0
Linear	84.5	79.5	99	100	95.5	61.0	61.0
Polynomial Order 3	82.0	80.0	99	100	92	61.0	61.0

Table 7.5   Time domain feature-based classification accuracy (%) between seizure (E) and non-seizure (AD) EEG signal

SVM kernel	Max. amp.	Min. amp.	Mean amp.	Std. deviation	Var.	Shannon entropy	Skewness	Kurtosis
RBF	92.7	94.4	65.7	95.4	92.7	96.4	77.4	70.0
Linear	92.7	93.4	66.4	94	92.4	95.7	83.4	77.4
Polynomial Order 3	91.7	93	66.7	93	91.7	95.7	66.7	66.7

Table 7.6   Frequency domain feature-based classification accuracy (%) between seizure (E) and non-seizure (AD) EEG signal

SVM kernel	Max. amp.	Min. amp.	Mean amp.	Std. deviation	Var.	Skewness	Kurtosis
RBF	80.4	80.4	96	95.7	92	66.7	66.7
Linear	80.4	82.4	96	95	92	66.7	66.7
Polynomial order 3	78.7	81.7	95.7	92.4	91.0	66.7	66.7

Table 7.7   Time domain feature-based classification accuracy (%) between seizure (E) and inter-seizure (CD) EEG signal

SVM kernel	Max. amp.	Min. amp.	Mean amp.	Std. deviation	Var.	Shannon entropy	Skewness	Kurtosis
RBF	91.4	92.7	66.4	93.7	92.7	96	72.7	74.0
Linear	91.0	92.4	66.4	94	93.4	95.7	78.4	75.4
Polynomial Order 3	90.34	93	66.7	92.7	91.4	93.7	66.7	66.7

Table 7.8   Frequency domain feature-based classification accuracy (%) between seizure (E) and inter-seizure (CD) EEG signal

SVM kernel	Max. amp.	Min. amp.	Mean amp.	Std. deviation	Var.	Skewness	Kurtosis
RBF	80.4	79.7	96	94.7	92.4	75.0	66.7
Linear	80.0	82.4	95.4	94	92.7	75.4	66.7
Polynomial Order 3	81.0	81.7	94.4	92	91.4	75.4	66.7

achieved 96% accuracy. Among the frequency domain features, skewness and kurtosis achieved the lowest accuracy.

Tables 7.7 and 7.8 represent the classification accuracy achieved by SVM model in classifying seizure and inter-seizure EEG signals. The maximum accuracy was achieved by Shannon entropy extracted directly from the signal. The maximum accuracy achieved was 96% using an SVM with RBF kernel. From the frequency domain features, the mean amplitude achieved the highest accuracy, i.e. 96% using an SVM with RBF kernel. The skewness and kurtosis features achieved the lowest accuracy, i.e. 66.7% using an SVM with polynomial order 3. The maximum accuracy was achieved by an SVM linear kernel using skewness and kurtosis features, i.e. 78.4% and 75.4%, respectively.

7.7   Deep learning techniques in seizure detection

Deep learning techniques are widely in use in processing biomedical signals. In contrast to the machine learning techniques, in a deep learning-based approach, the features were given directly as an input to the model. The mostly used deep learning algorithms are convolutional neural networks, recurrent neural networks and LSTM networks.

7.7.1   Methodology

7.7.1.1   LSTM network

An LSTM [27] is a special type of recurrent neural network capable of learning long-term dependencies. An LSTM model has a cell state and three gates. The cell state in an LSTM helps the information to flow without alternation. Each unit has an input, output and forget gate. The forget gate is used to decide which information is to be added or removed from the cell state. The input gate is used to control the flow of information to the cell gate. The output gate decides which information should be passed onto the next hidden state.

In this chapter, the LSTM model designed using MATLAB® 2021a software. The model had two hidden layers and two drop-out layers. The fifth layer is the fully connected layer followed by a softmax layer and a classification layer. The drop-out layer is used to avoid overfitting the model.

7.8 Results

Table 7.9 gives the accuracy achieved by the LSTM model in classifying healthy, seizure and inter-seizure EEG signals. Healthy-inter-seizure EEG signals were classified with 63.75% accuracy. Healthy-seizure EEG signals were classified with 100% accuracy. The inter-seizure and seizure EEG signals were classified with 94.17% accuracy. The non-seizure and seizure EEG signals were classified with 96.5% accuracy. So, the LSTM model classified the inter-seizure and seizure with good accuracy. This method is useful as this can be used to design a seizure prediction model.

7.9 State-of-the-art comparison of different techniques

In this section, different machine learning and deep learning techniques are compared. Different state-of-the-art methods are listed in Table 7.10. Widely used

Table 7.9 LSTM-based approach for seizure detection (combined time and frequency domain features)

Z-F	Z-S	ZN-S	ZF-S	FN-S
63.75	100	96.5	96.67	94.17

Table 7.10 State-of-the-art method comparison table

Authors	Features	Classifier
Mahmoodian *et al.* [24]	Cross-bispectrum	SVM classifier
Johnson *et al.* [1]	12 cepstral coefficients	SVM classifier
Omidvar *et al.* [2]	Spectral- and entropy-based features	ANN, SVM classifier
Chen *et al.* [7]	DTCWT FFT features	KNN classifier
Ra *et al.* [12]	Permutation entropy	KNN classifier
Akut *et al.* [3]	DWT	CNN classifier
Dash *et al.* [28]	Iterative filtering, power spectral density, fractal dimension	HMM classifier
Dash *et al.* [29]	Wavelet-based features	KNN classifier

classifiers are SVM and KNN classifiers in seizure detection. While considering the deep learning model, CNN model has wide application in seizure detection and prediction. Regarding features, the frequency domain features, wavelet transform and entropy features are widely used in seizure detection.

7.10   Future scope

Different authors have proposed various seizure detection methods using machine learning and deep learning techniques. Different wearable seizure detection instruments were proposed by state-of-the-art methods. In future, these approaches can be evaluated in a clinical set-up and can be validated to be used by the patients and clinicians. The effectiveness of the developed model can be evaluated for various types of seizures. Apart from seizure detection, seizure prediction algorithm can be validated in a controlled environment and can be validated to be used by the patients. The seizure prediction can actually be of immense help for the patients with epilepsy.

References

[1]   Johnson AN, Sow D, Biem A. A discriminative approach to EEG seizure detection. In *AMIA Annual Symposium Proceedings 2011* (Vol. 2011, p. 1309). American Medical Informatics Association.

[2]   Omidvar M, Zahedi A, Bakhshi H. EEG signal processing for epilepsy seizure detection using 5-level Db4 discrete wavelet transform, GA-based feature selection and ANN/SVM classifiers. *Journal of Ambient Intelligence and Humanized Computing*. 2021;12(11):10395–403.

[3]   Akut R. Wavelet based deep learning approach for epilepsy detection. *Health Information Science and Systems*. 2019;7:1–9.

[4]   Hussain SJ. Epileptic seizure detection using wavelets and EMD. In *2018 Fourth International Conference on Biosignals, Images and Instrumentation (ICBSII)* 2018 March 22 (pp. 206–212). IEEE.

[5]   Jana GC, Agrawal A, Pattnaik PK, Sain M. DWT-EMD feature level fusion based approach over multi and single channel EEG signals for seizure detection. *Diagnostics*. 2022;12:324.

[6]   Chen G. Automatic EEG seizure detection using dual-tree complex wavelet-Fourier features. *Expert Systems with Applications*. 2014;41:2391–4.

[7]   Al-Salman W, Li Y, Wen P, Miften FS, Oudah AY, Al Ghayab HR. Extracting epileptic features in EEGs using a dual-tree complex wavelet transform coupled with a classification algorithm. *Brain Research*. 2022; 1779:147777.

[8]   Murugavel AM, Ramakrishnan S. Tree based wavelet transform and DAG SVM for seizure detection. *Signal & Image Processing*. 2012;3:115.

[9]   Daoud H, Bayoumi MA. Efficient epileptic seizure prediction based on deep learning. *IEEE Transactions on Biomedical Circuits and Systems*. 2019; 13:804–13.

[10] Kiral-Kornek I, Roy S, Nurse E, *et al.* Epileptic seizure prediction using big data and deep learning: toward a mobile system. *EBioMedicine.* 2018; 27:103–11.

[11] Jana R, Mukherjee I. Deep learning based efficient epileptic seizure prediction with EEG channel optimization. *Biomedical Signal Processing and Control.* 2021;68:102767.

[12] Ra JS, Li T, Li Y. A novel permutation entropy-based EEG channel selection for improving epileptic seizure prediction. *Sensors.* 2021;21:7972.

[13] Beniczky S, Conradsen I, Henning O, Fabricius M, Wolf P. Automated real-time detection of tonic-clonic seizures using a wearable EMG device. *Neurology.* 2018;90:e428–34.

[14] Vandecasteele K, De Cooman T, Gu Y, *et al.* Automated epileptic seizure detection based on wearable ECG and PPG in a hospital environment. *Sensors.* 2017;17:2338.

[15] Dong C, Chen L, Ye T, *et al.* Home-based detection of epileptic seizures using a bracelet with motor sensors. In *10th International IEEE/EMBS Conference on Neural Engineering, NER 2021* (pp. 854–857). IEEE, 2021.

[16] Harishvijey A, Raja JB. Automated technique for EEG signal processing to detect seizure with optimized variable Gaussian filter and fuzzy RBFELM classifier. *Biomedical Signal Processing and Control.* 2022;74:103450.

[17] Garcés Correa A, Orosco LL, Diez P, Laciar Leber E. Adaptive filtering for epileptic event detection in the EEG. *Journal of Medical and Biological Engineering.* 2019;39:912–8.

[18] Malekzadeh A, Zare A, Yaghoobi M, Kobravi HR, Alizadehsani R. Epileptic seizures detection in EEG signals using fusion handcrafted and deep learning features. *Sensors.* 2021;21:7710.

[19] Shimamoto S, Waldman ZJ, Orosz I, *et al.* Utilization of independent component analysis for accurate pathological ripple detection in intracranial EEG recordings recorded extra-and intra-operatively. *Clinical Neurophysiology.* 2018;129:296–307.

[20] Sharmila A, Geethanjali P. DWT based time domain features on detection of epilepsy seizures from EEG signal. In *Biomedical Signal Processing* 2020 (pp. 181–200). Springer, Singapore.

[21] Shanir PP, Khan YU, Farooq O. Time domain analysis of EEG for automatic seizure detection. *Emerging Trends in Electrical and Electronics Engineering.* 2015.

[22] Haghighat M, Abdel-Mottaleb M, Alhalabi W. Discriminant correlation analysis for feature level fusion with application to multimodal biometrics. In *2016 IEEE International Conference on Acoustics, Speech and Signal Processing (ICASSP)*, 2016 March 20 (pp. 1866–1870), IEEE.

[23] Yavuz E, Kasapbaşı MC, Eyüpoğlu C, Yazıcı R. An epileptic seizure detection system based on cepstral analysis and generalized regression neural network. *Biocybernetics and Biomedical Engineering.* 2018;38:201–16.

[24] Mahmoodian N, Boese A, Friebe M, Haddadnia J. Epileptic seizure detection using cross-bispectrum of electroencephalogram signal. *Seizure.* 2019; 66:4–11.

[25]   Andrzejak RG, Lehnertz K, Mormann F, Rieke C, David P, Elger CE. Indications of nonlinear deterministic and finite-dimensional structures in time series of brain electrical activity: Dependence on recording region and brain state. *Physical Review E.* 2001;64:061907.

[26]   Kolekar MH, Dash DP, Patil PN. Support vector machine based extraction of crime information in human brain using ERP image. *In Proceedings of the International Conference on Computer Vision and Image Processing 2017* (pp. 163–174). Springer, Singapore.

[27]   Dash DP, Kolekar MH, Chakraborty C, Khosravi MR. Review of machine and deep learning techniques in epileptic seizure detection using physiological signals and sentiment analysis. *Transactions on Asian and Low-Resource Language Information Processing,* 2022.

[28]   Dash DP, Kolekar MH, Jha K. Multi-channel EEG based automatic epileptic seizure detection using iterative filtering decomposition and hidden Markov model. *Computers in Biology and Medicine.* 2020;116:103571.

[29]   Dash DP, Kolekar MH, Jha K. Surface EEG based epileptic seizure detection using wavelet based features and dynamic mode decomposition power along with KNN classifier. *Multimedia Tools and Applications.* 2022;81:42057–42077.

Chapter 8

Progress of deep learning in digital pathology detection of chest radiographs

K.A. Saneera Hemantha Kulathilake[1],
A.M. Randitha Ravimal Bandara[2],
Abhishek Shivanand Lachyan[3], Eric Chung[4] and
Khin Wee Lai[5]

Abstract

Chest radiographs are one of the primary diagnostic medical imaging modalities in the present clinical medicine. Compared to other medical imaging techniques, this non-invasive imaging modality is cost-effective. As a result, improving the radiography modality-based computer-aided diagnostic methods is a fruitful approach for obtaining reliable diagnostic results. Also, it facilitates a wider clinical community around the globe, especially in low-income countries. Recently, deep learning (DL) has led to a promising performance in pathology detection in chest radiography used for the diagnosis of cancers, respiratory diseases and some infectious diseases. As a result, various DL applications have been proposed for image enhancement, object detection and segmentation, localization and image generation. Therefore, the prime aim of this chapter is to critically review those recent applications to determine the performance gain, technical challenges and future research trends.

8.1 Introduction

Chest X-ray (CXR) imaging is one of the primary diagnostic medical imaging modalities in clinical medicine today. Low-radiation dose consumption, cost-

[1]Department of Computing, Faculty of Applied Sciences, Rajarata University of Sri Lanka, Mihintale, Sri Lanka
[2]Department of Computer Science, Faculty of Applied Sciences, University of Sri Jayewardenepura, Nugegoda, Sri Lanka
[3]Department of Social and Preventive Medicine, Faculty of Medicine, Universiti Malaya, Kuala Lumpur, Malaysia
[4]Department of Biomedical Imaging, Faculty of Medicine, Universiti Malaya, Kuala Lumpur, Malaysia
[5]Department of Biomedical Engineering, Faculty of Engineering, Universiti Malaya, Kuala Lumpur, Malaysia

effectiveness and reasonable sensitivity to various pathologies are the factors that drive this demand [1]. Generally, CXR images are obtained for screening, diagnosis and management of various disease conditions of the lungs and cardiovascular system. Although CXR images provide a detailed examination of the patient's thorax, image interpretation requires the services of a qualified radiologist.

However, the interpretation of CXR images is challenging even for experienced radiologists. Superimposition of organs along the projection direction, low contrast near the borders of organs and size variation in the shape of organs are the main reasons that increase the potential complexity of CXR interpretation [2]. Additionally, the increased workload and lack of specialist radiologists in the emergency department also stimulate opportunities for misinterpretation [2,3]. Also, it has been revealed that these constraints cause discrepancies in CXR-based diagnostic decisions [4–6]. Thus, implementing computer-aided diagnostic methods to obtain reliable results is the new trend in clinical medicine. Also, it caters to a broader clinical community around the globe, especially in low-income countries.

Among various algorithms, DL has attracted more attention in medical imaging with the rapid development of graphics processing unit (GPU) technology. Also, DL has shown higher performance than traditional machine learning algorithms in detecting various thoracic diseases due to its effective feature extraction and classification ability [7,8]. Moreover, recent studies have proven the efficacy and sensitivity of DL algorithms for clinical validation and real-time use in emergency departments [3]. In addition, the need to propose effective DL-based computer-aided diagnostic methods has increased worldwide since 2019, along with the COVID-19 pandemic [9,10].

Thus, this chapter aims to review DL algorithms proposed since 2019 for thoracic pathology detection using CXR images. The publications were retrieved by querying the Web of Science. Accordingly, the main contribution of this chapter is fourfold. (i) presenting a critical review of existing DL algorithms used for pathology detection in CXR images; (ii) investigating various performance characteristics considered in application design; (iii) presenting limitations of proposed DL applications for pathology detection in CXR images and (iv) summarizing research gaps in CXR-based pathology detection that can address in future studies.

The rest of the chapter is organized as follows. Section 8.2 analyses the DL algorithm for detecting CXR pathology. The third section describes common diseases that have been widely considered in the recent literature. Afterward, the fourth section reviews the performance characteristics considered in application design. Then, the fifth section presents the limitations and future direction of DL-based pathology detection in CXR images. Finally, the chapter ends with the conclusion section.

8.2   Overview of the CXR pathology

This section describes common pathologies reported in the published literature in the post- COVID period. Also, this section highlights how these pathologies are visualized on CXR images and the challenges of detection. Furthermore, graphical illustrations of the described pathologies are shown in Figure 8.1 for further clarification.

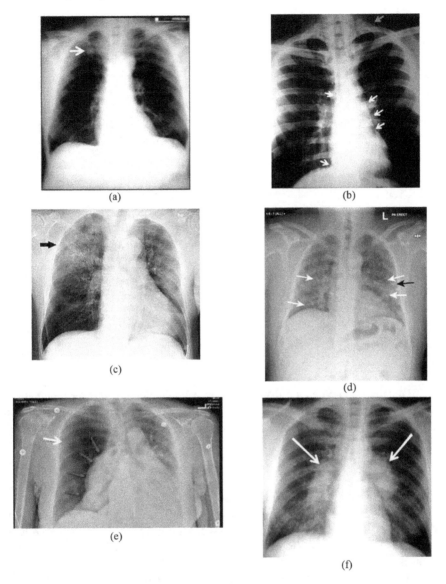

*Figure 8.1   Visualization of pathology on CXR images. (a) Pulmonary nodule
(arrowhead); (b) emphysema (red arrow) and pneumomediastinum
(white arrows) [12], (c) pneumonia; (d) detection of the ground glass
opacity in both mid and lower zones of the lungs of a COVID-19
patient [13]; (e) pneumothorax (white arrow) and right lung collapse
(red arrows) [14]; and (f) pulmonary tuberculosis (white arrows) [15]*

8.2.1   Lung nodule

The lung nodule is considered as another life-threatening condition that can lead to cancer if not detected at an early stage. It has no symptoms. Therefore, lung nodules can only be detected by screening. On CXR images, it is visible as a dense round area compared to normal tissue (Figure 8.1(a)). However, lung nodules of size 5–10 mm are not visible in CXR images. As a result, detecting the tiny lung nodules in CXR images is challenging. In some cases, those small lung nodules can be hidden in the clavicle or strong ribs [11].

8.2.2   Emphysema

Emphysema permanently enlarge and lose elasticity of the alveolar airspaces, the thin-walled air spaces at the ends of the lungs where oxygen and carbon dioxide are exchanged. As a result, individuals with emphysema typically have difficulty with exhaling. Therefore, Emphysema's grouped under the umbrella of chronic obstructive pulmonary disease, along with chronic bronchitis.

On screening CXR, emphysema shows several characteristics compared to a healthy CXR image. Accordingly, it increases the radiolucency of the lung field. Also, the rib spaces and cardiac shadows are visible as wider-spaced and tube-shaped, respectively. Additionally, the diaphragm is visible as a flat dome (Figure 8.1(b)).

8.2.3   Pneumonia

Pneumonia is a common fatal disease among young children and elderly people. It is caused by viral or bacterial infections or fungi that cause lung inflammation. On CXR examination, pneumonia can be detected as white spots or fluid around the lungs (Figure 8.1(c)).

8.2.4   COVID-19

COVID-19 is also an infectious disease caused by the SARS-Co-V-2 virus. COVID-19 became a global pandemic between 2019 and 2022, killing 6.47 million by the end of 2022. It can be diagnosed as a type of pneumonia. Compared to RT-PCR and antigen tests, CXR is cost-effective and one of the best pre-diagnostic medical imaging methods for COVID-19.

On CXR examination, the infected area is usually visible in the periphery (middle and lower regions) of the lungs. It does not represent pleural effusion (fluid in the pleural space), mediastinal lymphadenopathy and pericardial fluid collection. Also, the patient's CXR represents diffuse and bilateral consolidations (fluid-filled spaces) predominantly in the lower regions of the lungs. Also, the periphery of the lungs shows zones of ground-glass opacities (white spots with blood vessels passing through them) (Figure 8.1(d)). However, compared to computed tomography images, the sensitivity of ground glass opacities shown in CXR images is low. Therefore, it has become the main limitation of CXR imaging in the diagnosis of COVID-19.

8.2.5 *Pneumothorax*

Pneumothorax, also known as collapsed lung, is a condition in which air in the lungs leaks into the pleural cavity. This air puts pressure on the lungs and causes the lungs to collapse. The main cause of development of pneumothorax is chest injury and chest trauma. Sudden sharp pain and shortness of breath are the main symptoms of pneumothorax [7]. It is also a life-threatening disease if not detected early. The effect of pneumothorax can be clearly screened on erect chest radiograph. It visualizes the visceral pleural edge as a very thin sharp white line. Also, the edges of the lungs are not visible peripheral to this line. The peripheral space shows up radiolucent in contrast to the adjacent lung (Figure 8.1(e)).

8.2.6 *Pulmonary tuberculosis*

Pulmonary tuberculosis (TB) is a global infection that causes high morbidity and mortality, particularly in developing countries [16]. It forms tubercles in the tissue and can cause tissue death. Mantoux tuberculin skin test or TB blood tests are recommended in clinical practice to diagnose the disease and are expensive medical tests. Therefore, CXR is popular for over a hundred years as one of the cheap and highly sensitive tools for detecting TB. In CXR images, TB indicates as light areas of varying size (Figure 8.1(f)). However, CXR has low specificity for the diagnosis of TB because CXR abnormalities consistent with pulmonary TB are also noticed in several other pulmonary pathologies [17]. Consequently, CXR-based TB diagnosis leads to overdiagnosis and underdiagnosis.

8.3 Functional aspects of DL techniques

8.3.1 *Classification*

Classification is one of the preliminary steps in the analysis of CXR images for diagnosis. The problem of classification of CXR images is typically done in several levels of applications such as identifying anomalies, predicting the predisposition and even a set of potential diagnosis. Some studies have worked even up the extent of predicting the severity in terms of the visual clues found in CXR images [18–22].

Computerized digital Image classification is not a new problem even in the domain of medical imaging, although it has not been widely explored to the level of natural image domain. However, the existing studies prove the potential of utilizing a diverse set of techniques that has been introduced for classifying natural images, to the medical imaging with or without modifications. In addition to this, since CXR images help diagnosing a vast array of diseases from tumours to respiratory diseases at a lower cost it becomes one of the mostly accumulating image types in the medical domain [23–26]. Hence, the advancement of classification techniques for CXR images made it rapidly to the current level.

Recent literature suggests that vast majority of the studies has adapted DL techniques for solving several problems that includes the lack of labelled data in many of the related domains as well as the limitations of the existing DL models.

To learn the patterns well, the data set should include data representing all possible major variations that may contributes to accurate classification in a DL model. As the most DL models combinedly learns both the features and classification together, a good dataset is very critical for its performance. Transfer learning is widely used for adapting an existing trained model for a different domain by using less data. Reference [27] has proposed a method that consists of a several steps including decompose, transfer learning and composing to diagnose COVID-19 from CXR images. The authors have added a class decomposition layer to an existing Convolution Neural Network (CNN)s, that partitions each class in the dataset into several subclasses aiming the improvement of the performance when irregularities presence in the data distribution. The decomposed classes will then get composed back to get the final decision of the class label. The method is named as DeTraC and it has been used with pre-trained AlexNet, VGG19, GoogleNet, ResNet and SqueezNet for evaluation. The results show that DeTraC outperforms the both conventionally fine-tuned and deep-tuned CNNs and has achieved the best performance with VGG19 over several challenging datasets. The authors describe the term 'irregularity' by using an example namely the overlapping classes. Although it is an obvious problem that could occur in any domain, the study does not express any knowledge of the presence of irregularities in the dataset used in any qualitative or quantitative manner.

Reference [19] addresses the problem of lack of data by augmenting underrepresented class through generative modelling technique such that deep convolutional generative adversarial network (DCGAN). The proposed model consists of two neural networks, one for generating fake CXR images and the other for discriminating it to be a real of fake. The network has been trained by inputting a random noise to the generator and showing the output of it with a real image from the training dataset to the discriminator. The performance of the generative adversarial network (GAN) has been measured in terms of FréChet distance of inception. The study concludes that the proposed DCGAN can generate data for augmentation and ultimately improve the existing classification models. The authors further acknowledge that the synthesized images should be further inspect and validated by clinicians probably as a human moderator to the automated discriminator of DCGAN.

Reference [21] proposes another GAN named as random GAN (RANDGAN) to overcome the lack of annotated data in a specific domain by using the concept of one-class classifier. In use of this concept, the training does not require any annotated data from the unknown class (the class of interest) hence can utilize all the other existing labelled data for detecting any anomaly. In this study, the authors specifically have used CXR images with segmented lungs. RANDGAN generator consists of several inception blocks and residual blocks whereas the discriminator consists of two convolutional layers with a single dense layer. It has been evaluated for screening COVID-19 using a semi-supervised procedure, yet the model has been trained only using non-COVID-19 and unknown CXR images comparing with another similar work called as AnoGAN. RANDGAN marks the best performance in terms of area under the ROC curve claiming its significance at fast screening of a pandemic prone disease at its early stages, where not many annotated CXR images present. Authors in [21,28] have revealed that any model performs better with segmented images as the features outside of the area of interest cause many misclassifications. Segmentation also requires human effort as computer-based automatic segmentation may propagate the error further to the classification [21]. Hence, the technique still requires professional intervention for validating the outputs.

As already mentioned, that the segmentation of CXR images can substantially improves the classification performance, as it mitigates the effect of the noise outside the Region of Interest (ROI), many different types of noise even prevail within the ROI, that hinders achieving the required performance [24]. Hence, even though data is available, it will be still challenging to classify if the CXR images are noisy. Studies related to denoising of CXR images mainly focused on preparing the images for human expert inspection instead of improving computerized classification [29–31]. The existence of noise in CXR images is typically handled by making the classification models knowledgeable regarding the existence of different types of noise in images through data augmentation [32,33].

Li *et al.*'s [34] work is notable that has been carried out to cope with the impracticality of using the massive existing datasets for a newly emerged disease like COVID-19. An attention-guided augmentation is proposed in this study to reduce noise and generating meaningful augmented CXR images and used them with a multi-scale attention model to achieve better classification performance.

The usage of natural image classification models' parameters for CXR image classification is a questionable application as it solely based on an assumption that both the domains share the same set of features. Fricks *et al.* [23] have explored this question and revealed that deliberate sequential training yielded substantial improvement over classification accuracy compared to the traditional transfer learning initiated with ImageNet parameters. The study has used only DenseNet121 model with six different training schemes but without any pre-trained parameters to validate the claim and no further exploration has been done, whether any other model can do better with the pre-trained models with fine-tuning.

Li *et al.* [25] proposed a method to cope with the domain discrepancy by introducing a self-supervised plug-and-play feature-standardization-block (FSB) to the deep model. The FSB consists of contrast enhancement, boundary detection and a normalization operation to extract robust feature maps suitable for cross domain applications. The study validated the claim by using VGG, Xception and DenseNet models with FSB to CXR image classification tasks and has achieved at least 2% improvement over the classification accuracy. The study shows that the proposed method does not need images from the target domain to handle the domain discrepancies as the FSB works in self-supervised setup.

Filing the existing gaps in the CXR image classification domain has produced many different methods that have been validated using the existing data. As most of the methods have not been made to any real-world clinical platform, the effective capabilities of the methods are unknown. The work proposed in [35] discusses in detail about the practical limitations of the traditional procedure of making decisions based on CXR images relevant to COVID-19. The limitations include longer time consumption for identifying radiological signatures and the remaining error-prone process affected by riddling with intra-observer variability. [35] further argues that fully automating the end-to-end process of diagnosing CXR images at radiologist-level would be a better solution. Saying that, the authors have extensively explored over around 20 deep neural networks to find the best performing deep models for COVID-19 classification of CXR images and proposed two best models such that the ensemble deep transfer learning CNN model and hybrid LSTMCNN based on the results of experiments performed over four large datasets. The significance of the work is to mimic the challenges in practical usage by evaluating all the deep models with setting up different combination of datasets for training and testing phases. Nevertheless, there is no information regarding the clinical usage of the said methods beside the authors claims of their suitability. Further, the set of assumptions in the study [35] includes that patients have only one disease which may again introduces vulnerabilities in practical situations.

As per the literature most recent works that are related to CXR image classification concentrated on a few problems that include data deficiency and the limitations of the existing DL models. A summary of the research gaps that has been addressed by the recent research works with the proposed methods is shown in Figure 8.2. It shows that the main problems that are trying to solve through the studies mentioned in the chapter are annotated data deficiency, domain discrepancy, noisy image data, noisy annotations and the limitations of the existing DL models.

The studies reported in [19] and [21] address the annotated data deficiency by augmenting the under-represented class through generative modelling and a

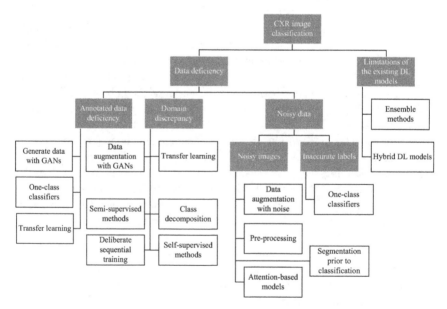

Figure 8.2   Summary of the research gaps that have been addressed by the majority of recent studies, with potential solutions

one-class classification method, respectively. Throughout the self-supervision, class decomposition, deliberate sequential training and data augmentation, [25,27,23,21] address the problem of domain discrepancy. The studies mentioned in [21,28], [32,33] and [35] use segmentation, data augmentation and attention guidance to address the noisy images. The one-class classifier which is proposed in [21] also addresses the problem of noisy labels among the other problems. Lastly, Khanna *et al.* [35] explored the problems of the existing DL methods and their limitations that prevent them from being used in practical situations. Apart from that [23] pointing out the re-usage of the existing DL models for CXR image classification with the pre-trained parameters might not be the optimal setup.

8.3.2   *Enhancement*

Image enhancement is an essential image pre-processing method in medical imaging to detect and localize any abnormalities in the image. Overall, image enhancement improves the visual quality of medical images and minimizes estimation errors in diagnostic procedures. Accordingly, a survey of the literature revealed noise, poor illumination, edge blurring and interference from bony structures as abnormalities in CXR images. Also, recently, a significant DL-based contribution to the suppression of those abnormalities has been suggested [36].

Generally, CXR images are contaminated with Gaussian noise. It occurs during acquisition, storage, transmission and processing of CXR images [37]. Noise in CXR images degrades image quality and makes them diagnostically unstable. This leads to poor diagnosis, treatment and discourages further decision-making in clinical procedures [38]. Recently, DL played an important role in CXR denoising. The availability of optimization algorithms, automatic adjustment of parameters and adaptive implementation are the main reasons for the popularity of DL in CXR denoising [39].

To suppress Gaussian noise and artefacts, Jin *et al.* [40] have proposed a model that combines depth separable convolution, batch normalization and residual learning. The significant design feature of this denoising model was the use of depth-separable convolution. This operation reduces network parameters. Also, the evaluation results of this denoising model have proven its fast training and robustness to minimize different noise levels. Later, Jiang, Zhu [39] proposed a multi-resolution residual CNN model to improve the complex edge structures and textures of CXR images to facilitate the detection of COVID-19 (MPR-CNN). Using multi-resolution learning enables the extraction of more sensitive spatial and semantic information recorded in CXR images. Therefore, the experimental results of this MPR-CNN model have revealed that this model also positively affects CXR image classification. On contrary to the convention real convolution models, Goyal *et al.* [38] proposed a CXR denoising model incorporating the complex-valued operations with the residual learning-based CNN model. The ability to enhance the representational capacity, improve the generalization, enhance the computational power and easy optimization motivates to use complex-valued neural networks than real-valued counterparts [41]. Also, the CXR denoising algorithms proposed during the post-COVID period were further analysed in Table 8.1.

Table 8.1 Comparison of CXR enhancement applications

Type of enhancement	Proposed model	Reference	Qualitative features enhanced	Strength	Limitation(s)
Noise suppression	ResNet	Jin et al. [40]	Preserving the edge details between the ribs much better while denoising.	Preserving the edge details between the ribs much better while denoising.	Texture loss.
		Jiang et al. [39] [MPR-CNN]	Improving sharpness of the tissues.	Better denoising performance in CXR images with different scaling factors, Robust solution for unseen data.	Degraded with artefacts.
	Complex valued CNN	Rawat et al. [41]	Retained the edges, boundaries and other small details in the image with higher quality than the rest.	Efficient than the conventional CNN model.	Poor generalizability. Low performance in feature similarity assessments.
Sharpening the edges	ResNet	Ghosh and Ghosh [44]	The microstructure of the lobar, bronchus and segmented bronchus are visually improved.	The proposed model improves the accuracy of the feature classification. No artefacts.	Not adaptable for the mutations of corona virus.
Suppression of the bony structures	CCN	Chen et al. [51] [Wavelet-CCN]	Bone regions were suppressed.	Wavelet reconstruction avoids the inconsistent background intensity; Provides all levels enriched contextual information.	Some anatomical regions were not improved (e.g., trachea).
		Zarshenas et al. [45]	Suppressed ribs near the lung wall and the clavicles, rib edges, enhanced the visualization of nodules of various sizes and vessels under the clavicles and with overlapping ribs.	Outperform MTANN model [49]. Providing a relatively simple model with fewer parameters and a large receptive field.	Poor hyper parameter optimization.

Convolutional neural filter	Matsubara et al. [52]	Visualize the lung nodules.	does not require the acquisition of a lung field mask or smoothing of the bone-extracted image.	Sub-optimal generated bone-only images are sub-optimal [53]
CNN with complex values.	Rajaraman et al. [53] [CVMIDNet]	Restoring the edges, boundaries and other small details. Sharpening the image.	Signifying the better generalizability and robustness	Low performance in structural similarity index (SSIM) analysis.
GAN	Liang et al. [54]	Bone regions were suppressed.	Introduce minimal motion artefacts. Unpaired training might be more robust to unseen CXRs	Model has trained with unpaired data.
	Eslami et al. [55] [Pix2Pix MTdG]	Bone regions were suppressed.	Facilitates the bone suppression and organ segmentation.	Long training time.
	Zhou et al. [57]	Bone shadows appear dimer and soft tissue texture is better preserved.	Improved the limitations mentioned in Eslami et al. [55]	Limitation on enhancing the lung nodules and lesions from the original CXR.
	Rani et al. [46] [SFRM-GAN]	Preserving the resolution and feature information; Generator is more aware of the spatial information of the image.	Loss function allows to capture high and low-frequency details in an image effectively.	VGG-19 does not reflect the real feature similarity of the medical images.

Apart from noise, poor illumination can cause the loss of many important details in CXR images. In the diagnosis of COVID-19, cases have been reported where medical professionals failed to distinguish corona from conventional pneumonia due to poor illumination of CXR images [41,43]. Also, due to the hardware architecture and the low signal-to-noise ratio (SNR) of the projections, visible edges in CXR images are blurred. The ResNet model proposed in [44] has overcome these limitations. Furthermore, empirical results have proven that CXR images sharpened through this model can improve the binary and multi-class classifications developed for the detection of COVID-19.

Bones such as the ribs and clavicles also make some disturbances to detect lung cancer nodules in CXR images [11]. Especially, the CXR-based computer-aided lung nodule detection applications report false-positive results due to overlap of lung nodules with bony structures [45]. However, the conventional bone suppression methods based on CXR images generally suffer from, blurring, low contrast, high computational cost, lack of retaining lung nodules and the loss of spatial information including lesions [46]. Therefore, DL becomes the state-of-the-art for bone suppression in CXR images and the literature proves that various supervised and unsupervised algorithms have been proposed during the post-COVID period.

The target of the unsupervised DL algorithms is to segment the bone structure and subtract it from the original CXR image. Blind source separation methods [47] or gradient modification [48] are used to extract bony structures from CXRs. However, the retention of bone shadows in the result is the main limitation of unsupervised bone suppression algorithms.

Also, the first supervised learning DL algorithm for bone suppression in CXR images was first proposed by Suzuki *et al.* [49]. This DL model was called massively trained artificial neural networks (MTANNs) and its objective was to find the relationship between CXRs and corresponding Dual-energy (DE) bone images. DE images are mainly used in the supervised DL models to prepare the teacher dataset. To obtain DE images, first, the patient is scanned at two different energy levels at short intervals to capture two radiographs. Then, the intensity difference between the two radiographs is used to identify and delineate bone structures [50]. Figure 8.3 demonstrates the difference between the original CXR and corresponding DE image for further clarifications.

After Suzuki *et al.* [49], several DL applications were developed for bone suppression based on the variants of CNN and GANs. Accordingly, Chen *et al.* [51] proposed a cascaded CNN model in the wavelet domain to suppress skeletal structures (Wavelet-CNN). As a result of using wavelet decomposition, this proposed model was able to use sparsity based multi-resolution analysis. Later, Zarshenas *et al.* [45] attempted to improve the MTANN model for lung nodule delineation through a CNN model coupled with two sub models. The two sub models are called the mixture of orientation-frequency-specific (OFS) specialists and anatomy-specific (AS) specialists. Accordingly, the OFS module assisted in delineating the rib structures in different orientations and the AS modules assisted in the separation of bony structures from soft tissues in different lung segments. Meanwhile, Matsubara *et al.* [52] proposed a CNN-based convolutional neural

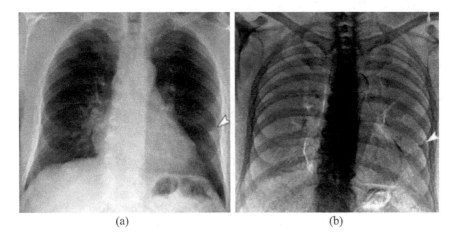

Figure 8.3   Difference between the CXR and DE images: (a) CXR, (b) DE image. Arrowhead points to a lung nodule. Source: Kuhlman, Collins [53].

filter that outputs a value for the bone component of the target pixel by analysing the input pixel values   in the neighbourhood of the target pixel. Although CNN models show high performance in bone suppression, they suffer from bias and variability problems that can adversely affect their interpretation. To overcome these problems, a new model in [53] has been proposed through ensemble learning. Accordingly, several state-of-the-art CNN architectures such as U-Nets and Feature Pyramid Networks were combined to find the best-performing models in this ensemble learning-based bone suppression model.

In parallel to CNN-based models, GAN models were also proposed to suppress bony structures depicted in CXR images. Generally, a GAN model can generate the bony structure of CXR images by learning the mapping between the DE radiograph and the original CXR. However, contrary to the use of paired data, Liang *et al.* [54] have attempted to train a GAN model using an unpaired CXR data set. This study has revealed that the unpaired training can be robust for the unseen CXRs that do not closely match the source distribution, e.g., antero-posterior CXRs unseen during training. In addition, Eslami *et al.* [55] modified the pix2pix model [56] to the image-to-image model (pix2pix MT) for the first time to accommodate the multi-task learning framework for bone suppression and organ segmentation. Accordingly, in contrast to other GAN models, the pix2pix MT generator creates two images to represent the results of bone suppression and organ segmentation. Additionally, to achieve an effective receptive field, the dilated convolution has been used in certain layers of pix2pix MT's generator model. However, Zhou *et al.* [57] have stated that the texture of bone-suppressed images generated by pix2pix MT is blurred due to small receptive fields caused by dilation. Therefore, different from [55], this study proposed gradually increased dilation factors (from 2 to 32) instead of fixed ones to overcome that problem. Also, the down sampling operations of the generative model are removed after dilation convolution compression to avoid the problem of loss of contextual information. Meanwhile, Rani *et al.* [46] have proposed a spatial feature and resolution maximization GAN (SFRM-GAN) using U-Net based generator and minibatch discrimination. This proposed model avoids treating bones as noise components. Consequently, this proposed model overcomes the loss of sharpness in the generated bone suppressed CXR images. Overall, Table 8.1 compares GAN-based bone suppression applications for further clarification.

8.3.3   Segmentation

Recent research of CXR image segmentation mainly focused on two main problems namely anatomical segmentation and separation of abnormal regions from a given organs. Anatomical segmentation of the heart, lungs, clavicles, or ribs, on chest radiographs, is a core part of many computer-aided detection pipelines [1]. Lung segmentation is a challenging task as there is variation in shape, size (due to age), gender and the overlapping of clavicles and rib cage. Many different segmentation methods were developed such as simple rule-based to adapting deformable models, but since the popularity of complex DL architectures, most of the segmentation studies are using them [2].

The usual procedure of segmentation starts with bone suppression and then the organ segmentation is applied separately [58]. [55] suggests that following the different steps in the procedure separately, limits gaining knowledge from the consolidation of parameters that could be utilizing for optimization the process and proposed a multitask organ segmentation and bone suppression method that utilizes an image-to-image network. The study revealed that the adaption to the image-to-image network not only improves the accuracy of segmentation but also the computational efficiency. The authors further explained that the models were trained using the images with 512×512 resolution yet, the same model can be further improved if a higher resolution can be used.

The study proposed in [59] also focuses on segmenting multiple organs such as the lungs, the heart and clavicles all at once by augmenting generic CNN models with image contours. The study augmented UNet, LinkNet and DenseNet with the contour and shows improved performance over non-augmented models in terms of Jaccard overlap coefficient. The poorly visible boundaries seem challenging to use with this system as the contours cannot be detected accurately. Hence, the authors predict that the method can be further improved by imposing additional anatomical constraints on contour detection.

Another notable study focuses on lung area segmentation with accurate organ boundaries based on a self-attention module [60]. The strength of this method relies on the two attention modules namely the channel attention which pays attention on 'what' features give clues on segmentation and spatial attention that pays attention of 'where' to segment. The method outperformed the state-of-the-art methods for majority of the data, but the presence of deformity and cardiac silhouette has exhibited low performance.

Reference [61] proposes a GAN based technique for lung segmentation in CXR images. The generator component of the proposed GAN generates the segmentation mask where the discriminator component attempt to distinguish it between the ground-truth and the generated mask. The study has explored through four different discriminators each with different patch sizes and network architectures. The results revealed that the proposed work with D3 discriminator which consists of the patch size from 16×16 to 70×70 with three batch normalized convolutional hidden layers activated with linear rectified unit. The authors further mention that the proposed method is computationally expensive and method generalization might be required for applying it for images acquired with different X-ray machines.

A-LugSeg is another notable lung segmentation method that utilizes two sub-networks for obtaining an accurate segmented regions through a stepwise refinement method [62]. Most importantly it uses RCNN for a coarse segmentation of the input and combined with an improved closed principal curve method the segmentation is further refined. Moreover, the proposed method even provides a mathematical model for obtaining a smooth contour of the segmentation. It is the first time that this type of guided model has not been investigated for machine learning-based segmentation ever. However, regardless of the good overall performance, the method still poorly performs with the extreme cases such as in the presence of bilateral pulmonary TB like diseases.

As per the literature, the problem of extreme deformations in organs due to various diseases makes the segmentation very challenging [63]. The study proposed in [63] directly addresses this problem through optimizing the base U-Net model with Bayesian optimization. Nevertheless, the method is yet to be generalized as it relies on very small datasets.

Besides the organ segmentation in CXR, many methods are proposed for lung segmentation to determine the ROI for specific abnormalities such as lung nodules, pulmonary TB, cavities, pulmonary opacity and consolidations. Usually, the whole X-ray is used for training purposes, but the presence of unnecessary organs can contribute to noise and false positive [2]. The study in [64] proposes a fully convolutional multi-scale DenseNet with spatial and channel squeezes and excitation modules for automated segmentation and diagnosis of pneumothorax. The method further utilizes a loss function with spatially weighted cross-entropy to obtain a precise boundary for the segmented regions. This retrospective study has utilized around 11 051 frontal-view CXR images to train and test the models and the optimized model has outperformed several state-of-the-art methods. Besides this DenseNet base method, there are several other methods are proposed for the segmentation of pneumothorax such as [65,66]. The study in [65] proposes an ensemble of multiple modified U-Net models whereas [66] proposes a new learning framework named as deep signed distance map (DeepSDM). Both the methods have been validated with external datasets and proved the generalizability of the models.

In summary, regardless of the segmentation of organs or regions of scars and abnormalities, the lack of annotated data seems greatly affect the generalizability and the validity of the methods in practical situations. Nevertheless, the recent methods mainly focus on precise segmentation of the organ regions and boundaries with or without unnecessary structure suppression (such as bones and organs' silhouette) under the presence of deformities.

8.4   Application design considerations

8.4.1   Data preparation

The core of most of the related research work relies on the data that is utilized throughout the studies. Various challenges imposed with the data such as the diversity, meta data, quality and format. Hence, some of the research works has paid a considerable attention on preparing data for designing the research. To compensate for the problem of lacking data and diversity, the usage of hybrid datasets has become a common practice among the related studies. The studies described in [28] and [27] have used several public datasets combined to improve the task accuracy by overcoming the lack of data and diversity. As usual, 30% of data is being used for the testing purpose [27], only a 70% of the data is being contributed to learn the detection. Given the fact, integrating multiple datasets regardless of their origin, source devices and their configurations has contributed to the improvement of the classification accuracy.

The hybrid dataset approach has mostly used in addition to the data augmentation that is a typical phase in the data preparation for any machine learning task. Usual data augmentation techniques used on CXR images are flipping up–down and right–left, random cropping and rotation using random angles [27,39,46,51,53]. However, [19] mentions that the advantages of data augmentation are not guaranteed in the domains like medical imaging, and it may lead to overfitting. The claim can be further supported with the fact that right–left flipping of an asymmetric structure creates a data that would never occur in the dataset, yet augmenting with it forces the model to learn that pattern.

Recent work has adapted generative models for augmenting CXR images from an external domain to the target domain [21,67]. These methods have proved to be well suited when there are less domain specific data available yet many data available from similar domains. However, generated CXR images may suffer from several known issues such as mode collapsed outputs or images with generative artefacts. Hence it is recommended to validate the generated data samples before augmenting the natural dataset.

Also, it has been observed that data sets can sometimes be prepared using simulations and devices. Especially in noise suppression experiments, Gaussian noise is simulated across test data sets to verify performance [39]. However, these simulation methods are sometimes biased and do not emphasize the true statistical noise distribution. In addition, as mentioned in Section 8.3.2, DE radiographs are acquired for training and testing bone suppression models. However, DE imaging has several limitations. Compared to conventional CXR imaging, DE imaging exposes patients to a higher radiation dose. Also, it can only produce the posterior–anterior view. Apart from that, the DE procedure is more expensive compared to CXR imaging because it relies on special hardware. Additionally, DE imaging is degraded with motion artefacts caused by patient movement and breathing [39,40]. Furthermore, several popular public datasets can be found in the applications reviewed in this study. These are listed in Table 8.2 for further information.

Table 8.2 Summary of datasets used in DL-based CXR pathology detection applications

Type	Dataset	Remarks	Applications
Classification	NIH Clinical Center CXR dataset	The dataset contains 112 120 frontal-view CXR images of 30 805 unique patients with cardiothoracic and pulmonary abnormalities.	[22]
	Kermany, Goldbaum [61]	It consists of 5 232 images. Further, it has 2 538, 1 345 and 1 349 images belonging to bacterial pneumonia, viral pneumonia and normal class.	[19]
	COVIDx	Consists of 14 198 images comprised of 573 COVID-19 cases, 5 559 Pneumonia cases and 8 066 normal-case images from multiple public databases.	[21]
	Prashant Patel, CXR (COVID-19 and pneumonia)	Consists of 6 432 total CXR images in which 1 583 of normal cases, 576 of COVID-19 cases and 4 273 of pneumonia cases.	[69]
	Japan Society of Radiological Technology (JSRT) dataset	247 chest radiographs (collected from 13 institutions in Japan and one in the United States). Image resolution is 2 048 × 2 048.	[27]
	Cohen *et al.* COVID-19 image data collection	Contains 105 and 11 samples of COVID-19 and SARS (with 4 248 × 3 480 pixels)	[27]
	UCSD-AI4H/COVID-CT	Total of 746 images with 349 COVID-19 cases and 397 of non-COVID-19 cases	[35]
	COVID-19 ACTION-RADIOLOGY-CXR	Total of 516 images with 278 COVID-19 cases and 238 of non-COVID-19 cases	[35]
	Cohen *et al.* – COVID-19 image data collection [66]	Consists of 258 COVID-19 images.	[34]
	CXR8	A hospital-scale CXR database	[34]
	BIMCV-COVID-19 dataset.	Dataset belongs to the Institute for Diagnostic and Interventional Radiology, Hannover Medical School, Hannover, Germany. It consists of 2 473 CXRs showing COVID-19-like manifestations	[34]
Segmentation	Japan Society of Radiological Technology (JSRT) dataset.	247 chest radiographs (collected from 13 institutions in Japan and one in the United States). Image resolution is 2 048 × 2 048,	[55,59, 61–63]
	'Multi-Atlas labelling beyond the cranial vault'	Contains CT scans and corresponding segmentation labels of 13 abdominal organs of 50 subjects	[55]

(Continues)

Table 8.2 (Continued)

Type	Dataset	Remarks	Applications
	Montgomery dataset	Consists of 138 CXR images with 58% of normal data, 41% of TB cases and 1% of cases with stable scars.	[61–63]
	Shenzhen dataset [67] PTX-498 [63]	Consists of 566 CXR images Includes 498 pneumothorax CXR images from three hospitals. with pixel-level annotations.	[61,62] [66]
	SIIM-ACR (Kaggle)	Data are comprised of images in DICOM format. Annotations are provided in terms of binary masks. Some images contain instances of pneumothorax (collapsed lung).	[65,66]
Enhancement	Japan Society of Radiological Technology (JSRT) dataset.	247 chest radiographs (collected from 13 institutions in Japan and one in the United States). Image resolution is 2 048 × 2 048,	[40,57,55, 52,56]
	NIH CXR dataset	Posterior anterior and anterior posterior radiographs. Also, contains 8 525 normal radiographs and abnormal 17 159 radiographs.	[54]
	Shenzhen TB dataset. et	Data are collected at Shenzhen Hospital, China. It consists of 662 frontal CXR (336 are TB infected and 326 are not TB-infected). Image resolution is 3K×3K pixels.	[72]
	Kermany, Goldbaum [69]	Data are collected at Guangzhou women and children's medical centre, China. It consists of 5 232 Further, it has 2 538, 1 345 and 1 349 images belonging to bacterial pneumonia, viral pneumonia and normal class.	[41]
	COVID-19 Radiography database.	Dataset belongs to Radiological Society of North America. It consists of 1 341, 1 345 and 219 CXR images representing normal CXR, viral pneumonia and COVID-19, respectively.	[39,44]
	BIMCV-COVID-19 dataset	Dataset belongs to the Institute for Diagnostic and Interventional Radiology, Hannover Medical School, Hannover, Germany. It consists of 2 473 CXRs showing COVID-19-like manifestations [22].	[53]
	RSNA CXR dataset	The dataset belongs to the Radiological Society of North America and the Society of Thoracic Radiology. It is an annotated dataset with possible Pneumonia.	[53]

8.4.2   Using transfer learning

In general, the accuracy of the results generated by the DL model is directly proportional to the number of samples in the training data sets. However, the acquisition of large data sets in the medical imaging domain is impractical due to various reasons such as patient privacy and hazards caused by the imaging source [73]. Also, the development of DL-based applications for pathological detection of CXR also suffers from the same data problem. As a solution to this problem, a supervised machine learning method called transfer learning has been used in DL applications.

Transfer learning can apply knowledge learned from a large data set to a small data set to improve the performance of DL models. Therefore, it speeds up training and gives excellent results for a small data set [74]. Generally, the transfer learning method consists of two steps, namely, selecting a pre-trained model and fine-tuning the DL model dataset based on the size of the target dataset and the similarity of the target dataset with the pre-trained model. Accordingly, if the target data set is large and different from the pre-trained model data set, training the entire DL model is necessary. Also, if the target data set is smaller than the pre-trained model data set, it is necessary to train some layers and freeze the other layers of the pre-trained model [75]. Table 8.3 summarizes an overview of commonly used pre-trained models for CXR pathology detection and applications that used knowledge of those models through transfer learning. In all these applications, prior-art models were used as feature extractors.

Table 8.3   Pre-trained models used for CXR-based disease detection applications

Model	Versions	Layers	Parameters (Millions)	Applications
AlexNet [80]		8	62	[81]
VGGNet [82]	VGG-16	16	138	[81,83,75,77,84,85]
	VGG-19	19	144	[81,83,84,85]
Inception (GoogleNet) [87]	Inception V2	20	11.2	[75,79]
	InceptionV3	48	27	[75,77,84,85,79,88,89]
ResNet [90]	ResNet-50	50	25.6	[81,75,84,85,91,92]
	ResNet-101	101	44.7	[75,88]
	ResNet-152	152	60.4	[75]
ResNetV2 [93]	ResNet50 V2	50	26.5	[75]
	ResNet101 V2	191	44.7	[75]
	ResNet152 V2	152	60.7	[75]
DenseNet [94]	DenseNet121	121	8	[75,77,84,88]
	DenseNet169	169	14.31	[75]
	DenseNet201	201	20.2	[75,85]
XCeption [95]		126	22.9	[75,77,79,88,96]
MobileNet [97]		88	4.25	[83,75,85,79,88]
InceptionResNet V2 [98]		572	55.87	[83,75,77,84,85,79]

Table 8.4 Analysis of quantitative measurements used in DL-based CXR pathology detection applications

Type	Reference (R)/non-reference (N)	Measurement	Purpose	Interpretation	Applications
Classification	N	AUC	To summarize the ROC curve for measuring the overall ability of classifying between classes	1.0 (best) 0.0 (worst)	[22,19,35]
		ROC	To see the performance of a classification model at all classification thresholds	Curves that follow from (0,0) through (0,1) to [1] denotes the best classifier. Curves closer to the straight line connecting (0,0) to [1] is a random classifier	[19,21]
		Accuracy	Determine how many times the model was correct in classification overall	100% (best) – 0% (worst)	[19,27,35,34]
		Precision	Determine how good the model is at predicting a specific category	100% (best) – 0% (worst)	[19,69]
		Recall	Determine how many times the model was able to detect a specific category	100% (best) – 0% (worst)	[19,69]
		False positive rate	To see how often the model wrongfully detects a class	0.0 (best) –1.0 (worst)	[19]
		True positive rate/sensitivity	To see how well the model detects the true cases	1.0 (best) –0.0 (worst)	[19,27,34]
		F1 score	To see the trade-off between the precision and recall	1.0 (best) –0.0 (worst)	[69,35,34]
Segmentation	R	SSIM	Measure similarity	1 (structurally similar), 0 (no structural similarity)	[55]
		Root mean squared error (RMSE)	Measures the difference between predicted and actual values	Lower means less different and higher means extremely different	[55]

		Metric	Description	Range	References
Enhancement	R	Jaccard overlap coefficient/intersection over union (IOU)	To measure the overlap between two sets. In segmentation it denotes how well the segments overlaps with the ground truth.	0 (no overlap) – 1 (complete overlap)	[59,61,62]
		Dice score	To measure overlap between two sets.	0 (no overlap) – 1 (complete overlap)	[61–66]
		Mean pixel-wise accuracy (MPA)	To measure the pixels-wise segmentation accuracy		[64]
		Mean absolute error (MAE)/root mean absolute error (RMAE)/Mean squared error (MSE)/Root mean squared error (RMSE)/Normalized mean squared error (NMSE)	Determine the error between the predicted and ground truth images.	0 (best) – 1 (worst)	[51,44,40,55,46]
		Peak signal-to-noise ratio (PSNR)	Computes the ratio between the peak power of the signal and the power of the contaminating noise that affects the fidelity of its representation.	The higher the value, the better.	[51,45,40,54,57, 52,41,39,53,46]
		SSIM	To determine the structure similarity between the predicted image and ground truth image.	0 (worst) – 1 (best)	[51,45,40,54,57, 55,52,41,39, 53, 46,44]
		Bone suppression rate (BSR)	To compute the BSR	100% (best) – 0% (worst)	[51,52]
	N	Entropy	Compute the information retention capability.	0 (low level disorder) – 1 (high level disorder)	[46]
		Blind Referenceless Image Spatial Quality Evaluator (BRISQUE) Score	It is a measure of distortions in an image from its natural appearance.	The lower the value, better perceptual quality.	[46]
		Universal quality index (UQI)	Measures the image quality with respect to the correlation loss, brightness distortion and contrast distortion	1 (best) – (-1) worst	[44]

Typically, the pre-trained models listed in Table 8.3 are trained based on the ImageNet feature space consisting of natural images. Therefore, it is revealed that these pre-trained models fail to achieve the best performance in the CXR domain. To overcome that performance bottleneck, problem-based transfer learning techniques [76] and pre-trained models combining modality-specific features [77] have been published. However, in CXR pathology detection, applying specific modifications to the pre-trained model, such as architectural adjustments and parameter tuning [78], has been suggested. In this way, only specific knowledge obtained from previous work is retained, and new trainable parameters are fed into the modified network [79].

8.4.3   Measurements

Choosing the right measurement is imperative to determine the gain of the proposed model. Accordingly, the literature survey emphasizes the various measurements used to quantitatively assess the target characteristics of outcomes. Some of them are non-reference measurements and others are reference measurements. Table 8.4 lists the measurements used in DL-based CXR pathology detection applications for further clarification.

8.4.4   Performance improvement techniques

8.4.4.1   Residual learning

In general, adding depth to the CNN model increases the performance of the DL model. However, increasing the depth may cause the vanishing gradient problem and adversely affect model training. To overcome this problem, residual learning [90] has been applied, especially for modelling in CXR enhancement and segmentation applications [40,44]. Figure 8.4 illustrates the visual comparison of the

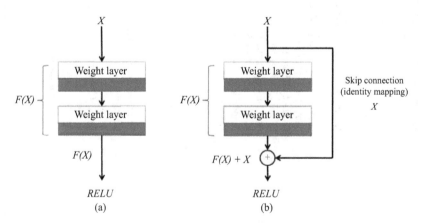

Figure 8.4   Visual comparison of conventional CNN model and residual learning framework: (a) conventional CNN framework and (b) residual learning framework

residual learning framework and the traditional CNN model. Compared to conventional CNN model, residual learning consists of a skip connection. It performs the identity mapping when the derivatives of the backpropagation algorithm updated to 0 during training. Mathematically, it can be expressed as changing the optimization target from $R(X) = F(X) + X$ to $R(X) - X$. In this representation, X, F (X) and $R(H)$ represent the original CXR image, mapping function and the resulting image, respectively. As a result of performing the identity mapping by residual learning at gradient vanishing time, the model can continue learning without interruption [40].

8.4.4.2   Convolution operations

In general, the basic mathematical operation of a typical computer vision system is based on convolution operations. Recently, various types of convolution operations have been introduced to increase the performance of DL models. Among them, depth-wise separable convolution (DSC) and dilation convolution are leading operations to improve the performance of DL modes, which are widely used in CXR enhancement applications.

One factor that affects the performance of a DL model is the number of learnable parameters. However, if the learnable parameters are less, the training time is faster. To achieve this objective, DSC is especially used in CXR enhancement applications [40]. Figure 8.5 shows how DSC reduces the number of learnable parameters in contrast to the traditional convolution operation. DSC decomposes the convolution operation into two steps namely depth-wise convolution and point-wise convolution. As shown in Figure 8.5, in depth-wise convolution, the convolution operation is applied to each channel of the same image. The number of output feature maps after depth-wise convolution is equal to the channel number of the previous layer. Since the convolution operation is performed independently on each channel of the input layer, depth-wise convolution fails to extract feature information from different channels at the same spatial location. To overcome this limitation, point-wise convolution is then applied to combine existing feature maps to generate new feature maps. Accordingly, as shown in Figure 8.5(b), DSC can greatly reduce the number of parameters that can be learned. Therefore, it can shorten the training time, accelerate the network convergence and improve the accuracy of the results [95].

Dilation convolution is a technique used in CXR enhancement models to improve the performance of the results [55,57]. In this technique, the convolution kernel is expanded by inserting holes between its successive elements. As a result, the dilation operation can cover a large area of the CXR image that needs to be processed. In DL models, the amount of dilation is controlled by a parameter called the dilation factor. Also, changing the dilation factor expand the effective receptive filed of the DL model. As a result, it allows to preserve more spatial information in the CXR image to be processed.

8.4.4.3   Objective function

The objective function of a DL model evaluates how well the data can be learned from a specific DL model according to the target. Therefore, some CXR pathology

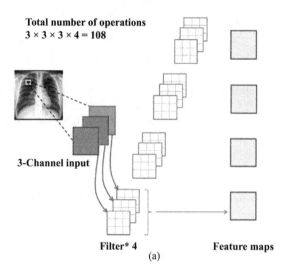

Total number of operations
$3 \times 3 \times 3 \times 4 = 108$

3-Channel input

Filter* 4   Feature maps

(a)

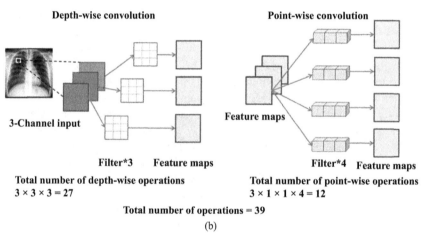

Depth-wise convolution   Point-wise convolution

3-Channel input

Feature maps

Filter*3   Feature maps   Filter*4   Feature maps

Total number of depth-wise operations   Total number of point-wise operations
$3 \times 3 \times 3 = 27$ $3 \times 1 \times 1 \times 4 = 12$

Total number of operations = 39

(b)

Figure 8.5   Total number of operations in convolution operations: (a) traditional
convolution operation and (b) DSC operations

detection applications, e.g., classifiers consist of error estimates based on the MSE as the objective function [41,45,52]. Although MSE is the most used objective function in many DL applications, it results in regression-mean error, especially in object detection and enhancement applications [51]. As a result, the results are degraded by texture loss, smoothing and false lesions artefact. These problems lead to misdiagnosis of pathology and over- or under-estimation in computer-aided diagnosis. Therefore, to avoid the problem of over smoothing, some applications have introduced the MAE as the ideal objective function for the proposed DL models [51].

However, most CXR-based segmentation and enhancement applications consist of composite objective functions constructed by combining different aspects to be learned from images. In those applications, MSE or MAE is used as the primary objective function. Besides that, objective functions especially in some CXR enhancement applications combine the VGG-16 pre-trained network to determine the perceptual loss between the enhanced and original CXR images [46]. Also, some CXR enhancement applications have used gradient loss and structural similarity [39,53] loss to learn the model effect for sharpening [46] and contextual similarity, respectively.

Recent contributions proposed to enhance CXR have uncovered GAN for the DL models [54,55,57]. These GAN-based applications mainly use adversarial loss as the objective function to perform the min–max game between generative and discriminative models. Furthermore, some of those applications have been proposed by integrating several other functional aspects into adversarial learning, such as noise reduction and perceptual similarity loss. Overall, proposing an objective function for the DL model is considered a significant contribution of the study, which is formulated by a thorough empirical analysis.

8.5 Limitations and future directions

8.5.1 Limitations

Although the rate of accumulation of CXR images all over the world is very high compared to the other domains, the effort of making them available to the research community is still lag. Ethical issues, the labour effort required to annotate and organize the data, and the interdisciplinary nature of data processing make this an inevitable challenge. Also, the less amount of available data for a certain domain of disease, lack of data with ground truths, annotations, or labels and lack of diversity in data further leverage the limitations for developing automated diagnosis applications.

Unlike natural images, the quality of CXR images is greatly compromised by noise. This problem is largely due to limits on the dose of X-rays used in imaging, which have been enforced to reduce the potential health hazards of human exposure to radiation. Therefore, noisy output from sensors is inevitable with current sensor technology and DL models should solve this problem on their own.

Moreover, the quality of the data can express how well it contributes to the diagnosis. There are many other factors, including the skill and experience of the radiologists/technicians, the capability of the imaging equipment, the calibration of the equipment and the practical limitations of exposing the subject to optimal placement in the imaging frame [35]. As identifying the suitability of a CXR image for a particular diagnosis requires expert-level domain knowledge with experience, this is a very difficult challenge for most automated classification systems.

Natural images typically consist of more complex and diverse sets of visual features yet do not require precise attention over all these features to do the different levels of classification and detection. However, CXR images from a particular domain should consist of a less diverse set of visual features yet need precise attention over the features to do the classification and detection. Studies [18,19] have achieved good performance using existing DL models. Therefore, it can be confirmed that there is a large overlap of significant visual features in classifying natural images and medical images. However, [21,25,27] showed that the existing models trained on natural images are not entirely suitable for CXR image classification.

Besides, there are many extensive efforts for new methods to detect pathology in CXR images, but most of them have not reached the practical world. Most of the contributions reviewed are validated using private or public datasets and have never undergone clinical validation. Therefore, there is a potential for data sets to be biased or adjusted with many assumptions that are not valid for all situations in the practical world.

8.5.2   Future directions

The COVID-19 pandemic that has been outbroken in the last three years seems to have motivated researchers to explore computer-aided pathology detection in CXR images, even by addressing sub-problems such as lack of data, lack of annotation data and domain switching. However, it is difficult to find solutions that incorporate different pathology detection requirements i.e., classification, localization and severity together. Addressing individual problems in different works has obviously provided more room for innovation, but has hindered the production of practical, automated solutions.

In addition, the lack of a completed overall CXR image classification is further apparent as many proposed methods have not been subjected to clinical validation. It would be better if the works could be validated at least as modules for developing CXR image classification frameworks.

Reframing existing works can lead to finding new areas to explore and ultimately reaching solutions. Tasks such as CXR image denoising are traditionally aimed at improving image quality to help human experts identify relevant radiological markers and come to a correct conclusion. However, how artificially denoised images can improve or degrade computer-aided classification has not been well explored.

Finally, there are many individual works that have independently improved the diagnosis of various diseases from CXR images. It is impractical to use multiple modalities to build CXR image-based solutions for disease diagnosis everywhere. It is an open area for integration or ensembles of best methods to form a single ubiquitous solution [75].

8.6   Conclusions

The improvement of computer-aided diagnosis based on CXR image is a significant contribution as it is one of the primary non-invasive and cost-effective diagnostic methods in clinical departments worldwide. Generally, CXR images are examined to diagnose various thoracic diseases and along with the COVID-19 pandemic, the demand for CXR has grown rapidly in clinical medicine. Also, due to new technological innovations, the need to develop computer-aided diagnostic methods using DL during CXR examination has become critical. Consequently, many DL-based CXR pathology detection algorithms have been proposed. Accordingly, the prime aim of this chapter is to critically review those recent applications published in the post-COVID period regarding key tasks such as detection, segmentation and optimization. Also, this chapter analysed the various factors considered to increase the performance of the proposed CXR-based DL models. Last but not the least, this chapter describes the limitations of the domain and future research directions that facilitate potential researchers to conduct new experiments as a new contribution to the industry.

References

[1] Calli E., Sogancioglu E., van Ginneken B, van Leeuwen K.G., Murphy K. 'Deep learning for chest X-ray analysis: A survey'. *Medical Image Analysis*. 2021;72(29):102125.

[2] Agrawal T., Choudhary P. 'Segmentation and classification on chest radiography: A systematic survey'. *The Visual Computer*. 2023:39:875–913.

[3] Hwang E.J., Nam J.G, Lim W.H., *et al.* 'Deep learning for chest radiograph diagnosis in the emergency department'. *Radiology*. 2019;293(3):573–80.

[4] Petinaux B., Bhat R., Boniface K., Aristizabal J. 'Accuracy of radiographic readings in the emergency department'. *The American Journal of Emergency Medicine*. 2011;29(1):18–25.

[5] Al Aseri Z. 'Accuracy of chest radiograph interpretation by emergency physicians'. *Emergency Radiology*. 2009;16(2):111–4.

[6] Eng J., Mysko W.K., Weller G.E., *et al.* 'Interpretation of emergency department radiographs: A comparison of emergency medicine physicians with radiologists, residents with faculty, and film with digital display'. *American Journal of Roentgenology*. 2000;175(5):1233–8.

[7] Iqbal T., Shaukat A., Akram M.U., Mustansar Z., Khan A. 'Automatic diagnosis of pneumothorax from chest radiographs: A systematic literature review'. *IEEE Access*. 2021;9:145817–39.

[8] Anis S., Lai K.W., Chuah J.H., *et al.* 'An overview of deep learning approaches in chest radiograph'. *IEEE Access*. 2020;8:182347–54.

[9] Heidari A., Navimipour N.J., Unal M., Toumaj S. 'The COVID-19 epidemic analysis and diagnosis using deep learning: A systematic literature review and future directions'. *Computers in Biology and Medicine*. 2022;141:24.

[10] Serena Low W.C., Chuah J.H., Tee C.A.T., *et al.* 'An overview of deep learning techniques on chest X-ray and CT scan identification of COVID-19'. *Computational and Mathematical Methods in Medicine*. 2021;21:1–17.

[11]   Shah P.K., Austin J.H., White C.S., *et al.* 'Missed non-small cell lung can-
       cer: radiographic findings of potentially resectable lesions evident only in
       retrospect'. *Radiology.* 2003;226(1):235–41.
[12]   Covantev S., Mazuruc N., Uzdenov R., Corlateanu A. 'Spontaneous pneu-
       momediastinum – a rare asthma complication'. *Folia Medica (Plovdiv).*
       2019;61(3):472–7.
[13]   Cleverley J., Piper J., Jones M.M. 'The role of chest radiography in con-
       firming covid-19 pneumonia'. *The British Medical Journal.* 2020;370:
       m2426.
[14]   Taha A., Hazam R., Tseng J., Nahapetyan L., Alzeerah M., Islam A.
       'Bubbles in the box: recurrent pneumothorax from bronchopleural fistula in
       rheumatoid arthritis'. *Journal of Investigative Medicine High Impact Case
       Reports.* 2019;7:2324709619860555.
[15]   Ubaidi B., Ubaidi B. 'The radiological diagnosis of pulmonary tuberculosis
       (TB) in primary care'. *Journal of Family Medicine and Disease Prevention.*
       2018;4:073.
[16]   Piccazzo R., Paparo F., Garlaschi G. 'Diagnostic accuracy of chest radiography
       for the diagnosis of tuberculosis (TB) and its role in the detection of latent TB
       infection: A systematic review'. *The Journal of Rheumatology.* 2014;41:32–40.
[17]   Organization W.H. *'Chest radiography in tuberculosis detection: summary
       of current WHO recommendations and guidance on programmatic approa-
       ches'.* World Health Organization; 2016. Report No.: 9241511508.
[18]   Jain R., Gupta M., Taneja S., Hemanth D.J. 'Deep learning based detection
       and analysis of COVID-19 on chest X-ray images'. *Applied Intelligence.*
       2021;51(3):1690–700.
[19]   Kora Venu S., Ravula S. 'Evaluation of deep convolutional generative
       adversarial networks for data augmentation of chest X-ray images'. *Future
       Internet.* 2020;13(1):8.
[20]   Madani A., Moradi M., Karargyris A., Syeda-Mahmood T., (eds.). 'Semi-
       supervised learning with generative adversarial networks for chest X-ray
       classification with ability of data domain adaptation'. *2018 IEEE 15th
       International Symposium on Biomedical Imaging (ISBI 2018) 2018*:
       Washington, DC, USA. IEEE; 2018.
[21]   Motamed S., Rogalla P., Khalvati F. 'RANDGAN: Randomized generative
       adversarial network for detection of COVID-19 in chest X-ray'. *Scientific
       Reports.* 2021;11(1):1–10.
[22]   Tang Y-X., Tang Y-B., Han M., Xiao J., Summers R.M., (eds.). 'Abnormal
       chest X-ray identification with generative adversarial one-class classifier'.
       *2019 IEEE 16th International Symposium on Biomedical Imaging (ISBI
       2019)*; Venice, Italy, April 8–11 2019. IEEE; 2019.
[23]   Fricks R.B., Ria F., Chalian H., *et al.* 'Deep learning classification of
       COVID-19 in chest radiographs: Performance and influence of supplemental
       training'. *Journal of Medical Imaging.* 2021;8(6):064501.
[24]   Jain P.K., Sharma N., Kalra M.K., Viskovic K., Saba L., Suri J.S. 'Four
       types of multiclass frameworks for pneumonia classification and its

validation in X-ray scans using seven types of deep learning artificial intelligence models'. *Diagnostics.* 2022;12(3):652.

[25] Li X., Shen L., Lai Z., *et al.* 'A self-supervised feature-standardization-block for cross-domain lung disease classification'. *Methods.* 2022;202:70–77.

[26] Sundaram S.G., Aloyuni S.A., Alharbi R.A., Alqahtani T., Sikkandar Y., Subbiah C. 'Deep transfer learning based unified framework for COVID-19 classification and infection detection from chest X-ray images'. *Arabian Journal for Science and Engineering.* 2022;47(2):1675–92.

[27] Abbas A., Abdelsamea M.M., Gaber M.M. 'Classification of COVID-19 in chest X-ray images using DeTraC deep convolutional neural network'. *Applied Intelligence.* 2021;51(2):854–64.

[28] Rahman T., Khandakar A., Kadir M.A., *et al.* 'Reliable tuberculosis detection using chest X-ray with deep learning, segmentation and visualization'. *IEEE Access.* 2020;8:191586–601.

[29] Kulathilake K.A.S.H., Abdullah N.A., Lachyan A.S., Bandara A.M.R.R., Patel D.D., Lai K.W., (eds.). 'Restoring lesions in low-dose computed tomography images of COVID-19 using deep learning'. *Kuala Lumpur International Conference on Biomedical Engineering*; Kuala Lumpur, Malaysia, 2021: Berlin: Springer; 2022. pp. 405–413.

[30] Kulathilake K.A.S.H., Abdullah N.A., Sabri A.Q.M., Bandara A.M.R.R., Lai K.W. 'A review on self-adaptation approaches and techniques in medical image denoising algorithms'. *Multimedia Tools and Applications.* 2022:1–36.

[31] Kulathilake K.A.S.H., Abdullah N.A., Bandara A.M.R.R., Lai K.W. 'InNetGAN: Inception network-based generative adversarial network for denoising low-dose computed tomography'. *Journal of Healthcare Engineering.* 2021.

[32] Akbarimajd A., Hoertel N., Hussain M.A., *et al.* 'Learning-to-augment incorporated noise-robust deep CNN for detection of COVID-19 in noisy X-ray images'. *Journal of Computational Science.* 2022;63:101763.

[33] Momeny M., Neshat A.A., Hussain M.A., *et al.* 'Learning-to-augment strategy using noisy and denoised data: Improving generalizability of deep CNN for the detection of COVID-19 in X-ray images'. *Computers in Biology and Medicine.* 2021;136:104704.

[34] Li J., Wang Y., Wang S., *et al.* 'Multiscale attention guided network for COVID-19 diagnosis using chest X-ray images'. *IEEE Journal of Biomedical and Health Informatics.* 2021;25(5):1336–46.

[35] Khanna M., Agarwal A., Singh L.K., Thawkar S., Khanna A., Gupta D. 'Radiologist-level two novel and robust automated computer-aided prediction models for early detection of COVID-19 infection from chest X-ray images'. *Arabian Journal for Science and Engineering.* 2021:1–33.

[36] Shazia A., Xuan T.Z., Chuah J.H., Usman J., Qian P., Lai K.W. 'A comparative study of multiple neural network for detection of COVID-19 on chest X-ray'. *EURASIP Journal on Advances in Signal Processing.* 2021;2021(1):1–16.

[37] Turajlić, E., Karahodzic, V. (eds.). 'An adaptive scheme for X-ray medical image denoising using artificial neural networks and additive white Gaussian

noise level estimation in SVD domain'. *CMBEBIH 2017: Proceedings of the International Conference on Medical and Biological Engineering*; Singapore: Springer; 2017. pp. 36–40.

[38]   Goyal B., Agrawal S., Sohi B. 'Noise issues prevailing in various types of medical images'. *Biomedical & Pharmacology Journal*. 2018;11(3):1227.

[39]   Jiang X.B., Zhu Y., Zheng B.B., Yang D.W. 'Images denoising for COVID-19 chest X-ray based on multi-resolution parallel residual CNN'. *Machine Vision and Applications*. 2021;32(4):15.

[40]   Jin Y., Jiang X.B., Wei Z.K., Li Y. 'Chest X-ray image denoising method based on deep convolution neural network'. *IET Image Processing*. 2019;13 (11):1970–8.

[41]   Rawat S. Rana K.P.S., Kumar V. 'A novel complex-valued convolutional neural network for medical image denoising'. *Biomedical Signal Processing and Control*. 2021;69:102859.

[42]   Ghosh S.K., Ghosh A. 'ENResNet: A novel residual neural network for chest X-ray enhancement based COVID-19 detection'. *Biomed Signal Processing and Control*. 2022;72:14.

[43]   Chen Y.Y., Gou X.F., Feng X.X., *et al.* 'Bone suppression of chest radiographs with cascaded convolutional networks in wavelet domain'. *IEEE Access*. 2019;7:8346–57.

[44]   Zarshenas A., Liu J.C., Forti P., Suzuki K. 'Separation of bones from soft tissue in chest radiographs: Anatomy-specific orientation-frequency-specific deep neural network convolution'. *Medical Physics*. 2019;46(5):2232–42.

[45]   Suzuki K., Abe H., MacMahon H., Doi K. 'Image-processing technique for suppressing ribs in chest radiographs by means of massive training artificial neural network (MTANN)'. *IEEE Transactions on Medical Imaging*. 2006;25(4):406–16.

[46]   Matsubara N., Teramoto A., Saito K., Fujita H. 'Bone suppression for chest X-ray image using a convolutional neural filter'. *Physical and Engineering Sciences in Medicine*. 2020;43(1):97–108.

[47]   Rajaraman S., Cohen G., Spear L., Folio L., Antani S. 'DeBoNet: A deep bone suppression model ensemble to improve disease detection in chest radiographs'. *PLoS One*. 2022;17(3):22.

[48]   Liang J., Tang Y.X., Tang Y.B., Xiao J., Summers R.M., (eds.). 'Bone suppression on chest radiographs with adversarial learning'. *Conference on Medical Imaging – Computer-Aided Diagnosis*; 2020 February 16–19; Houston, TX. BELLINGHAM: Spie-Int Soc Optical Engineering; 2020.

[49]   Eslami M., Tabarestani S., Albarqouni S., Adeli E., Navab N., Adjouadi M. 'Image-to-Images translation for multi-task organ segmentation and bone suppression in chest X-ray radiography'. *IEEE Transactions on Medical Imaging*. 2020;39(7):2553–65.

[50]   Zhou Z.Z., Zhou L.P., Shen K.K. 'Dilated conditional GAN for bone suppression in chest radiographs with enforced semantic features'. *Medical Physics*. 2020;47(12):6207–15.

[51]   Rani G., Misra A., Dhaka V.S., Zumpano E., Vocaturo E. 'Spatial feature and resolution maximization GAN for bone suppression in chest radiographs'. *Computer Methods and Programs in Biomedicine*. 2022;224: 107024.

[52]   Chowdhury M.E.H., Rahman T., Khandakar A., *et al.* 'Can AI help in screening viral and COVID-19 pneumonia?'. *IEEE Access*. 2020;8:132665–76.

[53]   Rasheed T, Ahmed B, Khan MAU, Bettayeb M, Sungyoung L, Tae-Seong K, (eds.). 'Rib suppression in frontal chest radiographs: a blind source separation approach'. *2007 9th International Symposium on Signal Processing and Its Applications*; 2007 12–15 February 2007.

[54]   Simkó G., Orbán G., Máday P., Horváth G., (eds.). 'Elimination of clavicle shadows to help automatic lung nodule detection on chest radiographs'. *4th European Conference of the International Federation for Medical and Biological Engineering; 2009*. Berlin: Springer; 2009.

[55]   Kuhlman J.E., Collins J., Brooks G.N., Yandow D.R., Broderick L.S. 'Dual-energy subtraction chest radiography: What to look for beyond calcified nodules'. *RadioGraphics*. 2006;26(1):79–92.

[56]   Isola P., Zhu J-Y., Zhou T., Efros A.A., (eds.). 'Image-to-image translation with conditional adversarial networks'. *Proceedings of the IEEE Conference on Computer Vision and Pattern Recognition*; 2017. pp. 1125–1134

[57]   Faisal A., Khalil A., Chai H.Y., Lai K.W. 'X-ray carpal bone segmentation and area measurement'. *Multimedia Tools and Applications*. 2022;81: 37321–37332.

[58]   Kholiavchenko M., Sirazitdinov I., Kubrak K., *et al.* 'Contour-aware multi-label chest X-ray organ segmentation'. *International Journal of Computer Assisted Radiology and Surgery*. 2020;15(3):425–36.

[59]   Kim M., Lee B.D. 'Automatic lung segmentation on chest X-rays using self-attention deep neural network'. *Sensors*. 2021;21(2):12.

[60]   Munawar F., Azmat S., Iqbal T., Gronlund C., Ali H. 'Segmentation of lungs in chest X-ray image using generative adversarial networks'. *IEEE Access*. 2020;8:153535–45.

[61]   Peng T., Gu Y.D., Ye Z.Y., Cheng X.X., Wang J. 'A-LugSeg: Automatic and explainability-guided multi-site lung detection in chest X-ray images'. *Expert Systems with Applications*. 2022;198:116873.

[62]   Nishio M., Fujimoto K., Togashi K. 'Lung segmentation on chest X-ray images in patients with severe abnormal findings using deep learning'. *International Journal of Imaging Systems and Technology*. 2021;31 (2):1002–8.

[63]   Wang Q.F., Liu Q.Y., Luo G.T., *et al.* 'Automated segmentation and diagnosis of pneumothorax on chest X-rays with fully convolutional multi-scale ScSE-DenseNet: A retrospective study'. *BMC Medical Informatics and Decision Making*. 2020;20:317.

[64]   Wang X.Y., Yang S., Lan J., *et al.* 'Automatic segmentation of Pneumothorax in chest radiographs based on a two-stage deep learning method'. *IEEE Transactions on Cognitive and Developmental Systems*. 2022;14(1):205–18.

[65] Wang Y.P., Wang K., Peng X.Q., *et al.* 'DeepSDM: Boundary-aware pneumothorax segmentation in chest X-ray images'. *Neurocomputing.* 2021;454:201–11.

[66] Chartsias A., Joyce T., Dharmakumar R., Tsaftaris S.A., (eds.). 'Adversarial image synthesis for unpaired multi-modal cardiac data'. *Simulation and Synthesis in Medical Imaging: Second International Workshop, SASHIMI 2017,* Held in Conjunction with MICCAI 2017, Québec City, QC, Canada, September 10, 2017, Proceedings 2; 2017: Berlin: Springer.

[67] Jain R., Gupta M., Taneja S., Hemanth D.J. 'Deep learning based detection and analysis of COVID-19 on chest X-ray images'. *Applied Intelligence.* 2021;51(3):1690–700.

[68] Cohen J.P., Morrison P., Dao L., Roth K., Duong T.Q., Ghassemi M. 'Covid-19 image data collection: Prospective predictions are the future'. *Journal of Machine Learning for Biomedical Imaging.* 2020;2:128–166.

[69] Jaeger S., Karargyris A., Candemir S., *et al.* 'Automatic tuberculosis screening using chest radiographs'. *IEEE Transactions on Medical Imaging.* 2013;33(2):233–45.

[70] Munadi K., Muchtar K., Maulina N., Pradhan B. 'Image enhancement for tuberculosis detection using deep learning'. *IEEE Access.* 2020;8:217897–907.

[71] Kermany D.S., Goldbaum M., Cai W., *et al.* 'Identifying medical diagnoses and treatable diseases by image-based deep learning'. *Cell.* 2018;172 (5):1122–31.

[72] Liang G.B., Zheng L.X. 'A transfer learning method with deep residual network for pediatric pneumonia diagnosis'. *Computer Methods and Programs in Biomedicine.* 2020;187:104964.

[73] Pan S.J., Yang Q. 'A survey on transfer learning'. *IEEE Transactions on Knowledge and Data Engineering.* 2010;22(10):1345–59.

[74] Rahaman M.M., Li C., Yao Y.D., *et al.* 'Identification of COVID-19 samples from chest X-ray images using deep learning: A comparison of transfer learning approaches'. *Journal of X-Ray Science and Technology.* 2020;28 (5):821–39.

[75] Krizhevsky A., Sutskever I., Hinton G.E. 'Imagenet classification with deep convolutional neural networks'. *Communications of the ACM.* 2017;60(6):84–90.

[76] Dey N., Zhang Y.D., Rajinikanth V., Pugalenthi R., Raja N.S.M. 'Customized VGG19 architecture for pneumonia detection in chest X-rays. *Pattern Recognition Letters.* 2021;143:67–74.

[77] Simonyan K., Zisserman A. 'Very deep convolutional networks for large-scale image recognition'. *arXiv preprint arXiv:1409.1556.* 2014.

[78] Mohammadi, R., Salehi, M., Ghaffari, H., Rohani, A. A., and Reiazi, R. 'Transfer learning-based automatic detection of coronavirus disease 2019 (COVID-19) from chest X-ray images'. *Journal of Biomedical Physics & Engineering.* 2020;10:559–68.

[79] Rajaraman S., Antani S.K. 'Modality-specific deep learning model ensembles toward improving TB detection in chest radiographs'. *IEEE Access.* 2020;8:27318–26.

[80]   Sekeroglu B., Ozsahin I. 'Detection of COVID-19 from chest X-ray images using convolutional neural networks'. *SLAS Technology.* 2020;25(6):553–65.

[81]   El Asnaoui K., Chawki Y. 'Using X-ray images and deep learning for automated detection of coronavirus disease'. *Journal of Biomolecular Structure and Dynamics.* 2021;39(10):3615–26.

[82]   Zheng R., Zhang L.L., Jin H. 'Pneumoconiosis identification in chest X-ray films with CNN-based transfer learning'. *CCF Transactions on High Performance Computing.* 2021;3(2):186–200.

[83]   Szegedy C., Liu W., Jia Y., *et al.* (eds.). 'Going deeper with convolutions'. *Proceedings of the IEEE Conference on Computer Vision and Pattern Recognition*; 2015. pp. 1–9.

[84]   Apostolopoulos I.D., Mpesiana T.A. 'Covid-19: Automatic detection from X-ray images utilizing transfer learning with convolutional neural networks'. *Physical and Engineering Sciences in Medicine.* 2020;43(2):635–40.

[85]   Hashmi M.F., Katiyar S., Keskar A.G., Bokde N.D., Geem Z.W. 'Efficient pneumonia detection in chest X-ray images using deep transfer learning'. *Diagnostics.* 2020;10(6):23.

[86]   Chhikara P., Gupta P., Singh P., Bhatia T. 'A deep transfer learning based model for automatic detection of COVID-19 from chest X-rays'. *Turkish Journal of Electrical Engineering and Computer Sciences.* 2021;29:2663–79.

[87]   He K., Zhang X., Ren S., Sun J., (eds.). 'Deep residual learning for image recognition'. *Proceedings of the IEEE Conference on Computer Vision and Pattern Recognition*; 2016. pp.770–778.

[88]   Zhang R., Guo Z., Sun Y., *et al.* 'COVID19XrayNet: A two-step transfer learning model for the COVID-19 detecting problem based on a limited number of chest X-ray images'. *Interdisciplinary Sciences: Computational Life Sciences.* 2020;12(4):555–65.

[89]   Rajpal S., Lakhyani N., Singh A.K., Kohli R., Kumar N. 'Using handpicked features in conjunction with ResNet-50 for improved detection of COVID-19 from chest X-ray images'. *Chaos, Solitons & Fractals.* 2021;145:110749.

[90]   He K., Zhang X., Ren S., Sun J., (eds.). 'Identity mappings in deep residual networks'. *Computer Vision–ECCV 2016: 14th European Conference*; Amsterdam, The Netherlands, October 11–14, 2016, Proceedings, Part IV 14; 2016: Berlin: Springer; pp. 630–645.

[91]   Huang G., Liu Z., Van Der Maaten L., Weinberger K.Q., (eds.). 'Densely connected convolutional networks'. *Proceedings of the IEEE Conference on Computer Vision and Pattern Recognition*; 2017. pp. 4700–4708.

[92]   Chollet F., 'Xception: Deep learning with depthwise separable convolutions'. *Proceedings of the IEEE Conference on Computer Vision and Pattern Recognition*; 2017. pp. 1251–1258.

[93]   Khan A.I., Shah J.L., Bhat M.M. 'CoroNet: A deep neural network for detection and diagnosis of COVID-19 from chest X-ray images'. *Computer Methods and Programs in Biomedicine.* 2020;196:105581.

[94]   Howard A.G., Zhu M., Chen B., *et al.* 'Mobilenets: Efficient convolutional neural networks for mobile vision applications. *arXiv preprint arXiv:170404861*. 2017.

[95]   Szegedy C., Ioffe S., Vanhoucke V., Alemi A., (eds.). 'Inception-v4, inception-resnet and the impact of residual connections on learning'. *Proceedings of the AAAI Conference on Artificial Intelligence*; 2017.

[96]   Behzadi-khormouji H., Rostami H., Salehi S., *et al.* 'Deep learning, reusable and problem-based architectures for detection of consolidation on chest X-ray images'. *Computer Methods and Programs in Biomedicine*. 2020;185:105162.

[97]   Mahmud T., Rahman M.A., Fattah S.A. 'CovXNet: A multi-dilation convolutional neural network for automatic COVID-19 and other pneumonia detection from chest X-ray images with transferable multi-receptive feature optimization'. *Computers in Biology and Medicine*. 2020;122:103869.

[98]   Khalifa N.E.M., Taha M.H.N., Hassanien A.E., Elghamrawy S. 'Detection of coronavirus (covid-19) associated pneumonia based on generative adversarial networks and a fine-tuned deep transfer learning model using chest X-ray dataset'. *arXiv preprint arXiv:200401184*. 2020.

Chapter 9

Computer vision and modern machine learning techniques for autonomous driving

Sobhan Siamak[1] and Eghbal Mansoori[1]

Abstract

Human vision is one of the most important senses for receiving visual perception. When humans as the most intelligent living creatures look at a scene, they always perform a feature extraction from the information of that scene in order to understand its content. Using the extracted features, humans pay attention to part of the scene that contains more valuable information and then turn their gaze to other parts of it, until they have analyzed all the relevant information. This is a natural and instinctive behavior of humans to gather information from the scenery and the surrounding environment and it happens very quickly. Understanding the content of images in computer vision is not as fast as the human understanding of the observer's scenery, but over many years, there has been an effort to increase the accuracy and speed of computer vision by imitating the behavior of human vision. In recent years, due to significant advances in artificial intelligence and the emergence of deep learning, we are witnessing an increasing growth in computer vision and its related areas, including autonomous driving. Recent works have demonstrated the incredible successes of computer vision and deep learning algorithms in various domains including autonomous driving and robotics. In this chapter, we provide a detailed review of the state-of-the-art computer vision techniques for self-driving cars and some recent research advances in this field. After perceiving the challenges of autonomous driving, we concentrate on five perspectives of autonomous driving from visual perception and computer vision viewpoints. These include: (a) object detection, (b) object tracking, (c) segmentation, (d) deep reinforcement learning, and (e) 3D scene analysis. Each of these viewpoints are then analyzed and evaluated via computer vision techniques using some datasets about object detection, object tracking, segmentation, lane detection, and localization as well as mapping in computer vision. Moreover, we introduce sensors as well as CARLA simulator. Finally, we provide a comprehensive analysis of the localization, mapping, and simultaneously both of them related to computer vision for autonomous driving systems (ADS).

[1]School of Electrical and Computer Engineering, Shiraz University, Shiraz, Iran

9.1   Introduction and challenges of autonomous driving

The question of whether humans have dreamed of moving from one place to another without the intervention of hands has persisted ever since the invention of the automobile, but it is evident that there is not much longer for such a desire is accomplished. Perhaps, the best definition of an autonomous driving car as a highly advanced robot can be provided by looking at Isaac Asimov's famous triple rule. In these three principles, it has been clearly stated that the robot not only must not harm the human, but also must execute his/her orders and not harm itself. Therefore, any robot system based on autonomy, its first and most important goal should be to maintain the health and safety of humans and all living things in contact with the environment.

An autonomous vehicle can be defined as a machine that uses a variety of sensors such as cameras, laser radar (LiDAR), radar, and sonar, as well as artificial intelligence algorithms, to interact with its environment and move between locations without human assistance. Completely autonomous navigation in a dynamic general environment has not yet been achieved, even though the technology for autonomous vehicles has advanced significantly. One of the reasons for this that can be mentioned is the generalizability to all environments, which has not yet been fully realized. Modeling that generalize to unknown circumstances and reason quickly are essential for autonomous systems functioning in complicated dynamic environments. Another reason is that, despite the usage of numerous types of sensors in autonomous systems, the reception of these perceptions has not yet approached human precision and comprehension.

9.1.1   Autonomous levels of driving

The Society of Automotive Engineers (SAE) presented their categorization of ADS in 2014, as shown in Figure 9.1, with levels ranging from 0 (no autonomy) being the lowest to 5 being the highest (full autonomy). Level zero refers to the typical vehicles that people drive, while the subsequent levels range from driver-aided features to fully autonomous vehicles.

If we define an advanced driving assistance system (ADAS) as having features like a vibrating seat alert to inform drivers when they are drifting out of their lane, then at level one, ADAS aids the human driver with steering, braking, or accelerating but not simultaneously. At level two, the ADAS can steer and brake or accelerate simultaneously while the driver remains fully alert behind the wheel and controls the vehicle. An ADS is capable of performing all driving duties under certain conditions, such as parking the car at level three. A human driver must remain in charge of the vehicle in this scenario and be prepared to regain control of the vehicle. At the fourth level, an ADS can manage the driving environment under certain circumstances and handle all driving activities. Because ADS is reliable enough in this scenario, a human driver does not need to pay attention. At the ultimate level, the vehicle's ADS functions as a virtual driver and does all the driving in any situation. Human occupants are passengers and are never expected to drive the vehicle [1,2].

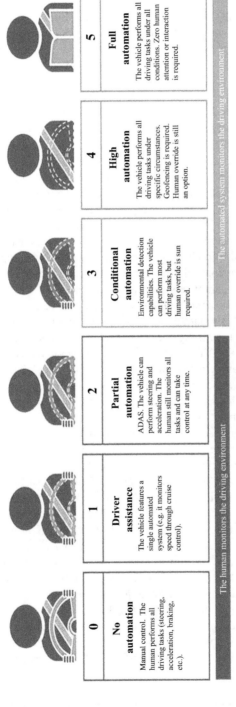

Figure 9.1   SAE levels of autonomy [image source: Synopsys]

9.1.2   *Modular strategy for autonomous driving systems*

Recent autonomous driving techniques can be divided into two groups: modular pipelines and unified end-to-end methods of learning. End-to-end learning strategy will be briefly discussed in the following parts. A modular pipeline is widely used in the industry as a common method for autonomous driving, and we will go through this further. Sensing, perception, prediction, planning, and control are the five components that constitute an ADS in terms of the modular design. Large volumes of information are typically gathered by the sensing component from numerous resources such as cameras, LiDAR, global positioning system (GPS), or other measurement devices mounted on autonomous systems just like Figure 9.3. The perception parts, which usually perform functions like detection and tracking, process the information. In one scenario, these data can be frames acquired from cameras mounted in the autonomous system and delivered to the object detection division, which would then identify pedestrians and other objects in the scene. The prediction module uses a subset of the perception module's outputs to forecast the trajectories of any identified motion. For instance, these trajectories are used for the planning section to use them to determine and plan routes that are safer for the vehicle and do not lead to collisions. Aimed at the vehicle to properly follow the planned path, the central controller interprets the intended route into commands for the vehicle that specify parameters such as the acceleration or steering angle that should be used. The main purpose behind the modular strategy is to be able to take high-dimensional tasks as separate modules, turn them into low-dimensional tasks, train them, and then put them together to provide the autonomous system for evaluation and testing [1]. The deployment of human-explainable intermediary demonstrations, such as detected objects or tracking data, which enable understanding system damage modes is the main benefit of modular streams. However, modular design with human-explainable intermediary demonstrations does not necessarily mean optimality for autonomous systems and may even increase the number of learning parameters, such as loss functions. Explainable autonomous vehicle [1], whose structure is illustrated in Figure 9.2, can be used as an instance of ADS that are constructed in a modular approach.

According to Figure 9.2, the inputs received from the sensors are entered into the perception module, and in this module, a complete understanding of the surrounding environment, such as object recognition, multiple object tracking, 3-dimensional scene understanding, and object localization and position, is sent to the next module, planning. In the planning module, decisions concerning the behavior and movement are made based on factors such as risk estimation, and a trajectory is sent to the control module. In the control module, a quick reaction to the observations of the sensors and their information processed by the previous modules is done. The explainer unit is placed at a higher level, where the event data recorder captures all bottom-level behaviors and transfers them as required to the explainer unit. At the highest level, there is also a user who can communicate with the autonomous vehicle in vocal or visual form and ask it queries or make requests to perform [1].

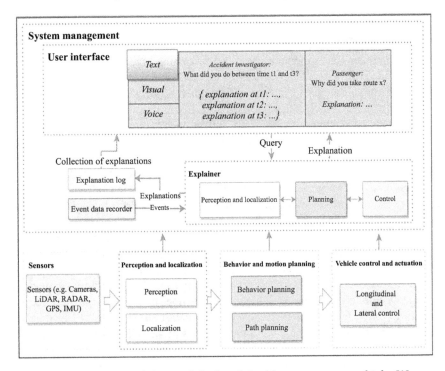

Figure 9.2   A modular model of explainable autonomous vehicle [1]

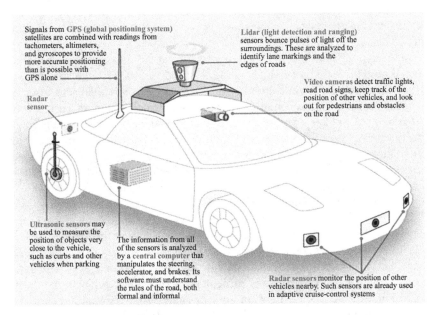

Figure 9.3   Variety of sensors in autonomous driving vehicle [image source: The Economist]

9.1.3   Challenges of computer vision in autonomous driving systems

Modern computer vision methods are currently finding usage in several of the most difficult and inspiring sectors, including autonomous driving. The ability of computer vision in autonomous systems to distinguish between a pedestrian and a tree or a bicycle and a vehicle does not, however, imply that it can compete with the human driver's perception senses. This skill is merely a stepping stone to much more advanced technologies. There are new challenges for computer vision related to ADS, nevertheless, as a result of the expanding requirement. The following part discusses the most major challenges in this field [1,2].

First of all, data is an important thing in the learning paradigm, and collecting data is a very challenging issue. In fact, each algorithm needs its own dataset for the learning process, which must be prepared in advance. Another difficult task that will be encountered during data collection is data labeling. The labeling of the data, which necessitates physically demanding activity, is another challenging task that will be experienced throughout data gathering. Data labeling is extremely reliant on human labor to detect unlabeled objects in original images, especially for datasets as large as autonomous driving vehicles. Meanwhile, in order to operate effective modern machine learning projects, the labeled data must be precise and reliable. One of the most important and well-known works in the field of data gathering for computer vision, known as ImageNet [3], was done by the research group of Professor Fei-Fei Li. Another challenge of data collection is its generalization, which means that the data collected in each region is specific to that region and mostly cannot be generalized. This phenomenon is also known as out of distribution, because the new data are completely distinct from the distribution in which the gathered data were trained [1,2].

Another significant challenge is the sensors and the data that is received and gathered from them for processing and use at various stages. Just like humans, who must perform their tasks while driving with the collaboration of their senses such as vision and hearing, ADS accomplish this task with a combination of sensors. If the settings of a sensor have a problem even a small amount, and intelligent algorithms and deep neural networks suffer a slight calculation error in reading and interpreting information, a disaster will occur, and even human lives may be in danger. Therefore, a complete understanding of the scene and an external environment by autonomous systems is very important for correct processing [1,2].

Object detection is another important challenge in the field of computer vision for autonomous systems. The fact that object detection must be done in real time is considered a major obstacle. An additional major problem in this field is the confusion of the detection system by objects that it has never seen or that are located in a strange place compared to the autonomous vehicle, such as images on billboards. Recognizing traffic signs can also be difficult due to being covered by leaves, being dirty and unreadable, and having poor viewing angles. Another important task is to detect pedestrians, which is very difficult due to several reasons, such as the uncertainty of their movements and changing body positions [1,2].

The purpose of object tracking is to provide data to the control component of an ADS regarding the current motion of an object as well as information about its anticipated future motion. This portion needs to be able to predict behavior along with motion. The other challenge in this portion is changing the background. Additionally, it is challenging to track many items from the same instance, such as vehicles, even when their colors are similar. The tracking of multiple objects, where numerous objects must be tracked simultaneously over time, poses the greatest issue in this field [1,2].

Identifying several items in a single image and assigning a unique label to each of them is the aim of semantic segmentation. Finding the distinctions between each individual object in the scene is the goal of semantic instance segmentation. Almost every obstacle to object detection, including poor illumination or changing weather, is present in this context. The issue of real time still exists and must be addressed in this area, much like it did with object recognition [1,2].

One of the most important tasks that autonomous systems must perform when interacting with the environment is 3-dimensional representation, and this function also relates to the control section in addition to the signal received from sensors. Minor mistakes in 3-dimensional scene analysis have a tendency to compound into larger flaws and cause a deviation. At low speeds, anything that seems safe may become noticeable as the speed increases. Furthermore, the circumstances of various environments vary; for instance, the complexity of objects on a highway differs significantly from that of objects in congested urban traffic [1,2].

These challenges are explained in more detail in the following sections.

9.2 Visual perception and object detection for autonomous driving

One of the most fundamental components of autonomous vehicles is a highly effective and powerful object detection algorithm. Due to the fact that autonomous vehicles deal with a dynamic and nondeterministic environment where the probability of the presence of other vehicles, pedestrians, and other obstacles is very high, the design of object detection algorithms for such environments is very complex. There are many challenges that make detection difficult, such as great variety and similarity of objects to each other along with their different scale ratios, view-point, illumination, and occlusion of objects by other objects. Furthermore, weather conditions and urban areas add to the difficulty of the detection. Due to the importance of pedestrian detection, pedestrian protection systems have been placed in smart cars and utilized to warn the driver when approaching pedestrians in perilous scenarios from the not-too-distant past to the present [2].

9.2.1 Methods for detection

A growing diversity of applications and advancements in computer science and technology have made object detection a prominent topic in recent years. Researchers and major technology corporations are interested in this area of computer vision for both academic and industrial purposes.

Finding the locations of objects in an image or video frame, localization, and the classes to which they each belong, classification, are the goals of object detection and as a result, one of the most important challenges is to perform these two tasks together. Therefore, detecting objects has two important tasks as follows: First, detecting all the objects in the image which is a regression problem and has the task of finding the bounding boxes that contain the objects in the image. One of the most important functions in this section is the localization of objects, which means that the algorithm goes to the location of objects in the image. Second, determining the class of objects in the image, which is a classification problem. The variety of objects in the image with various sizes, the variation in brightness and light, and the similarity of the objects to the foreground of the image are some of the major challenges faced with object detection [4,5].

9.2.1.1 Traditional methods for object detection

A majority of traditional object detection approaches used a multiple pipeline that included picking a portion of the image, extraction of features, and classification. In the first stage of the pipeline, a part of the visual environment that can be an image was selected, and the sliding window technique was used to select it in traditional methods. In this technique, some windows were defined and slid over the visual environment, and this work had to be done on all parts of the image. Whether these windows are variable or a fixed window is defined was also an issue. With these interpretations, this step had many defects such as a very high and tedious computational overhead along with the generated redundant windows [4,5]. In order to properly recognize objects, some good features must be extracted from the visual environment. The traditional approaches used several methods such as SIFT [6] and HOG [7] for this task in the second stage of the pipeline. At the end of the pipeline, a classifier was needed to distinguish the specified object class from the rest, and although DPBM [8] and other methods were used, the most common method has been the support vector machine [9] method [4].

Traditional methods manually (hand-crafted) extract features and are not suitable and robust for the challenges of object detection that were mentioned, and more importantly, they cannot be used in practical applications. Therefore, there is not much attention and emphasis on traditional methods [4,5].

9.2.1.2 Modern object detection methods based on deep learning

In recent years, deep learning [10] has overcome the limitations of computer vision and helped solve problems such as object detection, classification, and image segmentation. One of the success factors of deep neural networks, which is a turning point in computer vision and artificial intelligence and goes back to 2012 and the AlexNet [11] network, is the use of convolutional neural networks (CNNs) [12] and learning a very high amount of labeled data, ImageNet [3], on them. As a result, modern methods of detecting objects based on deep learning were also introduced, which were able to outperform traditional approaches in terms of accuracy. They are divided into two main categories: two-stage and one-stage approaches.

Two-stage detectors

In these methods, the model first proposes a series of interested areas as potential regions for bonding boxes. Next, it performs regression among them more precisely and then selects the best ones. The detected objects are then classified. The first stage, also called region proposal, can be performed by an algorithm or a network similar to CNNs. The methods in this category perform well in terms of accuracy, but they take a lot of time and suffer from high computational complexity. One of the most important two-stage algorithms is R-CNN [13], which uses a search algorithm called selective search [14] to suggest regions containing objects. This method first selects about 2 000 candidate areas and then extracts the features of each of these areas with a deep CNN. Next, it carries out regression or illustrates a bounding box around the objects and classifies each object separately with a support vector machine [9]. Since the inputs of fully-connected layers must have the same size, the R-CNN's input is partially cropped or warped from the region proposal of the input image, causing some objects to be inputted incompletely or some objects to be geometrically disordered which will reduce the accuracy in turn. To resolve these R-CNN issues, a new type of CNN structure called SPP-Net [15] was introduced, in which the spatial pyramid matching [16] structure was used. By spreading out the cost of computing among the many proposals, this method improves outcomes by accurately estimating various region proposals on their appropriate scales which in turn increases the detection efficiency during the testing phase.

In [17], another two-stage detector named Fast R-CNN was introduced. Unlike R-CNN, the entire image is fed into a deep CNN along with some regions of interest that have been gathered in advance (pooling), and the probability of objects in them is high. Finally, the output of the CNN is given to a classifier like support vector machine for classification and simultaneously to a regression to draw a box around the objects. In other words, it is fast because unlike the prior method, regression and classification are done simultaneously. Faster R-CNN, a two-stage detector with a higher speed than the preceding approaches, was introduced in [18]. This approach is similar to Fast R-CNN, except that instead of the selective search algorithm, a deep neural network, called RPN, is used to suggest candidate regions in the input image which contain objects. It should be noted that there is also an extended Faster R-CNN method called Mask R-CNN [19], which is used for image segmentation, and its difference with Faster R-CNN is the change in the cost function and pooling layer.

One-stage detectors

The second category consists of one-stage object detectors, which detect the objects in an integrated network without performing the region proposal stage of two-stage systems. They try to identify objects in the image by processing the regions of a set of pre-specified dense points that they have generated from the image. These methods are quicker and more suited to real-time work than two-stage approaches, although they are not as accurate. To name several of the most important one-stage algorithms, a significant one-stage detector called YOLO was introduced in [20]. it was utilized in real-time applications with the aim of finding objects in the image by viewing only once. This algorithm uses a deep convolutional integrated network, which first extracts image features before doing classification, and the output of this network is a grid image with specific dimensions. This output contains important features that, when combined with a number of mathematical and probabilistic relationships, allow for the rapid detection of objects in the image. However, YOLO has some drawbacks, such as difficulty of finding small objects and objects with disproportionate dimensions.

Another notable one-stage detector named YOLO9000 was released in [21]. It was offered to tackle the issues of the previous method and had the best results until then. YOLO9000 claimed that it can discover up to 9000 classifications of distinct objects in real-time. As an improvement over them, the YOLOv3 [22] method was introduced, which trained a larger network than before and simultaneously increased the accuracy. In recent years, different versions of the YOLO family have been developed, all of which have attempted to boost the precision of this well-known one-stage approach. RetinaNet, as a one-stage detector introduced in [23], is important for identifying and classifying objects in input images that fall into unbalanced categories. RetinaNet uses the well-known focal loss cost function.

Pedestrian detection

One of the important components of ADS is pedestrian detection with high accuracy and appropriate reasoning speed to avoid collisions. Important challenges in this field include pedestrians obstructing one another, pedestrians unexpectedly changing tracks, disorganized urban environments with wide variations in illumination and harsh weather conditions, multiple pedestrians present at once in various scales, and conflicting pedestrian appearance.

A CNN approach based on VGG-16 [24] as the backbone is presented in [25] in order to obtain high accuracy and deal with dynamic environment elements related to pedestrian detection in smart cities. A method based on k-means, YOLOv3, and CNNs was presented in [26] to solve the problem of falsely negative pedestrians and occlusions caused by human skin under complex conditions such as illuminations and variations in images. In order to combine numerous deep neural networks with the well-known one-stage detector to form an ensemble learning network with high performance, some methods such as [27] have been proposed. However, ensemble networks have the drawback of demanding an increasing amount of memory usage as the networks get larger.

In [28], a series-connected cascade network with multiple learning algorithms is employed to decrease the amount of memory utilized. Since the learned information is transmitted from one network to another, less memory is used while improving the accuracy. In recent years, cross-dataset assessment and pipeline techniques for training have been used to increase the performance and generalization of the detection algorithms. Cross-dataset assessment utilizes numerous datasets to train and test the detection system, in which a learning algorithm is trained using two or further combined datasets and then tested using a separate dataset, increasing generalization. A cross-dataset strategy was employed for evaluation in [29], which was a cascade R-CNN method, and the acquired results revealed an improvement in accuracy due to an increase in generalization. Occlusion limitation, as mentioned above, is one of the issues in this part, and approaches based on deep learning have been proposed in [30] and [31] to address this problem.

Vehicle detection

Vehicle detection is another component of ADS. According to the use of cameras as one of the receivers of visual perception in these systems, autonomous systems must first detect another vehicle in the surrounding environment before tracking and predicting other vehicle behavior. A vehicle detection system should be reliable, quick, and precise, regardless of cost. The challenges that this portion faces can be poor weather conditions and lack of illumination in the daytime, a wide range of different classes for vehicles, vehicles being observed from various angles (front or right side), vehicle size scale variation (leading to a diversified feature map for the same object), crowds and complex traffic sights, and similar categories of vehicles differing in size, form, color, and architecture. The usage of a 2D deep belief network in [32] allowed for the extraction of additional discriminatory features, making the system more resistant to complicated scenarios and producing superior outcomes to those of the conventional approaches.

The specific network, known as backward feature enhancement, which attaches discriminatory features from low-level layers to high-level layers (and vice versa) with the purpose of obtaining excellent region proposals and having the ability to boost recall for tiny objects, was proposed in [33]. This is a solution to the problem that algorithms like R-CNN have trouble detecting tiny objects because the feature maps used for region proposal have limited discriminatory features. A particular module known as split transform and merge, used in the specific network, which swaps out the traditional fully-connected layers, are used to further improve the produced regional suggestions. An innovative recurrent rolling CNN was introduced in [34] to enhance the mean average precision of a single-stage method. The system is capable of performing feature collection and combining it to retrieve more additional context due to the network's rolling and recurrent components.

Another method that employed a cascaded strategy and combined traditional detectors such as HOG with deep learning classifiers was introduced in [35] for vehicle detection. Since traditional classification methods such as support vector machine are ineffective at classifying objects in this field, this method uses a combination of deep learning and traditional methods for classification. On the scale of issues for vehicle detection, certain approaches [36] and [37] have worked and were substantially successful. In order to increase the detection accuracy, a specific network is described in [38] that substitutes Gabor filters and multishape for the low-level convolutional kernel. Additionally, it contains a module known as "dynamic region enlargement" that enlarges specific areas of the image where tiny objects are situated.

Faster R-CNN exhibits suitable vehicle detection results on some datasets but does not perform well on specific datasets that have more various angle views, occluded vehicles, and multiscale vehicles [39,40]. As a result, upon improving the Faster R-CNN algorithm, acceptable outcomes were able to be achieved on datasets with much more challenging circumstances, like KITTI. An innovative ensemble deep CNN and multitask learning in [41] increased the robustness of vehicle detection via a novel voting approach. In order to improve the effectiveness of detection, a graph-based strategy is introduced in [42] that reduces the number of candidate regions in contrast to the conventional sliding-window method, which attains higher speed than previous algorithms in this field. A novel method for reducing necessities with the intention of increasing detection speed based on a deep CNN known as DenseLightNet is presented in [43]. Another technique that attempted to improve detection quality and accuracy was the cascade R-CNN method [44].

Traffic sign detection

Another element of an ADS that must be reliable, accurate, and behave like a person, is the traffic sign detector. Although traditional object detection methods such as [45] were previously used to detect traffic signs, the introduction of deep learning in recent years has led in methods with significantly superior results to categorize traffic signs [46–48].

A multilayer perceptron trained on conventional feature descriptors and a CNN trained on images were used to classify traffic signs in [46]. Instead of employing manually created features like HOG, [48] proposes a multiscale CNN to learn relevant features for traffic sign identification. A quicker approach for sign identification using stochastic gradient descent is presented in [47] with a cost function that resembles the support vector machine's objective function. In [49], a sliding window detector that extracts features using a CNN was proposed. To train the identification of traffic signs at various scales, this approach uses CNN with specific convolutions on a number of resolutions and, to categorize the retrieved features, trains a fully-connected convolutional network. According to [50], the evaluation of modern object detection algorithms based on one of the well-known traffic sign recognition datasets [51] indicated that two-stage object detection methods (e.g., R-CNN, Fast R-CNN, and SPP-Net) as well as one-stage detection approaches (e.g., YOLO and YOLO9000) did not yield acceptable results. The mentioned approaches struggle to handle traffic signs because, based on their size, scale, occlusion, and distance, they can be very tiny in the image.

In an innovative approach [18], Inception V2 [52] was applied for feature extraction in conjunction with the two-stage Faster R-CNN method, yielding promising results close to one of the excellent methods [49] in this field. The two-stage Faster R-CNN method was modified by applying a technique, called coarse-to-fine, to extract regions and also offered an attention network to operate on specific regions in another inventive method [53] that was evaluated on two significant datasets [51,54]. The German Traffic Sign Recognition Benchmark [55] and the German Traffic Sign Detection Benchmark [51] are two of the earliest traffic sign datasets, and new algorithms based on CNNs have achieved great accuracies on them. As a result of this, particularly in recent years, a new dataset known as

Tsinghua-Tencent [54] has been introduced. It has more appealing and more challenges in the field of traffic sign detection.

9.3   Visual perception and object tracking for autonomous driving

Despite the fact that in object detection, each frame is usually processed individually and no relationships across moments are made, the main objective of tracking is to approximate the status of one or more objects across time using information gathered through sensors, which each status or state characterizes at a specific time via position, acceleration, and velocity. An essential aspect of ADS, especially in traffic situations, is keeping track of other road users. The sophistication of motion, crowded environments, and occlusions are only a few of the challenges that the tracking section has to overcome. The partial or complete occlusion of objects by other objects is one of the primary challenges to tracking, and this occlusion intensifies when interacting with the dynamic environment of ADS, particularly pedestrians. Another challenge is tracking similar objects belonging to the same class over time due to their resemblance. Other kinds of difficulties include changing illumination, the similarity of background elements to the targets, background clutter, scale invariance, and deformation of some objects, like the rotation of pedestrians.

9.3.1   Methods for visual tracking

In general, there are two kinds of tracking, known as single-object tracking and multiobject tracking. The first category contains five solutions for tracking, include feature-based, segmentation-based, appearance-based, estimation-based, and learning-based tracking [56]. Basic approach to object tracking is the feature-based methodology, in which features like color, texture, optical flow, and other attributes are first extracted and then used to track the target object [56]. In order to simply recognize the objects in the feature space and distinguish them, the features extracted by the strategies must be unique. It is necessary to employ similarity criteria to find the most comparable objects in the following frame after extracting and applying the features. A major flaw in these methods is the requirement to extract exclusive, reliable, and robust features, which are unable to provide.

For segmentation-based approaches, there are two sets of objects in a video frame: the background and the foreground. Because the foreground objects move within the scene environment, they must be distinguished from the background in order to be tracked [56]. The estimating approach converts the tracking challenge into an estimation problem where a state vector represents parameters of an object such as location, velocity, and acceleration. Bayesian approaches are utilized to estimate these vectors, which represent the system's dynamic mode. Using the most recent sensor information, it is possible to constantly adjust the target's coordinate system placement thanks to the Bayesian filters. The prediction and adjusting parts of this recursive method are also included in this approach. While the adjusting part modifies the coordinates using the present observation and the observed model, the prediction part utilizes the state model to anticipate the new location of the target in the subsequent step. Most estimation approaches are either based on the non-linear particle filter [56] or the linear Kalman filter [56]. Although the concept behind appearance-based approaches is interesting, no approach or body of research has so far been able to come to a sound conclusion [56]. In these methods, it is argued that most objects in reality are very complex and may even change shape over time. Therefore, in order to track such objects, the changes in their appearance must be considered in their visual tracking.

The final approach in this category is learning-based methods that learn the features of different objects related to the next frame, including predicting the trajectory of objects. They can track different objects during testing time based on their learnings. Among the approaches considered in this category are reinforcement learning and deep learning [56]. However, on the odd occasion does a solitary target appear in the scenes engaged in autonomous driving applications. Typically, multiple objects should be simultaneously detected and tracked and some of targets possibly will be moving with respect to the vehicle and to other objects. As a result, the majority of strategies in the associated research deal with numerous objects and are designed to address challenges with multiple object tracking.

9.3.1.1 Can we perform tracking using detection?

Tracking objects through detection is a standard methodology that is frequently utilized due to the effectiveness of object detectors. Objects must be detected first in these approaches, and then associated detections related to similar objects must be performed in the following step and over time for tracking. Due to the fact that the tracking challenge has been simplified to a data association in these methods, tracking objects through detection has gained enormous acceptance. However, because the detection method contains faults such as missing and incorrect detection, tracking algorithms must address and resolve these issues. Therefore, data association is a fundamental challenge when working with detection-based tracking methods.

In tracking, graph models are commonly used to infer associations. A mutual matching between the two distinct subsets of nodes that are defined as detection and trajectory in a graph-based scenario can be performed from scratch. Some methods have used the optimal Hungarian approach such as that discussed in [57], which runs in polynomial time, to allocate two disjoint subsets of detection and trajectory, while others have done this using greedy methods like that discussed in [58]. In other graph-based approaches known as network flow including that in [59] nodes are considered as detections, and edges between nodes as spatial and temporal events across detections. In addition, a straightforward subset of constraints as an integer program is provided to guarantee that the tracks generated are legitimate and consistent throughout the beginning and finishing nodes.

To prevent the NP-Hard of the integer program, these constraints are frequently reduced to a linear program. In some approaches to address the network flow issue for optimization shortest pathways [60], linear programming [59], or set cover algorithm [61] utilized. Other graph-based methods, such as min cost multicut [62] and Minimum Clique [63], discover a graph decomposition with the lowest total cost and treat tracking as a clustering approach. The paired association issue is initially separately solved in Max-weight independent set approaches like [64], and then the paired outcomes are joined utilizing a measurement of learned distance. An energy function determined on the nodes with pairs and specific potentials is minimized in graphic model approaches such as those discussed in [65]. Regarding extremely non-convex challenges, continuous energy minimizing methods including [66] have been suggested as a substitute to discretization. Several methods such as those discussed in [67] are proposed in order to improve the reliability and robustness of tracking objects.

9.3.1.2 Pedestrian tracking

Pedestrian tracking is one of the most challenging tasks in ADS, made further difficult by drawbacks such as false positives in the detection part. To overcome some of these problems, a more reliable method based on the combination of human pose tracking and detection was proposed in [68], which uses a hierarchical Gaussian model with latent variables for effective detection. As an improvement on the previous method, an idea to accurately estimate the 3D human position of the multiple persons only from monocular image information was proposed in [69]. This approach can be used together with a hidden Markov model to track each person in long sequences. The 2D viewpoint and human position are estimated in the initial stage and linked throughout a limited group of frames. The hierarchical Gaussian model with latent variables is then utilized to estimate the three-dimensional position using the gathered 2D image information. Some methods based on a network flow were proposed [70] to resolve the detection and association cooperatively by learning a model for each goal and changing the graph to determine the probabilities between both the goals and nodes. This idea differs from the usual object tracking via detection, which supposes that detections are accessible.

9.3.1.3 Multiple object tracking

Another challenge of computer vision is the multiple objects tracking (MOT), where moving targets must be tracked over time. Multiobject tracking has many applications in the real world, as in ADS. Typically, multiple objects should be simultaneously detected and tracked while some of targets possibly are moving with respect to the vehicle and to other objects. As a result, the majority of strategies in the associated research deal with numerous objects and are designed to address challenges with multiple object tracking. Although there are methods in the framework of multiobject tracking that track objects individually, in most of the multiple methods, the goal is to identify and track several objects simultaneously. The input of these algorithms can either be through the cameras mounted in the autonomous driving cars, or the data received through LiDAR sensors. Commonly, the combination of these two data is used for evaluation.

Unlike some other tracking methods that do not use detection and have to be manually initialized over time, the object tracking through detection model is used by new multiple object trackers. They start tracking objects using detection data like bounding boxes from regression and object labels from classification via object detection model. Since the environment of ADS is highly dynamic, it is almost impossible to predict the number and location of objects in that environment in advance as the objects enter or leave over time. So, tracking methods based on the detection of these environments are very appropriate.

A question now arises here: if the input data in all frames come from the camera or other sensors in real-time, how will detection methods help in tracking objects? In answer, it should be noted that estimation methods are widely used here. During detection updates for each frame, target locations will be estimated by algorithms related to the tracker. Every track using identified locations can be accurately adjusted by the tracker as soon as it acquires the detection output. Another application of detection is that with different detections of a target, a model of the velocity of that target can be created, which can be used over time to precisely estimate the location of that target in tracking. If this velocity model is made with more data (i.e., it uses a greater number of detections in the middle frames for tracking), the tracking of objects will be more reliable, especially in the middle frames.

In most detection-based tracking methods and in the detection-related parts, each target must have a unique identifier in order to perform more accurate tracking. Therefore, the total of these object location estimates during detection over time upon several frames or trajectory, the multiple object tracking can be viewed as an output that is entered into the modules of the next steps. Now, if unique identifiers are not defined for each of the targets, this scenario will encounter problems. If the detection and unique identifier pairs are viewed as nodes in a weighted bipartite graph, a distance criterion based on the features shared by each node can be created, and the edges between each node can be identified based on the value of these distances. The ultimate goal of multiple object tracking can be summarized in two problems: (a) minimizing incorrect matches between detection pairs and unique identifiers, and (b) accurately estimating the location of each target. The target location's uncertain estimation and deviation from the indicated graph's optimal match are two issues with reaching this goal.

Multiple object tracking based on deep learning

In recent years, deep learning and sequential models have been used for learning of track representation [71]. Some methods have used deep learning for association and confirmed the detections related to the same object with the help of deep and representation learning such as [72]. It has been demonstrated that sequential models integrated with a conventional model for association outperform their antecedents. The method based on CNNs that learns the multiple tracking space [73], the method relied on hand-crafted features that learns the tracking with the Markov decision process [74], and the Siamese network-based method that functions as multicut [75] can all be mentioned as more traditional approaches. The innovative combined approaches, on the other hand, include the bi-linear long short-term memory network based on modification [71], the interaction long short-term memory network based on combining motion and appearance [76], and the hierarchical method based on recurrent neural networks that serves as clustering [77]. The basic methodology in the instances that follow is to first learn a solid track representation before attempting an association strategy.

Multiple object tracking based on end-to-end learning has been introduced in recent years [78], [79], which has been struggling with challenges such as specific search space issues and limited availability of labeled data. In [78], a network layer based on manually created bounding box representations was proposed to learn cost functions of a network flow. A particular recurrent neural network is used to estimate the target states and long short-term memory networks are used to estimate the association in the initial end-to-end learning method for tracking given in [79]. However, the approach cannot be compared to the results of earlier methods because it was trained on artificial data and does not include an appearance model. In conclusion, the four general steps of the majority of modern multiple objects tracking systems are detection, feature extraction, comparison, and association [80].

A distinct object detection approach generally handles the detection phase, processing a camera frame and producing bounding boxes and corresponding labels for specific frames of objects. The precision of an object tracker is hugely reliant on the precision of the bounding boxes that it receives from the object detector because this outcome is needed to initialize and modify the tracker over time. Following the detection phase, the feature extraction phase employs networks to convert each bounding box from the camera frame into features. The pair of detection and feature vectors is valued in the comparison phase using a distance measurement such as cosine similarity or Euclidean distance. The association phase manages feature vector replacement for any unmatched detections, removing old feature vectors, and matching detections to feature vectors using the specific cost matrix.

9.4 Visual perception and segmentation for autonomous driving

Another vital challenge in computer vision that is an intermediary objective to resolve increasing problems such as scene understanding is semantic segmentation. Assigning a label from a predetermined category list to every pixel of the image is the aim of semantic segmentation. Because of the complex object borders, the scene's ambiguity, the tiny objects, and a sizable label space, the segmentation is difficult. The navigation module related to ADS requires a thorough awareness of the environment that can be achieved by segmenting images into semantic areas that are frequently present in street scenes, like pedestrians, vehicles, sky, or roadways.

9.4.1 Methods of segmentation

As mentioned before, semantic segmentation tries to classify each pixel of an image into a related class such as street, sidewalk, or pedestrian. To accomplish these goals, some traditional methods were defined. They are based on conditional random fields on the specific pixels known as super pixels [81,82] or ordinary pixels [83,84] and use maximum a posteriori deduction. To overcome the drawbacks of conditional random fields with local connections and also to follow lengthy interactions inside the image, hierarchy approaches [83,85] and lengthy connectivity, as well as greater potentials defined on image areas [81,82], have been implemented.

Despite former approaches, which were limited to using fully-connected conditional random fields on a minor portion of images due to high computational complexity related to memory, an innovation method with the pairwise possibilities across each couple of pixels in the image via fully-connected conditional random field pattern based on a tractable inference at pixel-level was introduced in [86]. An approach which relies on a hierarchical sequence of inference patterns that can cover more regions of the environment for semantic segmentation was proposed in [87] as a replacement for ordinary inference. By avoiding the obstacles of training structural forecasting patterns in these situations, this methodology is able to produce a technique of scene understanding with extremely effective and precise outcomes. A method based on new features known as the texture-layout filter with stronger potential that uses conventional features such as color and texture was introduced in [88]. This approach uses conditional random fields in combination with low-level image and texture-layout features. It takes advantage of an object's texture, achieves pixel-level semantic segmentation.

Considering that the independence of the class of each object in the scene is a very wrong assumption, some methods [89,90] tried not to consider this assumption. In fact, if a street scene class such as a pedestrian occurs, the probability of other classes of this type of scene occurring is very high, and this phenomenon is called co-occurrence. An optimized method based on co-occurrence theory as features into a conditional random field that utilizing graph cuts was proposed in [89] along with enhance performance than pairwise approaches. As an improvement on the previous method, a technique based on coding the order of different classes was presented in [90]. In [91], another method based on retrieval is described for obtaining context associations from pairs of labeled regions.

9.4.1.1   Semantic segmentation based on deep learning

Deep CNNs have been successful at classifying images and identifying objects, which caused curiosity in how well suited they are for pixel-level problems like semantic segmentation. One of the initial attempts to use CNN to tackle the image segmentation challenge is the fully CNN [92]. By sequentially layers such as subsampling that reduce the resolution, CNNs for image classification in the recent years integrate multiscale context information. However, dense forecasts or full-resolution forecasts, along with multiscale context inference are needed for semantic segmentation. Therefore, in order to address the different demands of multiscale reasoning and full-resolution outcomes, multiple approaches [93,94] have been developed. The receptive field of neural networks is expanded by dilated convolutions [93,94] without reducing the resolution. The dilated convolution procedure is equivalent to a conventional convolution in which some pixels are ignored whereas the filter is utilized. As a result, effective multiscale inferring is possible without adding more parameters to the model. Through employing numerous parallel dilated convolutions with various sampling frequencies, the model in [95] is developed.

Integrating CNNs with conditional random field models is an alternative approach to meeting the demands of multiscale reasoning and full resolution forecasting. Several methods [93,95] suggest utilizing a fully connected conditional random field model [86] to improve the label mapping produced by a CNN. The CNN outcome lacks fine details because of the limited spatial precision, but the conditional random field enables them to retain these features based on the raw RGB inputs. According to some methods [24,96], a CNN depth is essential for accurately representing powerful features. But as a network gets deeper, its complexity rises, it becomes saturated, and its accuracy suffers as a result. To solve this issue, the deep residual learning framework was introduced in [97].

9.4.1.2   Semantic segmentation for video frames

Videos, as compared to solitary image frames, are generally available in robotic applications like autonomous driving. To increase the segmentation performance, effectiveness, and robustness, it is possible to take use of the temporal correlation among nearby frames. In most cases, there is little to no change in the scene between two frames. Semantic labeling can therefore be rectified using temporal features or transmitted over time given correspondences across two frames. One method for semantic segmentation [98] that works on video structures provided a graphical model to ensure temporal coherence relating frames. This approach particularly provides a conditional random field that links relevant image pixels to the deduced 3D scene locations produced via structure-from-motion in order to achieve temporal coherence across following video sequences.

The segmentation of street side images (e.g., building appearances) into its ingredient parts (e.g., walls, doors, windows, and plants) is one particular function paradigm of semantic segmentation that has significant applications for ADS. This type of semantic segmentations is important for path planning, memory-efficient 3D mapping, reliable localization [99], and precise 3D reconstruction [100]. In 3D reconstruction functionalities, for instance, using side data enables for the omission of plants that is challenging to represent and may vary over time. In [101], a model enabling multiview semantic segmentation of images taken via a camera placed on a moving vehicle was proposed.

9.4.1.3   Semantic instance segmentation

Detection, classification, and segmentation of each unique object in an image is the purpose of semantic instance segmentation at the same time. This approach has significant functions in autonomous driving because, despite semantic segmentation, the response includes details about the location, geometry, semantics, and quantity of each object. Proposal-based and proposal-free instance segmentation are the mainly two study areas for the subject of semantic instance segmentation. Proposal-free models forecast pixel labels straight through the image, in contrast to proposal-based models, which typically involve two steps: proposal extraction and proposal classification. The goal of proposal-based instance segmentation techniques is to achieve pixel-level cases from class-independent proposals that are identified as cases of a semantic group.

SharpMask [102], DeepMask [103], and Constrained Parametric Min-Cut [104] are some of the region proposal methodologies that yield general class-independent region proposals to utilize as instance segments straight away. In order to increase the detection accuracy to aid segmentation, a number of object detection classifiers were proposed, including Simultaneous Detection and Segmentation [105], Convolutional Feature Masking [106], and HyperColumn [107]. These classifiers handle object detection and semantic segmentation by utilizing region features from instance segments at the same time. Because of the time-consuming and costly proposal generating process, proposal-based methods are sluggish during inference phase. A three-stage fully CNN, known as Multitask Network Cascade, was proposed in [108] to overcome this issue. With this technique, box suggestions are extracted, enhanced to segments using shared features, and afterwards categorized into semantic groups.

Latest research [19,109] proposes to simultaneously solve the detection and segmentation challenges, whereas previous techniques addressed these issues using two separate sub-networks in sequence. Faster R-CNN is the foundation for both MaskLab [109] and Mask R-CNN. The method in [19] adds a new branching to Faster R-CNN to estimate segmentation masks. A combination method including semantic segmentation logits for pixel-wise categorization in addition to Faster R-CNN box predictions in [109] was introduced. In this strategy, orientation prediction logits approximate the orientation near centers of instances. In fact, the instances belonging to the same class can finally be separated thanks to the orientation towards centers of instances.

In response to the issue with proposal-based techniques for inheriting the mistakes of the proposal-generating part, several alternative strategies have recently been developed. Through immediately transforming instance segmentation into a problem of pixel labeling, these approaches simultaneously estimate the segmentation and the semantic class of particular instances. Depth information has the ability to distinguish between various object instances, as demonstrated by a number of methods [110,111]. A neural network based on fully convolutional layers is trained by a variety of methods [110,111] to correctly forecast the pixel-level instance segmentation of densely observed image patches whereas the instance identity carries a depth arranging. These techniques reinforce coherence with a specific Markov random field and so enhance the forecasts. Parallel work [112,113] presents proposal-free methods based on an initial semantic segmentation rather than depending on depth information. In another study [112], semantic instance segmentation is inferred by a multicut paradigm that integrates semantic segmentation and object border detection using globally inference. Classes that are not suitable for instance segmentation purposes (e.g., roadway or sky), are generally neglected via this approach, which emphasizes instances of objects. As a result, panoptic segmentation [114] deals with the dense estimate of an instance identification and semantic label. Following that, numerous approaches to dealing with the problem were proposed [115,116].

9.5   Visual perception and deep reinforcement learning for autonomous driving

The modular approach is one of the techniques that ADS can practically implement. It combines and assembles various components, such as object detection, object segmentation, multiple object tracking, etc., for many purposes, such as pedestrian detection. This approach is currently used in the industry and has produced the best results. The planning module takes the outcomes of the preceding modules and sends the decision-making program (e.g., motion) to the control module for performance. To manage the velocity and route of the vehicle, solid solutions to a number of outstanding issues in scene comprehension are required. Moreover, in order to train each component individually, extra loss functions are needed. This consequently pays little attention to the real goals of the autonomous driving mission, including journey time, security, and enjoyment.

As another strategy, a number of approaches regard ADS as an end-to-end learning challenge. All of the components, including perception, planning, and control, are merged in these methods, and via deep neural networks, one model is trained end to end. Through receiving input from the camera sensors, the desired end-to-end learning technique directly processes and converts this information into the data required for the steering angle of the ADS before delivering it.

9.5.1   Method

There are two types of end-to-end learning strategies that can be utilized in ADS. The first is to train the system policies using the commands of an expert and then imitate the behavior of the expert to execute the driving commands. The second strategy uses reinforcement learning and, more recently, deep reinforcement learning and exploring or exploiting in interaction with the environment for training, which is often used in the simulation environment.

9.5.1.1   Deep reinforcement learning

In general, sequential decision-making describes a situation in which a decision-maker (e.g., an agent) makes successive observations of a process before making a final decision. In most sequential decision problems, there is an implicit or explicit cost for each observation, the aim is to find a stopping rule that optimizes the decision in terms of the minimum loss or maximum profit, including the observation costs, and the observation repetition procedure terminates at a point that depends on the problem. Optimal strategy or policy is also another name for the optimal terminating rule. Learning problems are one of the branches in which sequential decision-making is applied.

Reinforcement learning is the most similar to human and animal learning, and many of the primary reinforcement learning algorithms are influenced by biological learning systems [117]. An agent is a learner or decision-maker who aims to maximize a defined reward while interacting with the environment. Therefore, in reinforcement learning, we are dealing with an agent in search of a goal that interacts with the environment and influences the environment with its movements in order to achieve an implicit purpose. Through describing the preferences and objectives of the driving agent, the reward in the ADS is specified. A method based on deep reinforcement learning that integrated numerous characteristics (e.g., speed, distance traveled to the target) as well as used a reward function, defined in the CARLA simulator was introduced in [118]. The benefit of an asynchronous actor-critic approach [119] is applied to train the agent and policy of actor updates, utilizing the learned value function from the critic section. Also, even though that the reinforcement learning agent was trained on a substantially bigger group of visual data than a behavior cloning agent trained via conditionally imitation, this approach [118] detects that the reinforcement learning agent behaves noticeably terrible. A reinforcement learning model was also used [120] to demonstrate stated intention in learning to drive in an actual environment. This strategy trains the reinforcement learning agent using the deep specific policy gradients technique, and the distance the car travels without the security driver taking over is used to determine the reward.

All the methods mentioned so far used model-free techniques for learning. Model-free approaches have the drawback of frequently requiring plenty of inter-actions with the surroundings and being data-inefficient. The model-based rein-forcement learning techniques, in contrast, use observable information to create a framework for the dynamics of the surroundings, which is then used to train a policy related to driving systems. The quantity of environmental interaction necessary to train a successful policy has been proven to really be greatly reduced by model-based approaches. Model-based approaches, however, frequently need for an interactive setting because a dynamic model trained on a predetermined set of performances could produce inaccurate forecasts unfamiliar the learning area. Nevertheless, in the actual world, when such interactions are time-consuming and unsafe, the ongoing learning scenario is not effective. In order to address this issue, another approach [121] suggests training a model-based policy that is inspired to develop actions where the forward dynamics framework is optimistic. In this approach, uncertainty is defined as a difference between the states of the training data and the triggered states, and the learnt policy aims to minimize this cost of uncertainty.

9.5.1.2   Inverse reinforcement learning

Since the exploration and exploitation only occur from possible states, training from several suboptimal educators enables more rapid learning than with purely reinforcement learning agents. In fact, the real application of reinforcement learn-ing is constrained by the necessity to define the reward function. Parameter opti-mization is difficult and computational cost is ineffective in order to precisely specify the reward function. Despite activity clone methods that supervise straight learning of the evaluation mapping, inverse reinforcement learning techniques attempt to provide improved generalization by learning a reward function that describes expertise action. As an example in ADS, this method [122] suggests using inverse reinforcement learning to understand the unfamiliar reward function of the driving action behavior through expert presentations.

9.6 3D scene analysis, sensors, datasets, and CARLA simulator for autonomous driving

9.6.1 3D scene analysis

Perfect understanding of the local environment, such as a complicated traffic condition, is among the fundamental prerequisites of ADS. As the tasks were stated in the preceding sections, each of these tasks, such as object detection, tracking, etc., can be considered as a subtask for the entire analysis of outdoor scene perception. To take advantage of the corresponding characteristics of the several hints in the environment and to develop a much more comprehensive understanding, it can be useful to model some of these components together. In fact, gaining a strong representation of the scene environment that involves all of its components (e.g., the order of scene elements, traffic users, and their relationships with one another) is the objective of scene understanding approaches. The world is perceived by humans as having 3Ds; hence, a 3D analysis of the environment will provide the greatest reasoning from the surroundings. As a result, a much more accurate representation of the scene, especially in ADS, is produced by 3D object patterns, layout components, and occlusion connections thanks to 3D reasoning, which enables geometric scene interpretation. Urban environments are one of the main challenges in 3D scene analysis, especially in the case of traffic, due to the complexity that exists there compared to rural environments and highways. Urban scenes differ from highways and country roads in that they contain moving objects, a great deal of variation in the geometric arrangement of roadways and intersections, and a higher level of complexity brought on by confusing visual characteristics, occlusions, and tough illumination conditions.

9.6.1.1 3D scene analysis methods

In recent years, direct learning of complicated relationships from data is a goal of advance approaches. One innovative approach, for instance [123], gathers the entire 3D construction of an outdoor environment from a solitary image frame. A combination of rough geometrical categories with specific directions (e.g., back, vertical, and sky) are used to depict the shallow structure. Through learning a pattern based on appearance for each category, these components are implied. Through a combination of 2D polygons feature in the function of initial samples, a time variable 3D demonstration method was presented in [124]. This approach determines the strengthen plane using RANSAC and then performs clustering inliers to distinguish samples from 3D LiDAR point clouds. As an enhancement on a prior method [125], a creative content [126] to a stochastic 3D scene understanding pattern that includes object identification based on multiclass, tracking, scene tagging, and inference about geometric connections was given. The 3D scene structure of joints, in addition to the positioning and direction of the cars in the scene, are all considered at the same time in a different approach [127]. By using car tracking, semantic tags, scene flowing, and occupied some grids technique, this approach delivers a generative probabilistic pattern that captures the scene topological, geometrical, and traffic behaviors.

There are alternative improved approaches to depict a street scene than 3D primitive-based models such as [128], which suggest a more precise model of the route. In comparison, some methods [129,130] take into account a passing car as the viewer and create representative 3D scene patterns via considering traffic conditions and occlusions. Regarding precise object occlusion inference compare to other objects, some approaches [129,130] combine numerous object detection component [126] into the 3D scene understanding pattern. Additionally, through eliminating geometric impossible detection, these techniques ensure physically acceptable trajectory. A descriptive generation system of 3D urban scenes is proposed in [131], which is comparable to [127]. Although the independent feature vector, known as Tracklets in [127] can cause unreasonable reasoning outcomes, this strategy avoids the mentioned issue and forces the resolution to comply with traffic regulations by reasoning on high-level semantics in the arrangement of traffic conditions. As a result, their scene evaluation and car-to-lane relationship outcomes are greatly improved. Another approach [132] suggests employing a deep network to derive an upper edge depiction for complicated road scenes from a camera.

3D convolutional neural network

In this brief section, we will introduce the 3D CNN, which is employed in a variety of applications for ADS. They have been quite effective at semantic segmentation of 2D images, however there has been relatively little research about applying them to label 3D data. In this context, a specific 3D CNN known as VoxNet [133], intended for object detection of volumetric 3D information was proposed. VoxNet is one of the first usage of 3D CNN for categorized particular volume of data, known as Voxel.

A 3D CNN is proposed as a framework in [134] to instantly tag 3D point cloud information. This method generates 3-dimensional occupant grids of a specific size that are precisely focused on a series of randomly chosen important spots. A 3D CNN made up of max-pooling, a fully connected output layer, convolutional layers, as well as a logistic regression layer, which receives its input from the occupant grids and the tags. Another strategy [135] suggests Oct-Net, a 3D convolutional network, which enables training deep structures at noticeably high-level resolutions and therefore can analyze greater quantities. This approach is based on the finding that 3D information of data (e.g., point clouds), because of sparsity, is frequently lacking in detail. Through hierarchical dividing the 3D area into a collection of octrees and employing pooling layer in a specific adaptive data, Oct-Net takes advantage of this sparsity characteristic. As a result, since the convolutional network functions are based on the architecture of these data structures, there is a decrease in the amount of processing and the required storage, and relying on the input's architecture, resources can be assigned flexibly.

9.6.2   Sensors

Nowadays, numerous sensors such as cameras, gyroscopes, wheel odometry, and range sensors are used in various applications to imitate the diverse senses of humans. Even in many cases, such as LiDAR, RADAR, and SONAR (ultrasonic sensors) which are components of range sensors or thermal cameras, they outperform humans. Generally, a sensor package, made up of numerous kinds of sensors, is used to assist the navigation of ADS. For instance, Tesla's advanced driver assistance system, called Autopilot, makes use of many cameras, RADAR, and ultrasonic sensors. Interestingly, this big company and tech giant does not use LiDAR sensors in its autonomous cars. In order to overcome the shortcomings of individual sensors, such as the lack of structural features in cameras or the absence of color channels in range data, information from multiple sensors must be fused. The wheel rotation is determined via wheel odometry sensors, which can be utilized to calculate how far the autonomous vehicle has traveled. Wheel odometry often works in conjunction with visual odometry or the simultaneous localization and mapping (SLAM) approaches covered in other section because it is unable to capture the car body position in all orientations [2]. LiDAR and other range sensors offer extra details relation to the scene's geometry and framework. Sound waves with high frequency are produced by ultrasonic sensors, which track how long the waves take to reach surrounding objects. Given that the sound wave's velocity is determined, the range to objects can be calculated from the transit time. The similar theories regulate both RADAR and LiDAR, instead of using sound signals, they use electromagnetic waves and laser light beams. Although RADAR sensors have a lower level of precision than other range sensors, because of their longer wavelength, they have a greater working distance. Cameras are an appealing sensor option for autonomous driving vehicles as they are inexpensive, passive, and simple to mount. Many current autonomous systems rely on cameras for activities such as pedestrian detection.

9.6.3   Datasets

In this part, different datasets related to ADS are introduced in the order of their tasks. Table 9.1 illustrates the datasets for object detection and tracking that are widely used in ADS. As can be observed, the number of frames in some datasets is very significant, indicating that the research is close to real world, and given that many of these datasets were generated by big companies, it demonstrates the industry's acceptance of ADS. Furthermore, datasets with plenty of frames seem to be more beneficial for the modern artificial intelligence algorithms, which frequently use deep learning and have a special place in autonomous systems. Despite the high cost, there has been an increase in 3D object labeling and interest in employing LiDAR sensors in recent years. The video camera is one of the most common and straightforward sensors, according to the presented data, and the majority of these datasets have been sampled in urban environments. Referring to MOT challenge benchmarks [136], which evaluate the performance of various multiple object trackers on a benchmark, will be very beneficial given the significance of multiple object tracking.

The datasets for object segmentation, particularly semantic instance segmentation, are shown in Table 9.2 and are frequently utilized in ADS. The high cost and

Table 9.1 Object detection datasets for ADS

Dataset	Organization	Sensors	Annotation	Tracking	Frames	Classes
PandaSet [158]	Hesai & Scale	Video, LiDAR, GPS	2D, 3D	No	60.000	28
nuScences [159]	Aptiv	Video, LiDAR, GPS, Radar	2D, 3D	Yes	40.000	23
Waymo Open [160]	Waymo Inc.	Video, LiDAR	2D, 3D	Yes	200.000	5
Lyft Level5 [161]	Lyft	Video, LiDAR, GPS	2D, 3D	Yes	55.000	23
H3D [162]	Honda Res. Inst.	Video, LiDAR, GPS	3D	Yes	27.000	8
Boxy [163]	Bosch N.A. Res.	Video	2D, 3D	No	200.000	1
Road Damage [164]	U. of Tokyo	Video	2D	No	9.000	8
KAIST Multispect [165]	KAIST	Video, LiDAR, GPS, Thermal	2D	Yes	8.900	6
BDD [166]	U. of California	Video, GPS	2D	Yes	100.000	10
Apollo Open Plat [167]	Baidu Inc.	Video, LiDAR	2D, 3D	Yes	20.000	5
EuroCity [168]	Delft U. of Tech.	Video	2D	Yes	47.000	7
CityPersons [169]	Max Planck Inst.	Video, GPS	2D	No	5.000	4
Electra (CVC-14) [170]	Auton. U. of Barcelona	Video, Infrared Camera	2D	Yes	10.000	1
KITTI [171]	Karlsruhe Inst. of Tech.	Video, LiDAR, GPS	2D, 3D	Yes	15.000	2
German Tarff Sign [55]	Ruhr U.	Video	2D	No	5.000	43
TUD Pedestrian [172]	Max Planck Inst.	Video	2D	Yes	1.600	1
ETH Pedestrian [173]	ETH Zürich	Video	2D, 3D	Yes	4.800	1
Caltech Pedestrian [174]	Caltech	Video	2D	Yes	250.000	1

Table 9.2 *Segmentation datasets for ADS*

Dataset	Organization	Sensors	Annotation	Frames	Classes
PandaSet [158]	Hesai & Scale	Video, LiDAR, GPS	Pixel, Point Cloud	60.000	37
Semantic Kitti [175]	University of Bonn	LiDAR, GPS	Point Cloud	43.000	23
Highway Driving [176]	KAIST	Video	Pixel	1200	10
Apollo Space [177]	Baidu Inc.	Video, LiDAR, GPS	Pixel, Point Cloud, Instance	147.000	35
BDD [166]	U. of California	Video, GPS	Point Cloud, Instance	10.000	40
Wilddash [178]	Austrian Inst. of Tech.	Video	Point Cloud, Instance	226.000	30
Raincouver [179]	U. of British Columbia	Video	Pixel	326.000	3
CitySpace [180]	Max Planck Inst.	Video, GPS	Pixel, Instance	5.000	30
KITTI Semantics [171]	Karlsruhe Inst. of Tech.	Video, LiDAR, GPS	Pixel, Instance	200.000	34
Stanford Track [181]	Stanford University	LiDAR, GPS	Point Cloud, Instance	14.000	3
CamVid [182]	University of Cambridge	Video	Pixel	700.000	32

time complexity are the reasons why segmentation datasets are less than object detection and tracking datasets. Moreover, there are very huge datasets with many frames, allowing us to infer here, as with the previous analysis, that these datasets are suitable for modern machine learning approaches such as deep learning for autonomous systems.

An important part related to ADS is lane detection, which can also be considered related to the detection and segmentation of objects. Table 9.3 shows the datasets applied in this field and features such as spline, point cloud, bounding box, and pixel are used to describe lines. Table 9.4 depicts the datasets related to localization/mapping. From Table 9.4, it can be understood that these datasets are less popular compared to object detection datasets. A large amount of data is not very important in algorithms related to alpha, and maybe that is the reason why deep learning methods are less used in these algorithms. In some of these datasets, RTK and DGPS have been used for centimeter accuracy, and in others, special importance has been given to long distances. However, achieving very high accuracy in the methods that are implemented on these datasets depends on many parameters.

9.6.4   CARLA simulator

For imitated vehicle behaviors, the CARLA simulator [118] gives many forms of sensor information, such as cameras and LiDAR. Furthermore, CARLA offers assistance for planning and analyzing performance in specified scenarios. As an example, we will explain some tracking scenarios that can be implemented in CARLA.

9.6.4.1   Multiple scenarios in CARLA

The three scenarios TrackPedestrians, ManyPedestrians, and ManyPedestriansWithTurn that can be utilized with CARLA will be discussed in the following. The personal vehicle is positioned at a crossroads ahead of a green light in the first scenario, TrackPedestrians. The streets on either side of the roadway are packed with three or five people walking away from the car. The street is vacant of any other vehicles. The pedestrians can all be tracked accurately with less sophisticated trackers because they all move at the same specific speed. As a result, the TrackPedestrians scenario provides a simple setting for evaluating trackers, and trials conducted there should yield starting point for each tracker's performance and precision.

Another scenario, called ManyPedestrians, pursues the previous scenario with the exception that there are twice as many pedestrians viewable in each frame. Although the increased quantity of pedestrians is intended to provide additional occlusions, the pedestrians continue to move at a constant speed, which makes their motion predictable across time. To comprehend how tracker behavior and precisions are impacted when the quantity of targets rises, tests that are done in this scenario are evaluated with equivalent operations in the prior scenario. The third scenario, ManyPedestriansWithTurn, uses the same arrangement of pedestrians as the second one. The vehicle, on the other hand, moves far away from the road in the corner and purposes to provide the target speed at a certain value higher than in the preceding scenarios. In fact, the vehicle in the third scenario performs the following

Table 9.3 Lane detection datasets for ADS

Dataset	Organization	Sensors	Annotation	Frames	Classes
Unsupervised Llamas [183]	Bosch N. A. Research	Video, LiDAR, GPS	Pixel, Point Cloud	100.000	5
BDD [166]	U. of California	Video, GPS	Spline	80.000	11
ApolloScape [177]	Baidu Inc.	Video, LiDAR, GPS	Pixel, Point Cloud	170.000	27
VPGNet [184]	KAIST	Video, GPS	Spline	21.000	17
KITTI Road [171]	Karlsruhe Inst. of Tech.	Video, LiDAR, GPS	Pixel	579.000	2
Road Marking [185]	Honda Research Institute	Video	Bounding box	14.00	23
CalTech Lanes [186]	Caltech	Video	Spline	12.00	2

Table 9.4 Localization and mapping datasets for ADS

Dataset	Organization	Sensors	Length	Frames	Ground Truth
StreetLearn [187]	Deep Mind	Video	1100 km	114.000	GPS, Map
UTBM RoboCar [188]	U. of Tech. of Belfort	Video, LiDAR	63.4 km	220.000	RTK
Multi VSEC [189]	U. of Pennsylvania	Video, LiDAR, ECamera	9.6 km	36000	GPS, IMU, Map
Complex Urban [190]	KAIST	3D LiDAR, 2D LiDAR	44.8 km	unknown	RTK, Map
Oxford RobotCar [191]	Oxford University	Video, LiDAR, GPS	1.01 km	1000.000	DGPS
KITTI Odometry [171]	Karlsruhe Inst. of Tech.	Video, LiDAR	39.2 km	41.000	RTK
Ford [192]	U. of Michigan	Video, LiDAR	5.1 km	7.000	DGPS

actions before reaching the starting point of the car in the second scenario: it first drives about five meters, also turns right along the road, and finally drives another five meters. Regarding the other scenarios, feature straightforward trajectories evaluations in this scenario are performed to establish how the efficiency of the trackers is impacted by rotating camera movements.

Graphics in CARLA

In addition to letting collective various driving scenarios in diverse maps, CARLA also gives users a number of options to customize how the scenarios seem when captured via virtual cams. Users can choose between daylight and overnight settings in recent versions to adjust illumination [118]. Additionally, there are other weather settings that let users define the sun's direction, the amount of cloud cover, the wind velocity, and the amount of rainfall. Numerous camera settings are adjustable by the operator, such as the color intensity, blurriness, and lens length. CARLA has announced that further possibilities for scenario personalization will be made available in addition to all of these. The CARLA team wants to increase the variety of apparel, skins, and hair of pedestrians, for instance [118]. Although CARLA keeps adding more choices for scenario modification, the simulator's presentation remains considerably different from that of the actual world. Due to the constraints of the visual graphics related to the CARLA simulator, input perception in simulations is easier to achieve compared to the actual world. The effectiveness of perceptual elements that depend on cameras as entrance information is influenced by this difference between the CARLA and the real environment. In order for the models trained on the simulator to function reasonably well in the actual world, the training circumstances on the simulator should be diversified enough to avoid overfitting the data on the simulator conditions and to have an acceptable performance in the actual world as much as possible. Additionally, it is challenging for the CARLA simulator to implement multiple objects tracking that is acquired from the real world. The CARLA simulator's circumstances are sufficiently complicated, nevertheless, that the overall outcomes from every simulation are applicable to ADS in the actual world.

In addition to major corporations like Tesla and Uber in the field of autonomous vehicles, as well as thanks to Professor Thrun and the Udacity company, who have been researching in this field for many years, one of the best companies functioning in this field is the Waabi Company, under the direction of Professor Urtasun. The Wayve research company has also experienced impressive development recently in the area of autonomous mobility.

9.7   Localization and mapping for autonomous driving

An accurate knowledge of the location and orientation of the vehicle is necessary for navigation. In high-tech fields such as robotics and computer vision, localization is a well-researched issue that has given rise to a variety of solutions, from indoor localization utilizing incorrect sensory readings to identifying the location of an image. Localizing the car on a map is the main objective of ADS so that it can take advantage of the specific features that extracted from the map. The mapping challenge is characterized as the problem of generating a map of the interacting environment depicted by entire world.

In general, there are two approaches for generating maps: metric and semantic. Semantic maps offer information particular to a given problem, like the position of parking spaces, whereas metric maps enable precise localization. It is important to note that through the utilization of precise but computationally costly optimization approaches, offline mapping can be produced for localization.

9.7.1   Mapping

The production of accurate metric and semantic maps is made possible by satellite, aerial, and street images. Different computer vision approaches, such as semantic segmentation or scene understanding, are commonly used for map generation based on the needed degree of detail.

9.7.1.1   Metric approaches for generating maps

The 2D maps from metric approaches, which depict knowledge from a bird's-eye perspective, are typically adequate for localization in autonomous vehicles. A notable case of a significant gathering of panoramas images which are recorded with respect to one another to create a globe map is the Google Street View project [137]. This work [137] estimates the position of the car using several resources, such as navigation [138], GPS data fusion, and a Kalman filter, with the purpose of recording the information. A probabilistic graphical model is used to enhance the position estimations, and then specific meshes are reliably fitted to the 3D observations to reconstruct the geometric features of the 3-dimentional view. To create a map using pooled reflectivity data from a LiDAR scanner, a method [139] was proposed. During the DARPA Urban Challenge, this technique made use of generated maps for accurate data based on LiDAR localization.

9.7.1.2   Semantic approaches for generating maps

To perform some tasks such as automatic vehicle parking, it is very important to have semantic information while metric maps do not have this information. Semantic maps overcome this weakness of metric maps and several important semantic approaches were introduced for this task [140,141]. While not producing a semantic map, some scene understanding techniques such as [142] approximate semantic categories to retrieve path geometries.

9.7.2   Localization

Both visual data basis of images and a sensor like GPS can be utilized for localization. A precision of about five meters is often provided through using GPS exclusively. In an ideal environment, it is possible to achieve centimeter-level accuracy with the presence of multiple sensors along with the signal correction technique as in the KITTI car [143]. The question is whether all environments are ideal. In response it should be stated that in environments such as urban traffic, due to the presence of some buildings or trees and vegetation, there is a possibility of occlusion, and this phenomenon is known as disturbing effects. As a result, localization based on images that is not relying on satellite systems is still extremely important. Generally, metric and topological approaches are used to categorize visual localization strategies. Through estimating the 3D position in relation to a map, metric localization [144] is accomplished. On the contrary, using a limited number of potential spots that are depicted as a graph's nodes and linked by edges that interconnect them in accordance with certain proximity or visual parameters, topological localization approaches [145,146] offer a rough estimation. In comparing these two methods, it should be mentioned that topological localization may be more dependable but only make available coarse estimation, whereas metric localization can be quite precise but is naturally not appropriate for very lengthy sequences scene.

9.7.3 Simultaneous localization and mapping (SLAM)

In general, planning and navigation in ADS are made easier with a thorough environmental mapping. Nevertheless, there are some conditions under which ADS have to perform localization when generating the map, such as places where the map is old and outdated or places for which no map is provided at all. The mapping also has to be revised frequently to indicate continual varies in the environment. The process of constantly generating a map of the agent environments while simultaneously estimating the agent's location is known as SLAM, which concentrates on real-time applications and large-scale environments.

By applying extended particle filters [147] or Kalman filters [148], initial SLAM methods could handle the issue with Bayesian assumptions. The current state, defined by position, velocity, and the coordinates of the markers, is iteratively revised in based on the previous state and incoming information. On the other hand, due to the volume of markers on the map has a quadratic relationship with the belief state and computation cost of the filtering upgrade, this strategy incompetent to apply in enormous environs. Given that stereo cameras, contrary to LiDAR sensors, they enable depth estimation while simultaneously offering rich knowledge on an object's form. Moreover, they are a popular option for addressing the SLAM, and perhaps this is the reason, beside to its cost, why one of the major companies in the field of autonomous vehicles does not use LiDAR sensors.

A visual SLAM approach based on dense stereo that estimates a dense 3D map is introduced in [149]. This approach achieves a sparse map and the position. In fact, stereo cameras generate a dense model for the 3D map in a local coordinate, and then utilizing a SLAM based on sparsity to follow the local coordinate to constantly update the map. LSD-SLAM, a large-scale direct SLAM approach for real-time performance that integrates multiview and static stereo from a camera configuration was proposed in [150]. This approach prevents scale-drift that happens when utilizing multiview stereo and enables it to approximate the depths of cells that are restricted in static stereo. Depending on the image coherence of high contrast cells, the images are closely aligned.

One of the most important and commonly used SLAM methods, entitled ORB-SLAM, was introduced in [151]. It uses specific features called ORB [152] for mapping, localization, tracking, and an important function related to loops called loop closure. Actually, this strategy uses a mixture of methods, such as position optimization of graphs [153], loop closing [154], and loop detection [155], to achieve its goal. A significant problem in SLAM approaches is dealing with modifications in the environment that may perhaps not be depicted on the map. With generating a map including features that are inclined to remain static across time in [156], mentioned earlier SLAM issues have almost been overcome. In order to generate an infra-red specific map of the roadways from overhead sights, this strategy exclusively remain at surfaces via 3D LiDAR scanning sensor. In a real-time process, a particle filter is then utilized to find a vehicle through the specific map, known as the reflectance map. A novel strategy that regards map-pings as probability distributions across environmental attributes instead of a static depiction was presented in [157] as an improvement on previous work. To be more precise, each cell of the probabilistic map is defined by a separate distribution of Gaussian which enables this method to localize with less mistakes and depict the environment more precisely. This method also aligns numerous passes of the same environs made at various periods utilizing offline SLAM to build up a more comprehensive understanding of the environment.

References

[1]   D. Omeiza, H. Webb, M. Jirotka, and L. Kunze, "Explanations in Autonomous Driving: A Survey," *IEEE Transactions on Intelligent Transportation Systems*, vol. 23, pp. 10142–10162, 2021.

[2]   L. G. Galvao, M. Abbod, T. Kalganova, V. Palade, and M. N. Huda, "Pedestrian and Vehicle Detection in Autonomous Vehicle Perception Systems—A Review," *Sensors*, vol. 21, no. 21, p. 7267, 2021.

[3]   J. Deng, W. Dong, R. Socher, L. Li, L. Kai, and F.-F. Li, "ImageNet: A Large-Scale Hierarchical Image Database," in *2009 IEEE Conference on Computer Vision and Pattern Recognition*, 2009, pp. 248–255.

[4]   Z. Zhao, P. Zheng, S. Xu, and X. Wu, "Object Detection With Deep Learning: A Review," *IEEE Transactions on Neural Networks and Learning Systems*, vol. 30, no. 11, pp. 3212–3232, 2019.

[5]   X. Wu, D. Sahoo, and S. C. H. Hoi, "Recent Advances in Deep Learning for Object Detection," *Neurocomputing*, vol. 396, pp. 39–64, 2020.

[6]   D. G. Lowe, "Distinctive Image Features from Scale-Invariant Keypoints," *International Journal of Computer Vision*, vol. 60, no. 2, pp. 91–110, 2004.

[7]   N. Dalal and B. Triggs, "Histograms of Oriented Gradients for Human Detection," in *2005 IEEE Computer Society Conference on Computer Vision and Pattern Recognition (CVPR'05)*, 2005, vol. 1, pp. 886–893.

[8]   P. F. Felzenszwalb, R. B. Girshick, D. McAllester, and D. Ramanan, "Object Detection with Discriminatively Trained Part-Based Models,"

       IEEE Transactions on Pattern Analysis and Machine Intelligence, vol. 32, no. 9, pp. 1627–1645, 2010.

[9]   C. Cortes and V. Vapnik, "Support-Vector Networks," *Machine Learning*, vol. 20, no. 3, pp. 273–297, 1995.

[10]   Y. LeCun, Y. Bengio, and G. Hinton, "Deep Learning," *Nature*, vol. 521, no. 7553, pp. 436–444, 2015.

[11]   A. Krizhevsky, I. Sutskever, and G. E. Hinton, "ImageNet Classification with Deep Convolutional Neural Networks," presented at the *Proceedings of the 25th International Conference on Neural Information Processing Systems* – Volume 1, Lake Tahoe, Nevada, 2012.

[12]   Y. Lecun, L. Bottou, Y. Bengio, and P. Haffner, "Gradient-Based Learning Applied to Document Recognition," *Proceedings of the IEEE*, vol. 86, no. 11, pp. 2278–2324, 1998.

[13]   R. Girshick, J. Donahue, T. Darrell, and J. Malik, "Rich Feature Hierarchies for Accurate Object Detection and Semantic Segmentation," in *2014 IEEE Conference on Computer Vision and Pattern Recognition*, 2014, pp. 580–587.

[14]   J. Uijlings, K. V. D. Sande, T. Gevers, and A. Smeulders, "Selective Search for Object Recognition," *International Journal of Computer Vision*, vol. 104, pp. 154–171, 2013.

[15]   K. He, X. Zhang, S. Ren, and J. Sun, "Spatial Pyramid Pooling in Deep Convolutional Networks for Visual Recognition," *IEEE Transactions on Pattern Analysis and Machine Intelligence*, vol. 37, no. 9, pp. 1904–1916, 2015.

[16]   S. Lazebnik, C. Schmid, and J. Ponce, "Beyond Bags of Features: Spatial Pyramid Matching for Recognizing Natural Scene Categories," in *2006 IEEE Computer Society Conference on Computer Vision and Pattern Recognition (CVPR'06)*, 2006, vol. 2, pp. 2169–2178.

[17]   R. Girshick, "Fast R-CNN," in *2015 IEEE International Conference on Computer Vision (ICCV)*, 2015, pp. 1440–1448.

[18]   S. Ren, K. He, R. Girshick, and J. Sun, "Faster R-CNN: Towards Real-Time Object Detection with Region Proposal Networks," *IEEE Transactions on Pattern Analysis and Machine Intelligence*, vol. 39, no. 6, pp. 1137–1149, 2017.

[19]   K. He, G. Gkioxari, P. Dollár, and R. Girshick, "Mask R-CNN," in *2017 IEEE International Conference on Computer Vision (ICCV)*, 2017, pp. 2980–2988.

[20]   J. Redmon, S. Divvala, R. Girshick, and A. Farhadi, "You Only Look Once: Unified, Real-Time Object Detection," in *2016 IEEE Conference on Computer Vision and Pattern Recognition (CVPR)*, 2016, pp. 779–788.

[21]   J. Redmon and A. Farhadi, "YOLO9000: Better, Faster, Stronger," in *2017 IEEE Conference on Computer Vision and Pattern Recognition (CVPR)*, 2017, pp. 6517–6525.

[22]   J. Redmon and A. Farhadi, "YOLOv3: An Incremental Improvement," ArXiv:1804.02767, 2018.

[23] T. Lin, P. Goyal, R. Girshick, K. He, and P. Dollár, "Focal Loss for Dense Object Detection," *IEEE Transactions on Pattern Analysis and Machine Intelligence*, vol. 42, no. 2, pp. 318–327, 2020.

[24] K. Simonyan and A. Zisserman, "Very Deep Convolutional Networks for Large-Scale Image Recognition," ArXiv:1409.1556, 2015.

[25] B. Kim, N. Yuvaraj, K. R. Sri Preethaa, R. Santhosh, and A. Sabari, "Enhanced Pedestrian Detection Using Optimized Deep Convolution Neural Network for Smart Building Surveillance," *Soft Computing*, vol. 24, no. 22, pp. 17081–17092, 2020.

[26] M. Aledhari, R. Razzak, R. M. Parizi, and G. Srivastava, "Multimodal Machine Learning for Pedestrian Detection," in *2021 IEEE 93rd Vehicular Technology Conference (VTC2021–Spring)*, 2021, pp. 1–7.

[27] X. Du, M. El-Khamy, J. Lee, and L. Davis, "Fused DNN: A Deep Neural Network Fusion Approach to Fast and Robust Pedestrian Detection," in *2017 IEEE Winter Conference on Applications of Computer Vision (WACV)*, 2017, pp. 953–961.

[28] G. Brazil and X. Liu, "Pedestrian Detection With Autoregressive Network Phases," in *2019 IEEE/CVF Conference on Computer Vision and Pattern Recognition (CVPR)*, 2019, pp. 7224–7233.

[29] I. Hasan, S. Liao, J. Li, S. U. Akram, and L. Shao, "Generalizable Pedestrian Detection: The Elephant In The Room," *2021 IEEE/CVF Conference on Computer Vision and Pattern Recognition (CVPR)*, pp. 11323–11332, 2020.

[30] W. Ouyang and X. Wang, "A Discriminative Deep Model for Pedestrian Detection with Occlusion Handling," in *2012 IEEE Conference on Computer Vision and Pattern Recognition*, 2012, pp. 3258–3265.

[31] P. Luo, Y. Tian, X. Wang, and X. Tang, "Switchable Deep Network for Pedestrian Detection," in *2014 IEEE Conference on Computer Vision and Pattern Recognition*, 2014, pp. 899–906.

[32] H. Wang, Y. Cai, and L. Chen, "A Vehicle Detection Algorithm Based on Deep Belief Network," *The Scientific World Journal*, vol. 2014, p. 647380, 2014.

[33] W. Liu, S. Liao, W. Hu, X. Liang, and Y. Zhang, "Improving Tiny Vehicle Detection in Complex Scenes," in *2018 IEEE International Conference on Multimedia and Expo (ICME)*, 2018, pp. 1–6.

[34] J. Ren, X. Chen, J. Liu, *et al.*, "Accurate Single Stage Detector Using Recurrent Rolling Convolution," *2017 IEEE Conference on Computer Vision and Pattern Recognition (CVPR)*, pp. 752–760, 2017.

[35] J. Hu, Y. Sun, and S. Xiong, "Research on the Cascade Vehicle Detection Method Based on CNN," *Electronics*, vol. 10, no. 4, p. 481, 2021.

[36] X. Hu, X. Xu, Y. Xiao, *et al.*, "SINet: A Scale-Insensitive Convolutional Neural Network for Fast Vehicle Detection," *IEEE Transactions on Intelligent Transportation Systems*, vol. 20, pp. 1010–1019, 2018.

[37] Z. Cai, Q. Fan, R. S. Feris, and N. Vasconcelos, "A Unified Multi-scale Deep Convolutional Neural Network for Fast Object Detection," ArXiv: 1607.07155, 2016.

[38]   X. Wang, X. Hua, F. Xiao, Y. Li, X. Hu, and P. Sun, "Multi-Object Detection in Traffic Scenes Based on Improved SSD," *Electronics*, vol. 7, no. 11, p. 302, 2018.

[39]   Q. Fan, L. Brown, and J. Smith, "A Closer Look at Faster R-CNN for Vehicle Detection," in *2016 IEEE Intelligent Vehicles Symposium (IV)*, 2016, pp. 124–129.

[40]   Y. Gao, S. Guo, K. Haung, *et al.*, "Scale Optimization for Full-Image-CNN Vehicle Detection," in *2017 IEEE Intelligent Vehicles Symposium (IV)*, 2017, pp. 785–791.

[41]   W. Chu, Y. Liu, C. Shen, D. Cai, and X. S. Hua, "Multi-Task Vehicle Detection With Region-of-Interest Voting," *IEEE Transactions on Image Processing*, vol. 27, no. 1, pp. 432–441, 2018.

[42]   X. Yuan, S. Su, and H. Chen, "A Graph-Based Vehicle Proposal Location and Detection Algorithm," *IEEE Transactions on Intelligent Transportation Systems*, vol. 18, no. 12, pp. 3282–3289, 2017.

[43]   L. Chen, Q. Ding, Q. Zou, Z. Chen, and L. Li, "DenseLightNet: A Light-Weight Vehicle Detection Network for Autonomous Driving," *IEEE Transactions on Industrial Electronics*, vol. 67, no. 12, pp. 10600–10609, 2020.

[44]   Z. Cai and N. Vasconcelos, "Cascade R-CNN: High Quality Object Detection and Instance Segmentation," *IEEE Transactions on Pattern Analysis and Machine Intelligence*, vol. 43, no. 5, pp. 1483–1498, 2021.

[45]   A. Broggi, P. Cerri, P. Medici, P. P. Porta, and G. Ghisio, "Real Time Road Signs Recognition," in *2007 IEEE Intelligent Vehicles Symposium*, 2007, pp. 981–986.

[46]   D. Cireşan, U. Meier, J. Masci, and J. Schmidhuber, "A Committee of Neural Networks for Traffic Sign Classification," in *The 2011 International Joint Conference on Neural Networks*, 2011, pp. 1918–1921.

[47]   J. Jin, K. Fu, and C. Zhang, "Traffic Sign Recognition With Hinge Loss Trained Convolutional Neural Networks," *IEEE Transactions on Intelligent Transportation Systems*, vol. 15, no. 5, pp. 1991–2000, 2014.

[48]   P. Sermanet and Y. LeCun, "Traffic Sign Recognition with Multi-Scale Convolutional Networks," in *The 2011 International Joint Conference on Neural Networks*, 2011, pp. 2809–2813.

[49]   H. Habibi Aghdam, E. Jahani Heravi, and D. Puig, "A Practical Approach for Detection and Classification of Traffic Signs Using Convolutional Neural Networks," *Robotics and Autonomous Systems*, vol. 84, pp. 97–112, 2016.

[50]   Á. Arcos-García, J. A. Álvarez-García, and L. M. Soria-Morillo, "Evaluation of Deep Neural Networks for Traffic Sign Detection Systems," *Neurocomputing*, vol. 316, pp. 332–344, 2018.

[51]   S. Houben, J. Stallkamp, J. Salmen, M. Schlipsing, and C. Igel, "Detection of Traffic Signs in Real-World Images: The German Traffic Sign Detection Benchmark," in *The 2013 International Joint Conference on Neural Networks (IJCNN)*, 2013, pp. 1–8.

[52]   S. Ioffe and C. Szegedy, "Batch Normalization: Accelerating Deep Network Training by Reducing Internal Covariate Shift," ArXiv:1502.03167, 2015.

[53]   T. Yang, X. Long, A. K. Sangaiah, Z. Zheng, and C. Tong, "Deep Detection Network for Real-Life Traffic Sign in Vehicular Networks," *Computer Networks*, vol. 136, pp. 95–104, 2018.

[54]   Z. Zhu, D. Liang, S. Zhang, X. Huang, B. Li, and S. Hu, "Traffic-Sign Detection and Classification in the Wild," in *2016 IEEE Conference on Computer Vision and Pattern Recognition (CVPR)*, 2016, pp. 2110–2118.

[55]   J. Stallkamp, M. Schlipsing, J. Salmen, and C. Igel, "The German Traffic Sign Recognition Benchmark: A Multi-class Classification Competition," in *The 2011 International Joint Conference on Neural Networks*, 2011, pp. 1453–1460.

[56]   R. Ravindran, M. J. Santora, and M. M. Jamali, "Multi-Object Detection and Tracking, Based on DNN, for Autonomous Vehicles: A Review," *IEEE Sensors Journal*, vol. 21, no. 5, pp. 5668–5677, 2021.

[57]   A. G. A. Perera, C. Srinivas, A. Hoogs, G. Brooksby, and H. Wensheng, "Multi-Object Tracking Through Simultaneous Long Occlusions and Split-Merge Conditions," in *2006 IEEE Computer Society Conference on Computer Vision and Pattern Recognition (CVPR'06)*, 2006, vol. 1, pp. 666–673.

[58]   M. D. Breitenstein, F. Reichlin, B. Leibe, E. Koller-Meier, and L. V. Gool, "Robust Tracking-by-Detection Using a Detector Confidence Particle Filter," in *2009 IEEE 12th International Conference on Computer Vision*, 2009, pp. 1515–1522.

[59]   H. Jiang, S. Fels, and J. J. Little, "A Linear Programming Approach for Multiple Object Tracking," in *2007 IEEE Conference on Computer Vision and Pattern Recognition*, 2007, pp. 1–8.

[60]   J. Berclaz, F. Fleuret, E. Turetken, and P. Fua, "Multiple Object Tracking Using K-Shortest Paths Optimization," *IEEE Transactions on Pattern Analysis and Machine Intelligence*, vol. 33, no. 9, pp. 1806–1819, 2011.

[61]   Z. Wu, T. H. Kunz, and M. Betke, "Efficient Track Linking Methods for Track Graphs Using Network-Flow and Set-Cover Techniques," in *CVPR 2011*, 2011, pp. 1185–1192.

[62]   S. Tang, B. Andres, M. Andriluka, and B. Schiele, "Subgraph Decomposition for Multi-Target Tracking," in *2015 IEEE Conference on Computer Vision and Pattern Recognition (CVPR)*, 2015, pp. 5033–5041.

[63]   A. Dehghan, S. M. Assari, and M. Shah, "GMMCP Tracker: Globally Optimal Generalized Maximum Multi Clique problem for Multiple Object Tracking," in *2015 IEEE Conference on Computer Vision and Pattern Recognition (CVPR)*, 2015, pp. 4091–4099.

[64]   W. Brendel, M. Amer, and S. Todorovic, "Multiobject Tracking as Maximum Weight Independent Set," in *CVPR 2011*, 2011, pp. 1273–1280.

[65]   B. Yang and R. Nevatia, "An Online Learned CRF Model for Multi-Target Tracking," in *2012 IEEE Conference on Computer Vision and Pattern Recognition*, 2012, pp. 2034–2041.

[66] A. Andriyenko, K. Schindler, and S. Roth, "Discrete-Continuous Optimization for Multi-Target Tracking," in *2012 IEEE Conference on Computer Vision and Pattern Recognition*, 2012, pp. 1926–1933.

[67] J. Giebel, D. M. Gavrila, and C. Schnörr, "A Bayesian Framework for Multi-cue 3D Object Tracking," in *Computer Vision – ECCV 2004*, Berlin, Heidelberg, 2004, pp. 241–252: Springer Berlin Heidelberg.

[68] M. Andriluka, S. Roth, and B. Schiele, "People-Tracking-by-Detection and People-Detection-by-Tracking," in *2008 IEEE Conference on Computer Vision and Pattern Recognition*, 2008, pp. 1–8.

[69] M. Andriluka, S. Roth, and B. Schiele, "Monocular 3D Pose Estimation and Tracking by Detection," in *2010 IEEE Computer Society Conference on Computer Vision and Pattern Recognition*, 2010, pp. 623–630.

[70] Y. Tian, A. Dehghan, and M. Shah, "On Detection, Data Association and Segmentation for Multi-Target Tracking," *IEEE Transactions on Pattern Analysis and Machine Intelligence*, vol. 41, no. 9, pp. 2146–2160, 2019.

[71] C. Kim, F. Li, and J. M. Rehg, "Multi-object Tracking with Neural Gating Using Bilinear LSTM," in *Computer Vision – ECCV 2018*, Cham, 2018, pp. 208–224: Springer International Publishing.

[72] S. Tang, B. Andres, M. Andriluka, and B. Schiele, "Multi-Person Tracking by Multicut and Deep Matching," ArXiv:1608.05404, 2016.

[73] C. Kim, F. Li, A. Ciptadi, and J. M. Rehg, "Multiple Hypothesis Tracking Revisited," in *2015 IEEE International Conference on Computer Vision (ICCV)*, 2015, pp. 4696–4704.

[74] Y. Xiang, A. Alahi, and S. Savarese, "Learning to Track: Online Multi-object Tracking by Decision Making," in *2015 IEEE International Conference on Computer Vision (ICCV)*, 2015, pp. 4705–4713.

[75] S. Tang, M. Andriluka, B. Andres, and B. Schiele, "Multiple People Tracking by Lifted Multicut and Person Re-identification," in *2017 IEEE Conference on Computer Vision and Pattern Recognition (CVPR)*, 2017, pp. 3701–3710.

[76] A. Sadeghian, A. Alahi, and S. Savarese, "Tracking the Untrackable: Learning to Track Multiple Cues with Long-Term Dependencies," *2017 IEEE International Conference on Computer Vision (ICCV)*, pp. 300–311, 2017.

[77] M. Babaee, A. Athar, and G. Rigoll, "Multiple People Tracking Using Hierarchical Deep Tracklet Re-identification," ArXiv:1811.04091, 2018.

[78] S. Schulter, P. Vernaza, W. Choi, and M. Chandraker, "Deep Network Flow for Multi-object Tracking," *2017 IEEE Conference on Computer Vision and Pattern Recognition (CVPR)*, pp. 2730–2739, 2017.

[79] A. Milan, S. H. Rezatofighi, A. R. Dick, I. D. Reid, and K. Schindler, "Online Multi-Target Tracking Using Recurrent Neural Networks," in *AAAI Conference on Artificial Intelligence*, 2016.

[80] G. Ciaparrone, F. Luque Sánchez, S. Tabik, L. Troiano, R. Tagliaferri, and F. Herrera, "Deep Learning in Video Multi-object Tracking: A Survey," *Neurocomputing*, vol. 381, pp. 61–88, 2020.

[81]   X. He, R. S. Zemel, and D. Ray, "Learning and Incorporating Top-Down Cues in Image Segmentation," in *Computer Vision – ECCV 2006*, Berlin, Heidelberg, 2006, pp. 338–351: Springer Berlin Heidelberg.

[82]   P. Kohli, L. Ladicky, and P. H. S. Torr, "Robust Higher Order Potentials for Enforcing Label Consistency," in *2008 IEEE Conference on Computer Vision and Pattern Recognition*, 2008, pp. 1–8.

[83]   H. Xuming, R. S. Zemel, and M. A. Carreira-Perpinan, "Multiscale Conditional Random Fields for Image Labeling," in *Proceedings of the 2004 IEEE Computer Society Conference on Computer Vision and Pattern Recognition, 2004. CVPR 2004*, 2004, vol. 2, pp. 695–702.

[84]   J. J. Verbeek and B. Triggs, "Scene Segmentation with CRFs Learned from Partially Labeled Images," in *NIPS*, 2007.

[85]   S. Kumar and M. Hebert, "A Hierarchical Field Framework for Unified Context-Based Classification," in *Tenth IEEE International Conference on Computer Vision (ICCV'05) Volume 1*, 2005, vol. 2, pp. 1284–1291.

[86]   P. Krähenbühl and V. Koltun, "Efficient Inference in Fully Connected CRFs with Gaussian Edge Potentials," in *NIPS*, 2011.

[87]   D. Munoz, J. A. Bagnell, and M. Hebert, "Stacked Hierarchical Labeling," in *Computer Vision – ECCV 2010*, Berlin, Heidelberg, 2010, pp. 57–70: Springer Berlin Heidelberg.

[88]   J. Shotton, J. Winn, C. Rother, and A. Criminisi, "TextonBoost for Image Understanding: Multi-Class Object Recognition and Segmentation by Jointly Modeling Texture, Layout, and Context," *International Journal of Computer Vision*, vol. 81, no. 1, pp. 2–23, 2009.

[89]   L. Ladicky, C. Russell, P. Kohli, and P. H. S. Torr, "Graph Cut Based Inference with Co-Occurrence Statistics," in *Computer Vision – ECCV 2010*, Berlin, Heidelberg, 2010, pp. 239–253: Springer Berlin Heidelberg.

[90]   Y. Zhang and T. Chen, "Efficient Inference for Fully-Connected CRFs with Stationarity," in *2012 IEEE Conference on Computer Vision and Pattern Recognition*, 2012, pp. 582–589.

[91]   H. Myeong, J. Y. Chang, and K. M. Lee, "Learning Object Relationships via Graph-Based Context Model," in *2012 IEEE Conference on Computer Vision and Pattern Recognition*, 2012, pp. 2727–2734.

[92]   E. Shelhamer, J. Long, and T. Darrell, "Fully Convolutional Networks for Semantic Segmentation," *2015 IEEE Conference on Computer Vision and Pattern Recognition (CVPR)*, pp. 3431–3440, 2014.

[93]   L.-C. Chen, G. Papandreou, I. Kokkinos, K. P. Murphy, and A. L. Yuille, "Semantic Image Segmentation with Deep Convolutional Nets and Fully Connected CRFs," ArXiv:1412.7062, 2014.

[94]   F. Yu and V. Koltun, "Multi-Scale Context Aggregation by Dilated Convolutions," ArXiv:1511.07122, 2015.

[95]   L.-C. Chen, G. Papandreou, I. Kokkinos, K. P. Murphy, and A. L. Yuille, "DeepLab: Semantic Image Segmentation with Deep Convolutional Nets, Atrous Convolution, and Fully Connected CRFs," *IEEE Transactions on Pattern Analysis and Machine Intelligence*, vol. 40, pp. 834–848, 2016.

[96] C. Szegedy, W. Liu, Y. Jia, *et al.*, "Going Deeper with Convolutions," in *2015 IEEE Conference on Computer Vision and Pattern Recognition (CVPR)*, 2015, pp. 1–9.

[97] K. He, X. Zhang, S. Ren, and J. Sun, "Deep Residual Learning for Image Recognition," *2016 IEEE Conference on Computer Vision and Pattern Recognition (CVPR)*, pp. 770–778, 2016.

[98] G. Floros and B. Leibe, "Joint 2D-3D Temporally Consistent Semantic Segmentation of Street Scenes," in *2012 IEEE Conference on Computer Vision and Pattern Recognition*, 2012, pp. 2823–2830.

[99] J. L. Schönberger, M. Pollefeys, A. Geiger, and T. Sattler, "Semantic Visual Localization," *2018 IEEE/CVF Conference on Computer Vision and Pattern Recognition*, pp. 6896–6906, 2017.

[100] C. Häne, N. Savinov, and M. Pollefeys, "Class Specific 3D Object Shape Priors Using Surface Normals," in *2014 IEEE Conference on Computer Vision and Pattern Recognition*, 2014, pp. 652–659.

[101] J. Xiao and L. Quan, "Multiple View Semantic Segmentation for Street View Images," *2009 IEEE 12th International Conference on Computer Vision*, pp. 686–693, 2009.

[102] P. O. Pinheiro, T.-Y. Lin, R. Collobert, and P. Dollár, "Learning to Refine Object Segments," in *Computer Vision – ECCV 2016*, Cham, 2016, pp. 75–91: Springer International Publishing.

[103] P. H. O. Pinheiro, R. Collobert, and P. Dollár, "Learning to Segment Object Candidates," in *NIPS*, 2015.

[104] J. Carreira and C. Sminchisescu, "CPMC: Automatic Object Segmentation Using Constrained Parametric Min-Cuts," *IEEE Transactions on Pattern Analysis and Machine Intelligence*, vol. 34, no. 7, pp. 1312–1328, 2012.

[105] J. Carreira, R. Caseiro, J. Batista, and C. Sminchisescu, "Semantic Segmentation with Second-Order Pooling," in *Computer Vision – ECCV 2012*, Berlin, Heidelberg, 2012, pp. 430–443: Springer Berlin Heidelberg.

[106] J. Dai, K. He, and J. Sun, "Convolutional Feature Masking for Joint Object and Stuff Segmentation," *2015 IEEE Conference on Computer Vision and Pattern Recognition (CVPR)*, pp. 3992–4000, 2014.

[107] B. Hariharan, P. Arbeláez, R. B. Girshick, and J. Malik, "Hypercolumns for Object Segmentation and Fine-Grained Localization," *2015 IEEE Conference on Computer Vision and Pattern Recognition (CVPR)*, pp. 447–456, 2014.

[108] J. Dai, K. He, and J. Sun, "Instance-Aware Semantic Segmentation via Multi-Task Network Cascades," *2016 IEEE Conference on Computer Vision and Pattern Recognition (CVPR)*, pp. 3150–3158, 2015.

[109] L.-C. Chen, A. Hermans, G. Papandreou, F. Schroff, P. Wang, and H. Adam, "MaskLab: Instance Segmentation by Refining Object Detection with Semantic and Direction Features," *2018 IEEE/CVF Conference on Computer Vision and Pattern Recognition*, pp. 4013–4022, 2017.

[110] Z. Zhang, A. G. Schwing, S. Fidler, and R. Urtasun, "Monocular Object Instance Segmentation and Depth Ordering with CNNs," *2015 IEEE*

International Conference on Computer Vision (ICCV), pp. 2614–2622, 2015.

[111] Z. Zhang, S. Fidler, and R. Urtasun, "Instance-Level Segmentation for Autonomous Driving with Deep Densely Connected MRFs," *2016 IEEE Conference on Computer Vision and Pattern Recognition (CVPR)*, pp. 669–677, 2015.

[112] A. Kirillov, E. Levinkov, B. Andres, B. Savchynskyy, and C. Rother, "InstanceCut: From Edges to Instances with MultiCut," *2017 IEEE Conference on Computer Vision and Pattern Recognition (CVPR)*, pp. 7322–7331, 2016.

[113] M. Bai and R. Urtasun, "Deep Watershed Transform for Instance Segmentation," *2017 IEEE Conference on Computer Vision and Pattern Recognition (CVPR)*, pp. 2858–2866, 2016.

[114] A. Kirillov, K. He, R. B. Girshick, C. Rother, and P. Dollár, "Panoptic Segmentation," *2019 IEEE/CVF Conference on Computer Vision and Pattern Recognition (CVPR)*, pp. 9396–9405, 2018.

[115] Q. Li, A. Arnab, and P. H. S. Torr, "Weakly- and Semi-Supervised Panoptic Segmentation," ArXiv:1808.03575, 2018.

[116] A. D. Costea, A. Petrovai, and S. Nedevschi, "Fusion Scheme for Semantic and Instance-Level Segmentation," in *2018 21st International Conference on Intelligent Transportation Systems (ITSC)*, 2018, pp. 3469–3475.

[117] R. S. Sutton and A. G. Barto, *Reinforcement Learning: An Introduction*. A Bradford Book, 2018.

[118] A. Dosovitskiy, G. Ros, F. Codevilla, A. Lopez, and V. Koltun, "CARLA: An Open Urban Driving Simulator," presented at the *Proceedings of the 1st Annual Conference on Robot Learning, Proceedings of Machine Learning Research*, 2017. Available: https://proceedings.mlr.press/v78/dosovitskiy17a.html

[119] V. R. Konda and J. N. Tsitsiklis, "Actor-Critic Algorithms," in *NIPS*, 1999.

[120] A. Kendall, J. Hawke, D. Janz, *et al.*, "Learning to Drive in a Day," in *2019 International Conference on Robotics and Automation (ICRA)*, 2019, pp. 8248–8254.

[121] M. Henaff, A. Canziani, and Y. LeCun, "Model-Predictive Policy Learning with Uncertainty Regularization for Driving in Dense Traffic," ArXiv:1901.02705, 2019.

[122] S. Sharifzadeh, I. Chiotellis, R. Triebel, and D. Cremers, "Learning to Drive using Inverse Reinforcement Learning and Deep Q-Networks," ArXiv:1612.03653, 2016.

[123] D. Hoiem, A. A. Efros, and M. Hebert, "Recovering Surface Layout from an Image," *International Journal of Computer Vision*, vol. 75, pp. 151–172, 2007.

[124] M. Oliveira, V. Santos, A. D. Sappa, P. Dias, and A. P. Moreira, "Incremental Scenario Representations for Autonomous Driving Using Geometric Polygonal Primitives," *Robotics and Autonomous Systems*, vol. 83, pp. 312–325, 2016.

[125] C. Wojek and B. Schiele, "A Dynamic Conditional Random Field Model for Joint Labeling of Object and Scene Classes," in *Computer Vision –*

ECCV 2008, Berlin, Heidelberg, 2008, pp. 733–747: Springer Berlin Heidelberg.

[126] C. Wojek, S. Roth, K. Schindler, and B. Schiele, "Monocular 3D Scene Modeling and Inference: Understanding Multi-Object Traffic Scenes," in *Computer Vision – ECCV 2010*, Berlin, Heidelberg, 2010, pp. 467–481: Springer Berlin, Heidelberg.

[127] A. Geiger, M. Lauer, C. Wojek, C. Stiller, and R. Urtasun, "3D Traffic Scene Understanding From Movable Platforms," *IEEE Transactions on Pattern Analysis and Machine Intelligence*, vol. 36, pp. 1012–1025, 2014.

[128] D. Töpfer, J. Spehr, J. Effertz, and C. Stiller, "Efficient Road Scene Understanding for Intelligent Vehicles Using Compositional Hierarchical Models," *IEEE Transactions on Intelligent Transportation Systems*, vol. 16, no. 1, pp. 441–451, 2015.

[129] C. Wojek, S. Walk, S. Roth, and B. Schiele, "Monocular 3D scene understanding with explicit occlusion reasoning," in *CVPR 2011*, 2011, pp. 1993–2000.

[130] C. Wojek, S. Walk, S. Roth, K. Schindler, and B. Schiele, "Monocular Visual Scene Understanding: Understanding Multi-Object Traffic Scenes," *IEEE Transactions on Pattern Analysis and Machine Intelligence*, vol. 35, no. 4, pp. 882–897, 2013.

[131] H. Zhang, A. Geiger, and R. Urtasun, "Understanding High-Level Semantics by Modeling Traffic Patterns," in *2013 IEEE International Conference on Computer Vision*, 2013, pp. 3056–3063.

[132] Z. Wang, B. Liu, S. Schulter, and M. Chandraker, "A Parametric Top-View Representation of Complex Road Scenes," *2019 IEEE/CVF Conference on Computer Vision and Pattern Recognition (CVPR)*, pp. 10317–10325, 2018.

[133] D. Maturana and S. Scherer, "VoxNet: A 3D Convolutional Neural Network for Real-Time Object Recognition," in *2015 IEEE/RSJ International Conference on Intelligent Robots and Systems (IROS)*, 2015, pp. 922–928.

[134] H. Jing and Y. Suya, "Point Cloud Labeling Using 3D Convolutional Neural Network," in *2016 23rd International Conference on Pattern Recognition (ICPR)*, 2016, pp. 2670–2675.

[135] G. Riegler, A. O. Ulusoy, and A. Geiger, "OctNet: Learning Deep 3D Representations at High Resolutions," *2017 IEEE Conference on Computer Vision and Pattern Recognition (CVPR)*, pp. 6620–6629, 2016.

[136] P. Dendorfer, H. Rezatofighi, A. Milan, *et al.*, "MOT20: A Benchmark for Multiobject Tracking in Crowded Scenes," ArXiv:2003.09003, 2020.

[137] D. Anguelov, C. Dulong, D. Filip, *et al.*, "Google Street View: Capturing the World at Street Level," *Computer*, vol. 43, no. 6, pp. 32–38, 2010.

[138] B. Klingner, D. Martin, and J. Roseborough, "Street View Motion-from-Structure-from-Motion," in *2013 IEEE International Conference on Computer Vision*, 2013, pp. 953–960.

[139]   J. Levinson, M. Montemerlo, and S. Thrun, "Map-Based Precision Vehicle Localization in Urban Environments," in *Robotics: Science and Systems*, 2007.

[140]   J. D. Wegner, J. A. Montoya-Zegarra, and K. Schindler, "A Higher-Order CRF Model for Road Network Extraction," in *2013 IEEE Conference on Computer Vision and Pattern Recognition*, 2013, pp. 1698–1705.

[141]   J. D. Wegner, J. A. Montoya-Zegarra, and K. Schindler, "Road Networks as Collections of Minimum Cost Paths," *ISPRS Journal of Photogrammetry and Remote Sensing*, vol. 108, pp. 128–137, 2015.

[142]   A. Ess, T. Mueller, H. Grabner, and L. V. Gool, "Segmentation-Based Urban Traffic Scene Understanding," in *British Machine Vision Conference*, 2009.

[143]   A. Geiger, P. Lenz, and R. Urtasun, "Are We Ready for Autonomous Driving? The KITTI Vision Benchmark Suite," *2012 IEEE Conference on Computer Vision and Pattern Recognition*, pp. 3354–3361, 2012.

[144]   F. Dellaert, D. Fox, W. Burgard, and S. Thrun, "Monte Carlo Localization for Mobile Robots," *Proceedings of the 1999 IEEE International Conference on Robotics and Automation (Cat. No.99CH36288C)*, vol. 2, pp. 1322–1328, 1999.

[145]   Y. Li, D. J. Crandall, and D. P. Huttenlocher, "Landmark Classification in Large-Scale Image Collections," *2009 IEEE 12th International Conference on Computer Vision*, pp. 1957–1964, 2009.

[146]   Y. Zheng, M. Zhao, Y. Song, *et al.*, "Tour the World: Building a Web-Scale Landmark Recognition Engine," *2009 IEEE Conference on Computer Vision and Pattern Recognition*, pp. 1085–1092, 2009.

[147]   M. Montemerlo, S. Thrun, D. Koller, and B. Wegbreit, "FastSLAM: A Factored Solution to the Simultaneous Localization and Mapping Problem," in *AAAI/IAAI*, 2002.

[148]   R. C. Smith, M. Self, and P. C. Cheeseman, "Estimating Uncertain Spatial Relationships in Robotics," *Proceedings of the 1987 IEEE International Conference on Robotics and Automation*, vol. 4, pp. 850–850, 1986.

[149]   H. Lategahn, A. Geiger, and B. Kitt, "Visual SLAM for Autonomous Ground Vehicles," *2011 IEEE International Conference on Robotics and Automation*, pp. 1732–1737, 2011.

[150]   J. J. Engel, J. Stückler, and D. Cremers, "Large-Scale Direct SLAM with Stereo Cameras," *2015 IEEE/RSJ International Conference on Intelligent Robots and Systems (IROS)*, pp. 1935–1942, 2015.

[151]   R. Mur-Artal, J. M. M. Montiel, and J. D. Tardós, "ORB-SLAM: A Versatile and Accurate Monocular SLAM System," *IEEE Transactions on Robotics*, vol. 31, pp. 1147–1163, 2015.

[152]   E. Rublee, V. Rabaud, K. Konolige, and G. R. Bradski, "ORB: An Efficient Alternative to SIFT or SURF," *2011 International Conference on Computer Vision*, pp. 2564–2571, 2011.

[153]   R. Kümmerle, G. Grisetti, H. M. Strasdat, K. Konolige, and W. Burgard, "G2o: A General Framework for Graph Optimization," *2011 IEEE International Conference on Robotics and Automation*, pp. 3607–3613, 2011.

[154]   H. M. Strasdat, A. J. Davison, J. M. M. Montiel, and K. Konolige, "Double Window Optimisation for Constant Time Visual SLAM," *2011 International Conference on Computer Vision*, pp. 2352–2359, 2011.

[155]   D. Gálvez-López and J. D. Tardós, "Bags of Binary Words for Fast Place Recognition in Image Sequences," *IEEE Transactions on Robotics*, vol. 28, pp. 1188–1197, 2012.

[156]   B. Wolfram, B. Oliver, and S. Cyrill, "Map-Based Precision Vehicle Localization in Urban Environments," in *Robotics: Science and Systems III*: MIT Press, 2008, pp. 121–128.

[157]   J. Levinson and S. Thrun, "Robust Vehicle Localization in Urban Environments Using Probabilistic Maps," in *2010 IEEE International Conference on Robotics and Automation*, 2010, pp. 4372–4378.

[158]   P. Xiao, Z. Shao, S. Hao, *et al.*, "PandaSet: Advanced Sensor Suite Dataset for Autonomous Driving," *2021 IEEE International Intelligent Transportation Systems Conference (ITSC)*, pp. 3095–3101, 2021.

[159]   H. Caesar, V. Bankiti, A. H. Lang, *et al.*, "nuScenes: A Multimodal Dataset for Autonomous Driving," *2020 IEEE/CVF Conference on Computer Vision and Pattern Recognition (CVPR)*, pp. 11618–11628, 2019.

[160]   P. Sun, H. Kretzschmar, X. Dotiwalla, *et al.*, "Scalability in Perception for Autonomous Driving: Waymo Open Dataset," *2020 IEEE/CVF Conference on Computer Vision and Pattern Recognition (CVPR)*, pp. 2443–2451, 2019.

[161]   J. Houston, G. Zuidhof, L. Bergamini, *et al.*, "One Thousand and One Hours: Self-driving Motion Prediction Dataset," in *Conference on Robot Learning*, 2020.

[162]   A. Patil, S. Malla, H. Gang, and Y.-T. Chen, "The H3D Dataset for Full-Surround 3D Multi-Object Detection and Tracking in Crowded Urban Scenes," 2019 *International Conference on Robotics and Automation (ICRA)*, pp. 9552–9557, 2019.

[163]   K. Behrendt, "Boxy Vehicle Detection in Large Images," in *2019 IEEE/CVF International Conference on Computer Vision Workshop (ICCVW)*, 2019, pp. 840–846.

[164]   H. Maeda, Y. Sekimoto, T. Seto, T. Kashiyama, and H. Omata, "Road Damage Detection Using Deep Neural Networks with Images Captured Through a Smartphone," ArXiv:1801.09454, 2018.

[165]   Y. Choi, N. Kim, S. Hwang, *et al.*, "KAIST Multi-Spectral Day/Night Data Set for Autonomous and Assisted Driving," *IEEE Transactions on Intelligent Transportation Systems*, vol. 19, no. 3, pp. 934–948, 2018.

[166]   F. Yu, H. Chen, X. Wang, *et al.*, "BDD100K: A Diverse Driving Dataset for Heterogeneous Multitask Learning," *2020 IEEE/CVF Conference on Computer Vision and Pattern Recognition (CVPR)*, pp. 2633–2642, 2018.

[167]   M. Feng and H. Zhang, "Application of Baidu Apollo Open Platform in a Course of Control Simulation Experiments," *Computer Applications in Engineering Education*, vol. 30, no. 3, pp. 892–906, 2022.

[168]   M. Braun, S. Krebs, F. Flohr, and D. M. Gavrila, "EuroCity Persons: A Novel Benchmark for Person Detection in Traffic Scenes," *IEEE Transactions on Pattern Analysis and Machine Intelligence*, vol. 41, no. 8, pp. 1844–1861, 2019.

[169]   S. Zhang, R. Benenson, and B. Schiele, "CityPersons: A Diverse Dataset for Pedestrian Detection," *2017 IEEE Conference on Computer Vision and Pattern Recognition (CVPR)*, pp. 4457–4465, 2017.

[170]   Y. Socarrás, S. Ramos, D. Vázquez, A. M. López, and T. Gevers, "Adapting Pedestrian Detection from Synthetic to Far Infrared Images," *International Conference on Computer Vision (ICCV) Workshops*, 2013, pp. 1–3.

[171]   N. Smolyanskiy, A. Kamenev, and S. Birchfield, "On the Importance of Stereo for Accurate Depth Estimation: An Efficient Semi-Supervised Deep Neural Network Approach," *2018 IEEE/CVF Conference on Computer Vision and Pattern Recognition Workshops (CVPRW)*, pp. 1120–11208, 2018.

[172]   C. Wojek, S. Walk, and B. Schiele, "Multi-Cue Onboard Pedestrian Detection," in *2009 IEEE Conference on Computer Vision and Pattern Recognition*, 2009, pp. 794–801.

[173]   A. Ess, B. Leibe, K. Schindler, and L. V. Gool, "A Mobile Vision System for Robust Multi-Person Tracking," in *2008 IEEE Conference on Computer Vision and Pattern Recognition*, 2008, pp. 1–8.

[174]   P. Dollar, C. Wojek, B. Schiele, and P. Perona, "Pedestrian Detection: A Benchmark," in *2009 IEEE Conference on Computer Vision and Pattern Recognition*, 2009, pp. 304–311.

[175]   J. Behley, M. Garbade, A. Milioto, *et al.*, "SemanticKITTI: A Dataset for Semantic Scene Understanding of LiDAR Sequences," ArXiv:1904.01416, 2019.

[176]   B. Kim, J. Yim, and J. Kim, "Highway Driving Dataset for Semantic Video Segmentation,"ArXiv:2011.00674, 2020.

[177]   P. Wang, X. Huang, X. Cheng, D. Zhou, Q. Geng, and R. Yang, "The ApolloScape Open Dataset for Autonomous Driving and Its Application," *IEEE Transactions on Pattern Analysis and Machine Intelligence*, vol. 42, pp. 2702–2719, 2018.

[178]   O. Zendel, K. Honauer, M. Murschitz, D. Steininger, and G. F. Domínguez, "WildDash – Creating Hazard-Aware Benchmarks," in *Computer Vision – ECCV 2018*, Cham, 2018, pp. 407–421: Springer International Publishing.

[179]   F. Tung, J. Chen, L. Meng, and J. J. Little, "The Raincouver Scene Parsing Benchmark for Self-Driving in Adverse Weather and at Night," *IEEE Robotics and Automation Letters*, vol. 2, no. 4, pp. 2188–2193, 2017.

[180]   M. Cordts, M. Omran, S. Ramos, *et al.*, "The Cityscapes Dataset for Semantic Urban Scene Understanding," *2016 IEEE Conference on Computer Vision and Pattern Recognition (CVPR)*, pp. 3213–3223, 2016.

[181]   A. Teichman, J. Levinson, and S. Thrun, "Towards 3D Object Recognition via Classification of Arbitrary Object Tracks," in *2011 IEEE International Conference on Robotics and Automation*, 2011, pp. 4034–4041.

[182]   G. J. Brostow, J. Fauqueur, and R. Cipolla, "Semantic Object Classes in Video: A High-Definition Ground Truth Database," *Pattern Recognit. Lett.*, vol. 30, pp. 88–97, 2009.

[183]   K. Behrendt and R. Soussan, "Unsupervised Labeled Lane Markers Using Maps," *2019 IEEE/CVF International Conference on Computer Vision Workshop (ICCVW)*, pp. 832–839, 2019.

[184]   S. Lee, J. Kim, J. S. Yoon, *et al.*, "VPGNet: Vanishing Point Guided Network for Lane and Road Marking Detection and Recognition," *2017 IEEE International Conference on Computer Vision (ICCV)*, pp. 1965–1973, 2017.

[185]   T. Wu and A. Ranganathan, "A Practical System for Road Marking Detection and Recognition," in *2012 IEEE Intelligent Vehicles Symposium*, pp. 25–30, 2012.

[186]   M. Aly, "Real Time Detection of Lane Markers in Urban Streets," 2008 *IEEE Intelligent Vehicles Symposium*, pp. 7–12, 2008.

[187]   P. Mirowski, A. B. Horvath, K. Anderson, *et al.*, "The StreetLearn Environment and Dataset," ArXiv:1903.01292, 2019.

[188]   Z. Yan, L. Sun, T. Krajník, and Y. Ruichek, "EU Long-Term Dataset with Multiple Sensors for Autonomous Driving," *2020 IEEE/RSJ International Conference on Intelligent Robots and Systems (IROS)*, pp. 10697–10704, 2019.

[189]   A. Z. Zhu, D. Thakur, T. Özaslan, B. Pfrommer, V. R. Kumar, and K. Daniilidis, "The Multivehicle Stereo Event Camera Dataset: An Event Camera Dataset for 3D Perception," *IEEE Robotics and Automation Letters*, vol. 3, pp. 2032–2039, 2018.

[190]   J. Jeong, Y. Cho, Y.-S. Shin, H. Roh, and A. Kim, "Complex Urban Dataset with Multi-Level Sensors from Highly Diverse Urban Environments," *The International Journal of Robotics Research*, vol. 38, no. 6, pp. 642–657, 2019.

[191]   W. Maddern, G. Pascoe, C. Linegar, and P. Newman, "1 year, 1000 km: The Oxford RobotCar dataset," *The International Journal of Robotics Research*, vol. 36, no. 1, pp. 3–15, 2017.

[192]   G. Pandey, J. R. McBride, and R. M. Eustice, "Ford Campus Vision and Lidar Data Set," *The International Journal of Robotics Research*, vol. 30, no. 13, pp. 1543–1552, 2011.

Chapter 10

Dehazing and vision enhancement: challenges and future scope

Sattwik Barua[1], Tannistha Pal[2] and Mritunjoy Halder[3]

Abstract

Poor visibility of outdoor images has been drastically increased. Applications using computer vision, including surveillance systems, intelligent transportation systems, are not able to function properly due to limited visibility. Numerous image dehazing methods have been introduced as a solution to this problem, and they are crucial in enhancing the functionality of several computer vision systems. The dehazing approaches are intriguing to researchers as a consequence. In order to demonstrate that dehazing techniques could be successfully used in actual practice, this study conducts an extensive examination of the state-of-the-art dehazing approaches. In contrast, it motivates scholars to apply some of these methods for removing haze from hazy images. In this chapter, we discuss several robust mathematical models along with some neural network-based approaches and their implementations in various aspects. Finally, we address several concerns about difficulties and potential future applications of dehazing approaches.

Due to poor visibility conditions, the visibility of outdoor images is drastically decreased. Applications using computer vision, including surveillance systems, intelligent transportation systems, etc., are not able to function properly due to limited visibility. Numerous image dehazing methods have been introduced as a solution to this issue, and they are crucial in enhancing the functionality of several computer vision systems. The dehazing approaches are intriguing to researchers as a consequence. In order to demonstrate that dehazing techniques could be successfully used in actual practice, this study conducts an extensive examination of the state-of-the-art dehazing approaches. In contrast, it motivates scholars to apply some of these methods for removing haze from hazy images. We keep an eye on the robust mathematical models along with some neural network-based approaches and their implementations in

[1]Computer Science & Engineering Department, Indian Institute of Engineering Science and Technology, Shibpur, India
[2]Computer Science & Engineering Department, National Institute of Technology, Agartala, India
[3]Information Technology, Indian Institute of Engineering Science and Technology, Shibpur, India

various aspects. Finally, we address several concerns about difficulties and potential future applications of dehazing approaches.

10.1 Introduction

Poor visibility conditions are a major cause of vehicle accidents in highly motorized economies affecting commuters of each and every socio-economic level. It is hard for a motorist to see clearly visible cars, warnings and objects from the other direction if the motorist is driving on a road under poor visibility conditions. Because of this reason, the locomotive pilot is unable to view the signal and stop with ease when a train is in operation. Nonetheless, it is exceedingly difficult for a pilot to take off or land in poor visibility conditions. In many ways, poor visibility conditions weaken driving consciousness and distort driving speed and makes it impossible to drive at real speed. Thus, the total travel time increases over real travel time. In a level co-occurrence, more than 600 people have died and over 16 300 have been injured. The extent to which the eyesight is decreased leads to vehicle accident that varies amongst nations and travellers. Poor visibility conditions caused 65% of vehicles and two-wheel motor vehicle collision in the State of Victoria, in Australia. Two-wheelers are less apparent than other vehicles throughout the day because of their size and shape. For instance, during the hours of daylight, most of the motorbike accidents occur in Malaysia. An European study has revealed two-fifth of the drivers find the pedestrians difficult to view. Almost 1.4 million people die each year and an average of 3 287 die every day due to traffic accidents worldwide and 20–50 million individuals suffer from injuries or disabilities. More than 0.147 million people are killed in India and over 0.47 million are wounded each year. In India, every year more than 11 000 people have died of foggy road conditions and almost 24 000 are injured.

The primary reasons for poor visibility conditions include fog, snow-blowing, smoke, dust and heavy precipitation. One of the primary contributors in decreasing the visibility is fog. There are several ice crystals or liquid droplets in a small volume of air perched on the ground. It affects a wide variety of environmental components including the national and domestic temperature, thermal and radiative balances of the atmosphere, flora and fauna, water, air quality, interaction between air and the surface, etc. Simultaneously, depending on the concentration of the droplets, it can disrupt and significantly impact human civilization and its functionality. It can cause direct or indirect damage to human health like secondary health effects, skin and eye damages, radiation and respiratory diseases depending on their physical and chemical structural features.

Foggy weather conditions have become more common, as a result of contemporary industrial air pollution, resulting in a drastic fall of visibility, which has a serious impact on outdoor video acquisition and processing. Reportedly, video capture surveillance technology is being used in a variety of fields, but in foggy weather and poor visibility environments, the frames of recorded videos, for example, deteriorating contrast, low glow, restricted dynamic range, poorer resolution details, non-bright natural landscape colours and reduced saturation are subject to various degrees of influence and deterioration. Such deteriorations have resulted in considerable discomfort for the responsible personnel in extraction of video data, especially in the area of line control station.

Videos and images have grown in popularity as a mean of transmitting information over networks in recent years. Machine vision and multimedia researchers have traditionally tried to defog a video using an effective technique of image dehazing for each frame of the video. He *et al.* [1] made the first substantial breakthrough in image haze removal by suggesting the idea of the dark channel prior (DCP). As a result, DCP interpretations in bright areas of the image and the sky are incorrect, since dark channel pixels in these regions are definitively unreachable. Several procedures for improving the framework at particular areas in an image have been described in [2–4].

Tasks like recognizing a video or an image whether it is foggy or non-foggy, or identifying objects in an image or a video or has predominantly been difficult for an automated machine learning (ML) algorithm. Deep learning (DL) [5,6] has recently proved to be accurate in certain tasks which go beyond cognitive abilities. In fact, even a decade ago, most of the computer vision researchers would not have imagined the latest achievements of profound learning algorithms that surpass the human performance [7] in image or video processing. Deep neural networks (DNNs) [8] show that neuronal biological networks also get much of their potential from their own dimension. An example of such a sort of topology is the usage of convolutional neural network (CNN) [5] for image processing. This architecture has been influenced by Hubel and Wiesel's [9] researches on neuron architecture in the visual cortex of cat. The neocognitron [10] was the precursor of CNN, and was directly based on these insights. More than eons have passed in evolving the structure of human synaptic pathways to optimize the sustainability efficacy; the structure of survivors is intimately linked to the fact that robotic systems are not capable of combining sensation and intuition.

High-quality images are sought for a number of computer vision-based applications, including image classification, autonomous driving, outdoor and traffic security surveillance and drone and object identification. Poor weather, however, degrades outdoor scenes; for instance, fog significantly reduces the clarity of a captured scene. Several atmospheric particles that hover in the air impair images captured in an outdoor space. The two most frequent natural phenomena resulting from suspended air particles, fog and haze, are the leading cause of degradation in vision. Both human observers and computer vision algorithms underperform in foggy weather conditions due to poor visibility. Water vapour condenses around these minuscule solid particles, and the molecules of water vapour combine during condensation to form tiny liquid water droplets that hover in the air, leading to fog. It reduces eyesight to less than 1 km; haze, on the other hand, is a phenomenon characterized by a suspension in an atmosphere of dry particles such as dust, salt and aerosols that can restrict visibility to 2 to 5 km [11]. Foggy weather conditions have become more common, resulting in a drastic fall in visibility, seriously impacting vehicular accidents. Suppose we look at the statistics of vehicular accidents caused by fog. In that case, it can be perceived that there is a need to remove fog from the degraded images. As a result, dealing with natural phenomena like fog, haze and mist is crucial from a practical standpoint. On images captured in a hazy or foggy environment, dehazing enhances the performance of computer vision systems or algorithms. The image-based dehazing field is developing rapidly due to its practical use and academic importance. Several techniques have been presented for image dehazing and vision enhancement. Dehazing is a significant challenge, and up to this point, there has been a few systematic assessments of the scientific work that covers the past, current and future capabilities. We discuss the significant approaches taken towards addressing the issue to date.

10.2   Organizing the survey

The main contribution of this research is the comprehensive review of dehazing techniques that it offers. We thoroughly describe the daytime atmospheric scattering model and the impact that various atmospheric conditions have on the scattering model. The domain we are concentrating on is highlighted when we suggest a taxonomy for dehazing techniques. We discuss several vision enhancement techniques and vision restoration techniques [1,3,5,6,8,12–17], which are the state-of-the-art approaches to resolve the problem. The traditional atmospheric scattering model serves as the foundation for model restoration methods, while noise reduction or removal techniques improve the visual features that may contain information about the image. These methods do not really rely on any underlying physical theory of degradation of an image. Some of the main methods include frequency modulation, fuzzy enhancement, and histogram equalization. Learning-based image dehazing employs a technique that may be expressed as a combination of ML and conventional approaches to anticipate the unknowns, predicated on the fundamental supposition that transmission estimation is accurate. Another approach is to use a neural network that learns the unknown jointly [5], i.e., the atmospheric light and transmission from the training data points and then reconstruct the clear image. In a nutshell, we shall discuss CNN [6,18–21], autoencoder [7,22–26], generative adversarial network-based approaches [4,22,27–30], i.e., the neural network-based approaches along with the mentioned classical approaches.

10.3   Classification and comparison of haze removal techniques

Numerous studies have been conducted over the past ten years to develop different haze removal techniques. This section provides a thorough overview of the most popular dehazing techniques currently in use. Several review articles on image dehazing may be found in the literature. Different dehazing procedures are categorized in some review papers, while others compare different dehazing approaches. Authors in [31–33] have classified the techniques into single image and multiple image-based dehazing based on the number of input images. In [34],

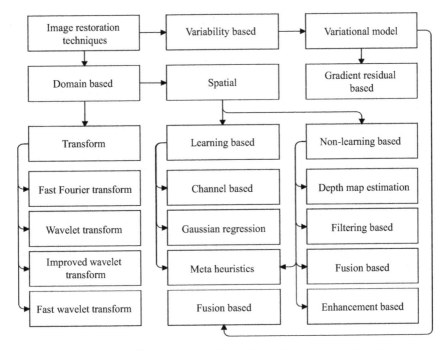

Figure 10.1   Classification of techniques for image restoration

Chengtao *et al.* classified into physical model-based and enhancement-based techniques. Five dehazing algorithm-based on physical model are compared in [35]. Several haze removal techniques based on enhancement and restoration are explored in [36,37]. Authors in [11,38] categorize all the dehazing techniques based on their previous work. The image restoration techniques are divided into various categories, including the most recent research, taking into account all the factors. According to Figure 10.1, the image restoration techniques are fundamentally categorized in terms of the domain and variability. Spatial and temporal domain-based approaches are divided into two categories. While transform domain-based techniques successfully analyse the data in the frequency plane and restore the image, spatial domain-based methods explicitly define alternative learning and non-learning models of image restoration. There includes a thorough discussion of the eight primary categories of image restoration procedures.

10.3.1   Depth map estimation-based dehazing

A majority of haze reduction techniques rely on depth map estimation. Priors and assumptions must be taken into account while evaluating these procedures at the outset. Based on the assessed depth map, an estimate of the transmission map and atmospheric light is made. These methods' effectiveness is totally dependent on the presumptions made. Edge preservation, colour distortion, halo artefacts, large haze gradients, gradient inversion artefacts, blocking artefacts, speed, etc. are just a few of the issues these techniques frequently encounter.

10.3.2   Filtering-based dehazing

Several scholars in the literature have put forth a variety of filter-based dehazing strategies to improve the depth map, transmission map and estimate of atmospheric light. Those filters include weighted guided image filter [39], median filter [40], bilateral filter [41], L2-norm with guided filter [42] and Koschmiedars law, etc. However, these techniques completely rely on the estimated results of previous priors. They suffer from the problem of computational speed.

In [43], Pal presents a method for image dehazing in sky region that frequently suffers from noise and colour distortion. An enhanced DCP technique is provided in this study, which first identifies the sky region, separates the picture into sky region and non-sky region, estimates the transmission of each component independently, then combines and refines the results. Additionally, the suggested technique precisely corrects the sky region's transmission to prevent colour and noise deformation. The quality of the output images is improved more by experimental findings than by using the current methods.

10.3.3   Fusion-based dehazing

Another interesting and effective method for removing haze is the fusion of images [44]. A guided fusion-based technique was introduced by Riaz *et al.*, in [45], which efficiently reduces the potential for failures of DCP and artefacts for restoration. Another dehazing technique is proposed in [46] that combines linear transformation output with guided image filtering, which results in improving the visibility at good computational constraints.

Zhu *et al.* [47] proposed an artificial multi-exposure-based image fusion method. The visual impairment brought on by bad weather cannot be adequately and efficiently mitigated in real time by the existing imaging systems. Using current physical framework techniques, hazy effects are removed using images depth map. Dehazing effectiveness, meanwhile, is constantly impacted by the inaccurate comprehensive data. The accuracy and stability of image dehazing are improved by the automated system which is outlined in this chapter [47]. By evaluating both global and local exposure to direct the hybrid transformation, sparse representation mappings are built using a collection of alpha desaturated images. Their method balances the oversaturated colours of the merged image while minimizing the correlation structure of its intensity. Both conceptual research and comparison experiments demonstrate that the suggested approach performs as expected.

10.3.4   Enhancement-based dehazing

The basic objective of image enhancement techniques is to simultaneously improve the crucial details and eliminate the undesired noise. There are several image enhancement methods, such as bi-histogram modification [39], Retinex [48], histogram equalization, weighted histogram [49], histogram modification [44], fuzzy enhancement [50], etc. However, these methods work inefficiently in case of pictures with larger haze gradients or when the scene contains non-homogeneous haze. Also, these methods suffer from problems related to saturation pixels and over/under-estimation.

Pal and Bhattacharjee [51] present a paper to analyse the images that are impacted by fog in the field of image processing. An adaptive-function-based picture-defogging strategy is suggested in this study since there are currently no traditional image-processing methods to reduce the effects of high-density fog. The suggested method precisely improves such damaged photos by modifying the contrast and brightness depending on an appropriate threshold operator. On the basis of an objective assessment, the photographs are then classified as foggy or non-foggy. Additionally, the suggested approach can be very effective for real-time applications with very less computational time.

10.3.5 Meta-heuristic method-based dehazing

One of the key components of the majority of dehazing techniques is parameter tuning, which is recognized as a difficult task in current research. It was discovered that variables like patch size, white balance factor, restore value and others can all be efficiently modified to improve the general effectiveness of the present dehazing approaches. Zhang *et al.* [48] implemented genetic algorithm-based dehazing from premature method to optimize the assessment of depth map by utilizing DCP. But these methods suffer convergence and low convergence speed problems. Bui and Kim [52] used the combination of genetic algorithm and particle swam optimization to enhance the visibility of hazy images. Similarly, an ant colony algorithm was designed by Zhao *et al.* [53] for the estimation of atmospheric light.

Pal [54] narrates that several computer vision programs have a difficult problem when trying to improve the visibility of photographs taken in foggy conditions. So, the major objective of improving vision is to clear the fog. An approach for picture defogging based on dark channel previous strategy has also been presented after this chapter's investigation of numerous state-of-the-art fog removal strategies. According to experimental findings, the suggested approach improves the visibility of pictures that have been negatively affected by fog more effectively than several state-of-the-art solutions. The proposed method has been used in this study to reduce the significantly greater computing times of the current methodologies. Additionally, benchmark data sets are subjected to qualitative assessment evaluation to ascertain the method's effectiveness.

10.3.6 Transform-based dehazing

Transform-based dehazing methods were introduced to improve the efficiency of restoration methods and decrease the colour distortions. When a hazy image is recovered using a pair of mathematical processes called transform domain-based dehazing methods, the image is transformed into time, frequency or wavelet domains [55]. Babu and Venkatram *et al.* [56] proposed a simple and powerful fog removal technique based on DCP knowledge after fast Fourier transform noise removal. When compared to time domain and discrete Fourier transform approaches, the fast Fourier transform increases the visibility by converting the time domain image into the frequency domain. However, these methods result in some colour distortion. In order to resolve this problem, modified dehazing techniques have been proposed in the literature [57]. A combination of wavelet and DCP methods are used to enhance the restored images quality. Qiao *et al.*, in [58], utilized the combination of adaptive histogram equalization and wavelet transformation approach. Liu *et al.* [59] introduced the wavelet strategy to eliminate the fog impact and improve the design quality in conjunction.

10.3.7 *Variational-based dehazing*

Due to the negligence of some physical assumptions, depth map and transmission map estimation methodologies do have some problems. Additionally, enhancement-based approaches have issues with oversaturation and wide hazy gradients. Numerous variational-based haze removal techniques have been developed recently with the goal of resolving these issues [60,61]. An enhanced variation image dehazing energy minimization function has been designed in [62] to restore the degraded image. In [63], Wang *et al.* proposed the combination of three variation models to degrade and denoise the image. These methods however suffer from less computational speed.

Fang *et al.* [64] examined the difficult challenge of eliminating haze from a single natural photograph. The examination of the haze creation model reveals that the ambient mist has considerably less bearing on chromaticity than luminance, which encourages to focus on the luminance channel during the dehazing process and ignore the haze in a chrominance channel. Additionally, the empirical analysis shows that the YUV colour space is the best for image dehazing. In the light of this, the reformulation of the haze model and the two effective priors are combined to suggest a discretization model in the Y channel of the YUV colour domain. A majority of the image's luminance data is kept post dehazing since they primarily concentrate on the Y channel.

10.3.8 *Learning-based dehazing*

Despite the fact that several dehazing methods have been put forth in the literature, they are limited to particular hand-crafted elements. The issue of effectively and reliably restoring photos is still difficult. Recent studies have started to concentrate on applying DL and ML techniques for quick and accurate image restoration. These approaches such as linear model [65], dehazeNet [18], two-layer Gaussian regression [66], kernel regression [67], MSCNN (multiscale CNN) [19], AOD-Net [6], GFN (gated fusion network), LDTNet (light weight dual-task network) [68] and GMAN (generic model-agnostic CNN) [69], etc. are proposed for dehazing with good computational speed compared to others. However, the requirement of number of images with distinct scenes to train a specific model makes it harder to implement in real time.

Tarel and Hautiere [12] present a novel visibility restoration technique and its variants from a single image. The key benefit of the suggested technique over alternatives is that it has a temporal complexity that is linearly proportional to the number of pixels. With this speed, vision restoration may finally be used for real-time processing tasks like sign-and-obstacle identification from an in-car camera. Since the discrepancy between the presence of fog and the items with low colour saturation is resolved by assuming only small objects can have low colour saturation, the ability to handle both colour images and grey-level images is another advantage. The algorithm, which is only affected by a small number of parameters, consists of tone-mapping, image restoration and smoothing, and atmospheric veil inference.

The all-in-one dehazing network, a CNN-based picture dehazing model, is suggested in [6]. Based on a revised atmospheric scattering model, it was created. As opposed to most earlier models, which estimated the transmission matrix and atmospheric light separately, AOD-Net directly generates the clean image using a lightweight CNN. It is simple to incorporate AOD-Net into other deep models, such as Faster R-CNN, for improving high-level tasks on hazy images thanks to this innovative end-to-end design.

This study in [16] suggests a brand-new technique for restoring clear photos from the damaged ones. To accomplish this, the proposed algorithm makes use of a novel compensation strategy to correct the post-dehazing erroneous enlargement of white objects and a supervised ML-based technique to predict the pixel-wise extinction coefficients of the transmission medium. Additionally, a comparable hardware accelerator built on a field-programmable gate array chip is required to support real-time processing, which is a vital component of workable camera-based systems.

The single image haze removal algorithm proposed in [14] significantly outperforms the colour attenuation prior-based approach. It is found that there are issues in the colour attenuation prior, such as colour distortion and background noise, which arise because the priors do not hold true in all situations through a huge number of experiments on a wide variety of images.

In [15], Van Nguyen *et al.* present a single illumination-based illumination decomposition-based maritime picture defogging technique. In order to deconstruct a hazy input image into glow and glow-free layers, an optimization problem must first be formulated and then successfully solved, with closed-form solutions used to update the optimization variables. Then, a defogging algorithm is used to remove the fog components from a glow-free layer. To get the final, fog-free image, the glow layer's natural illumination is recovered using a compensation strategy.

In [70], CNNs are investigated to directly train a nonlinear function between hazy photos and the equivalent clear ones. They introduce a perceptual pyramid deep network-based multi-scale picture dehazing technique that is based on the recently well-liked dense blocks and residual blocks. The suggested solution uses an encoder–decoder structure with a pyramid pooling module in the decoder to take context from the scene into account as it decodes. By reducing mean-squared error (MSE) and perceptual losses, the network is trained. To further enhance the performance, multi-scale patches are used during the training and inference processes.

Shin *et al.* [8] present a brand-new dehazing approach based on optimization that combines reflectance and radiance components with an additional refinement made with a structure-guided 1 0-norm filter. More specifically, we improve the transmission map based on the predicted reflectance map after initially estimating a weak reflectance map. To eliminate the dehazing artefacts, we then estimate the structure-guided 1 0 transmission map. Additionally, the results of the real-world enhancement show that the suggested method can deliver a high-quality image free of unwanted artefacts. Furthermore, for general image enhancement algorithms, the guided 1 0-norm filter can eliminate textures while maintaining edges.

Salazar-Colores *et al.* [5] present a framework based on segmenting the sky and non-sky regions and recovering the sky and non-sky components individually. Here, the floodfill algorithm's binary mask is used to separate the sky from the rest of the image. Contrast limited adaptive histogram equalization is used to restore the hazy sky portion, and modified DCP is used to restore the non-sky portion. For the final image, the restored pieces are combined. Both artificial and actual real-world foggy images are used to compare the proposed method to state-of-the-art methods.

By applying a white balance and a contrast-enhancing approach to two initial hazy image inputs, Ancuti and Ancuti's [17] method creates a fusion-based strategy. They filter the key aspects of the derived inputs by computing three measures (weight maps): brightness, chromaticity and saliency in order to combine the information of the derived inputs efficiently and maintain the regions with good visibility. Our method uses a Laplacian pyramid representation and is developed in a multiscale manner to reduce artefacts caused by the weight maps. This research is the first to show the value and potency of a fusion-based dehazing technique using a single degraded image. The technique operates in a simple-to-implement per-pixel fashion.

10.4   Experiments and results

In order to effectively compare the various dehazing techniques currently used, we present detailed qualitative and quantitative statistics. For evaluation, both real and synthetic images were taken into account. For our research, we took into account datasets with various classes of haze. NYU [71], RESIDE-HSTS [72] and RESIDE-SOTS [72] datasets are taken into consideration. Ten strenuous and challenging real-world images are also chosen to evaluate the dehazing approaches, as these methods are sensitive to and white pixels and sky.

Image quality assessment is regarded as a distinguishing attribute of an image. Image quality evaluation measures the degradation of perceived pictures. Typically, degradation is estimated in comparison to a reference picture, which is an ideal image.

To show the departure from an ideal or a reference model, image quality can be objectively and technically characterized. It also has to do with the subjective interpretation or forecast of a picture, like an image of a human appearance. The noise has an impact on the decline in image quality. Depending on how it corresponds to the data the viewer is looking for in the image, this noise can be

Figure 10.2 Some outputs from different methods from the considered datasets. Row-wise, the inputs are hazy input image, and others are the method of [1,3,5,6,8,12–17] and finally the ground truths

Figure 10.2   (Continued)

considered. Acquiring, enhancing, compressing or transmitting visual information are only a few of the many possible features processes.

After all of the processing is done, some of the information that an image's characteristics give might become distorted. The human view perceptron should thus assess the quality. Subjective and objective evaluations are the two categories that exist in practice. Implementing subjective evaluation requires a lot of effort and money. The objective picture quality measurements are then generated based on many factors.

10.4.1   Metrics used

10.4.1.1   Structural similarity index

Structural SIMilarity (SSIM) was first introduced in the study [73] proposed by Wang *et al.* The visibility of mistakes (differences) between a distorted image and a reference image was previously sought to be quantified using a range of known aspects of the human visual system. This method presents a different supplementary paradigm for quality evaluation based on the deterioration of structural information, supposing that human visual perception is well suited for obtaining structural information from a scene. The structural similarity scores depends mainly on three different aspect of image. They are as follows:

- Luminance: Luminance is nothing but the mean of the all pixel values. It is calculated using the formula

$$\mu_x = \frac{1}{N} \sum_{i=1}^{N} x_i \qquad (10.1)$$

- Contrast: The standard deviation (square root of variance) of all the pixel values is used to calculate it. Its symbol is sigma, and the following formula serves as its representation:

$$\sigma_x = \left(\frac{1}{N-1} \sum_{i=1}^{N} (x_i - \mu_x)^2 \right)^{0.5} \qquad (10.2)$$

- Structure: A condensed formula is used to do the structural comparison, but essentially, we divide the input signal by its standard deviation to get a result with a unit standard deviation, enabling a more reliable comparison.

$$\text{Structure} = \frac{(x - \mu_x)}{\sigma_x} \qquad (10.3)$$

What we now require is a combination function that combines all of the parameters, comparison algorithms that can compare the two provided photos on these parameters, and so on. Here, we define the comparison functions and, ultimately, the combination function that results in the value of the similarity index. Equation (10.4) gives the luminance, (10.5) gives the contrast and (10.6) comparison functions.

$$l(x,y) = \frac{2\mu_x\mu_y + C}{\mu_x^2 + \mu_y^2 + C} \qquad (10.4)$$

$$c(x,y) = \frac{2\sigma_x\sigma_y + C}{\sigma_x^2 + \sigma_y^2 + C} \qquad (10.5)$$

$$s(x,y) = \frac{\sigma_{xy} + C}{\sigma_x + \sigma_y + C} \qquad (10.6)$$

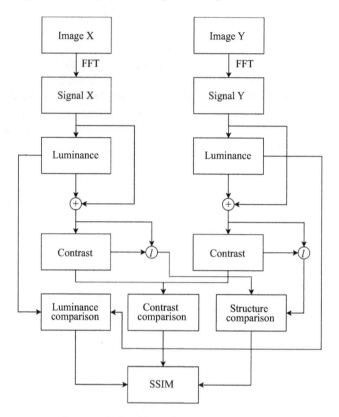

Figure 10.3   SSIM detailed explanation

Frequency domain analysis is mainly done on an image to calculate the SSIM score. The illustration is given in Figure 10.3. The final comparison function is given by (10.7)

$$SSIM = \frac{2\mu_x\mu_y + C_1}{\mu_x^2 + \mu_y^2 + C_1} \times \frac{2\sigma_{xy} + C_2}{\sigma_x^2 + \sigma_y^2 + C_2} \qquad (10.7)$$

10.4.1.2   Mean-squared error

The most popular estimate of the metric used to measure picture quality is the MSE. The values that are nearer to zero are preferable since it is a full reference measure. This is the second instance of the mistake. MSE takes into account both the estimator's bias and variation. In the case of an unbiased estimator, the MSE is the estimator's variance. The variance square has the same units of measurement as the variance square of the quantity being calculated. The root-mean-square error (RMSE), also known as the root-mean-square deviation (RMSD), or standard deviation of the variance, is introduced by the MSE.

The mean squared deviation (MSD) of an estimator can also be used to refer to the MSE. The process for estimating an unseen quantity of an image is known as an estimator. The average of the square of the mistakes is measured by the MSE or MSD. The error is the discrepancy between the estimator's prediction and the actual result. It is a function of risk when taking into account the anticipated value of the quadratic or squared error loss.

The MSE of two images is given by (10.8).

$$MSE = \frac{1}{MN} \sum_{n=0}^{M} \sum_{m=1}^{N} |f'(n,m) - f(n,m)|^2 \tag{10.8}$$

10.4.1.3   Peak signal-to-noise ratio

The peak signal-to-noise ratio (PSNR) formula is used to determine the ratio between the maximum signal strength and the power of the noise that distorts the signal's representation. The decibel form of this ratio between the two pictures is computed. Due of the signals' extremely large dynamic range, the PSNR is typically computed as the logarithm term of decibel scale. The greatest and lowest potential values, which are modifiable by their quality, are covered by this dynamic range. The most popular method for evaluating the quality of lossy image compression codec reconstruction is the PSNR. The noise is the mistake produced by compression or distortion, whereas the signal is thought of as the original data.

The formula given below is used to calculate the PSNR,

$$\text{PSNR} = 10\log_{10}\left(\frac{R^2}{MSE}\right) \tag{10.9}$$

In comparison to compression codecs, the PSNR is an approximation of the human impression of reconstruction quality. The PSNR value fluctuates from 30 to 50 dB for 8-bit data representation and from 60 to 80 dB for 16-bit data when it comes to picture and video compression quality deterioration. The recognized range of quality loss in wireless transmission is between 20 and 25 dB [74].

10.4.1.4   Normalized absolute error

The normalized absolute error, with a value of zero indicating a perfect match, is a measurement of how distant the reconstructed picture is from the original image. A picture with a high value of the normalized absolute error is of poor quality, whereas the one with a low value is of high quality.

The normalized absolute error is given by (10.10).

$$NAE = \sum_{j=1}^{M} \sum_{k=1}^{N} \frac{||x(j,k) - x'(j,k)||}{\sum_{j=1}^{M} \sum_{k=1}^{N} ||x(j,k)||} \tag{10.10}$$

The reference scores of the different DL-based methods are depicted in Table 10.1. Table 10.2 lists the reference scores of different image processing-based

Table 10.1   Comparative analysis between various methods which uses DL

Method name	SSIM	MSE	PSNR	NAE
Salazar-Colores *et al.* [5]	0.90	431.27	22.82	0.14
Li *et al.* [6]	0.90	490.38	22.24	0.15
Ngo *et al.* [13]	0.84	650.26	20.40	0.19

Table 10.2   Comparative analysis between various methods which uses image processing

Method name	SSIM	MSE	PSNR	NAE
He *et al.* [1]	0.89	1 538.45	17.68	0.24
Zhao *et al.* [3]	0.80	3 103.57	13.93	0.35
Shin *et al.* [8]	0.82	1 117.07	18.53	0.22
Tarel *et al.* [12]	0.79	1 994.76	5.54	0.35
Ngo *et al.* [14]	0.85	660.21	20.77	0.18
Van Nguyen *et al.* [15]	0.70	2 834.08	15.68	0.34
Ngo *et al.* [16]	0.77	1 418.487	17.11	0.27
Ancuti and Ancuti [17]	0.86	1 225.63	19.12	0.23

methods. Tables 10.1 and 10.2 show the comparative analysis on the SOTS dataset. As seen, the methods described in [5,6] and have the highest SSIM value and the lowest MSE value. These two methods are neural network-based methods and others with significantly low score are conventional scattering model-based methods.

In the methods detailed in [1,3,8,12,14,16,17], traditional image processing-based approach is used. The results are described in [3]. The method of [1] surpasses all other method in terms of the SSIM score. But the MSE score obtained by [14] is better than all other methods.

The methods proposed by Salazar-Colores *et al.*, Li *et al.* and Ngo *et al.* [5,6,13] used DL-based approach. Though SSIM score obtained by Salazar-Colores *et al.* [5] and Li *et al.* [6] is equal but the MSE score obtained by Salazar-Colores *et al.* [5] is better. The result is shown in Table 10.2. It can also be seen that the DL-based approach has achieved better score that of other methods.

Table 10.2 shows the qualitative analysis of different data of SOTS, NYU and HSTS datasets.

10.5   Conclusions

Single image dehazing is a significant domain of research with some important real-world applications. The aim of this chapter is to examine several image dehazing techniques in traditional classification benchmark, The significant growth of learning-based architectures for visibility enhancement and dehazing is a result of the success of ML techniques in other domains. This chapter performs a thorough analysis of existing dehazing methods under the categories of model restoration, image enhancement and ML and draws a conclusion about the performances of each approach in terms of both quantitative and qualitative metrics.

Image enhancement and physical model restoration are the two primary categories into which the various haze removal procedure approaches are divided in this research. It is clear from the analysis of image dehazing methods that each method has its own drawbacks. This research presents a thorough analysis of many cutting-edge image dehazing techniques. It has been discovered that traditional approaches do not work in areas where the intensity of the scene's colour becomes similar with the transmission light. These techniques also produces many artefacts and may generate a halo effect in the output images. On the majority of the images, the learning-based techniques worked well.

The disparity between learning-based approaches and traditional image enhancement approaches is comparable. The learning-based technique works noticeably well when analysing the qualitative data. Enhanced previous information and parameters can enhance the performance of traditional approaches. For assessing the performances in the various methodologies indicated in our research, some quantized evaluation measurements are also covered in detail. Several studies are conducted to show the effectiveness and impacts of visualization. In discussing the applications and usage of these techniques, we try to analyse the future research direction, which draws a conclusion to our study.

References

[1]   He K, Sun J, Tang X. Single image haze removal using dark channel prior. *IEEE Transactions on Pattern Analysis and Machine Intelligence*. 2010;33 (12):2341–2353.

[2]   Tan RT. Visibility in bad weather from a single image. In: 2008 *IEEE Conference on Computer Vision and Pattern Recognition. IEEE*; 2008. p. 1–8.

[3]   Zhao D, Xu L, Yan Y, *et al.* Multi-scale optimal fusion model for single image dehazing. *Signal Processing: Image Communication*. 2019;74:253–265.

[4]   Li R, Pan J, Li Z, *et al.* Single image dehazing via conditional generative adversarial network. In: *Proceedings of the IEEE Conference on Computer Vision and Pattern Recognition*; 2018. p. 8202–8211.

[5]   Salazar-Colores S, Cruz-Aceves I, Ramos-Arreguin JM. Single image dehazing using a multilayer perceptron. *Journal of Electronic Imaging*. 2018;27(4):1–11. Available from: https://doi.org/10.1117/1.JEI.27.4.043022.

[6]   Li B, Peng X, Wang Z, *et al.* AOD-net: All-in-one dehazing network. In: *Proceedings of the IEEE International Conference on Computer Vision*; 2017. p. 4770–4778.

[7]   He K, Zhang X, Ren S, *et al.* Deep residual learning for image recognition. In: *Proceedings of the IEEE Conference on Computer Vision and Pattern Recognition*; 2016. p. 770–778.

[8]   Shin J, Kim M, Paik J, *et al.* Radiance–reflectance combined optimization and structure-guided 0-norm for single image dehazing. *IEEE Transactions on Multimedia.* 2019;22(1):30–44.

[9]   Barta A, Suhai B, Horváth G. Polarization cloud detection with imaging polarimetry. In: *Polarized Light and Polarization Vision in Animal Sciences.* Springer; 2014. p. 585–602.

[10]   Fukushima K. Neocognitron: A hierarchical neural network capable of visual pattern recognition. *Neural Networks.* 1988;1(2):119–130.

[11]   Narasimhan SG, Nayar SK. Vision and the atmosphere. *International Journal of Computer Vision.* 2002;48(3):233–254.

[12]   Tarel JP, Hautiere N. Fast visibility restoration from a single color or gray level image. In: *2009 IEEE 12th International Conference on Computer Vision.* IEEE; 2009. p. 2201–2208.

[13]   Ngo D, Lee S, Lee GD, *et al.* Single-image visibility restoration: A machine learning approach and its 4K-capable hardware accelerator. *Sensors.* 2020;20(20):5795.

[14]   Ngo D, Lee GD, Kang B. Improved color attenuation prior for single-image haze removal. *Applied Sciences.* 2019;9(19):4011.

[15]   Van Nguyen T, Mai TTN, Lee C. Single maritime image defogging based on illumination decomposition using texture and structure priors. *IEEE Access.* 2021;9:34590–34603.

[16]   Ngo D, Lee S, Nguyen QH, *et al.* Single image haze removal from image enhancement perspective for real-time vision-based systems. *Sensors.* 2020;20(18):5170.

[17]   Ancuti CO, Ancuti C. Single image dehazing by multi-scale fusion. *IEEE Transactions on Image Processing.* 2013;22(8):3271–3282.

[18]   Cai B, Xu X, Jia K, *et al.* Dehazenet: An end-to-end system for single image haze removal. *IEEE Transactions on Image Processing.* 2016;25(11):5187–5198.

[19]   Ren W, Liu S, Zhang H, *et al.* Single image dehazing via multi-scale convolutional neural networks. In: *European Conference on Computer Vision.* Springer; 2016. p. 154–169.

[20]   Liu X, Ma Y, Shi Z, *et al.* Griddehazenet: Attention-based multi-scale network for image dehazing. In: *Proceedings of the IEEE/CVF International Conference on Computer Vision*; 2019. p. 7314–7323.

[21]   Deng Z, Zhu L, Hu X, *et al.* Deep multi-model fusion for single-image dehazing. In: *Proceedings of the IEEE/CVF International Conference on Computer Vision*; 2019. p. 2453–2462.

[22]   Zhang H, Patel VM. Densely connected pyramid dehazing network. In: *Proceedings of the IEEE Conference on Computer Vision and Pattern Recognition*; 2018. p. 3194–3203.

[23]   Mei K, Jiang A, Li J, *et al.* Progressive feature fusion network for realistic image dehazing. In: *Asian Conference on Computer Vision.* Springer; 2018. p. 203–215.

[24] Morales P, Klinghoffer T, Jae Lee S. Feature forwarding for efficient single image dehazing. In: *Proceedings of the IEEE/CVF Conference on Computer Vision and Pattern Recognition Workshops*; 2019. p. 0–0.

[25] Pang Y, Nie J, Xie J, *et al.* BidNet: Binocular image dehazing without explicit disparity estimation. In: *Proceedings of the IEEE/CVF Conference on Computer Vision and Pattern Recognition*; 2020. p. 5931–5940.

[26] Yin S, Wang Y, Yang YH. A novel image-dehazing network with a parallel attention block. *Pattern Recognition.* 2020;102:107255.

[27] Ren W, Ma L, Zhang J, *et al.* Gated fusion network for single image dehazing. In: *Proceedings of the IEEE Conference on Computer Vision and Pattern Recognition*; 2018. p. 3253–3261.

[28] Zhang H, Sindagi V, Patel VM. Joint transmission map estimation and dehazing using deep networks. *IEEE Transactions on Circuits and Systems for Video Technology.* 2019;30(7):1975–1986.

[29] Dudhane A, Biradar KM, Patil PW, *et al.* Varicolored image de-hazing. In: *Proceedings of the IEEE/CVF Conference on Computer Vision and Pattern Recognition*; 2020. p. 4564–4573.

[30] Chen WT, Fang HY, Ding JJ, *et al.* PMHLD: Patch map-based hybrid learning DehazeNet for single image haze removal. *IEEE Transactions on Image Processing.* 2020;29:6773–6788.

[31] Guo JM, Syue Jy, Radzicki VR, *et al.* An efficient fusion-based defogging. *IEEE Transactions on Image Processing.* 2017;26(9):4217–4228.

[32] Senthilkumar K, Sivakumar P. A review on haze removal techniques. *Computer Aided Intervention and Diagnostics in Clinical and Medical Images.* 2019;113–123.

[33] Patel SP, Nakrani M. A review on methods of image dehazing. *International Journal of Computer Applications.* 2016;133(12):44–49.

[34] Chengtao C, Qiuyu Z, Yanhua L. A survey of image dehazing approaches. In: *The 27th Chinese Control and Decision Conference (2015 CCDC).* IEEE; 2015. p. 3964–3969.

[35] Liu Q, Zhang H, Lin M, *et al.* Research on image dehazing algorithms based on physical model. In: *2011 International Conference on Multimedia Technology.* IEEE; 2011. p. 467–470.

[36] Saggu MK, Singh S. A review on various haze removal techniques for image processing. *International Journal of Current Engineering and Technology.* 2015;5(3):1500–1505.

[37] Tripathi AK, Mukhopadhyay S. Removal of fog from images: A review. *IETE Technical Review.* 2012;29(2):148–156.

[38] Singh D, Kumar V. A comprehensive review of computational dehazing techniques. *Archives of Computational Methods in Engineering.* 2019;26:1395–1413.

[39] Li Z, Zheng J, Zhu Z, *et al.* Weighted guided image filtering. *IEEE Transactions on Image Processing.* 2014;24(1):120–129.

[40] Zhang YQ, Ding Y, Xiao JS, *et al.* Visibility enhancement using an image filtering approach. *EURASIP Journal on Advances in Signal Processing.* 2012;2012(1):1–6.

[41] He S, Yang Q, Lau RW, *et al.* Fast weighted histograms for bilateral filtering and nearest neighbor searching. *IEEE Transactions on Circuits and Systems for Video Technology.* 2015;26(5):891–902.

[42] Kim JH, Jang WD, Sim JY, *et al.* Optimized contrast enhancement for real-time image and video dehazing. *Journal of Visual Communication and Image Representation.* 2013;24(3):410–425.

[43] Pal T. A robust method for dehazing of single image with sky region detection and segmentation. *International Journal of Image and Graphics.* 2021;21(04):2150045.

[44] Wang YK, Fan CT. Single image defogging by multiscale depth fusion. *IEEE Transactions on Image Processing.* 2014;23(11):4826–4837.

[45] Riaz I, Yu T, Rehman Y, *et al.* Single image dehazing via reliability guided fusion. *Journal of Visual Communication and Image Representation.* 2016;40:85–97.

[46] Ma Z, Wen J, Zhang C, *et al.* An effective fusion defogging approach for single sea fog image. *Neurocomputing.* 2016;173:1257–1267.

[47] Zhu Z, Wei H, Hu G, *et al.* A novel fast single image dehazing algorithm based on artificial multi exposure image fusion. *IEEE Transactions on Instrumentation and Measurement.* 2020;70:1–23.

[48] Zhang Y, Wang X, Bi X, *et al.* A light dual-task neural network for haze removal. *IEEE Signal Processing Letters.* 2018;25(8):1231–1235.

[49] Chen BH, Huang SC, Ye JH. Hazy image restoration by bi-histogram modification. *ACM Transactions on Intelligent Systems and Technology (TIST).* 2015;6(4):1–17.

[50] Ding M, Wei L. Single-image haze removal using the mean vector l2-norm of RGB image sample window. *Optik.* 2015;126(23):3522–3528.

[51] Pal T, Bhattacharjee D. Visibility enhancement of fog degraded images using adaptive defogging function. *Multimedia Tools and Applications.* 2022;1–31.

[52] Bui TM, Kim W. Single image dehazing using color ellipsoid prior. *IEEE Transactions on Image Processing.* 2017;27(2):999–1009.

[53] Zhao X, Ding W, Liu C, *et al.* Haze removal for unmanned aerial vehicle aerial video based on spatial-temporal coherence optimisation. *IET Image Processing.* 2018;12(1):88–97.

[54] Pal T. A fast method for defogging of outdoor visual images. *Recent Advances in Computer Science and Communications (Formerly: Recent Patents on Computer Science).* 2021;14(2):416–428.

[55] Rong Z, Jun WL. Improved wavelet transform algorithm for single image dehazing. *Optik.* 2014;125(13):3064–3066.

[56] Babu GH, Venkatram N. A survey on analysis and implementation of state-of-the-art haze removal techniques. *Journal of Visual Communication and Image Representation.* 2020;72:102912.

[57] Khmag A, Al-Haddad S, Ramli AR, *et al.* Single image dehazing using second-generation wavelet transforms and the mean vector L2-norm. *The Visual Computer.* 2018;34:675–688.

[58] Qiao X, Bao J, Zhang H, *et al.* Underwater image quality enhancement of sea cucumbers based on improved histogram equalization and wavelet transform. *Information Processing in Agriculture.* 2017;4(3):206–213.

[59] Liu X, Zhang H, Cheung Ym, *et al.* Efficient single image dehazing and denoising: An efficient multi-scale correlated wavelet approach. *Computer Vision and Image Understanding.* 2017;162:23–33.

[60] Chen C, Do MN, Wang J. Robust image and video dehazing with visual artifact suppression via gradient residual minimization. In: *Computer Vision–ECCV 2016: 14th European Conference*, Amsterdam, The Netherlands, October 11–14, 2016, Proceedings, Part II 14. Springer; 2016. p. 576–591.

[61] Galdran A, Vazquez-Corral J, Pardo D, *et al.* Fusion-based variational image dehazing. *IEEE Signal Processing Letters.* 2016;24(2):151–155.

[62] Galdran A, Vazquez-Corral J, Pardo D, *et al.* Enhanced variational image dehazing. *SIAM Journal on Imaging Sciences.* 2015;8(3):1519–1546.

[63] Wang Z, Hou G, Pan Z, *et al.* Single image dehazing and denoising combining dark channel prior and variational models. *IET Computer Vision.* 2018;12(4):393–402.

[64] Fang F, Wang T, Wang Y, *et al.* Variational single image dehazing for enhanced visualization. *IEEE Transactions on Multimedia.* 2019;22 (10):2537–2550.

[65] Mccartney E, Hall F. Scattering phenomena (Book reviews: Optics of the atmosphere. scattering by molecules and particles). *Science.* 1977;196 (4294):1084–1085.

[66] Fan X, Wang Y, Tang X, *et al.* Two-layer Gaussian process regression with example selection for image dehazing. *IEEE Transactions on Circuits and Systems for Video Technology.* 2016;27(12):2505–2517.

[67] Xie CH, Qiao WW, Liu Z, *et al.* Single image dehazing using kernel regression model and dark channel prior. *Signal, Image and Video Processing.* 2017;11:705–712.

[68] Li C, Guo J, Porikli F, *et al.* A cascaded convolutional neural network for single image dehazing. *IEEE Access.* 2018;6:24877–24887.

[69] Kang HJ, Kim YH, Lee YH. FPGA implementation for enhancing image using pixel-based median channel prior. *International Journal of Multimedia and Ubiquitous Engineering.* 2015;10(9):147–154.

[70] Zhang H, Sindagi V, Patel VM. Multi-scale single image dehazing using perceptual pyramid deep network. In: *Proceedings of the IEEE Conference on Computer Vision and Pattern Recognition (CVPR) Workshops*; 2018.

[71] Nathan Silberman PK Derek Hoiem, Fergus R. Indoor segmentation and support inference from RGBD images. In: ECCV; 2012.

[72] Li B, Ren W, Fu D, *et al.* Benchmarking single-image dehazing and beyond. *IEEE Transactions on Image Processing.* 2019;28(1):492–505.

[73]   Wang Z, Bovik AC, Sheikh HR, *et al.* Image quality assessment: From error visibility to structural similarity. *IEEE Transactions on Image Processing.* 2004;13(4):600–612.

[74]   Deshpande RG, Ragha LL, Sharma SK. Video quality assessment through PSNR estimation for different compression standards. *Indonesian Journal of Electrical Engineering and Computer Science.* 2018;11(3):918–924.

Chapter 11

Machine learning and revolution in agriculture: past, present and future

*Deep Suman Dev[1], Rinku Datta Rakshit[2],
Nabanita Choudhury[3] and Dakshina Ranjan Kisku[4]*

Abstract

Agriculture is one of the potential parameters in the economic sector. Traditional modes of farming are not able to meet the growing need of food as the population is increasing rapidly. Agricultural automation is very much essential to meet the supply–demand requirement of food and to minimize the employment issue and problems of food security. The introduction of artificial intelligence (AI) in agriculture has brought revolution by improving the overall accuracy and harvest quality, detecting pests and diseases in plants using applications like drones, smart monitoring systems and robots. Agricultural AI bots can harvest crops in a fast manner and in higher volume, which reduces the need of workers in higher numbers. Machine learning (ML), a subdomain under the umbrella of AI, is also used to capture the quality of seeds, pruning, parameters of soil, application of fertilizer and environmental conditions. In addition, using AI and ML, farmers can solve other challenges like forecasting crop prices, market demand analysis, finding optimal time and conditions for harvesting and sowing, nutrient deficiencies in soil, weight–diet balance using weight prediction systems. Using predictive analysis, ML techniques help to predict right genes for different weather conditions and to reduce chances of crop failures. The aim of this chapter is to provide an insight into the effectiveness of introducing ML in the field of agricultural applications. This chapter includes present scenarios of agricultural need, challenges, application of ML techniques and future development of agricultural applications using ML.

[1]Department of Computer Science and Engineering, School of Science and Technology, The Neotia University, Sarisha, India
[2]School of Computer Engineering, KIIT Deemed to be University, Bhubaneswar, India
[3]Faculty of Computer Technology, Assam down town University, Guwahati, India
[4]Department of Computer Science and Engineering, National Institute of Technology Durgapur, Durgapur, India

11.1   Introduction

Food security is one of the biggest challenges in human life. Agriculture plays a significant role for providing this. Nowadays, food production gets reduced due to unusual climatic variation, which becomes a threat for all human beings. Therefore, a sufficient amount of food production is essential for the survival of human beings. In agricultural production systems, to confront the ever-growing intricate problems and to address agricultural sustainability challenges, progression in smart farming and precision agriculture is an essential part. Agriculture sustainability is the key to assure food security and hunger removal for the ever-growing population. Agriculture is the backbone of any country's economy and considered as the source of employment. For the Indian economy, agriculture is one of the pillars contributing '15.4%' of the country's overall gross domestic product. The significant limbs of agriculture are agronomy, horticulture, fisheries, economics, livestock, agricultural engineering and forestry.

As the world population continues to increase and land becomes unavailable, there is an increasing need of ingenious and more skilful farming to produce more crops by using less space. Food safety, impoverishment and the general sustainability of the food and agricultural systems are all influenced by global trends. Around the world, the topic of agricultural automation is becoming more popular. Recently ML concepts are applied directly in agriculture. The use of ML in agricultural solutions will boost farmers to produce more with a smaller number of resources. The use of ML in agriculture will also improve the crop quality and reduce the time it takes for goods to reach the market. ML, IoT, computer vision applications help to elevate the profitability of the farmers by maintaining a balance between need–production cycle and also improves the quality. By using precision learning, significant improvement can be achieved on total yield of harvesting. Farmers are getting benefitted by the predictions of ML algorithms. These algorithms help in minimizing the casualties in farming. These algorithms are basically recommending affluent predictions and perceptivity about the crops. Farmers always must be in touch with latest information about crop, seed, soil, weather, environment, market trend, etc., as 'information is the power'.

Agricultural activities are mainly classified into three phases: pre-harvesting, harvesting and post-harvesting.

Pre-harvesting measures the overall growth of fruits/crops. Crops selection, preparation of soil/land, seeds quality, sowing of seed, inundation, spraying, maintenance of crop (utilization of fertilizer/pesticide, cropping), selection of cultivar, genetic conditions, environmental conditions, crop load, detection of weed, detection of disease and yield estimation (yield mapping, fruit number counting for production prediction) are basically included in this phase. The parameters considered in this stage are (captured by ML): parameters of soil, fertilizer application, seeds quality, genetic and environmental conditions, pruning and irrigation.

Profit is correlated with right and careful harvesting. Loss in harvesting stage is still a matter of concern. The use of ML, deep-learning methodologies and auto-harvesting robots are good candidates to be used to help farmers by reducing this loss [1]. The profit factors of the farmers depend on production increase and minimal harvesting time. Automatic intelligent harvesting robots can be used in horticulture to achieve production increase with minimal harvesting time [2,3]. Single shot detector algorithm (YOLO) is used to develop a CNN model (small size: number of layers = 6) and a Visual Geometry Group-16 fine-tuned deep learning model for on-tree fruit detection and achieve more than 90% accuracy. Both real and synthetic pear, apple fruits images are utilized for training using ACP (Amazon-cloud-platform) [4]. The performance of a neural network can be enhanced not only by changing the network architecture but also by increasing the neural network depth and by fusing bio-inspired features. Using bio-inspired features, generalization capabilities and model complexity for having better accuracy can be avoided [5]. Depending upon the type, maturity stage and are they harvestable or not, three classification models have been proposed to classify date fruit by using transfer learning from VGGNet and AlexNet (both are CNN models), considering the pre-maturity and maturity stages of date fruit. A total number of 8,072 images were considered in the dataset which contain images of five date types: Barhi, Sullaj, Naboot Saif, Meneifi and Khalas. VGG-16 model performs well in comparison with other models. The parameters considered in harvesting stage are skin colour, size of fruit/crop, taste, durability, maturity stage, trait, classification for harvesting and fruit detection market window.

Post-harvesting is a very crucial and the final stage of agriculture. Though from yield-estimation to harvesting, every stage is completed successfully, farmers may face severe loss due to laxity in post-harvesting. The shelf-life of vegetables and fruits, post-harvesting grading (varies with respect to the standard rules of different countries) [6–8] and export are considered in this stage. In this stage, a reference material for post-harvesting management of SQA (safety and quality assurance) must be prepared for different types of fruits and vegetables, which help stakeholders present in the horticulture supply chain. Fruit quantity and quality depend on proper handling of post-harvesting methods. Improper handling increases the overall loss. Overall loss also depends on improper packaging, careless handling, carriage conditions and poor harvesting. In [9], four levelled categories of tomato images are considered depending upon the parameters healthy, ripeness and defect. Four distinct models were proposed to classify the RGB tomato images in any one of the pre-specified categories (for post-harvest tomato grading). Fruit shelf-life is affected by humidity, temperature, chemical use in post-harvest phase, gasses used in fruit containers, and process to handle fruit to restrain the quality, grading of fruit with respect to quality.

Sequential flow of steps for farming can be like the selection of crops, preparation of land, sowing of seed, spraying, flooding, germinating, maintenance of crops by doing using pesticides, crop pruning, harvesting and post-harvesting activities.

Soil, seeds, pesticide detection and disease detection are very important components in farming life cycle.

Soil

- Analysis of the pre-harvesting parameter: soil.
- Parameters for the identification or prediction of soil property: soil temperature, moisture content and soil drying [10,11], pH values [12], soil fertility [12], OC (organic carbon), MC (moisture content) and TN (nitrogen) [13].

- ML algorithms with auto-regressive error function (AREF) are used to estimate the moisture content of soil [14].
- Soil attributes categorization help farmers in following way:
  - ○ Minimizes the dependencies of experts who do soil analysis [10,11]
  - ○ Improve the health of soil [10,11]
  - ○ Increase the profitability [10,11]
  - ○ Minimize extra cost on fertilizers [10,11]
- Indicators of soil fertility [15] are pH values and soil organic matter.

Seeds

Seed quality is a decisive constituent of production quality and yield. In contrast, seed quality is assessed with respect to the germination of seeds. CNNs are used to work out the seed germination rate and to mechanize the process of seed sorting [16–18]. Seed sorting has been done with high accuracy in [19] by using image recognition technique. High-quality seeds are separated from low-quality seeds using a classification method with enhanced accuracy by using a multilayer perceptron neural network model [20]. To assess the seed quantity per pod and to sort haploid seed with respect to the phenotypic expression, embryo pose and shape are implemented using a deep neural network (DNN) based on CNNs [21,22]. Classification of plant seedlings into 12 species is done through a CNN-based model [23]. By reducing features needed for clustering, PCA and image analysis technique are used to save the cost and time of placement of seeds in distinct clusters [24].

Pesticides and disease detection

Erroneous human experience is used in the detection of crop or leaves disease. Saving crops from major loss, disease detection is a vital step. Farmers generally analyse branches of tree and leaves in the growing phase to identify the disease or spreading pesticides on the crops with desired proportion (which they think). Disease type, disease stage and the affected area are the critical factors to decide pesticide type, time of applying the pesticide and the place to apply the pesticide. The improper use of fertilizer may harm the crop health as well as farmer health. Choice of relevant pesticide at desired land with legitimate proportion at an appropriate time can be implemented by precision agriculture. In [25], support vector machine (SVM) with two types of kernels (linear and polynomial) and extreme learning machine (ELM) have been used for plant disease identification by deploying decision support system with camera sensor in real-time scenario. The effect of crop losses in food security and global food production losses has been explored in [26]. Crop loss happens due to diseases. A comparative study has been shown between DL algorithms (VGG-16, Inception-v3 and VGG-19) and ML algorithms (RF, SVM and SGD) on disease detection, where DL methods are better performer. Naïve Bayes (NB), K-nearest neighbour (kNN) and artificial neural network (ANN) are used to detect fusarium and healthy diseased peppers by obtaining reflections from pepper leaves [27]. Different kinds of pesticides with their applications and environmental percussion of them are presented in [28]. Challenges present for the existing DL methods in the detection of plant disease are discussed in [29]. A two-stage architecture Disease Net model has been proposed to classify plant diseases. Without considering the entire leaf, only distinct spots and lesions are used to pinpoint plant diseases using the DL method [30]. Different diseases of plant are envisioned in [31] with respect to different DL methods used for that purpose. However, research gaps are pointed out and suggested that DL algorithms with advance features can be used to minimize gaps and increase the accuracy. Fuzzy rule-based approach for disease detection (FRADD) was presented in [32] for the classification and disease detection of apple by considering named 'scab' and couple of fruit types. Another CNN model has been proposed to detect diseases on apple leaf and as well as on fruit [33,34]. The proposed model classified apple leaf diseases into Rust, Brown, Altenaria and Mosaic leaf spot categories after having a training over newly created diseased leaves dataset with 13,689 images. Citrus fruit diseases have been detected in [35] by considering a couple of informative physical attributes such as hole structure on fruit, colour, morphology and texture. The prospected model for citrus fruit disease detection was possessed for ANN, SVM algorithms and K-means clustering technique. SVM with ANN improves disease detection and the classification rate significantly.

The use of farming techniques with AI/ML has several benefits:

- Profit margin being increased within the agriculture industry.
- It will increase the job scope.
- It provides new means to feed population with increasing rate.
- It offers new opportunities for the species management.
- Considering the fluctuation of ecological conditions, it can felicitate farmers by giving guidance to manage their land in better way by composing real-time models that can estimate evaporation rates, water content and soil temperature to deprecate costs that farmers are spending in maintenance of their lands and in effect it helps to escalate crop production.
- In addition to these, by using AI–ML techniques, farmers can predict the crop quality, crop yield and the presence of weeds. Also, farmers can make efficient price prediction and grown food allocation which in turn give benefits for both farmers and consumers.

Still there are serious obstacles in the integration of AI/ML techniques into agricultural production. These obstacles need to be addressed before the use of these technologies in the farming industry. Agricultural producers are facing problems due to the upliftment of these techniques, which requires enormous testing, promotion, investment and production costs. Acquire the knowledge about these technologies and implement them into agricultural farms is not an easy task for farmers due to the educational and time barriers. Economic growth and social production can be increased by integrating AI/ML technology into agricultural production. It also helps to relieve societies current most critical problems such as problems resulting from labour shifts, population growth and global warming.

The accuracy of AI/ML enabled agriculture system depends on the collection, analysis and processing of data related with potent agricultural production. Data collection can be done with the use of advanced technology like, GPS-based soil sampling, variable rate technology, cameras, robots, automated hardware, autonomous vehicles, GPS guidance and control systems, software, telematics, sensors and drones.

For accurate decision-making and better prediction, the following parameters are considered with different ML methodologies:

• Temperature, rainfall, area and humidity [36,37]
• To foresee the boom and diseases of plants, name of the crop, type of seed, area of land, pH value, type of soil and water can be considered with data-mining techniques [38].
• Place, temperature, precipitation and manufacturing can be used with SVM [39].
• Farming data like meteorological data, usage of pesticides can be used data mining [40]
• K-means algorithm is used to section soil [41].

11.2   Challenges and present scenario in agricultural applications

• Many countries are still using traditional means of agriculture.
• Due to lack of knowledge, unawareness about the advancement of technologies and heavy cost, farmers are hesitant in using the latest methodologies.
• Inadequate knowledge about crops, yields, types of soil, weather, lack of information about market trend, problems in irrigation, improper use of pesticides and erroneous harvesting → are the main causes for which farmers face loss or increase expenses.
• Loss in harvesting stage is still a matter of concern.
• Data operation (availability of data, quality of data, quantity of data, check for extraneous feature rich data, etc.).
• Pre-processing of data is done by applying techniques to prepare data suitable for training, validation and testing. The techniques are also used to remove data redundancy, missing data and non-informative data.
• Camera configuration at the user end.
• Predicting suitable crops in particular piece of land takes time and also a complex work.
• Rapid pace of population growth is one of the biggest preoccupations of our society.
• Due to urbanization and globalization, it is very challenging to find land (in terms of the area of land and the quality of land for agriculture).
• Crop cultivation prediction is even more challenging due to the hysterical use of fertilizers encompassing micronutrients, potassium and nitrogen.
• Input parameters selection for agriculture varies from region to region.
• Climatic change has negative impact on the corn yield.
• Cost of subsidies and fertilizers have been increased day by day, which are proven to be extra matter of concern for the government and agriculturist.
• Increase in agricultural production has a proportional dependency on the increase in population.

- Imperative need is that the environment must be saved from farming pollutants.
- Productivity of crops has been declined in the present decade. This declination is majorly due to illiteracy of Indian farmers, crippled holdings of land, lack of irrigational facilities, lack of decision-making capacity in choosing good manure, seeds, etc.
- The declining value for India (per hectare yield) is just because of improper pest management, scarce storage facilities, shortfall of irrigational facilities, unavailability of capital, lack of transportation, soil erosion due to natural calamities, etc.
- Farmers are illiterate and poor. Farmers cannot buy modern fertilizers and good-quality seeds, and as they are illiterate, they even cannot take decisions which in turn help them to increase the crop yield.
- Methods used to check the seed quality under quality assurance programs have constraints pertinent to subjectivity, time depletion and calamitous means of estimating the quality of seed [42–44].
- Production quality and yield is dependent on the germination of seed. Seed germination rate is calculated by using manual process and it is time-consuming and erroneous.

11.3   Need for ML in agricultural applications

Competent and decisive agriculture with high-quality production and less work-force can be achieved by applying ML in farming. Image recognition and ML techniques are used to mechanize seed sorting process and calculation of the seed germination rate. Efficient ML models can detect plant disease as well as pesticide prediction simultaneously.

The need for ML in farming applications can be seen as:

- Detection and classification of object in each farming stage can be done using ML algorithms.
- To mitigate the challenges related with training time requirement, small dataset and model accuracy enhancement, transfer learning process can be used.
- Farming gains can be achieved by using IoT with ML methods. Real-time data with respect to different farm parameters are collected using IoT and these can be used with ML methods to forecast the way of improvements in farming to the farmers.
- To make ML and deep learning model implementation more accurate, fast, deployable and smooth, following recommendations can be considered:
- Specific ML model can be built for classification and recommendation.
- Authentic and informative dataset must be created for specific type of ML algorithms.
- It is preferable to test and validate the model on public dataset.
- Transfer learning can be used to reduce the training time requirement of the model.
- Auto-ML approach can be used to create good quality, accurate ML models in a very short period.

11.4   State-of-the-art ML techniques in agricultural applications

11.4.1   Crop and fertilizer prediction

Generally, farmers have a common understanding that, same crop (if it is profitable) can be grown in all seasons by applying large quantity of fertilizers without having the idea about amount of fertilizers to be used and the proportion and combination of fertilizers. They do not even think for the improper use of fertilizer may degrade the soil quality and soil fertility. A combination of fertilizer and proportion of the fertilizer components are mainly dependent on the soil quality, weather conditions and crop to grow. Climatic change and varying weather conditions have a significant impact on crop production. Requirement of water, humidity is greatly affected by change in different climatic parameters [45].

The factors for better prediction of crops are weather conditions, environmental changes, rainfall (totally uncertain time to time and place to place), water availability and the utilization of pesticides.

The proposed system in [45] does the prediction about:

- Most suitable fertilizer and crop which are to be seeded for distinct land depending on the contents of soil (pH) and parameters of weather such as humidity, temperature and annual rainfall.
- The amount of nutrients to be added to grow new crops in different seasons, by which profit can be maximized and soil pollution can be reduced.
- Market price of the crop, required seed for cultivation in kg/acre, comparative yield in q/acre and required NPK for recommended crop.

ML has been used in the proposed system to excel and enhance the crop yield and crop quality. For crop prediction, XGBoost, random forest (RF) and KNN are used with parameters humidity, rainfall, N, P, K, and temperature. For fertilizer prediction, SVM and RF are used with parameters N, P, K, temperature, humidity and rainfall. The parameters used in ML methods (to figure our data and process pattern with respect to input conditions) are temperature, humidity and pH (SVM and decision tree (DT)).

11.4.2   Land area-specific prediction of suitable crops

Cultivation of crops can never be done on hand-on experience, because, in many cases it has been seen that farmers are not able to choose appropriate land for crops keeping in mind climatic factors and soil properties. Increase in crop production is mutually dependent on the accurate prediction of crop. Crop prediction relies on geographic, climatic attributes, soil. Relevant informative features for right crops [46] are selected by using feature selection techniques.

The production level of crop increases with respect to the accurate prediction of crop in appropriate land. To predict crop, genotype, climate and interaction between two are considered as attributes [47].

A hybrid feature selection method has been proposed using a boosting technique by keeping in mind the limitations of filter as well as wrapper feature selection methods [48]. Filter and wrapper approach-based feature selection method has been used, ranking of feature and multivariate feature selection has been done [49]. Induction and wrapper methods are compared without feature subset selection and compared after that with Relief (another filter method) [50]. Minimum spanning tree used for a hybrid model which was replaced by the first nearest neighbour [51]. For feature selection from a dataset, a hybrid combination method is proposed with the application of particle swarm optimization – support vector machine (PSO-SVM) [52]. An RF model is developed with RFE to improve accuracy of prediction [53]. For the prediction of crop yield, performance of ML methodologies is analysed with multiple feature selection techniques. It has been seen that RF come up with higher accuracy among other ML algorithms. Key attributes are selected from the dataset by suing feature selection techniques. Because achieving good prediction accuracy, information and relevant attributes play a vital role. Wrapper feature selection methods such as Boruta, RFE and sequential forward feature selection (SFFS) have been implemented to find the best features from the dataset. SFFS suffers when optimal subset is large. It selects one feature per unit time and loop continues for individual attribute selection. For this, its time requirement is high. In Boruta, both selection and rejection of features are coordinated concurrently. For this, it takes less time. However, ranking process has not been followed by it. RFE selects most important features with respect to the ranking method.

Classification is needed to classify the crop record accurately for a particular piece of land. To handle high-dimensional data, supervised learning-based classifiers like RF, SVM, kNN, DT, NB and bagging are used.

Steps followed for predicting suitable crop in specific area of land in [46] are as follows: initially, crop database data containing soil conditions and environmental factors are pre-processed. Filter (rapid execution), wrapper (better recognition rate) and embedded feature selection methods are used. Then RFE, Boruta and SFFS are used to select features along with classifiers RF, SVM, kNN, DT, NB and bagging for crop prediction, followed by the performance analysis of all the methods to select the best feature selection methodology with classifier.

The objective of the work is to find the best classification method-based feature selection technique to envision the most advisable crop for farming on particular piece of land. It is done by finding a functional relationship between cultivation and interactive factors such as climate, soil and genotype.

11.4.3   *Crop yield prediction and climate change impact assessment*

Weather change has a great impact on the crop yield. Anthropogenic change in climate affects the farming domain as this domain has a dependency on weather. Weather to crop yield mapping is necessary to project climate change impact on agriculture, environmental and economic outcomes to formulate adaptation and mitigation policy. This mapping depends on biophysical and deterministic crop models. It has been found that, the timing of moisture and heat are important to predict corn yields, with considering simple accumulation of heat. This model is better in prediction for challenges like probably rudimentary preceding knowledge about the function used to map the inputs to the outputs and longitudinal or other structure present within the data [54].

The objective of the work is to model yield using a semi-parametric variant of DNN to consider complex non-linear relationships in parametric structure, high-dimensional datasets and unobserved cross-sectional heterogeneity. A semi-parametric neural network has been deployed using parametric statistical models with DNN for crop yield prediction.

Future work options:

- Domain-area knowledge can be represented in a better way in the process of parametric component parameterization of the model.
- Combining non-parametric part of the model with ML.
- For the obligation to model the elements (such as CO_2 fertilization) statistically, new ways can be implemented to integrate elements generated from deterministic crop models.

11.4.4   *Extraction of fertilizer dosages for precision agriculture*

Technology can be implemented to obtain maximum yield by adding a precise number of fertilizers. The proposed model is deployed for areas of India where irrigated wheat is grown and can be protracted for different crops irrespective to any place in the world [55].

ML is used to forecast the presence of phosphorous, potassium and nitrogen for fertigation. The amount of fertilizer needed is dependent on different soil types, the need for different crops and crop varieties. World population may breach to 9.1 billion by 2050.

To achieve the increasing demand of food products, intensive farming can be applied. Intensive farming, a type of agriculture or system of cultivation which includes both crop plants and animals, uses huge amount of input and output per unit of agricultural land area, which is similar to housing very high densities of fish in artificial tanks, which allows farmers to control oxygen level, feed, and other factors to increase in yield.

As it has been reported in [56] that 67% of nitrogen fertilizers is lost in the environment, where only 33% of nitrogen fertilizer has been used by the plants. This unused nitrogen may be emitted as nitrous oxide into the atmosphere or can be released as a pollutant in ground water [57]. Phosphorous from different industries can get into water stream. Algal blooms (toxin-producing algae grow excessively in a body of water) and ultimately dead zones [58,59] happen due to this.

In general, agriculturists suggest blanket recommendation for individual crop, like blanket recommendations for different varieties of wheat for N:P:K was

80:40:40. In recent times, another approach is used, where fertilizers are recommended to each zone of a nation crop wise and soil category wise. Soil is categorized in terms of the amount of nutrients present in it and the categories are VL (very low), L (low), M (medium), H (high) and VH (very high).

Precision agriculture can be a preventive measure to lessen the peril caused due to agricultural practices to the nature. Precision agriculture can be applied to solve this challenging problem by predicting the correct proportion of fertilizer to be sprayed in each land separately. Proposed model predicts the specific values of fertilizers (nitrogen, phosphorous and potassium) to be sprayed in each land for distinctive target yields and different values of soil nutrients.

In the proposed model, target yield is considered as input parameters. After data collection, data preparation has been done to train and evaluate the model performance. Features used in the dataset are pH, zone, EC (electrical conductivity), soil nitrogen, OC (organic carbon content), soil potassium, soil phosphorus, recommended nitrogen, recommended potassium and recommended phosphorus. CART regression model is used to recommend nitrogen, phosphorous and potassium.

A comparative analysis of the proposed model for nitrogen, phosphorous and potassium recommendation is done using R-squared, mean absolute deviation (MAD), mean absolute per cent error (MAPE), mean squared error (MSE) and root mean squared error (RMSE).

Relative variable importance for nitrogen, phosphorous, potassium recommendations are done with the variables zone, target yield, N, OC, EC, pH, P and K.

11.4.5 Predicting fertilizer usage in agriculture production (crop yield-based on fertilizer consumption)

India is the second leading producer of pulses [60]. In comparison to other countries, India's per hectare yield of India is 3 tonnes. Farming issues can be solved using rule-based systems [61] and data mining techniques [61,62]. Farmers can take decision very easily by using rule-based systems about the usage of pesticides in accurate quantity and in choosing good-quality seeds, etc. However, its operation cost is very high. For all the situations, if the decision to be taken is known, then it performs well.

Productivity can be increased using ML in the following dimensions:

- Quality and the rational use of inputs such as seeds, water, pesticides and fertilizers.
- Using modern technology, safe and judicious exploitation of genetically modified seeds.
- Changing the scale to high-value commodities.

Solution to the improper use of fertilizer in agriculture is implemented by using supervised-ML algorithms such as SVM, regression and multi-layer perceptron, etc. Predicted fertilizer consumed in kg/ha for a given farmland after studying agricultural profile of different crops grown in India.

In the proposed model, Weka tool is used to compare the performance of algorithms. Farming data for different types of crops from 1965 to 2007 were collected [63]. ML algorithms along with WEKA tool with 10-fold cross validation are applied on the data.

Based on fertilizer consumption, supervised ML algorithms like SVM, SMOreg, regression and multi-layer perceptron are used to predict the crop yield. A statistical model MLR algorithm is applied on the existing data, followed by result analysis.

- *Simple linear regression*: This method models a linear relationship between the predictand and predictor. For the matter of fertilizer consumption prediction model for rice crop, fertilizer consumption is predictand and productivity (kg/ha) is predictor.
- *Multiple linear regression*: Here, more than one predictor variable is used. This method models a linear relationship between one predictand and many predictors. Here, fertilizer consumption is predictand and yield, productivity (kg/ha) and cropping area, are predictors.
- *Multilayer perceptron (MLP)*: MLP (based on supervised ML) is a feed-forward ANN model. It correlates a set of input data such as the productivity, cropping area, yield and year to a set of relevant output such as fertilizer consumed in kg per hectare.
- *Support vector machine*: SVM, a supervised ML algorithm, is used by setting the RegOptimizer in WEKA. Using productivity per hectare and cropping area, it can prognosis consumption of fertilizer.

RMSE, correlation coefficient and MAE are used as performance measures.

11.4.6   Seed quality classification

Optical sensors with ML algorithms are used in the evolution of prosperous advents to build the decision support system for the seed industry related to marketing of seed. X-ray imaging techniques and Fourier transform near-infrared (FT-NIR) spectroscopy are used to implement classifier models to forecast vigour and germination of seeds. This method uses a model species named forage grass (*Urochloa brizantha*). From individual seeds, radiographic images and FT-NIR spectroscopy data are captured.

In agricultural production, seed quality is one of the important factors. The yield is also dependent on the seed quality [64]. To reduce the cost of field experiments and to increase the probability for identifying better crop variety, high-quality seeds are much required matter in plant breeding. Seed quality is generally tested by quality assurance programs using different methods based on attributed like vigour tests and germination [65]. The loss of viability and vigour are dependent on the changes in internal anatomical characteristics of seed and chemical composition [44]. However, visual identification cannot identify these changes. Spectrometry and methods based on X-ray imaging techniques are efficient to capture data on complex trait associated with the quality of seeds and accuracy to classify the seed quality. By acquiring a large number of spectral details, FT-NIR spectroscopy can detect a seed compound [66–72]. Electromagnetic radiation with wavelengths from 780 to 2 500 nm is absorbed in FT-NIR spectroscopy [73]. In effect of this, simultaneous and direct measurements of different ingredients of seed sample are done accurately [70,74]. The internal morphology of seed (physical state) is revealed using an X-ray imaging technique, where differences between X-ray attenuation in several tissue types are measured [44,75]. Optical-based methods can induce discriminative information about the seed quality. However, classification performance can be improved by combining different datasets using ML algorithms. Similar to FT-NIR data, X-ray image data can be combined to classify the seed quality.

Motivation is to implement an efficient method which has the potential to provide reliable, quick, objective and non-destructive detection of seed quality. By selecting quality attributed of seed, ML algorithms can enhance classification accuracy, as they are able to confiscate linear and non-linear relationships.

A seed quality classification has been proposed and implemented using a comprehensive way. Germination prediction (FT-NIR and X-ray data) and seed vigour prediction (X-ray and FT-NIR data) have been done also by the model.

In the proposed model, partial least-squares discriminant analysis (PLS-DA), SVM with radial basis (SVM-r) kernel, LDA, NB and RF ML algorithms are used to create predictive models. R-software with 'caret' package [76] is used for data analysis. Caret package is also useful in calculation of informative predictor variables for the models. With respect to germination capacity, seeds are classified into non-germinated seeds, rapid germination (seedlings produced within 9 days) and slow germination (seedlings produced in more than 9 days). Germination speed is used to calculate seed vigour. X-ray and FT-NIT datasets are analysed separately, followed by the creation of another dataset, by combining these two datasets.

11.4.7 Soil property prediction

For efficient and effective farming, soil property plays an important role. Knowledge of soil property helps to yield crops sufficiently with minimum requirement of resources.

Modernization happens due to enhancement of technology which has advantageous impact over the society. In agricultural domain, technology helps a farmer by providing good-quality seeds (high-yielding variety seeds), advanced farming techniques, facilities of irrigation, chemical fertilizers, mechanized farm tools and electrical energy [77]. In recent times, it has been seen that the crop productivity is increased due to chemical fertilizers. The misuse or overuse of chemical fertilizers may be pernicious for soil fertility and crop productivity. The misuse or overuse of chemical fertilizers caused to improper recommendations of fertilizer (type and amount) which may not match with need of soil. To reduce the use of chemical fertilizers, contamination of ground water and preventing the deterioration of soil health and environment, it is recommended that soil must be balanced and test based and both organic and inorganic sources of plant nutrients may be used for integrated nutrient management of soil [78].

Objective has to get accurate fertilizer recommendation for the farmer and accurate analysis of soil properties. For this, soil property has to be predicted accurately for precision agriculture.

Factors for soil property prediction are soil organic carbon, calcium, pH, sand and phosphorus → these affects crop production.

In the proposed model, RF regression, multivariate regression, gradient boosting and SVM are used for prediction. In terms of the coefficient of determination, gradient boosting outruns other models. However, it suffers in the prediction of phosphorous presence in soil accurately. SVM is best in the prediction of phosphorous component in soil. Soil organic carbon, calcium, pH, sand and phosphorus are predicted by using ML models.

11.5 Application areas

ML has the potential to be utilized in farming with increasing results. It is as efficient to detect weeds and diseases, predict the quality of crops and yield, gather data, providing observations and offer predictions for livestock forecasting. Digital farming always gives an idea to the growers how the inputs are chosen to escalate the profit and yield. In addition, it also helps to figure out the field-wise actual cost.

Some of the ML applications in agricultural industry are discussed as follows:

- **Robots** – Hyper-efficient AI harvesting bots can reduce the dependency over human workers and thus it decreases labour costs. Also, robots help farmers to protect their crops by spraying weeds.
- **Watering** – Growing areas are monitored by using ML for temperature, crop humidity and soil composition. By the application of ML, usage of water and fertilizer is optimized and the yields are increased.
- **Resource management** – Using ML, farmers can save energy, reduce the improper use of pesticides, and shorten the time to make the product sellable.
- **Optimization of nitrogen in the soil** – Plant growth is much more dependent on one of the important nutrients – nitrogen. However, the use of nitrogen by plants is lesser range, through nitrogen is present both in the atmosphere and the ground. The level of inorganic nitrogen can be kept within optimum levels by using ML techniques to model nitrogen modelling. Simulation software checks for the availability of nitrogen and finds the appropriate time to add nitrogen to the soil.
- **Species breeding** – To effectively ensure the responsiveness to nutrients and water, specific genes are to be searched. Ideal plant species can cope with changes in climate, are very much defiant to disease, carries nutritional content in the higher margin, and that also better in taste. By studying huge amount of data, ML model can figure out accurate crop performance analysis.
- **Species recognition** – In general, the shape and colour of the leaves are used to classify plants. By using vein morphology, ML methods can do accurate, faster plant analysis.

Practical applications of AI in agriculture

11.5.1 Crop and soil monitoring

The decisive factors for quality and quantity of yield and health of crop are macro and micronutrients present in soil. The growth stages of crop must be monitored to optimize the production efficiency. Still, it is observed that human judgement and observations are used to determine the crop health and soil quality. But the efficiency may not reach to the expected level. To achieve good accuracy, unmanned aerial vehicles (drones) can be used to capture aerial image and that data can be trained to ML models for intelligent monitoring of soil and crop conditions and having this, farmers can take immediate actions.

Head growth stages give an idea of crop maturity. For this, farmers have to do regular observation of head growth. And human observation of daily growth may not be accurate for all the time. Using drones, images of different growth stages can be taken and in later time, ML models can differentiate the growth rate to decide the next action to be taken.

ML methods are also used to characterize soil organic matter (SOM) and soil texture. ML-based methodologies reduced the extra work to be done in other approach, where soil has to be dig up first, followed by energy intensive analysis has to be done on that. In ML methodologies, handheld microscope is used to train the algorithm to do the same work.

11.5.2 Insect and plant disease detection

Pests' detection and plant disease detection can be automated by using image recognition technology. The phases used in the image recognition technology are image classification, image detection, image segmentation, as shown in Figure 11.1. DNN can be trained with different images of different types of fruits with different levels of severity. This will minimize the dependency on labour-intensive human searching. YOLO v3 algorithm is also used to detect multiple tests or diseases on plants.

In addition to these, ML models are also efficient to find out whether pests are present in the crops or not and also what type of pests are they and how many pests are there. From an image with flying insects, detection and coarse counting

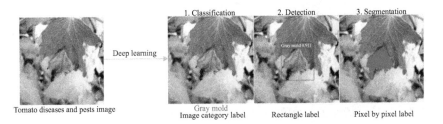

Figure 11.1   Image recognition steps

methods are used by ML algorithms on YOLO object detection and then it can count the number of insects is present, followed by fine counting on SVM and the classification on SVM using global features.

11.5.3 Livestock health monitoring

Apart from the plants, animals are also important component in the agricultural systems. However, some more close tracking is needed for animals. So, when ML model can identify an insect within an image, ML model are also efficient to figure out any animal using a bounding box process.

A camera is used to capture the images with animals and ML models will monitor the cattle behaviour and health. So, cattle can be monitored from remote location and a real-time scenario, farmers can be informed about any certain developed problem. So, an ML model can also count animals, detect disease in the animal, detect very significant and specific activities like giving birth and detect general activity of the animal like sleeping, eating, drinking or doing an unusual behaviour.

11.5.4 Intelligent spraying

An ML model also helps to prevent any disorder present in any activity. Drones automated with the ML model can spray pesticides or fertilizers automatically and also uniformly across a huge land. This automated process minimizes the risk of contaminating crops, water resources, animals and human. However, some challenges still persist. It is very tricky to assign specific task sequence for individual crafts. However, it is a good practice to spray a large land with multiple drones. A camera can be mounted over the sprayer which records geo-location of weeds and analyses the colour, size and shape of each plant to decide the amount of herbicides to be sprayed accurately to achieve precision targeting.

11.5.5 Automatic weeding

The way an insect can be spotted, weed can also be spotted. Weed removal, not only saves the farmers' work, but also reduces the need for herbicides. By this way, entire farming becomes very much environment-friendly and sustainable. Object detection, using ML methods, helps to discriminate weeds from crops following image training on the colour, shape and leaf size.

11.5.6 Aerial survey and imaging

Aerial imaging through camera or satellites gives a clear idea about livestock and crops with full accuracy. With respect to this, for any uneven situation, decisions can be made very faster by informing the farmer about the intensity of the situation. Aerial imaging is also helpful for efficient pesticide spraying and precision and this ensures that pesticides must go only to that place where it is intended for.

11.5.7 Produce grading and sorting

After crops are being harvested, ML models are also helping in finding the defects, disease and pests present on the plants. Sorting and grading process can also be automated using ML models by inspecting vegetables and fruits for the volume, shape, size and colour.

11.6   Future trends

Technology brings the advancement in the farming industry in a very efficient way. It also reduces dependency on human labour requirement for farming.

With respect to considerable changes in the environment, global food requirement and climate, ML has transformed agriculture of the twenty-first century by:

- Increasing the efficiency of resources, labour and time.
- Environmental sustainability is improved.
- Resource allocation is done in a more 'smarter' way.
- Real-time monitoring is done to promote the quality of produce and greater health.

ML methodology definitely elevates the agricultural industry to a certain level. Farmers' in-depth knowledge of their 'land' is being transformed to ML training. However, this requires greater educational and technical investments within agriculture sector. For this development, farmers are adopting the latest way of using ML and agricultural robotics to meet the increasing food demands and food security.

11.7   Summary

ML, a subsection of computer vision, is becoming a global need in maximum sectors in our daily life to meet our increasing needs. Agriculture is one of the sectors which seems to be the backbone for those countries where agriculture is the main source of economy. Like in every sector, agriculture also has some challenges. The challenges are the supply–demand need for food, food security, employment issues, over dependency on human labour, lack of literacy of farmers on knowledge of seed, soil, herbicide, pesticide, pests, etc. There are other challenges like climatic changes, crop selection with respect to climatic changes, finding good quality of seeds, pruning, learning properly parameters of soil, how the proportion of fertilizer is applied, actual forecasting of crop prices, market demand analysis, finding optimal time and conditions for harvesting and sowing, etc. ML basically studies the evidences collected in runtime and decides what to do, when to do and also forecast the things to be done when some difficulty arises. It is one of the most promising areas, which analyses and forecasted in advance and by which it become very easier to the farmers to decide what to do and when by which profit can be maximized.

References

[1]   Hua Y, Zhang N, Yuan X, *et al* . Recent advances in intelligent automated fruit harvesting robots. *Open Agricul J* 2019;13:101–6.

[2]   Kushtrim B, Demetrio P, Alexandra B, Brunella M, and Grappa C. Single-shot convolution neural networks for real-time fruit detection within the tree. *Front Plant Sci* 2019;10:611.

[3]   Hossain MS, Al-Hammadi M, and Muhammad G. Automatic fruit classification using deep learning for industrial applications. *IEEE Trans Ind Inf* 2019;15.

[4]   Kirk R, Cielniak G, and Mangan M. L * a * b * fruits: A rapid and robust outdoor fruit detection system combining bio-inspired features with one-stage deep learning networks. *Sensors* 2020;20:275.

[5]   Altaheri H, Alsulaiman M, and Muhammad G. Date fruit classification for robotic harvesting in a natural environment using deep learning. *IEEE Access* 2019;7:117115–33.

[6]   United States Department of Agriculture (USDA). Grade standards for fruits, https://www.ams.usda.gov/grades-standards/fruits (Accessed: July 2021).

[7]   EU, Fruit and Vegetables. Marketing standards, 2011, https://ec.europa.eu/agriculture/fruit-and-vegetables/marketing-standards_en (accepted in 2021).

[8]   Government of India, AGMARK ("Agricultural Marketing Adviser"), 2004, https://upload.indiacode.nic.in/showfile?actid=AC_CEN_23_31_00011_193701_1535099362507&type=rule&filename=fruits_and_vegetables_grading_and_marking_rules,_2004.pdf (accessed: July 2021).

[9]   Ireri D, Belal E, Okinda C, Makange N, and Ji C. A computer vision system for defect discrimination and grading in tomatoes using machine learning and image processing. *Artif Intell Agricul* 2019;2:28–37.

[10]   Liakos KG, Busato P, Moshou D, Pearson S, and Bochtis D. Machine learning in agriculture: a review. *Sensors (Switzerland)* 2018;18:1–29.

[11]   Sharma A, Jain A, Gupta P, and Chowdary V. Machine learning applications for precision agriculture: A comprehensive review. *IEEE Access* 2021;9:4843–73.

[12]   Suchithra MS and Pai ML. Improving the prediction accuracy of soil nutrient classification by optimizing extreme learning machine parameters. *Inf Process Agricul* 2019;7:72–82.

[13]   Morellos A, Pantazi X, Moshou D, *et al.* Machine learning based prediction of soil total nitrogen, organic carbon and moisture content by using VIS-NIR spectroscopy. *Biosyst Eng* 2016;152:104–16.

[14]   Johann AL, de Araújo AG, Delalibera HC, and Hirakawa AR. Soil moisture modeling based on stochastic behavior of forces on a no-till chisel opener. *Comput Electron Agricul* 2016;121:420–8.

[15]   Yang M, Xu D, Chen S, Li H, and Shi Z. Evaluation of machine learning approaches to predict soil organic matter and pH using vis-NIR spectra. *Sensors (Switzerland)* 2019;19:263–77.

[16]   Sivakumar D, Suriya Krishnaan K, Akshaya P, Anuja GV, and Devadharshini GT. Computerized growth analysis of seeds using deep learning method. *Int J Recent Technol Eng* 2019;7(6S5):1885–1892.

[17]   Huang S, Fan X, Sun L, Shen Y, and Suo X. Research on classification method of maize seed defect based on machine vision. *J Sens* 2019;2019:2716975.

[18] Zhu S, Zhou L, Gao P, Bao Y, He Y, and Feng L. Near-infrared hyper-spectral imaging combined with deep learning to identify cotton seed varieties. *Molecules* 2019;24:3268.

[19] Young J, Se JK, Dayeon K, Keondo L, and Wan CK. Super-high-purity seed sorter using low-latency image-recognition based on deep learning. *IEEE Robot Autom Lett* 2018;3:3035–3042.

[20] Ke-ling TU, Lin-Juan LI, Li-ming YANG, Jian-hua WANG, and Qun SUN. Selection for high quality pepper seeds by machine vision and classifiers. *J Integr Agric* 2018;17:1999–2006.

[21] Uzal LC, Grinblat GL, Namias R, *et al*. Seed-per-pod estimation for plant breeding using deep learning. *Comput Electron Agricul* 2018;150:196–204.

[22] Veeramani B, Raymond JW, and Chanda P. DeepSort: deep convolutional networks for sorting haploid maize seeds. *BMC Bioinformatics* 2018;19:289.

[23] Nkemelu D, Omeiza D, and Lubalo N. Deep convolutional neural network for plant seedlings classification, 2018, *arXiv*:1811.08404v1 [cs.CV].

[24] Amiryousefi MR, Mohebbi M, and Tehranifar A. Pomegranate seed clustering by machine vision. *Food Sci Nutr* 2017;6:18–26.

[25] Alagumariappan P, Dewan NJ, Muthukrishnan GN, Bojji Raju BK, Bilal RAA, and Sankaran V. Intelligent plant disease identification system using machine learning. *Eng Proc* 2020;2:49.

[26] Savary S, Ficke A, Aubertot J-N, and Hollier C. Crop losses due to diseases and their implications for global food production losses and food security. *Food Secur* 2012;4:519–537.

[27] Karadağ K, Tenekeci ME, Taşaltın R, and Bilgili A. Detection of pepper fusarium disease using machine learning algorithms based on spectral reflectance. *Sustain Comput* 2018;28:100299.

[28] Pandya IY. Pesticides and their applications in agriculture. *Asian J Appl Sci Technol (AJAST)* 2018;2:894–900.

[29] Arsenovic M, Karanovic M, Sladojevic S, Anderla A, and Stefanovic D. Solving current limitations of deep learning based approaches for plant disease detection. *Symmetry (Basel)* 2019;11:939.

[30] Barbedo JGA. Plant disease identification from individual lesions and spots using deep learning. *Biosyst Eng* 2019;180:96–107.

[31] Saleem MH, Potgieter J, and Arif KM. Plant disease detection and classification by deep learning. *Plants* 2019;8:468.

[32] Türkoğlu M and Hanbay D. Plant disease and pest detection using deep learning-based features. *Turk J Electr Eng Comput Sci* 2019;27:1636–51.

[33] Liu B, Zhang Y, He D, and Li Y. Identification of apple leaf diseases based on deep convolutional neural networks. *Symmetry (Basel)* 2018;10:11.

[34] Kour V and Arora S. Fruit disease detection using rule-based classification. In: *Proc Smart Innov Commun Comput Sci, Adv Intel Sys Compu (ICSICCS-2018)*; 2019. pp. 295–312.

[35] Doh B, Zhang D, Shen Y, Hussain F, Doh RF, and Ayepah K. Automatic citrus fruit is ease detection by phenotyping using machine learning. In: *Proc*

25th Int Conf Autom Comput Lancaster UK: Lancaster University; 2019. 5–7 September.

[36]   Vishnu Vardhanchowdary CH, and Venkataramana K. Tomato crop yield prediction using ID3, *Int J Innov Res Technol* 2018;4(10):662–665.

[37]   Veenadhari S, Misra B, and Singh C. Machine learning approach for forecasting crop yield based on climatic parameters, *2014 Int Conf Comp Commun Inform*, Coimbatore, 2014, pp. 1–5.

[38]   Sujatha R, and Isakki P. A study on crop yield forecasting using classification techniques, *2016 Int Conf Comput Technol Intell Data Eng (ICCTIDE'16)*, Kovilpatti, 2016, pp. 1–4.

[39]   Gandhi N, Armstrong LJ, Petkar O, and Tripathy AK. Rice crop yield prediction in India using support vector machines, *2016 13th Int Joint Conf Comp Sci Software Eng (JCSSE)*, KhonKaen, 2016, pp. 1–5.

[40]   KiranMai C, Murali Krishna IV, and Venugopal Reddy A. Data mining of geospatial database for agriculture related application, *Proc Map India*, New Delhi, 2006, pp. 83–96.

[41]   Verheyen K., Adrianens D, Hermy M, and Deckers S. High resolution continuous soil classification using morphological soil profile descriptions. *Geoderma* 2001;101:31–48.

[42]   Xia Y; Xu Y, Li J, Zhang C, and Fan S. Recent advances in emerging techniques for non-destructive detection of seed viability: A review. *Artif Intell Agric* 2019;1:35–47.

[43]   Wakholi C, Kandpal LM, Lee H, *et al.* Rapid assessment of corn seed viability using short wave infrared line-scan hyperspectral imaging and chemometrics. *Sens Actuators B Chem* 2018;255:498–507.

[44]   Ahmed MR, Yasmin J, Collins W, and Cho BK. X-ray CT image analysis for morphology of muskmelon seed in relation to germination. *Biosyst Eng* 2018;175:183–193.

[45]   Manoj Kumar DP, Malyadri N, Srikanth MS, and Ananda Babu J. A machine learning model for crop and fertilizer recommendation. *Nat Volatiles Essent Oils* 2021;8:10531–10539.

[46]   Suruliandi A, Mariammal G, and Raja SP. Crop prediction based on soil and environmental characteristics using feature selection techniques. *Mathem Comp Model Dyn Sys* 2021;27:117–140.

[47]   Das S. Filters, wrappers and a boosting-based hybrid for feature selection. In *Int Conf Mach Learn*, 2001, 1, pp. 74–81.

[48]   Guyon I, and Elisseeff A. An introduction to variable and feature selection. *J Mach Learn Res* 2003;3:1157–1182.

[49]   Kohavi R, and John GH. Wrappers for feature subset selection. *Artif Intell* 1997;97:273–324.

[50]   Sebban M and Nock R. A hybrid filter/wrapper approach of feature selection using information theory. *Pattern Recognit* 2002;35:835–846.

[51]   Chouhan S, Singh D, and Singh A. An improved feature selection and classification using decision tree for crop datasets. *Int J Comp Appl* 2016;142:5–8.

[52] Bahl A, Hellack B, Balas M, *et al.* Recursive feature elimination in random forest classification supports nanomaterial grouping. *NanoImpact* 2019; 15100179.

[53] Maya Gopal PS, and Bhargavi R. Performance evaluation of best feature subsets for crop yield prediction using machine learning algorithms. *Appl Artif Intell* 2019;33:621–642.

[54] Crane-Droesch A. Machine learning methods for crop yield prediction and climate change impact assessment in agriculture. *Environ Res Lett* 2018;13: 114003.

[55] Singh P, Garg Ch, Namdeo A. Applying machine learning techniques to extract dosages of fertilizers for precision agriculture, *IOP Conf Series: Earth Environ Sci* 614 (2020) 012136.

[56] López-Bellido RJ and López-Bellido L. Efficiency of nitrogen in wheat under Mediterranean conditions: Effect of tillage, crop rotation and N fertilization, *Field Crops Res* 2001;71:31–46.

[57] Praba R, Singh M, and Singh AB. Performance of macaroni (Triticum durum) and bread wheat (Triticum aestivum) varieties with organic and inorganic source of nutrients under limited irrigated conditions of vertisols, *Ind J Agr Sci* 2005;75:823–825.

[58] Mallarino AP and Haq MU. Phosphorus loss with runoff after applying fertilizer or manure as affected by the timing of rainfall, *Proc North Central Ext-Industry Soil Fert Conf*, Des Moines, *Int Plant Nutr Inst*, Peachtree Corners, GA, 2015, pp. 94–100.

[59] Singh B, Singh Y, and Sekhon GS. Fertilizer-N use efficiency and nitrate pollution of groundwater in developing countries, *Int J Env Sci* 1995; 20:167–184.

[60] Role of agrochemicals in sustainable farming. A report on Indian Agrochemical Industry, FICCI, 2019.

[61] Mercy Nesa Rani P, Rajesh T, and Saravanan R. Expert systems in agriculture. *J Comp Sci Appl* 2011;3:59–71.

[62] Milovic B and Radojevic V. Application of data mining in Agriculture, Agricultural Academy, *Bulg J Agricul Sci* 2015;21:26–34.

[63] Agriculture Database. ENVIS Centre, Punjab.

[64] Finch-Savage WEE and Bassel GWW. Seed vigour and crop establishment: Extending performance beyond adaptation. *J Exp Bot* 2016;67:567–591.

[65] ElMasry G, Mandour N, Al-Rejaie S, Belin E, and Rousseau D. Recent applications of multispectral imaging in seed phenotyping and quality monitoring—An overview. *Sensors* 2019;19:1090.

[66] De Medeiros AD, Pinheiro DT, Xavier WA, da Silva LJ, and dos Dias DCF. Quality classification of *Jatropha curcas* seeds using radiographic images and machine learning. *Ind Crops Prod* 2020;146:112162.

[67] De Medeiros AD, Zavala-León MJ, da Silva LJ, Oliveira AMS, and dos Dias DCF. Relationship between internal morphology and physiological quality of pepper seeds during fruit maturation and storage. *Agron J* 2020;112(1): 25–35.

[68]   Leão-Araújo ÉF, Gomes-Junior FG, da Silva AR, Peixoto N, and de Souza ERB. Evaluation of the desiccation of *Campomanesia adamantium* seed using radiographic analysis and the relation with physiological potential. *Agron J* 2019;111:592–600.

[69]   Kusumaningrum D, Lee H, Lohumi S, Mo C, Kim MS, and Cho BK. Non-destructive technique for determining the viability of soybean (*Glycine max*) seeds using FT-NIR spectroscopy. *J Sci Food Agric* 2018;98:1734–1742.

[70]   Seo YW, Ahn CK, Lee H, Park E, Mo C, and Cho BK. Non-destructive sorting techniques for viable pepper (*Capsicum annuum* L.) seeds using Fourier transform near-infrared and Raman spectroscopy. *J Biosyst Eng* 2016;41:51–59.

[71]   Andrade GC, Medeiros Coelho CM, and Uarrota VG. Modelling the vigour of maize seeds submitted to artificial accelerated ageing based on ATR-FTIR data and chemometric tools (PCA, HCA and PLS-DA). *Heliyon* 2020;6:e03477.

[72]   Ambrose A, Lohumi S, Lee WHH, and Cho BK. Comparative non-destructive measurement of corn seed viability using Fourier transform near-infrared (FT-NIR) and Raman spectroscopy. *Sens Actuators B Chem* 2016;224:500–506.

[73]   Silverstein RM, Webster FX, Kiemle D. *Spectrometric Identification of Organic Compounds*, 7th edn, John Wiley & Sons, Inc.: Hoboken, NJ, USA, 2005; pp. 72–126.

[74]   Li C, Zhao T, Li C, Mei L, Yu E, Dong Y, Chen J, and Zhu S. Determination of gossypol content in cottonseeds by near infrared spectroscopy based on Monte Carlo uninformative variable elimination and nonlinear calibration methods. *Food Chem* 2017;221:990–996.

[75]   Nugraha B, Verboven P, Janssen S, Wang Z, and Nicolaï BM. Non-destructive porosity mapping of fruit and vegetables using X-ray CT. *Postharvest Biol Technol* 2019;150:80–88.

[76]   Kuhn M. Building predictive models in R using the caret package. *J Stat Softw* 2008;28(5):1–26.

[77]   Yadav P. Agricultural situation in India, Junagadh Agricultural University, 2014.

[78]   Ministry of Agriculture, Overuse of fertilizer, https://pib.gov.in/Pressreleaseshare.aspx?PRID=1696465.

Chapter 12

AI- and ML-based multimedia processing for surveillance

Deepak Rai[1], Shyam Singh Rajput[2], K.V. Arya[3] and Poonam Sharma[4]

Abstract

Nowadays, surveillance systems are yielding the most critical and large volumes of data in the world from various sources. These data require proper management and analysis to produce relevant security information for modern security operations. However, it is still a challenge for humans to vigilantly monitor these large volumes of surveillance data for security assurance. Considering the upsurge in smart technologies, such as artificial intelligence (AI), machine learning (ML), deep learning (DL), and much more, the present security systems can be equipped with these technologies to radically increase the efficacy of the surveillance systems. The self-learning capabilities of AI and ML technologies make great impact on surveillance systems. This chapter comprehensively discusses the possible amalgamation of AI and ML technologies with the modern surveillance systems that will give them a technological edge. It also discusses all new findings based on object detection, visual sentiment analysis, video analytics, vehicle analytics, tracking people for potential crimes to ensure security for the society. Moreover, the specific types of AI and ML surveillance infrastructure being deployed are also discussed.

12.1 Introduction

Artificial intelligence (AI) is used in surveillance by utilizing computer programs to analyze the audio and visual data from cameras to identify various events, characteristics, and objects, including people and moving vehicles. Security personnel program the software to define restricted areas within the camera's view for

[1]School of Computer Science Engineering and Technology, Bennett University, Greater Noida, India
[2]Department of Computer Science and Engineering, National Institute of Technology Patna, Patna, India
[3]Department of Computer Science and Engineering, ABV-Indian Institute of Information Technology and Management, Gwalior, India
[4]Department of Computer Science and Engineering, Visvesvaraya National Institute of Technology, Nagpur, India

the property being protected by camera surveillance. If the AI finds a trespasser violating the rule set, it will send an alarm.

The AI surveillance program uses ML-based machine vision technologies to operate. Machine vision is a set of algorithms, or mathematical techniques, that compare the object observed with hundreds of thousands of different recorded reference images using a series of questions. AI asks itself a lot of questions, and when all the answers are combined, an overall ranking is created, which tells the AI probable value of the result. An alarm is sent if the value exceeds a predetermined limit. Such programs are distinctive in that they allow for some self-learning.

In addition to the basic rule, additional complex ones can be established. The AI has the capacity to keep track of hundreds of cameras at once. It is better than humans in spotting intruders in the distance, in rain, in bright light, or in various other circumstances. This kind of security AI is referred to as "rule-based" since a human programmer must create rules for each circumstance in which the user wants to get alerts. This type of AI for security is the most common. These days, a lot of security surveillance equipment have AI capabilities. Either the cameras' internal hard drives or a separate device that receives input from the cameras can hold the programs.

Behavioral analytics is a more recent, non-rule-based type of AI for security that has been created. This type of AI software is totally self-learning, without any initial programming input from the user or security contractor. In this sort of analytics, AI learns through its own observations of patterns with varied properties, such as the size, speed, reflectivity, color, grouping, vertical or horizontal orientation, and so on, what is typical behavior for humans, cars, equipment, and the environment. The AI normalizes the visual data by classifying and tagging the things and patterns it notices, which helps in constructing continuously improved definitions of what is normal or average behavior for the many observed objects. It can detect when something breaks the pattern after a few weeks of learning in this way. It sends an alarm when it notices these irregularities. For instance, driving in the street is commonplace. An unusual occurrence would be an automobile noticed pulling up onto a pavement. A person accessing a gated garden at night when it is often deserted would be unusual.

12.1.1 Need for AI and ML in surveillance

It makes sense to install and use CCTV cameras for security and surveillance. Although cameras are a necessary component for building any surveillance system, proactive surveillance and prompt response to breaches cannot be achieved by operators continuously watching hundreds or thousands of video streams.

AI was sought for because humans were unable to perform the duty of vigilantly watching live security camera material. When people view a single television display for more than 20 min, 95% of their capacity to pay attention long enough to notice important events is lost. This is again reduced in half when using two displays. It is obvious that the task is beyond the capacity of humans given that many sites have dozens or even hundreds of cameras. In general, camera shots of vacant buildings, parking lots, or hallways are incredibly uninteresting and quickly lose viewers' interest. The visual boredom rapidly becomes unbearable when numerous cameras are being watched, generally using views from bank of monitors having split screen or a wall monitor and switching between one set of cameras and the next every few seconds. Although surveillance cameras spread widely and were widely used by users including car dealerships, shopping malls, schools, businesses, and highly secured facilities like nuclear plants, it was later realized that video surveillance by human operators was inefficient and impractical. Large-scale monitoring systems for video surveillance were reduced to only capturing footage for potential forensic use to identify someone after a theft, fire, attack, or other incidents. When wide angle camera views were used, especially for broad outdoor regions, it was found that even for this purpose, there were serious limits because of poor resolution. Because the trespasser or perpetrator's image is so small on the display in these situations, it is hard to identify them. Overall, the key role that AI and its associated techniques plays in video surveillance is summarized as follows:

- It increases the detection accuracy without exponentially increasing hardware costs.
- For end-users, it significantly reduces the workload of security personnel.
- It provides substantial advantages by identifying unexpected occurrences and resolving numerous video forensic issues.
- It makes it possible to use the vast quantities of CCTV video data produced for system training purposes rather than having them gradually wiped.

In the future, the detection quality will continue to improve, increasing the application of AI in security and surveillance.

12.1.2 Impact of AI on surveillance

AI is having an immense impact because of its self-learning capabilities. The computer first honed its capacity for critical thought in relation to appealing objects in the scene. Now that it can identify objects in the real world, it compares its findings to the precise annotations (provided by humans) and continues to improve. As a result, it continues to learn and evolve. With each iteration, error is minimized, and approaches close to human error or even surpasses the same.

The intelligent software paradigm is replacing surveillance as a result of the self-learning capabilities that are proliferating in the market. The term "surveillance" has historically included the practice of following someone. Building a monitoring infrastructure has attracted enormous investment from governments all around the world. Although there are millions of cameras, no one is constantly keeping an eye on them. However, AI has the capacity to instantly analyze every frame and spare millions of lives. In order to accomplish a range of policy goals, many states are putting advanced AI surveillance technologies to use to map, track, and manage individuals. Some of these aims are legal, some violate human rights, and some fall somewhere in the middle.

Let us discuss a few crucial spying-related topics. Considerations should be made for things like monitoring traffic, parking availability, neighborhood monitoring, person tracking, and automobile analytics. Just after the Covid-19 tragedy, numerous businesses have spent a lot of time creating AI-based systems to enforce social division in public areas. AI has become so commonplace that it has developed to a degree of competence that was unimaginable just a couple of years ago. Real-time processing of video is used, for instance, in people tracking to examine and identify shady conduct that could jeopardize an enterprise's security. Surveillance software can identify anomalous behavior and notice unsafe behavior that a person might miss with the aid of video analytics technology.

12.1.3   Impact of ML on surveillance

Not only has ML changed how surveillance footage is seen, additionally how it may be applied to raise security and operational efficiency. Without having to manually maintain track of each video surveillance streaming and recorded video footage, security experts can react to crises, watch footage, and see trends to make greater use of video footage. Regional governments, law enforcement agencies, and commercial institutions including transit hubs, retail locations, event venues, and others will all benefit from the wide-ranging, positive effects this has on operations and security.

Even though CCTV monitoring has been around for more than 20 years, it has substantially improved thanks to technology developments like the high-speed Internet, IP cameras, and enhanced bandwidth. Security personnel and operations managers used to monitor CCTV in real time to look out for unusual behaviors or situations in areas that were being watched, or they would review hours or days' worth of footage for investigations after incidents to gather information and understand what occurred at the time. However, considering the time and assets required for completely evaluating the vast volumes of available video, it is difficult to fully utilize every useful detail that video data may offer. It can be more difficult to efficiently or successfully evaluate data from even a single video channel when using human monitors since they can be inaccurate and distracted. Therefore, a great deal of valuable video data is not utilized.

Because of this, the development of video intellect software that relies on ML, a kind of AI, has had a big impact on the video surveillance industry. A machine may develop the ability to classify and recognize patterns and objects on its own. As it becomes subjected to more data over time, it gets better.

12.1.4   Earlier attempts to surveillance

Before the use of AI-based technologies in surveillance domain there were other traditional methods which were utilized for surveillance purpose. Some of them are discussed in the following subsection.

12.1.4.1   Motion detection cameras

The initially proposed solution was to equip cameras with motion detectors. The theory was that a perpetrator's or intruder's motion would inform the remote monitoring officer, eliminating the need for ongoing human surveillance. The issue with this method was that the entire seen image on the screen is constantly moving or changing in an outside setting. Motion includes things like wind-blown leaves on trees, litter on the ground, insects, birds, and dogs, as well as shadows, headlights, sunbeams, and other things. This resulted in hundreds of thousands of false alarms every day, making this approach useless outside of interior settings outside of operating hours.

12.1.4.2   Advanced video motion detection

The subsequent evolution somewhat decreased false alarms, though at the expense of a time-consuming and laborious manual calibration. Here, shifts in a target's position in relation to a stationary backdrop, such as a person or car, are recognized. The reliability decreases over time when the background changes owing to seasonal changes or other changes. Again, proving to be a barrier, the economics of reacting to an excessive number of false warnings meant that this remedy was insufficient.

12.1.4.3   Advent of true video analytics

Patterns and their categorization are related to ML for visual recognition [1,2]. True analytics for video can tell apart between the motion of people, cars, boats, and other specific things from static images or pixel changes on the monitor. It accomplishes this by identifying patterns. An alert is sent when an object of interest, such as a person, transgresses a predetermined rule, such as the requirement that there be no more than zero persons in a certain location during a specified period. A brief video clip containing bounding boxes that usually automatically follows the identified intruder is delivered as the alarm.

12.2   Understanding AI and ML in surveillance

Many video surveillance professionals have come across the terms "AI" and "ML". But what do these terms mean, and how do they affect video surveillance?

The term "AI" broadly refers to the application of human intelligence to computer programs or to the process of allowing programs to learn over time with the aim of improving results over time. A method utilized to reach an AI level is ML, and DL is a development of ML. In essence, DL is an improved and more sophisticated version of ML, and both are ways to reach an AI level.

In video surveillance, object identification, classification, and property determination are accomplished using ML and DL techniques. Our brains try to make understanding of new information by comparing it to comparable information whenever we receive it. The ML and DL algorithms both make use of this comparison methodology.

The way that ML and DL algorithms are constructed to decide what qualifies as a known object differs. For ML to provide the correct results, additional human involvement from a programmer is needed to set the desired parameters. DL independently determines object attributes and may take into account traits that programmers would not. Both strategies discuss programming techniques that allow a system to learn from a set of data. When using ML, the characteristics of the data that a system searches for are typically predetermined or adjusted for by human programmers. For instance, the system might be trained to identify an object as a "person" if it is taller than it is wide, has limbs that move in a certain way, etc.

Since DL feeds the video analytic methods a large amount of data set that represents an object, it is thought to be superior to ML. The algorithm learns itself to recognize a certain sort of object during this phase, which is known as training. For instance, the system receives tens of thousands of photographs of people with diverse genders, clothing preferences, ethnicity, and more. The algorithm calculates how to weigh the importance of such features by identifying comparable and distinct attributes. Before a user uses the software, the system is trained by the software's creators. The procedure requires a significant amount of computational power—far more than what is needed when utilized in the field to identify and categorize items. The system consults the output file to determine whether a detected object corresponds to the classification. The development of analytics that can provide considerably more precise classification has resulted from the DL procedure, which employs the machine to ascertain object attributes. DL-based analytics, for example, can determine whether a person is a woman, man, or kid whereas previous methods may be able to recognize only a human. In addition, it might also be able to identify the type or manufacture of cars.

When used in the field, AI for video surveillance may not always get increasingly "smarter" because it is typically trained during design. However, DL and ML possess this capability and, when applied, can apply analytics that can improve over time. Systems that identify what is typical in a scene might be examples of typical applications. For instance, there is a surge of traffic in a school hallway every 45 min or so in between classes. The traffic is spread out and not focused in one spot during that busy period. In addition, the fact that everyone is moving so quickly is unique. A conflict may have broken out if the system notices an unusual focus on items. Outside of the typical inter-class period, if everyone is fleeing in the same direction, it might be a sign of an emergency.

12.2.1   Smarter systems, better results

Massive amounts of data are produced by video surveillance systems. Finding evidence and rapidly recognizing security problems are becoming more and more challenging due to the monitoring and filtering of such massive amounts of data. Better outcomes for your security program can be achieved with the aid of intelligent systems that use AI, ML, and DL to find evidence much more quickly and analyze video in real time to inform system operators of suspected activities.

12.3   AI- and ML-based models for multimedia

The overall AI- and ML-based models and technologies are basically categorized into two types: architectural models and learning models (refer Figure 12.1). The details about each are discussed in the following subsection.

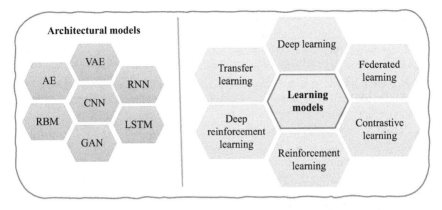

Figure 12.1   Different AI-based models and technologies for multimedia surveillance

12.3.1   Architectural models and technologies

For multimedia-based surveillance systems, there are various AI and ML architecture models that can be used. Convolutional neural networks (CNNs), recurrent neural networks (RNNs), long short-term memory (LSTM), generative adversarial networks (GANs), autoencoders (AEs), and restricted Boltzmann machines (RBMs) are some of the architectures described in this subsection.

12.3.1.1   Convolutional neural networks

CNNs are well-known and well-established deep neural network AI architectures that have been created to analyze spatial and multidimensional data, including the images. CNNs are frequently employed in applications that involve multimedia such as object identification, categorization, and computer vision. Multiple convolutional layers make up the CNN architecture, which is used to extract spatial information and correlations from data. CNNs are used in surveillance for a variety of purposes, including crowd analysis, fire detection, weapon identification, etc.

12.3.1.2   RNNs and LSTM

These are made to process time series or sequential data. To remember prior patterns of the time series data, the RNN architecture uses inputs from present and previous samples as well as the stored state from prior time steps. RNNs are frequently utilized in multimedia applications including voice or language processing and activity recognition. You may think of the LSTM as an expansion of the RNN model. In order to manage access to the memory cells, the LSTM model uses a neuron structure known as a memory cell that consists of a multiplicative forget gate, input gate, and output gate. The LSTM and RNN networks are employed in surveillance to track objects, detect anomalies in real time, track people, monitor targets, and perform other tasks.

12.3.1.3 Generative adversarial networks

It is an AI architecture that comprises two neural network topologies known as the generator network and the discriminator network. In order to solve the topic under investigation in the best possible way, the discriminator and generator networks collaborate. While the discriminator network's goal is to determine if the input data are coming from the generator network or the actual data stream, the generator network's goal is to generate new data after learning how the data are distributed. In order to train AI architecture models, extra data samples can be created using GANs (data augmentation). GAN-based networks have got very interesting applications in surveillance such as image de-raining (generate sharp images from a rainy image input), detection of anomaly during traffic monitoring, prediction of crowd trajectory, etc.

12.3.1.4 Restricted Boltzmann machine

An RBM is a probabilistic graphical model for a stochastic neural network architecture. The latent variables are contained in two levels (input and hidden layers) of the usual RBM architecture. RBMs are employed in real-time radar data recognition, handwritten digit recognition, and other surveillance applications.

12.3.1.5 Autoencoders

Another AI design that has an input layer, hidden layers, and an output layer is the AE. AEs are made up of two components: a decoder component that attempts to reconstruct the initial input information from the compressed state while minimizing the reconstruction error, and an encoder component that learns the representative properties of the data being processed in a compressed form. AEs are mostly utilized for smart surveillance via the identification of anomalous footage.

In addition to the methods listed above, contemporary AI architectures like the variational auto-encoder (VAE) architecture and transformer architecture have showed potential for multimedia AI. Applications involving object detection and localization can make use of the transformer architecture in conjunction with CNNs. A self-supervised network design called the VAE consists of a network of encoders and decoders. The image is mapped into the latent code space by the encoder network, and the image is generated from a latent code by the decoder network. The work provides additional details on current AI designs.

12.3.2 AI- and ML-based learning models

There are different AI learning models which can be deployed for multimedia-based surveillance systems. This subsection provides descriptions of several learning models which are proposed such as DL, reinforcement learning, deep reinforcement learning (DRL), federated learning and transfer learning.

- DL models are focused on building huge neural network models that can make correct data-driven decisions. When there are vast datasets available, this kind of AI method of learning is particularly well suited for training complex data.

- Reinforcement learning is a type of learning model used in cognitive science that is intended for situations where an agent communicates with an environment that offers rewards and/or penalties.
- Combining DL and reinforcement learning, DRL aims to create intelligent agents from vast datasets that can choose the optimal course of action to take for a variety of states through interactions with the environment. By maximizing the long-term accumulated profits, the DRL accomplishes this. In multimedia applications, DRL methods are frequently used for resource allocation (such as figuring out the best rate for video streaming) and suggestion. Policy-gradient-based and value-based models are the two main types for DRL.
- Transfer learning techniques can be used to reduce training costs for AI networks for surveillance applications. This method starts by training a base network (teacher network). In order to train a target data set, the learnt features are then sent to a target network (student network).
- Federated learning is a decentralized method of learning or training that may be applied to ensure edge device and information processing privacy. This method avoids sending and aggregating training data from devices at the edge on a centralized data center. By aggregating locally calculated updates, each edge or handheld device uses a distributed training strategy to train a model that is shared on the server.
- A recent AI learning approach called contrastive learning allocates a level of energy to training examples of a movie and a potential continuation. This learning model's goal is to assign a level of quality or badness to training instances that have few or no labels. By using this method, the neural network is trained to provide output vectors that are comparable for views of the same object from various angles and distinct for views of other things.

12.4 Multimedia processing for video surveillance

This section discusses some prominent AI- and ML-based multimedia work for surveillance.

A simple video preprocessing method based on AI and the Internet of Things (IoT) was suggested by the authors in [3], for use with wireless surveillance devices. The study used a lightweight DL analysis frame filter module built around dynamic backdrops modeling. Their strategy considers both static and dynamic surveillance situations. Obscure targets are found and recognized by a slave camera, which gives feedback to the primary camera to load resolutions as shown in Figure 12.2 [4–11]. Convolutional acceleration and channel pruning were coupled to create the object acquisition model. The accuracy loss brought on by model shrinkage and preservation of the environment is made up for by guaranteeing the incorporation of the adjacent cameras inside the one-hop range. Experiments on real-life footage show that the suggested approach can significantly cut the quantity of transmission while still maintaining a high level of system correctness and delay balancing. The technology was compared to green video transmission and found to save 64.4% of the bandwidth in a stable state and 61.1% in a flexible environment, making it a promising alternative.

Ahmed *et al.* [12] introduced a real-life top view-based person recognition method that employs a single step of CenterNet in a DL-based object identification approach. This method is illustrated in Figure 12.3. The approach identifies the human as a single point. In the work, a top view data set was used to train and test the model. The recognition results were compared with conventional

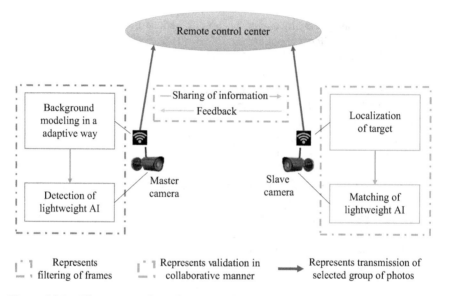

Figure 12.2   Illustration of wireless surveillance through one master slave camera pair

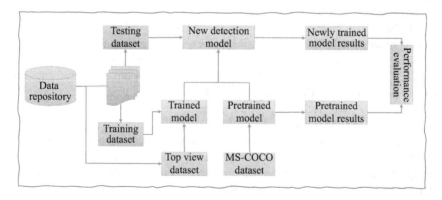

Figure 12.3   Surveillance-based DL detection model

recognition methods using an identical information set. Following further processing on a cloud computing layer, high-quality images are then delivered there, followed by a similar transmission to the multimedia processing unit. The work employed a CenterNet-based object identification system for person detection. More training is necessary to increase the efficacy of a recognition approach, according to the study, because the visual components of the human body differ noticeably from the top to bottom. Transfer learning was used to evaluate the new and improved trained tier for the top view information set after connecting it to the initial pretrained algorithm. The approach may obtain an identification precision of 89% and 94% with an already trained and newly trained model, respectively.

A distributed intelligent video surveillance (DIVS) system utilizing a DL approach was presented in the work from [13]. The work also produced a distributed DL training method-equipped multilayer computer system for the DIVS system. Their research suggested a flexible data transfer strategy to address the discrepancy between the edge devices' throughput and processing capacity. The authors used task-level parallel and design parallel training to expedite the video analysis process. To improve the efficiency of the DIVS system, two parallelization features were provided. Additionally, a key input value updating technique was advanced to ensure compatibility with all DL models globally. The process of video analysis was anticipated to proceed even more quickly with the application of compatible training techniques at the workplace. The test results demonstrated that the developed DIVS program could manage the video surveillance and analytical operations more effectively.

The work presented in [14] shows a customized intelligent video surveillance system known as EIVS. It is a platform for reliable edge computing that uses multitasking DL to carry out pertinent computer vision tasks. Video data from multiple cameras are standardized using a smart IoT device. Each EIVS node had the DL models installed in order to run computer vision operations on normalized data. This work used a multitask technique to implement the training depth classification model on a cloud server. The simulation results on the validated datasets shown that the system enables smart activity monitoring continuously and robustly and may increase the efficiency utilizing multitask learning.

The authors of [15] introduced SurveilEdge, a group-based cloud-edge system enabling real-time queries of substantial surveillance video streams. The research produced two new innovations: a smart load balancer that distributes the workload over different computing nodes and achieves the latency-accuracy trade off for real-time queries, and a CNN training approach to reduce training time while maintaining high accuracy. The suggested design offers a better balance between delay, bandwidth cost, and accuracy for future latency-sensitive applications. A prototype of the SurveilEdge was built using a lot of nodes at the edge and a public cloud. In comparison to the cloud-only solution, SurveilEdge reduced bandwidth requirements by up to 7% and improved query response times by 5.4%. It can also increase query precision by up to 43.9% and reach speedups of 15.8 when compared to conventional methods.

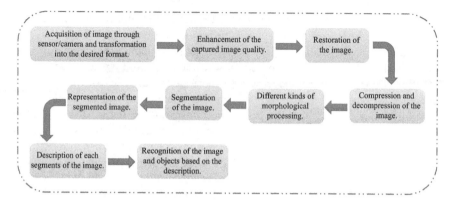

Figure 12.4   Workflow of a multimedia image-processing system

12.5   Image-processing working framework for surveillance systems

In order to learn from data, AI and ML methods typically employ a workflow. Think of a generalized representation of an effective algorithm for an image processing use case. To begin with, for AI algorithms to learn and make highly accurate predictions, they need a lot of high-quality data. We must ensure that the photos are correctly processed, labeled, and generic for AIML image processing, therefore. Computer vision can be used in this situation. To build the best dataset possible for the AI system, we can use computer vision to analyze, load, modify, and alter photos. Let us examine a fundamental image processing system's procedure. An overview of a typical image processing system is shown in Figure 12.4.

12.6   AI- and ML-based surveillance systems

Many surveillance cameras have previously been deployed along a crucial installation's fence/boundary. Modern cameras are typically digital IP-based, so a centralized monitoring station can access the video stream from all these cameras. The main goal is to spot behaviors like people loitering in a forbidden zone, approaching the fence, or crossing it. The following subsection discusses a few surveillance systems that use AI and ML.

12.6.1   Physical intrusion detection system

Physical intrusion detection system (PIDS) is a vision-based system that locates the 3D coordinates of human intrusions relative to camera coordinates system (CCS) and detects human intrusions. Geographic information system (GIS) is used to define CCS, with the camera's feet serving as the origin and the x-, y-, and z-axes pointing in the directions of geographic east, north, and upwards, respectively. This orientation assumption aids in the integration of real-time intrusion data from many video feeds onto a single fused map. The video stream from each camera is examined in PIDS to identify intrusions on an image-by-image basis. A DL model that has been trained to recognize items in the provided frame achieves the goal of discovering incursions in the frame. The DL model is built using SSD and is trained on huge datasets that are freely accessible to the public, such as MS-COCO. The Pytorch framework is used to train each DL model. The 2D location of humans is first determined in pixels, and then it is translated into a 3D CCS.

12.6.2   Stereo-based approach

Two cameras (designated as left (C_L) and right (C_R) cameras) are positioned in a stereo arrangement with parallel optical axes according to the stereo technique, as illustrated in Figure 12.5. Assuming a pin-hole camera model, (12.1) can be used to calculate the depth (a) of any object (O) in 3D space whose 2D pixel coordinates are known in both cameras.

$$\alpha = (f^l * b)(C_L - C_R) \tag{12.1}$$

where f^l represents the camera's focal length and b denotes the baseline of the setup. The term $C_L - C_R$ is the disparity which tells about the shift in the location of the pixel corresponding to the 3D points in both the images.

This system is being used for testing in the field within Bhabha Atomic Research Centre (BARC). The system spins to cover a wider field of vision because it also includes panning capabilities. On a computer with a GeForce RTX-2080 graphics card (4352 CUDA cores and 11 GB RAM), the processing time for one frame is roughly 20 ms.

12.6.3   Single camera approach

To estimate depth, a stereo vision-based configuration requires two cameras that are precisely parallel. The exact positioning of the cameras requires laborious mechanical work, which extends deployment time. A single camera solution is also

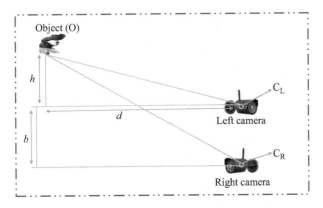

Figure 12.5   Illustration of the arrangement of a stereo camera

developed in order prevent the necessity of using two cameras and the associated alignment task. The 3D locations of the person are computed with the reasonable presumption that the human is standing on the ground. The trained DL system for object detection can be used to analyze the feed from any active surveillance camera to find intrusions. This system is also being used for testing in the field within BARC. Since a human always stands on the ground, it is obvious that the z position of the human feet position is always zero. On a computer with a GeForce RTX-2080 graphics card (4352 CUDA cores and 11 GB RAM), the processing time for one frame is roughly 20 ms.

12.6.4   Virtual fence

Virtual fences are created by recovering the three-dimensional positions of a plane's points from their 2D pixel locations. This program both recognizes and follows the user. Zones 1 and 2 are practically delineated on the ground in this location. An alarm is triggered if the person steps inside one of the exclusion zones. If a person crosses across from one zone to another, this also recognizes it. This is being used inside BARC for outside testing.

12.6.5   Suspicious behavior identification system (SBIS)

This application's goal is to identify suspicious behavior in people or other objects in the video feed. In order to anticipate suspicious actions, an end-to-end DL architecture is being developed. Small video clips of people acting are utilized to recognize the actions and then categorize them as normal or suspicious using the spatiotemporal characteristics of the main joints of the human body. Another option is to create a self-learning AI model that can be used to learn a person's typical and suspicious conduct.

12.7   Applications of AI and ML in surveillance

AI- and ML-based technologies have a wide range of applications in security video surveillance systems, such as:

- Detection of different kinds of anomalies.
- Detection and tracking of various types of objects.
- Development of various surveillance monitoring systems such as prevention systems, identification systems, warning systems and many more.
- Detection of individuals in crowd.
- Analysis of individuals movement in crowd.
- Biometric security.
- Use in behavioral biometrics.
- Understanding the behavior of human and other objects involved in security surveillance.
- Detection of any illegal activities.
- Development of different applications for traffic safety as well as safety of the driver.

12.8 Challenges and limitations of AI and ML in multimedia processing

There are several factors that make the real-life application of AI- and ML-based multimedia processing in surveillance domain very difficult. They are as follows:

- The primary concern for any effective AI and ML processing is the insufficiency of the real-life data.
- The extraction of features from videos becomes difficult in varying illumination conditions.
- Position and perspective of the camera is challenging because the appearance of individuals and objects varies with the change in their position and distance in reference to camera.
- Variability in the types of objects of interest in real world.
- Significant change in the performance of methods with variations in the density of the crowd being observed.
- Detection and tracking becomes difficult under occlusion effect.
- Lack of work for detection in domain-specific events.
- The skilled resource persons in the domain of AI and ML is still short.

References

[1] Davies ER. *Computer and Machine Vision: Theory, Algorithms, Practicalities*. Oxford: Academic Press; 2012.

[2] Domingos P. *The Master Algorithm: How the Quest for the Ultimate Learning Machine will Remake Our World*. New York, NY: Basic Books; 2015.

[3] Liu Y, Kong L, Chen G, *et al.* Light-weight AI and IoT collaboration for surveillance video pre-processing. *Journal of Systems Architecture*. 2021; 114:101934.

[4] Rajput SS, Arya K. A robust face super-resolution algorithm and its application in low-resolution face recognition system. *Multimedia Tools and Applications*. 2020;79:23909–23934.

[5] Rai D, Rajput SS. A new face reconstruction technique for noisy low-resolution images using regression learning. *Computers and Electrical Engineering*. 2023;107:108642.

[6] Rai D, Rajput SS. Robust face hallucination algorithm using motion blur embedded nearest proximate patch representation. *IEEE Transactions on Instrumentation and Measurement*. 2023;72:1–10.

[7] Kumar B, Rajput SS. Low-light robust face super resolution via morphological transformation based locality-constrained representation. *Computers and Electrical Engineering*. 2023;106:108612.

[8] Rajput SS, Arya K. Noise robust face hallucination via outlier regularized least square and neighbor representation. *IEEE Transactions on Biometrics, Behavior, and Identity Science*. 2019;1:252–263.

[9]   Rajput SS, Singh A, Arya K, *et al.* Noise robust face hallucination algorithm using local content prior based error shrunk nearest neighbors representation. *Signal Processing.* 2018;147:233–246.

[10]   Rajput SS, Arya K, Singh V. Robust face super-resolution via iterative sparsity and locality-constrained representation. *Information Sciences.* 2018;463:227–244.

[11]   Rajput SS. Mixed Gaussian-impulse noise robust face hallucination via noise suppressed low-and-high resolution space-based neighbor representation. *Multimedia Tools and Applications.* 2022;81:15997–16019.

[12]   Ahmed I, Ahmad M, Rodrigues JJ, *et al.* Edge computing-based person detection system for top view surveillance: using CenterNet with transfer learning. *Applied Soft Computing.* 2021;107:107489.

[13]   Chen J, Li K, Deng Q, *et al.* Distributed deep learning model for intelligent video surveillance systems with edge computing. *IEEE Transactions on Industrial Informatics.* 2019, doi: 10.1109/TII.2019.2909473.

[14]   Li J, Zheng Z, Li Y, *et al.* Multitask deep learning for edge intelligence video surveillance system. In: *2020 IEEE 18th International Conference on Industrial Informatics (INDIN).* vol. 1. IEEE; 2020. pp. 579–584.

[15]   Wang S, Yang S, Zhao C. SurveilEdge: real-time video query based on collaborative cloud-edge deep learning. In: *IEEE INFOCOM2020-IEEE Conference on Computer Communications.* IEEE; 2020. pp. 2519–2528.

Chapter 13

Action recognition techniques

Poonam Sharma[1], K.V. Arya[2] and Shyam Singh Rajput[3]

13.1 Introduction

Due to the common availability of surveillance as well as mobile camera, data generation in the form of images and videos has increased a lot. This in turn increased the requirement of data storage and, so manual analysis and interpretation is almost impracticable. Researchers have been working on the development of efficient as well as high-speed technologies capable of intelligent analysis and interpretation of visual data.

Video surveillance is in practice since long, but accuracy and high speed in detection and recognition still remain to be a challenge. This includes a variety of areas of research such as:

Pattern recognition: This aims at classifying the objects or data in the input images based on their inherent characteristic features.

Object tracking: It aims at tracking the object's location and movements in video sequences to monitor its activities and behavior.

Reconstruction: It typically aims at building two-dimensional or three-dimensional models of objects for advanced feature detailing.

Feature extraction: It is the process of reducing the dimensionality of the input image by extracting and selecting a subset of salient features representing the input data.

Segmentation: This provides for the extraction of the region of interest (ROI) from the gallery image based on different features. It divides the probe image into nonoverlapping areas, namely ROI areas and non-ROI areas.

Action recognition is a basic task in computer vision that focuses on identifying and understanding human activities from video stream. It is important for various applications, including video surveillance (static or dynamic), human–computer interaction (HCI), sports video analysis, and autonomous vehicles.

[1]Department of Computer Science and Engineering, Visvesvaraya National Institute of Technology, Nagpur, India
[2]Department of Computer Science Engineering, ABV-Indian Institute of Information Technology and Management, Gwalior, India
[3]Department of Computer Science and Engineering, National Institute of Technology Patna, Patna, India

Human action recognition covers an extremely large number of research topics in computer vision and has a wide range of applications in visual surveillance [1–4]. Action recognition in visual surveillance refers to the process of automatically analyzing and understanding human actions and activities captured by surveillance cameras or video feeds. This plays a crucial role in various applications, such as security monitoring, anomaly detection, and behavior understanding.

The following sections present a review of action recognition in visual surveillance, including its challenges, techniques, and recent advancements.

13.2   Challenges in action recognition in visual surveillance

Viewpoint variations: Surveillance cameras capture videos from different angles, leading to variations in human poses and appearances.

Occlusions: Objects or other people may obstruct the view of the person performing the action, making it challenging to accurately recognize actions.

Illumination changes: Lighting conditions in surveillance videos can vary significantly, affecting the visibility of actions.

Cluttered backgrounds: Surveillance scenes often contain complex backgrounds, which can interfere with action recognition algorithms.

Real-time processing: Surveillance systems typically require real-time or near-real-time action recognition to respond quickly to potential threats.

Basic techniques for action recognition in visual surveillance
Handcrafted features: Traditional approaches often use handcrafted features like histogram of oriented gradients [5], scale-invariant feature transform [6], or local binary patterns [7] to represent actions.

Deep learning-based methods: Convolutional neural networks (CNNs) [8] and recurrent neural networks (RNNs) [9] have shown remarkable success in action recognition. CNNs can learn spatial features, while RNNs capture temporal dependencies in actions.

Two-stream networks [8]: These models combine spatial information from still frames and temporal information from motion cues, typically extracted using optical flow, to improve the action recognition accuracy.

3D convolutional networks [10]: These networks operate directly on spatio-temporal volumes, capturing both spatial and temporal information in a unified manner.

Attention mechanisms [11]: Attention-based models focus on relevant spatial or temporal regions within a video to improve the action recognition performance.

13.3   Recent advancements

Graph convolutional networks (GCNs) [12]: GCNs capture interactions and relationships between different people in a scene, enabling better understanding of collective actions and group activities.

Transformer-based models [13]: Inspired by the success of transformers in natural language processing, researchers have applied transformer architectures to action recognition tasks, achieving state-of-the-art performance.

Weakly supervised learning [14]: With limited labeled data available, weakly supervised learning methods aim to learn action recognition models using only video-level annotations or a small number of weakly labeled samples.

Few-shot learning [15]: These approaches address the challenge of recognizing actions with minimal training samples by leveraging transfer learning or meta-learning techniques.

Online action recognition [16]: Real-time action recognition methods have been developed to process video streams in real time, allowing for immediate action detection and response.

13.4   Applications of action recognition

13.4.1   Video surveillance

Action recognition in visual surveillance is a challenging and an active research area. A combination of deep learning techniques, attention mechanisms, graph-based models, and advancements in weakly supervised and few-shot learning has significantly improved the accuracy and robustness of action recognition systems. These advancements contribute to enhancing the capabilities of visual surveillance systems for various applications, thereby improving public safety and security.

13.4.2   Industrial control [17–20]

Industrial control: Action recognition in industrial control refers to the process of automatically detecting and understanding human actions or machine operations in an industrial environment. It involves analyzing video or sensor data to recognize specific actions or activities, monitor production processes, detect anomalies, and improve the operational efficiency. This can be used for the following:

Quality control: Action recognition can be used to monitor and verify the correct execution of quality control procedures, such as inspections, measurements, or assembly processes.

Safety monitoring: By analyzing actions, industrial control systems can identify potentially hazardous situations or unsafe behaviors, enabling proactive safety measures.

Process optimization: Action recognition can help monitor and analyze the efficiency of production processes, identifying bottlenecks, optimizing workflows, and reducing downtime.

Predictive maintenance: By recognizing abnormal actions or patterns, industrial control systems can detect equipment malfunctions or maintenance needs, allowing for timely repairs and minimizing costly breakdowns.

Challenges in action recognition in industrial control
Variability in action execution: Industrial settings often involve complex and diverse actions that can vary due to factors such as operator skills, environmental conditions, or equipment configurations.

Data collection: Acquiring labeled data for training action recognition models in industrial control scenarios can be challenging, as it requires capturing and annotating large amount of real-world data.

Occlusions and cluttered environments: Industrial environments can be cluttered with machinery, tools, or other objects, leading to occlusions and complex backgrounds that hinder action recognition.

Sensor integration: Industrial control systems often rely on various sensors, such as cameras, depth sensors, or force sensors. Integrating data from multiple sensors and fusing them for action recognition poses technical and computational challenges.

Techniques for action recognition in industrial control
Deep learning: Similar to action recognition in other domains, deep learning techniques, such as CNNs [21] and RNNs [22], can be employed to learn spatio-temporal features and model complex action sequences.

Transfer learning [23]: Pretrained models on large-scale action recognition datasets can be fine-tuned on smaller industrial control datasets to leverage their learned features and enhance recognition accuracy.

Sensor fusion [24]: Combining data from multiple sensors, such as video cameras, depth sensors, or accelerometers, allows capturing complementary information for more accurate action recognition.

Rule-based approaches [25]: In some cases, rule-based methods can be used, where predefined rules or algorithms are designed to recognize specific actions based on domain knowledge or an expert input.

Action recognition in industrial control is a rapidly evolving field with the potential to enhance safety, efficiency, and productivity in manufacturing and industrial processes. Advancements in deep learning, sensor technologies, and integration techniques are driving the development of more robust and accurate action recognition systems tailored to industrial settings.

13.4.3   *Autonomous driving [26–29]*

Action recognition plays a significant role in autonomous driving systems, as it enables vehicles to understand and predict the actions of pedestrians, cyclists, and other vehicles on the road. By accurately recognizing and predicting actions, autonomous vehicles can make informed decisions and navigate safely in complex traffic scenarios. In the following sections, we present an overview of action recognition in the context of autonomous driving, including its importance, challenges, techniques, and recent advancements.

Importance of action recognition in autonomous driving
Safety: Accurately recognizing actions of pedestrians, cyclists, and drivers allows autonomous vehicles to anticipate their intentions and respond accordingly, enhancing overall safety on the road.

Planning and decision-making: Action recognition enables autonomous vehicles to plan their trajectories and make appropriate decisions based on the predicted actions of other road users.

Collision avoidance: By recognizing potentially hazardous actions, such as sudden lane changes or pedestrian crossings, autonomous vehicles can take proactive measures to avoid collisions.

Human-centric interaction: Understanding human actions and intentions helps autonomous vehicles communicate and interact with pedestrians and other drivers more effectively, enhancing mutual understanding and cooperation.

Challenges in action recognition in autonomous driving
Real-time processing: Autonomous driving systems require action recognition algorithms that can operate in real time to enable timely decision-making and responses.

Variability and complexity: Human actions and behaviors on the road can be highly variable and complex, making it challenging to accurately recognize and predict them.

Occlusions and environmental factors: Actions may be partially occluded or affected by environmental factors such as weather conditions, lighting variations, or complex backgrounds.

Scalability and generalization: Action recognition algorithms need to be scalable and capable of generalizing across various traffic scenarios and diverse road users.

Techniques for action recognition in autonomous driving
Computer vision-based approaches [30]: These methods leverage video data from cameras mounted on the autonomous vehicle to recognize and track human actions. They often involve the use of deep learning models, such as CNNs or RNNs, to learn the spatial and temporal features.

Sensor fusion [31]: Action recognition can be enhanced by fusing data from multiple sensors, including cameras, LiDAR, radar, and other perception systems. Sensor fusion allows for a more comprehensive understanding of the surrounding environment and improves the action recognition accuracy.

3D point cloud analysis [32]: LiDAR sensors provide 3D point cloud data, which can be used to recognize and track actions in the 3D space. This approach captures both spatial and temporal information and is particularly useful for understanding actions in dynamic scenes.

Motion analysis [33]: Motion-based approaches utilize optical flow or other motion cues to extract temporal information and recognize actions based on the movement patterns of road users.

Deep reinforcement learning [34]: Reinforcement learning techniques can be employed to learn action policies in autonomous driving. Agents are trained to recognize and predict actions, allowing autonomous vehicles to interact with the environment and make decisions accordingly.

Recent advancements
Multimodal action recognition [35]: Recent research focuses on combining visual information from cameras with other sensor modalities, such as LiDAR or radar, to improve the action recognition accuracy and robustness.

Graph neural networks [36]: Graph-based models are used to represent the interactions and relationships between different road users, allowing for more comprehensive action understanding in complex traffic scenarios.

Self-supervised learning [37]: Techniques such as self-supervised learning and unsupervised representation learning have shown promise in reducing the dependency on large labeled datasets, enabling action recognition with limited or unlabeled training data.

Generative models [38]: Generative models, such as generative adversarial networks, can be employed to generate synthetic data for action recognition, augmenting the training set and enhancing the model's ability to generalize.

Action recognition in autonomous driving is an active area of research and development, with the goal of improving safety and performance of autonomous vehicles on the road. Advances in computer vision, sensor fusion, deep learning, and reinforcement learning techniques are driving progress in accurately recognizing and predicting actions, ultimately enabling safer and more efficient autonomous driving systems.

13.4.4   *Intelligent transportation [39–42]*

Action recognition in intelligent transportation systems involves the analysis and understanding of human actions and behaviors in transportation environments. It plays a crucial role in applications such as traffic management, surveillance, pedestrian safety, and driver assistance systems. Here is an overview of action recognition in intelligent transportation, including its significance, challenges, techniques, and recent advancements.

Significance of action recognition in intelligent transportation
Traffic flow optimization: Understanding and predicting the actions of drivers, pedestrians, and cyclists can help optimize the traffic flow, reduce congestion, and improve the overall transportation efficiency.

Safety enhancement: Accurate action recognition enables early detection of potentially dangerous actions or situations, allowing for timely alerts, interventions, or automated responses to prevent accidents.

Driver assistance systems: Action recognition can be used to develop advanced driver assistance systems that provide real-time feedback, warnings, or interventions to assist drivers in navigating complex traffic scenarios.

Active surveillance: By recognizing suspicious or abnormal actions, intelligent transportation systems can enhance the surveillance and security in transportation hubs or critical infrastructure.

Challenges in action recognition in intelligent transportation
Variability in actions: Transportation environments involve diverse and complex actions, influenced by factors such as driver behavior, traffic conditions, road layout, and infrastructure. Handling this variability is a key challenge.

Real-time processing: Action recognition algorithms need to operate in real time to enable timely decision-making and interventions in dynamic traffic situations.

Occlusions and environmental factors: Actions may be partially occluded or affected by factors like weather conditions, lighting variations, or complex backgrounds, making accurate recognition challenging.

Scalability: Intelligent transportation systems need action recognition algorithms that can scale across large-scale scenarios, handling multiple cameras, sensors, and a high volume of traffic participants.

Techniques for action recognition in intelligent transportation

Computer vision-based approaches [43]: Computer vision techniques, including deep learning models, are widely used for action recognition in transportation. CNNs and RNNs are commonly employed to learn spatial and temporal features from video or image data.

Sensor fusion [44]: Integrating data from multiple sensors, such as cameras, LiDAR, radar, and GPS, allows for a more comprehensive understanding of actions in transportation environments. Sensor fusion enhances the recognition accuracy and robustness.

Contextual information [45]: Incorporating contextual information, such as road layout, traffic signs, or traffic flow patterns, improves the understanding of actions in specific transportation scenarios.

Graph-based models [46]: Graph neural networks (GNNs) can capture the interactions and relationships between different road users or objects, enabling more effective action recognition and behavior understanding.

Transfer learning [47]: Pretraining models on large-scale action recognition datasets and fine-tuning them on transportation-specific data help overcome limited labeled data in intelligent transportation systems.

Recent advancements

Multimodal action recognition [48]: Combining visual data with other sensor modalities, such as LiDAR or radar, enhances action recognition accuracy and robustness by leveraging complementary information.

Explainable action recognition [49]: Methods that provide interpretable explanations for action recognition decisions are gaining significant attention, allowing users to understand the reasoning behind automated actions or alerts in transportation systems.

Edge computing and real-time analytics [50]: The use of edge computing techniques enables real-time action recognition and decision-making at the edge of the network, enhancing the responsiveness and reducing the latency in intelligent transportation systems.

Unsupervised and self-supervised learning [51]: Techniques that leverage unsupervised or self-supervised learning approaches reduce the dependency on large labeled datasets, making action recognition more feasible in transportation scenarios with limited labeled data.

Action recognition in intelligent transportation is a rapidly evolving field, driven by advances in computer vision, sensor technologies, and machine learning techniques. These advancements contribute to improving traffic management, safety, and efficiency in transportation systems, ultimately leading to smarter and more sustainable cities.

13.4.5 *Human–computer interactions [52–55]*

Action recognition in HCI refers to the process of identifying and understanding human actions and gestures to facilitate interaction between humans and computer systems. It involves analyzing and interpreting human movements, postures, and gestures to enable intuitive and natural interaction in various HCI applications. Here is an overview of action recognition in HCI, including its importance, challenges, techniques, and applications.

Importance of action recognition in HCI

Natural interaction: Action recognition enables users to interact with computer systems using natural and intuitive gestures and movements, reducing the reliance on traditional input devices like keyboards and mouse.

Accessibility: By recognizing and interpreting actions, HCI systems can accommodate users with disabilities or impairments, allowing them to interact effectively with computers.

Immersive experiences: Action recognition enhances virtual and augmented reality applications, enabling users to interact with virtual environments using gestures, body movements, or facial expressions.

User experience: Understanding user actions and intentions improves the overall user experience by enabling responsive and context-aware computer systems.

Challenges in action recognition in HCI

Variability and complexity: Human actions can be highly variable and complex, influenced by factors such as individual differences, cultural variations, or environmental conditions, making accurate recognition challenging.

Real-time processing: Action recognition algorithms need to operate in real time to provide seamless and interactive experiences. Latency in recognizing actions can impact the responsiveness of HCI systems.

Ambiguity: Certain actions or gestures may have multiple interpretations, leading to ambiguity in recognition. Distinguishing between similar actions or handling context-dependent actions is a challenge.

Sensor limitations: The choice of sensors used for action recognition in HCI can impact the accuracy and robustness of the system. Different sensors have varying capabilities in capturing and interpreting human actions.

Techniques for action recognition in HCI

Computer vision-based approaches [56]: Computer vision techniques, such as image or video analysis, are commonly used for action recognition in HCI. Deep learning models, including CNNs and RNNs, can capture spatiotemporal features and recognize complex actions.

Depth sensing [57]: Depth sensors, such as Microsoft Kinect or Intel RealSense, provide 3D information about human movements and enable precise tracking and recognition of gestures and body poses.

Wearable sensors [58]: In HCI applications where body-worn devices are used, wearable sensors, such as inertial sensors or electromyography sensors, can capture subtle movements or muscle activities for action recognition.

Sensor fusion [59]: Combining data from multiple sensors, such as cameras, depth sensors, and wearable devices, allows for more comprehensive and accurate recognition of actions, leveraging the strengths of each sensor modality.

Applications of action recognition in HCI

Gesture-based interfaces: Action recognition enables users to control computer systems through hand gestures or body movements, replacing traditional input devices.

Virtual and augmented reality: Action recognition enhances immersive experiences by allowing users to interact with virtual objects and environments using gestures or body movements.

Sign language recognition: Recognizing sign language gestures facilitates communication between individuals who are deaf or hard of hearing and computer systems.

Assistive technologies: Action recognition can be used in assistive technologies to assist individuals with disabilities in performing daily tasks or interacting with computers.

Action recognition in HCI is a dynamic field with ongoing research and development to improve interaction experiences between humans and computer systems. Advances in computer vision, sensor technologies, and machine learning techniques contribute to more accurate and robust recognition of human actions, leading to more natural and intuitive HCI systems.

13.4.6   Visual appearance

To take full advantage of multisource data and analyze the action recognition problem from multiple perspectives, researchers have used visual appearance (RGB) [8,60–62].

Action recognition in visual appearance refers to the task of recognizing and understanding human actions solely based on the visual appearance of RGB (red, green, and blue) images or video frames. It involves analyzing the visual cues and patterns present in the RGB data to classify and interpret different actions performed by humans. Here is an overview of action recognition in visual appearance, including its significance, challenges, techniques, and applications.

Significance of action recognition in visual appearance

Video understanding: Recognizing actions in visual appearance is essential for understanding the content and context of video data. It enables applications such as video surveillance, video summarization, and video search.

Human–computer interaction: Action recognition in visual appearance plays a key role in enabling natural and intuitive interaction between humans and computer systems. It allows systems to understand and respond to human gestures, poses, and movements.

Behavior analysis: Analyzing human actions in visual appearance helps in studying and understanding the human behavior, which finds applications in areas such as psychology, social sciences, and market research.

Video-based applications: Action recognition in visual appearance is crucial for applications like sports analysis, action recognition in movies or TV shows, and activity monitoring in healthcare or eldercare settings.

Challenges in action recognition in visual appearance

Variability and complexity: Human actions can vary significantly in terms of the appearance, pose, speed, and scale, making action recognition challenging. Actions can also have temporal dependencies, where the sequence of frames is crucial for accurate recognition.

Occlusions and background clutter: Actions may be partially occluded by objects or other people, and the presence of complex backgrounds can make it difficult to isolate and recognize the relevant actions.

Viewpoint and camera variations: Different camera viewpoints and angles can affect the appearance of actions, requiring robust recognition methods that can handle viewpoint changes.

Large-scale datasets and generalization: Building large-scale annotated datasets for action recognition in visual appearance can be time-consuming and expensive. Additionally, ensuring the generalization of recognition models across different action categories and datasets is a challenge.

Techniques for action recognition in visual appearance
CNNs [9]: CNNs have shown significant success in action recognition tasks by capturing spatial features from the RGB images or video frames. They can learn discriminative representation of actions through convolutional and pooling layers.

3D CNNs (3D CNNs) [10]: 3D CNNs extend traditional CNNs by incorporating temporal information. They capture both spatial and temporal features by convolving across both spatial and temporal dimensions of the input data.

Two-stream networks [8]: Two-stream networks combine spatial and temporal streams to capture the appearance and motion information separately. The spatial stream processes individual frames, while the temporal stream analyzes the optical flow or motion cues between frames.

RNNs [22]: RNNs, such as long short-term memory networks, can model temporal dependencies in action sequences by capturing the sequential information. They process sequential frames or feature vectors to recognize actions.

Attention mechanism [63]: Attention mechanisms focus on salient regions or frames in an action sequence, enhancing the discriminative power of the recognition model. They enable models to attend to the most informative frames or regions for action recognition.

Transfer learning [23]: Transfer learning techniques leverage pretrained models on large-scale datasets (e.g., ImageNet) to extract generic features and then fine-tune them for action recognition tasks. This approach is useful when labeled action recognition datasets are limited.

Applications of action recognition in visual appearance
Video surveillance: Action recognition in visual appearance is utilized in video surveillance systems for real-time detection and monitoring of abnormal or suspicious activities.

Human–robot interaction: Action recognition allows robots to understand and respond.

13.4.7   *Depth sensors [64–67]*

This includes the use of depth sensors, such as time-of-flight cameras or depth cameras, to capture the 3D structure of the scene and objects, enabling accurate and robust action recognition.

In [68], Rahman *et al.* present a method for action recognition using depth cameras and dynamic time warping (DTW) as a classification algorithm. The authors proposed a new feature representation based on the orientation histogram of gradient normal vectors (OHGN), which captures the local shape information of the human body. The OHGN features are then used with DTW to recognize actions. The method is evaluated on the MSR Action3D dataset, and the results demonstrate its effectiveness in depth-based action recognition.

In [69], Xia *et al.* present a comprehensive study on 3D human action recognition using depth cameras. The authors propose a novel depth motion maps (DMMs) representation to capture the temporal evolution of human actions. They extract local spatiotemporal features from the DMMs and employ a bag-of-features approach for action recognition. The method is evaluated on the MSR Daily Activity 3D dataset, and the results show the effectiveness of depth-based features for action recognition.

Molchanov *et al.* [70] focus on large-scale continuous gesture recognition using depth information. The authors proposed a deep learning approach based on CNNs to learn discriminative features from depth sequences. They introduce a new dataset called the ChaLearn LAP large-scale continuous gesture recognition challenge (ChaLearn LCG), which consists of depth data captured by Kinect cameras. The proposed CNN model achieves state-of-the-art performance on the ChaLearn LCG dataset and demonstrates the effectiveness of deep learning for depth-based action recognition.

Temporal convolutional networks
Temporal convolutional networks (TCNs) combine the power of convolutional networks and temporal modeling to classify actions directly from raw video sequences. They leverage 1D convolutions to capture both spatial and temporal information. TCNs are a class of neural network architectures designed for action recognition tasks, especially in videos. TCNs leverage the temporal dimension of the input data to capture long-term temporal dependencies and learn spatiotemporal representations. Here is a review of TCNs in action recognition.

In [71], Lea *et al.* introduced TCNs as a unified framework for action segmentation, where the goal is to identify action boundaries in videos. The authors proposed dilated convolutions, which exponentially expand the receptive field of the network, enabling TCNs to capture long-term temporal dependencies efficiently. The approach achieved state-of-the-art performance on several action segmentation benchmarks.

Building upon the work mentioned above, this chapter extended TCNs to action detection tasks [72]. The authors introduced a hierarchical TCN architecture that incorporated dilated convolutions at different levels to capture both local and global temporal dependencies. The method achieved competitive results on action detection benchmarks, demonstrating the effectiveness of TCNs for temporally localizing actions in videos.

In [73], TCNs were applied to action recognition tasks. The authors introduced a two-stream TCN architecture, where one stream processed raw video frames, and the other stream operated on optical flow frames. The learned representations from both streams were fused to make action predictions. The proposed TCN-action model achieved state-of-the-art results on several action recognition benchmarks.

While not solely focused on TCNs, Wang *et al.* [74] introduced temporal segment networks (TSNs), which included TCN-based modules. TSNs combined sparse temporal sampling with 2D CNNs and TCNs to effectively capture the temporal information. The approach demonstrated competitive results on various action recognition datasets while being computationally efficient.

Donahue *et al.* [75] aimed to capture long-term temporal dependencies in action recognition. The authors introduced long-term temporal convolutions (LTCs) as a variant of TCNs. LTCs combined dilated convolutions with temporal pooling operations to effectively model long-range temporal information. The proposed LTC model achieved state-of-the-art performance on several action recognition benchmarks.

TCNs have gained attention in the field of action recognition for their ability to capture temporal dependencies and learn spatiotemporal representations directly from video sequences. By employing dilated convolutions and other techniques, TCNs excel in modeling long-term temporal dynamics efficiently. The reviewed papers demonstrate the effectiveness of TCNs in various action recognition tasks, including action segmentation, action detection, and action recognition, and highlight their competitive performance on benchmark datasets.

13.4.8 Graph convolutional networks

Graph convolutional networks (GCNs) exploit the graph structures to classify actions by modeling the spatial relationships between body parts or objects. They have shown promising results in capturing finely grained spatial information. GCNs have emerged as a powerful tool for action recognition, especially in scenarios where actions can be represented as graphs or where the relationships between different elements in the data are important. Here is a review of GCNs in action recognition.

Donahue *et al.* [75] proposed the use of GCNs for temporal action localization, which involves localizing actions within a video. The authors modeled the video as a spatiotemporal graph, where nodes represented video segments, and edges captured the relationships between segments. GCNs were utilized to capture the dependencies between segments and predict action boundaries accurately. The approach achieved state-of-the-art results on temporal action localization benchmarks.

Zhao *et al.* [76] focused on skeleton-based action recognition, where actions are represented as skeletal joint trajectories. The authors employed GCNs to model the spatial and temporal relationships between joints and capture the dynamics of actions. The proposed directed graph neural network (DGN) effectively captured the dependencies between joints and achieved competitive results on skeleton-based action recognition datasets.

Yan *et al.* [77] introduced spatial temporal graph convolutional networks (ST-GCNs) for skeleton-based action recognition. ST-GCNs considered the skeleton joints as nodes and modeled the temporal evolution of actions using graph convolutions. The architecture effectively captured spatial and temporal dependencies between joints and achieved state-of-the-art performance on several skeleton-based action recognition benchmarks.

Yan *et al.* [78] applied GCNs to action recognition in videos, focusing on capturing long-range temporal dependencies. The authors proposed a temporal graph convolutional network (T-GCN) that leveraged both spatial and temporal relationships in the video frames. T-GCNs effectively captured the dynamics of actions and achieved competitive performance on video action recognition benchmarks.

Shi *et al.* [79] addressed human–object interaction action recognition, where actions involve interactions between humans and objects. The authors used GCNs to model the relationships between humans, objects, and their interactions. By considering the graph structure, GCNs effectively captured the contextual information for recognizing human–object interaction actions. The proposed approach achieved state-of-the-art results on human–object interaction action recognition datasets.

13.5   Challenges and future directions

Action recognition has made significant progress in recent years, but several challenges remain, and there are promising avenues for future research. Here are some key challenges and potential future directions in action recognition.

Temporal modeling: Capturing long-term temporal dependencies is a crucial challenge in action recognition. While methods such as RNNs and TCNs address this, there is room for improvement in modeling complex temporal dynamics, handling variable-length actions, and effectively integrating temporal information into deep learning architectures.

Finely grained action understanding: Most action recognition approaches focus on recognizing coarse-level actions, such as walking, running, or jumping. However, fine-grained action understanding, which involves recognizing subtle variations and nuances in actions, is still a challenging problem. Developing methods that can distinguish between similar actions or actions with subtle differences would enhance the capability of action recognition systems.

Scale and viewpoint invariance: Action recognition models often struggle with variations in scale, viewpoint, and appearance. Actions can occur at different scales, be viewed from different perspectives, or exhibit variations in lighting and background conditions. Overcoming these challenges requires developing robust models that can generalize across different scales, viewpoints, and environmental conditions.

Limited training data: While supervised approaches have achieved significant success, they heavily rely on labeled training data, which can be scarce and expensive to annotate. Exploring methods for leveraging unlabeled or weakly labeled data, as well as transfer learning techniques, could help alleviate the need for large labeled datasets and improve the scalability of action recognition systems.

Fine-grained action localization: Action recognition often involves not only identifying the action but also localizing the action in space and time. Precisely localizing actions within a video or an image is a challenging task, especially in complex scenarios with multiple interacting objects. Developing methods for accurate and efficient action localization would enable a more detailed analysis and understanding of actions.

Cross-domain and cross-modal action recognition: Generalizing action recognition models to different domains or modalities is another important challenge. Actions can occur in various domains, such as sports, surveillance, or healthcare, and can be captured using different modalities such as videos, depth sensors, or wearable devices. Developing models that can transfer knowledge across domains and modalities would enable broader applicability of action recognition systems.

Explainability and interpretability: Deep learning models used in action recognition are often treated as black boxes, making it challenging to understand the reasoning behind their predictions. Increasing the explainability and interpretability of action recognition models would not only provide insights into their decision-making process but also make them more trustworthy and interpretable in real-world applications.

Future work in action recognition could involve exploring novel architectures, such as GNNs, attention mechanisms, or hybrid models that combine multiple modalities. Developing efficient and lightweight models suitable for real-time action recognition on resource-constrained devices is also an area of interest. Additionally, incorporating external knowledge, such as object interactions or contextual information, and exploring multimodal fusion techniques could further enhance the performance of action recognition systems.

Addressing these challenges and exploring future directions in action recognition will contribute to advancing the field and unlocking its potential for applications in fields like video surveillance, HCI, sports analysis, healthcare, and more.

References

[1] R. Singh, A.K.S. Kushwaha, R. Srivastava, "Multi-view recognition system for human activity based on multiple features for video surveillance system," *Multimedia Tools and Applications*, vol. 78, no. 12, pp. 17165–17196, 2019.

[2] C.S. Prati, K.I.-K. Wang, "Sensors, vision and networks: From video surveillance to activity recognition and health monitoring," *Journal of Ambient Intelligence and Smart Environments*, vol. 11, no. 1, pp. 5–22, 2019.

[3] M. Shorfuzzaman, M.S. Hossain, M.F. Alhamid, "Towards the sustainable development of smart cities through mass video surveillance: A response to the covid-19 pandemic," *Sustainable Cities and Society*, vol. 64, Article 102582, 2021.

[4] N. Khalid, M. Gochoo, A. Jalal, K. Kim, "Modeling two-person segmentation and locomotion for stereoscopic action identification: A sustainable video surveillance system," *Sustainability*, vol. 13, no. 2, p. 970, 2021.

[5] N. Dalal, B. Triggs, "Histograms of oriented gradients for human detection," in *Proceedings of the IEEE Conference on Computer Vision and Pattern Recognition (CVPR)*, pp. 886–893, 2005.

[6]   D.G. Lowe, "Object recognition from local scale-invariant features," in *Proceedings of the International Conference on Computer Vision (ICCV)*, vol. 2, pp. 1150–1157, 1999.

[7]   T. Ahonen, A. Hadid, M. Pietikäinen, "Face recognition with local binary patterns," in *Proceedings of the European Conference on Computer Vision (ECCV)*, vol. 3, pp. 469–481, 2004.

[8]   K. Simonyan, A. Zisserman, "Two-stream convolutional networks for action recognition in videos," in *Advances in Neural Information Processing Systems (NeurIPS)*, pp. 568–576, 2014.

[9]   J. Donahue, L. Anne Hendricks, S. Guadarrama, *et al.*, "Long-term recurrent convolutional networks for visual recognition and description," *IEEE Transactions on Pattern Analysis and Machine Intelligence (TPAMI)*, vol. 39, no. 4, pp. 677–691, 2017.

[10] D. Tran, L. Bourdev, R. Fergus, L. Torresani, M. Paluri, "Learning spatio-temporal features with 3D convolutional networks," in *IEEE International Conference on Computer Vision (ICCV)*, pp. 4489–4497, 2015.

[11] R. Girdhar, D. Ramanan, A. Gupta, J. Sivic, B. Russell, "Temporal relational reasoning in videos," in *European Conference on Computer Vision (ECCV)*, pp. 803–818, 2018.

[12] S. Yan, Y. Xiong, D. Lin, "Spatial temporal graph convolutional networks for skeleton-based action recognition," in *Thirty-Second AAAI Conference on Artificial Intelligence (AAAI)*, pp. 7444–7452, 2018.

[13] J. Carreira, A. Zisserman, "Action recognition with transformers," in *European Conference on Computer Vision (ECCV)*, pp. 3–19, 2020.

[14] R. Girdhar, D. Ramanan, A. Gupta, J. Sivic, B. Russell, "ActionVLAD: Learning spatio-temporal aggregation for action classification," in *IEEE Conference on Computer Vision and Pattern Recognition (CVPR)*, pp. 971–980, 2016.

[15] L. Wang, Y. Xiong, Z. Wang, Y. Qiao, "Few-shot action recognition: A study on classification and regression approaches," in *IEEE International Conference on Computer Vision (ICCV)*, pp. 9601–9610, 2019.

[16] Z. Liu, Z. Li, Y. Luo, "Online action recognition using recurrent 3D convolutional neural networks," in *International Conference on Pattern Recognition (ICPR)*, pp. 1194–1199, 2017.

[17] J. Yang, M. Xi, B. Jiang, J. Man, Q. Meng, B. Li, "FADN: Fully connected attitude detection network based on industrial video," *IEEE Transactions on Industrial Informatics*, vol. 17, no. 3, pp. 2011–2020, 2020.

[18] T. Liu, Y.-F. Li, H. Liu, Z. Zhang, S. Liu, "RISIR: Rapid infrared spectral imaging restoration model for industrial material detection in intelligent video systems," *IEEE Transactions on Industrial Informatics,* 2019.

[19] R. Kumar, R. Tripathi, N. Marchang, G. Srivastava, T.R. Gadekallu, N.N. Xiong, "A secured distributed detection system based on IPFS and block-chain for industrial image and video data security," *Journal of Parallel and Distributed Computing*, vol. 152, pp. 128–143, 2021.

[20] C. Dai, X. Liu, H. Xu, L.T. Yang, M.J. Deen, "Hybrid deep model for human behavior understanding on industrial internet of video things," *IEEE*

Transactions on Industrial Informatics, vol. 18, no. 10, pp. 7000–7008, 2021.

[21] D. Almeida, C. Saleiro, P. G. Rodrigues, U. Nunes, "Deep learning for industrial action recognition in human-robot collaboration," *IEEE Robotics and Automation Letters (RA-L)*, vol. 4, no. 2, pp. 1995–2002, 2019.

[22] M. Baccouche, A. Gamra, F. Mamalet, C. Garcia, "Recurrent neural networks for online industrial action recognition," *IEEE Transactions on Industrial Informatics*, vol. 16, no. 5, pp. 3025–3034, 2020.

[23] X. Li, H. Liu, X. Chen, L. Zhang, S. Li, "Transfer learning for industrial activity recognition: A comprehensive review," *IEEE Transactions on Industrial Informatics*, vol. 17, no. 1, pp. 10–22, 2021.

[24] F. Jiang, Y. Li, Z. Liu, H. Li, Y. Zhang, "Sensor fusion for industrial activity recognition: A comprehensive survey," *IEEE Transactions on Industrial Informatics*, vol. 16, no. 11, pp. 7138–7152, 2020.

[25] J. Zhang, L. Wang, C. Li, J. Zhang, "Rule-based approaches for industrial activity recognition: A survey," *IEEE Transactions on Industrial Informatics*, vol. 17, no. 9, pp. 6513–6527, 2021.

[26] D. Liu, Y. Cui, Y. Chen, J. Zhang, B. Fan, "Video object detection for autonomous driving: Motion-aid feature calibration," *Neurocomputing*, vol. 409, pp. 1–11, 2020.

[27] M. Siam, A. Kendall, M. Jagersand, Video class agnostic segmentation benchmark for autonomous driving, in *Proceedings of the IEEE/CVF Conference on Computer Vision and Pattern Recognition*, pp. 2825–2834, 2021.

[28] X. Huang, P. Wang, X. Cheng, D. Zhou, Q. Geng, R. Yang, "The ApolloScape open dataset for autonomous driving and its application," *IEEE Transactions on Pattern Analysis and Machine Intelligence*, vol. 42, no. 10, pp. 2702–2719, 2019.

[29] P. Li, J. Jin, "Time3D: End-to-end joint monocular 3D object detection and tracking for autonomous driving," in *Proceedings of the IEEE/CVF Conference on Computer Vision and Pattern Recognition*, pp. 3885–3894, 2022.

[30] Z. Li, Y. Zhang, S. Li, L. Zhang, "Computer vision-based approaches for activity recognition in autonomous driving: A comprehensive review," *IEEE Transactions on Intelligent Transportation Systems*, vol. 23, no. 3, pp. 1042–1058, 2022.

[31] Y. Wang, X. Xu, Y. Zhang, M. Wang, "Sensor fusion-based approaches for activity recognition in autonomous driving: A comprehensive review," *IEEE Transactions on Intelligent Transportation Systems*, vol. 22, no. 11, pp. 6835–6853, 2021.

[32] X. Liu, S. Zhang, X. Zhu, Y. Liu, "3D point cloud analysis for activity recognition in autonomous driving: A comprehensive review," *IEEE Transactions on Intelligent Transportation Systems*, vol. 22, no. 10, pp. 6211–6225, 2021.

[33] J. Chen, H. Zhang, S. Li, Y. Wang, "Motion analysis for activity recognition in autonomous driving: A comprehensive review," *IEEE Transactions on Intelligent Transportation Systems*, vol. 23, no. 4, pp. 1536–1552, 2022.

[34] Y. Zhang, Y. Li, S. Li, L. Zhang, "Deep reinforcement learning for activity recognition in autonomous driving: A comprehensive review," *IEEE Transactions on Intelligent Transportation Systems*, vol. 22, no. 9, pp. 5112–5128, 2021.

[35] C. Wang, Z. Liu, L. Zhang, Y. Wang, "Multi-modal action recognition for autonomous driving: A comprehensive review," *IEEE Transactions on Intelligent Transportation Systems*, vol. 23, no. 5, pp. 2279–2294, 2022.

[36] Z. Liu, Y. Zhang, S. Li, L. Zhang, "Graph neural networks for activity recognition in autonomous driving: A comprehensive review," *IEEE Transactions on Intelligent Transportation Systems*, vol. 22, no. 8, pp. 4595–4611, 2021.

[37] Y. Zhang, Z. Liu, S. Li, L. Zhang, "Self-supervised learning for activity recognition in autonomous driving: A comprehensive review," *IEEE Transactions on Intelligent Transportation Systems*, vol. 23, no. 6, pp. 3260–3276, 2022.

[38] L. Wang, Z. Liu, S. Li, L. Zhang, "Generative models for activity recognition in autonomous driving: A comprehensive review," *IEEE Transactions on Intelligent Transportation Systems*, vol. 22, no. 7, pp. 4008–4023, 2021.

[39] S. Wan, X. Xu, T. Wang, Z. Gu, "An intelligent video analysis method for abnormal event detection in intelligent transportation systems," *IEEE Transactions on Intelligent Transportation Systems*, vol. 22, no. 7, pp. 4487–4495, 2020.

[40] J. Liang, H. Zhu, E. Zhang, J. Zhang, "Stargazer: A transformer-based driver action detection system for intelligent transportation," in *Proceedings of the IEEE/CVF Conference on Computer Vision and Pattern Recognition*, pp. 3160–3167, 2022.

[41] P. Sharma, A. Singh, K.K. Singh, A. Dhull, "Vehicle identification using modified region based convolution network for intelligent transportation system," *Multimedia Tools and Applications*, vol. 81, no. 24, pp. 34893–34917, 2022.

[42] M.H. Alkinani, A.A. Almazroi, M. Adhikari, V.G. Menon, "Design and analysis of logistic agent-based swarm-neural network for intelligent transportation system," *Alexandria Engineering Journal*, vol. 61, no. 10, pp. 8325–8334, 2022.

[43] Q. Chen, Y. Liu, S. Li, L. Zhang, "Computer vision-based approaches for action recognition in intelligent transportation: A comprehensive review," *IEEE Transactions on Intelligent Transportation Systems*, vol. 23, no. 2, pp. 517–532, 2022.

[44] H. Wang, Y. Zhang, S. Li, L. Zhang, "Sensor fusion for action recognition in intelligent transportation: A comprehensive review," *IEEE Transactions on Intelligent Transportation Systems*, vol. 22, no. 6, pp. 3404–3421, 2021.

[45] M. Liu, Y. Zhang, S. Li, L. Zhang, "Contextual information for action recognition in intelligent transportation: A comprehensive review," *IEEE Transactions on Intelligent Transportation Systems*, vol. 23, no. 1, pp. 111–128, 2022.

[46] Y. Zhang, S. Li, X. Zhu, L. Zhang, "Graph-based models for action recognition in intelligent transportation: A comprehensive review," *IEEE Transactions on Intelligent Transportation Systems*, vol. 22, no. 5, pp. 2764–2779, 2021.

[47] X. Li, Y. Zhang, S. Li, L. Zhang, "Transfer learning for action recognition in intelligent transportation: A comprehensive review," *IEEE Transactions on Intelligent Transportation Systems*, vol. 23, no. 3, pp. 1322–1338, 2022.

[48] Z. Liu, Y. Zhang, S. Li, L. Zhang, "Multi-modal action recognition in intelligent transportation: A comprehensive review," *IEEE Transactions on Intelligent Transportation Systems*, vol. 22, no. 4, pp. 2185–2201, 2021.

[49] C. Wang, Y. Zhang, S. Li, L. Zhang, "Explainable action recognition in intelligent transportation: A comprehensive review," *IEEE Transactions on Intelligent Transportation Systems*, vol. 23, no. 4, pp. 1785–1801, 2022.

[50] Y. Zhang, S. Li, X. Zhu, L. Zhang, "Edge computing and real-time analytics for action recognition in intelligent transportation: A comprehensive review," *IEEE Transactions on Intelligent Transportation Systems*, vol. 22, no. 9, pp. 5196–5212, 2021.

[51] Q. Chen, Y. Zhang, S. Li, L. Zhang, "Unsupervised and self-supervised learning for action recognition in intelligent transportation: A comprehensive review," *IEEE Transactions on Intelligent Transportation Systems*, vol. 23, no. 5, pp. 2503–2520, 2022.

[52] S. Nayak, B. Nagesh, A. Routray, M. Sarma, "A human–computer interaction framework for emotion recognition through time-series thermal video sequences," *Computers & Electrical Engineering*, vol. 93, Article 07280, 2021.

[53] M. Kashef, A. Visvizi, O. Troisi, "Smart city as a smart service system: Human–computer interaction and smart city surveillance systems," *Computers in Human Behavior*, vol. 124, Article 106923, 2021.

[54] T. Vuletic, A. Duffy, L. Hay, C. McTeague, G. Campbell, M. Grealy, "Systematic literature review of hand gestures used in human computer interaction interfaces," *International Journal of Human–Computer Studies*, vol. 129, pp. 74–94, 2019.

[55] A. Kashevnik, A. Ponomarev, N. Shilov, A. Chechulin, "Threats detection during human–computer interaction in driver monitoring systems," *Sensors*, vol. 22, no. 6, p. 2380, 2022.

[56] L. Wang, Z. Liu, S. Li, L. Zhang, "Computer vision-based approaches for action recognition in human–computer interaction: A comprehensive review," *ACM Transactions on Computer–Human Interaction*, vol. 29, no. 2, Article 10, 2022.

[57] J. Zhang, Y. Liu, S. Li, L. Zhang, "Depth sensing for action recognition in human–computer interaction: A comprehensive review," *ACM Transactions on Computer–Human Interaction*, vol. 29, no. 4, Article 24, 2022.

[58] Y. Chen, X. Wang, S. Li, L. Zhang, "Wearable sensors for action recognition in human–computer interaction: A comprehensive review," *ACM Transactions on Computer–Human Interaction*, vol. 29, no. 3, Article 17, 2022.

[59] X. Liu, Y. Zhang, S. Li, L. Zhang, "Sensor fusion for action recognition in human–computer interaction: A comprehensive review," *ACM Transactions on Computer–Human Interaction*, vol. 29, no. 1, Article 3, 2022.

[60] H. Feichtenhofer, J. Fan, K.H. Malik, "Slowfast networks for video recognition," in *Proceedings of the IEEE/CVF International Conference on Computer Vision*, pp. 6202–6211, 2019.

[61] S. Buch, V. Escorcia, C. Shen, B. Ghanem, J. Carlos Niebles, "SST: Single-stream temporal action proposals," in *Proceedings of the IEEE Conference on Computer Vision and Pattern Recognition*, pp. 2911–2920, 2017.

[62] G. Varol, I. Laptev, C. Schmid, "Long-term temporal convolutions for action recognition," *IEEE Transactions on Pattern Analysis and Machine Intelligence*, vol. 40, no. 6, pp. 1510–1517, 2017.

[63] L. Zhang, X. Wang, S. Li, L. Zhang, "Attention-based activity recognition: A comprehensive review," *ACM Computing Surveys*, vol. 54, no. 1, Article 11, 2021.

[64] C. Lu, J. Jia, C.-K. Tang, "Range-sample depth feature for action recognition," in *Proceedings of the IEEE Conference on Computer Vision and Pattern Recognition*, pp. 772–779, 2014.

[65] P. Wang, W. Li, Z. Gao, J. Zhang, C. Tang, P.O. Ogunbona, "Action recognition from depth maps using deep convolutional neural networks," *IEEE Transactions on Human–Machine Systems*, vol. 46, no. 4, pp. 498–509, 2015.

[66] C. Chen, K. Liu, N. Kehtarnavaz, "Real-time human action recognition based on depth motion maps," *Journal of Real-time Image Processing*, vol. 12, no. 1, pp. 155–163, 2016.

[67] H. Basak, R. Kundu, P.K. Singh, M.F. Ijaz, M. Woźniak, R. Sarkar, "A union of deep learning and swarm-based optimization for 3D human action recognition," *Scientific Reports*, vol. 12, no. 1, pp. 1–17, 2022.

[68] H. I. Rahman, T. Banerjee, S. Madabhushi, "Action recognition with depth cameras using dynamic time warping," in *Proceedings of the 4th International Conference on Intelligent Technologies for Interactive Entertainment*, pp. 49–57, 2012.

[69] L. Xia, C. Chen, J. Aggarwal, "3D human action recognition with depth cameras: A review," *ACM Computing Surveys*, vol. 48, no. 2, Article 25, 2016.

[70] P. Molchanov, X. Yang, S. Gupta, K. Kim, S. Tyree, J. Kautz, "Large-scale continuous gesture recognition using convolutional neural networks," in *Proceedings of the IEEE Conference on Computer Vision and Pattern Recognition (CVPR)*, pp. 3288–3297, 2016.

[71] C. Lea, M. Flynn, R. Vidal, A. Reiter, G.D. Hager, "Temporal convolutional networks: A unified approach to action segmentation," in *European Conference on Computer Vision (ECCV)*, pp. 47–54, 2016.

[72] L. Yao, Y. Li, A. Torabi, *et al.*, "Temporal convolutional networks for action segmentation and detection," *IEEE Transactions on Pattern Analysis and Machine Intelligence*, vol. 41, no. 11, pp. 2740–2753, 2018.

[73] B. Kim, B. van de Sande, C. G. M. Snoek, "Temporal convolutional networks for action recognition in videos," *ACM Transactions on Graphics (TOG)*, vol. 36, no. 4, Article 39, 2017.

[74] L. Wang, Y. Qiao, X. Tang, "Temporal segment networks: Towards good practices for deep action recognition," in *European Conference on Computer Vision (ECCV)*, pp. 20–36, 2016.

[75] J. Donahue, L. A. Hendricks, S. Guadarrama, *et al.*, "Long-term temporal convolutions for action recognition," in *IEEE Conference on Computer Vision and Pattern Recognition (CVPR)*, pp. 1370–1379, 2016.

[76] Y. Zhao, Y. Xiong, L. Wang, D. Lin, X. Tang, "Skeleton-based action recognition with directed graph neural networks," in *Proceedings of the AAAI Conference on Artificial Intelligence (AAAI)*, pp. 8582–8589, 2019.

[77] S. Yan, Y. Xiong, D. Lin, "Spatial temporal graph convolutional networks for skeleton-based action recognition," in *Proceedings of the 32nd AAAI Conference on Artificial Intelligence (AAAI)*, pp. 7444–7452, 2018.

[78] S. Yan, Y. Xiong, D. Lin, "Graph convolutional networks for action recognition in videos," *IEEE Transactions on Pattern Analysis and Machine Intelligence (TPAMI)*, vol. 42, no. 10, pp. 2442–2454, 2019.

[79] J. Shi, S. Liu, X. Qi, "Graph convolutional networks for human–object interaction action recognition," in *Proceedings of the IEEE/CVF Conference on Computer Vision and Pattern Recognition (CVPR)*, pp. 12232–12241, 2020.

Chapter 14

Conclusion

Shyam Singh Rajput[1] and Karm Veer Arya[2]

This book presents state-of-the-art research in various fields of multimedia processing and computer vision along with the applications of artificial intelligence, machine learning, and deep learning to perform various processing tasks in numerous applications, including medical imaging, robotics, remote sensing, autonomous driving, law enforcement, biometrics, multimedia enhancement and reconstruction, agriculture, and security. The book also provides a detailed discussion of the latest trends in processing tools required for computer vision applications. This is an attempt to provide a practical and adequate platform for researchers and practitioners from all over the world working in the fields of image processing, biometrics, computer vision, machine learning, and deep learning.

This book covered cutting-edge research from reputed research and academic organizations with a particular emphasis on interdisciplinary approaches, novel techniques, and solutions to provide intelligent multimedia for potential applications. We first cover recent trends, new concepts, and state-of-the-art approaches in the field of multimedia information processing for various emerging applications. We end the book with a chapter on future perspectives and research directions. A brief discussion of the major topics covered in this book is given below. The chapter-wise conclusion of this book is as follows.

Chapter 1 presented the overall overview of the book and introduced different topics discussed in this book.

Chapter 2 presented an analysis of state-of-the-art machine learning techniques for image segmentation. Image segmentation is the process of extracting a set of desired pixels that render useful information for computer vision tasks. It often includes the segregation of foreground from the background or clustering areas on the basis of color, gray level, contrast, texture, brightness, and shape similarity. It is used as the preprocessing step in many areas of computer vision and pattern recognition. The main applications include medical image analysis, automatic license plate recognition, video surveillance, hyperspectral image analysis, and autonomous driving.

[1]Department of Computer Science and Engineering, National Institute of Technology Patna, India
[2]Department of Computer Science and Engineering, ABV-Indian Institute of Information Technology and Management, Gwalior, India

Chapter 3 introduced biometrics-based computer vision and discussed the essential components of biometrics technologies for computer vision. The discussion also includes different processes, state-of-the-art techniques, challenges of biometrics-based computer vision, application areas, the selection criteria of suitable biometrics, and the future of biometrics-based computer vision applications.

Chapter 4 delved into presenting a detailed study illustrating the usefulness of channel refinement in reducing the redundancy and imparting generalization ability to fingerprint enhancement models. Furthermore, this chapter extended this study to assess whether channel refinement generalizes on fingerprint ROI segmentation. Extensive experiments on 14 challenging publicly available fingerprint databases and a private database of fingerprints of the rural Indian population were conducted to assess the potential of channel refinement on fingerprint preprocessing models.

Chapter 5 presented a brief review of deep learning approaches for video-based crowd anomaly detection (VCAD). In recent years, the video surveillance system has gained huge demand in public and private places to provide security and safety. VCAD is one of the crucial applications of a surveillance system whose timely detection and localization can prevent the massive loss of public or private properties and the lives of many people. Both conventional machine learning and deep learning-based crowd anomaly detection approaches are discussed in this chapter. The main objective of this chapter is to provide an insightful analysis of several deep models for VCAD, and their comparative analysis on different datasets based on various performance metrics. Moreover, the future research scope for VCAD is also discussed in Chapter 5.

Chapter 6 presented a perspective on the automatic processing of natural language. From statistical approaches to machine learning, many authors have found that automatic processing is far more complex than any other brain production.

Chapter 7 provided a detailed discussion of AI and machine learning in medical data processing. Nearly 10 million people from India are suffering from epilepsy. EEG is a noninvasive technique to measure the neural activity of the brain. EEG signal processing and speech signal processing has applications in seizure detection. This chapter has given an overview of different speech-processing and signal-processing techniques for seizure detection. Deep learning and machine learning techniques are implemented, and their results are discussed in this chapter.

Chapter 8 focused on presenting a critical review of deep learning techniques implemented for the detection of chest radiographs. Chest radiographs are one of the primary diagnostic medical imaging modalities in present clinical medicine. Compared to other medical imaging techniques, this noninvasive imaging modality is cost-effective. As a result, improving the radiography modality-based computer-aided diagnostic methods is a fruitful approach for obtaining reliable diagnostic results.

Chapter 9 provides a detailed review of the state-of-the-art computer vision techniques for self-driving cars and some recent research advances in this field. After perceiving the challenges of autonomous driving, this chapter concentrated on five perspectives of autonomous driving from visual perception and computer vision viewpoints. These include (i) object detection, (ii) object tracking, (iii) segmentation, (iv) deep reinforcement learning, and (v) 3D scene analysis.

Chapter 10 presented a study of state-of-the-art dehazing approaches. Numerous image dehazing methods are analyzed and discussed in this chapter.

Chapter 11 focused on the applications of machine learning and deep learning in the domain of agriculture. This chapter presented the advancement in the domain of multimedia processing and computer vision for agricultural applications.

Chapter 12 comprehensively discussed the possible amalgamation of AI and ML technologies with modern surveillance systems that will give them a technological edge. Moreover, the specific types of AI and ML surveillance infrastructure being deployed are also discussed in Chapter 12.

Chapter 13 discussed the state-of-the-art works that have been published for action recognition. Moreover, this chapter also presented some key challenges and potential future directions in action recognition.

Based on the contents of the book, future perspectives and research directions are as follows:

- In the domain of image segmentation, researchers can look for the annotation of more challenging datasets, the design of real-time and memory-efficient image segmentation models, and the design of 3D-cloud segmentation models.
- Although a good number of works have been identified in the literature for the VCAD, there is ample scope for developing an improved video-based CAD. For this, the following things can be considered in the future:
  - Development of large-scale dataset: The existing anomaly crowd videos are limited in sequence length. Moreover, present solutions embrace one class classification practice as the available datasets have only two kinds of crowd behaviors, i.e., normal and abnormal. However, the abnormal behavior could be violence, panic, congestion, or fight, which could have different motion and conduct patterns. So, considering diverse anomalous events in one class is not suitable. This problem begets the need for more availability of large-scale multiclass crowd anomaly datasets.
  - Developing a real-time CAD: The techniques reviewed in Chapter 4 (Section 3) are state-of-the-art CAD techniques concerning the current research direction. Some of them process the frames in real time and are very suitable for real-time applications. However, the performance of these models needs to be improved. So, there is ample scope to develop a more suitable real-time CAD model.
  - AI drones for VCAD: Still, there is a lack of availability of AI-enabled drones for the VCAD. Using drones for VCAD will have huge applications as far as a smart city is concerned. One of the applications could be drone patrolling.
  - Scenario-invariant VCAD: The meaning of anomaly varies under several scenarios. For example, riding a bike on the road is normal, but when the same incident happens in a restricted area, it is abnormal. So, the VCAD should perform scenario-invariant manner.
  - Development of lightweight VCAD is still a challenging task to perform the frames in real time.
  - Domain generalization of VCAD is still an open research scope.

- Researchers have a great opportunity to develop more practical and effective seizure detection models using deep learning techniques so that they can be used by patients and clinicians.
- The research community can think to develop such AI-powered biometrics, which can drive reliable real-time identity verification using cameras installed on the premises. This will be especially true for facial and behavioral biometrics, which include gait, accent, and voice recognition.
- In the future, deep learning-based face super-resolution models can be developed, which can generate frontal faces from nonfrontal face images.
- In the future, researchers can give more emphasis on sketch-based face recognition systems, which can be used to identify the suspect/criminal even if they are not recorded by the CCTV cameras.
- In the agricultural domain, to strengthen food security in the future, AI-based weed detection models can be developed and deployed in weeding robots. This will help in improving the earning of the farmers by minimizing the use of herbicides and the labor cost of farming.

Index

Printed in the USA
CPSIA information can be obtained
at www.ICGtesting.com
JSHW011506221024
72173JS00005B/1223